Winner of the 2004 Jules and Frances Landry Award

The ties between Ireland and the American South span four centuries and include shared ancestries, cultures, and sympathies. The striking parallels between the two regions are all the more fascinating because, studded with contrasts, they are so complex. Kieran Quinlan, a native of Ireland who now resides in Alabama, is ideally suited to offer the first in-depth exploration of this neglected subject, which he does to a brilliant degree in *Strange Kin.*

The Irish relationship to the American South is unique, Quinlan explains, in that it involves both kin and kinship. He shows how a significant component of the southern population has Irish origins that are far more tangled than the simplistic distinction between Protestant Scotch Irish and plain Catholic Irish. African and Native Americans, too, have identified with the Irish through comparable experiences of subjugation, displacement, and starvation. The civil rights movement in the South and the peace initiative in Northern Ireland illustrate the tense intertwining that Quinlan addresses.

He offers a detailed look at the connections between Irish nationalists and the Confederate cause, revealing remarkably similar historical trajectories in Ireland and the South. Both suffered defeat; both have long been seen as problematic, if also highly romanticized, areas of otherwise "progressive" nations; both have been identified with religious prejudices; and both have witnessed

Strange Kin

Ireland and the American South

KIERAN QUINLAN

LOUISIANA STATE UNIVERSITY PRESS   BATON ROUGE

DESIGNER: Barbara Neely Bourgoyne
TYPEFACES: Whitman, text; Mason, display
TYPESETTER: Coghill Composition, Inc.
PRINTER AND BINDER: Thomson-Shore, Inc.

Library of Congress Cataloging-in-Publication Data

Quinlan, Kieran, 1945–
    Strange kin : Ireland and the American South / Kieran Quinlan.
        p.   cm.
    Includes bibliographical references and index.
    ISBN 0-8071-2983-6 (alk. paper)
    1. Irish Americans—Southern States.   2. Southern States—Civilization.   I. Title.
F220.I6Q56   2005
975'.0049162—dc22   2004011062

The paper in this book meets the guidelines for
permanence and durability of the Committee
on Production Guidelines for Book Longevity
of the Council on Library Resources. ∞

For Anna *and* David

who were born there

I had never heard any songs like those [sung by fellow slaves on allowance day] anywhere since I left slavery, except when in Ireland. There I heard the same *wailing notes*, and was much affected by them. It was during the famine of 1845–6.

—FREDERICK DOUGLASS, *My Bondage and My Freedom*, 1855

I die willingly for South Carolina, but oh! that it had been for Ireland!

—CAPT. JOHN C. MITCHEL, C.S.A., Fort Sumter, July 20, 1864

The case of the South in the civil war was to my mind much like that of Ireland today. It was a struggle for autonomy, self-government for a people . . . [P]eople must have freedom and autonomy before they are capable of their greatest result in the cause of progress. This is my feeling about the Southern people, as it is about my own people, the Irish.

—OSCAR WILDE, newspaper interview in New Orleans, 1882

[We Agrarians] used to talk about Yeats and Ireland vis-à-vis England as having a sort of parallel to the writer in the South, in a retarded and depressed society facing a big, booming, dominating society.

—ROBERT PENN WARREN, 1974

contents

ACKNOWLEDGMENTS xi

Introduction 1

KIN

1. Elusive Ancestries 21
2. Slaves and Slaveries 46
3. "An Unholy & Cruel War" 76
4. Defeat and Defiance 96
5. Tara Transplanted 118

KINSHIP

6. Causes Lost, Redemptions Found 139
7. Crackers, Celts, and Calibans 164
8. Writing with an Accent 191
9. The Experience of Reality 210
10. Remembering Things Past 235

Conclusion 265

CHRONOLOGIES 269
SELECTED BIBLIOGRAPHY 271
INDEX 281

ACKNOWLEDGMENTS

While a quarter-century of living in the American South has left me with more intellectual and personal debts than I care to list here, I want to thank in particular Derah Myers for originally making me aware that such a place and mindset really do exist, Lee Greene at Chapel Hill for forcing me to become aware that there are alternative interpretations, and DeeGee Lester for adding an Irish-Southern note. At a much later date, Bertram Wyatt-Brown at the University of Florida offered encouragement and gentle correction. Two separate travel grants from the University of Alabama at Birmingham also helped. Poet and novelist Jackie Kay in Britain responded to a belated query; from time to time friend and colleague Linda Frost and I discussed our respective interpretations of nineteenth-century American culture; Celeste Ray at Sewanee cautioned me that the "invention of tradition" would appear differently to an anthropologist than to a literary scholar. Eddie Luster and Rebecca Naramore at the Interlibrary Loan Desk at UAB's Sterne Library were unfailingly helpful and never rebuked me for my overdue books. Sylvia Frank Rodrigue got things off to a good start at LSU Press, and Glenn Perkins wrapped things up with the copy-editing. Finally, my wife and fellow academic Mary Kaiser has kept the bluest and most critical eye on my extended southern seduction, while our children Anna and David have instructed me daily on what it means—and does *not* mean—to have mongrel Yankee, French Alsatian, and Irish heritages in the American South at the beginning of the twenty-first century.

STRANGE KIN

iΠΤRΟDVCΤΙΟΠ

It was August 1977, just a couple of days, as it happened, before Elvis Presley's death in Memphis, Tennessee. In the noisy, bustling JFK airport, an immigration officer was examining my Irish passport with its accompanying J1 visa that would allow me to pursue graduate studies at Vanderbilt University in Nashville. "You won't understand the people down there," he remarked ominously without looking up at me. I was momentarily puzzled, even vaguely insulted. Had he just read the Irish Gaelic wording on my passport and assumed that English was only my second language, an "acquired speech" as James Joyce had called it? All of a sudden the officer's face lit up in a broad grin. "Say *y'all*," he teased, routinely stamping my documents and then shoving them back into my hand without waiting to hear my befuddled reply.

The immigration officer's poking fun at the Tennessee to which I was reluctantly going, rather than the Ireland from which I had just come, brought to mind once again all the negative comments I'd previously heard from American friends about the South, its cultural and economic backwardness, oppressive religious fundamentalism, and bitter racism. Drowned out were the often curious and even occasionally envious remarks of Irish and English fellow students who, however, hardly knew anything at all about the place. The more adventurous, or perhaps more cynical, among the latter even suggested that Music City was likely to be more exciting than staid Oxford, the proverbial "home of lost causes" from which I had received my undergraduate degree just weeks earlier. In any case, I now had to brace myself for my first encounter with this strange land seemingly so unlike my own, and even less, I suspected, like the England where I had been living for the previous four years.

A few days later, as I sat in the airport limo riding through downtown Nashville and recalling that I had seen it described as "the Athens of the South," I thought glumly of how little resemblance the city bore to its Grecian prototype. Even its famed replica of the Parthenon seemed no more than a pathetic and disorienting imitation, ill placed in a low-lying city park. Everything European was very far away, not least because of the oppressive heat of the place. I had indeed entered a "New World."

More than two decades later, the American South still seems to me to be no more like Ireland in a day-to-day sense—or any of the European nations for that matter—than it did then. A "very old place" for the likes of Alabama-born Albert Murray, it continues to strike me as relentlessly new. Of course, my perceptions *have* changed. What once was *so* different is now no longer such. Most of the time I don't think about the matter at all. I have certainly become more accepting and even celebratory of traditions and barely understood hierarchies not my own, phenomena to which many residents of European background remain jadedly condescending throughout their entire lifetimes in America. It takes the modern voluntary immigrant a while, and requires some empathy, to acknowledge that the Irish American, or German American, or even English American experience and history represents not a mere unfortunate cultural displacement but is just as valid as his own and has simply shaped communities and families in a different way from that which has formed his identity. More specifically, I am now aware that many of the South's inhabitants are my distant kin, and that its historical experience bears a striking, if somewhat unfamiliar, kinship with my own country's. That kin, often unknown and largely forgotten, and that kinship, passing mention of which crops up from time to time in journals and newspapers but without further examination, are the subjects of this study. Numerous defeated peoples—Poles, Japanese, those from the countries of the former Yugoslavia or of Latin and Central America, to mention just a few—have found it easier to identify their experience with that of the American South rather than with the more successful parts of the United States. Indeed, the traditional South in many of its social, political, and economic aspects is probably more typical of the struggling world at large than is the rest of the nation. What is unique about the Irish relationship with it, however, is that *both* kin and kinship are involved.[1]

Meanwhile, insofar as they are concerned with the matter at all, American southerners—or at least white southerners—tend to think of themselves primarily as English, with some admixture of Scottish, a perception that would be surprising to many of the present-day inhabitants of the Brit-

1. Albert Murray, *South to a Very Old Place* (New York, 1991); see, for example, the essays in *South Atlantic Review* 65, no. 4 (2000), devoted to "The Worldwide Face of Southern Literature."

ish Isles. Certainly, few of the standard histories of the South make even passing reference to Ireland or the Irish. It is as though the latter had never been there at all. The states of the former Confederacy instead are seen as the home of quintessential American Anglo-Saxonism. From 1607 when the Virginia Company of London founded the Jamestown colony (or even the slightly earlier "lost colony" of Roanoke in today's North Carolina) to the national presidency of Arkansas's William Jefferson Clinton, the dominant narrative of southern development has been characterized by its sequence of British names—in terms of its people and, for the most part, its places. There are tales of backwoods Scots and Scotch-Irish, wild men themselves pushing the frontier forward by dispossessing even wilder Native American tribes so that the land cleared could then be occupied by civilized Englishmen, but even many of these people have been so absorbed into the dominant Anglo-Saxon culture that it is hard to separate their existence from that of their former overlords. In either case, the plain, unhyphenated Irish, the Irish as they are usually thought of, are simply not part of the story of the South at all.

Despite its familiarity—and even without disputing its broad truth—the above account is obviously a simplified, not to say simplistic, one. It all too easily equates "British" with "English" and assumes, moreover, that the latter identification is without complication. It would be odd indeed if the long historical drama played out between English, Scottish, Welsh, and Irish peoples at home should not have transferred in some degree to the American colonies they founded. The perception of the American South as being essentially Anglo-Saxon minimizes the quite unique contribution the Scotch-Irish in particular have made to many areas of southern life, perhaps because, as E. Merton Coulter claimed in 1935, they "were individualistic and greatly lacking in self-consciousness." Even if the southern states of the eastern seaboard can be said to have a distinctly English origin, its western borders and Gulf coasts have been significantly influenced by Spanish and French incursions, nationalities also complex in their ethnic compositions. More to the point, it should hardly be surprising that a South that until recent times barely mentioned its Native and African American populations—despite that African Americans comprised at least a third of those living in the region—should also have passed over in complacent silence the untidy remnants of other cultural contributions.[2]

2. Quoted in Robert F. Durden, "A Half Century of Change in Southern History," *Journal of Southern History* 51, no. 1 (1985): 4.

There have always been anomalous counternarratives, of course. In his notorious 1920 essay "The Sahara of the Bozart," H. L. Mencken attributed the absence of a significant culture in the South to the fact that the people down there, in the post-Jeffersonian era at least, were predominantly Celtic rather than Anglo-Saxon, though he singled out Welsh Methodists rather than Irish Protestants or Catholics as the nefarious culprits. Some twenty years later, W. J. Cash's debunking parable of the development of the emblematic Southern plantation began with a surprising image: "A stout young Irishman brought his bride into the Carolina upcountry about 1800." *Gone with the Wind*, a novel and a movie perennially popular with diverse audiences and nations, has as its centerpiece an Irish Catholic family who are owners of a plantation named after the ancient seat of the high kings of Ireland. It could even be argued that since the last decade of the twentieth century, the rather novel idea of a *Celtic* South has come to receive the same kind of advocacy—and, unfortunately, claims of xenophobic exclusivity—that characterized the champions of Anglo-Saxonism in the 1890s.[3]

The Irish-southern connection, which tends to be seen as a component part of the broader Celtic-southern speculation of current emphasis, invites serious examination at a time when important distinctions need to be made in the field. To begin with, as the epigraphs from Frederick Douglass, Captain John C. Mitchel (son of pro-Confederate nineteenth-century Irish nationalist leader John Mitchel), Oscar Wilde, and Robert Penn Warren indicate, there are many different ways in which Ireland figures in the southern drama: as a country from which a not-insignificant component of the southern population originated; as a land with a strikingly similar historical experience of defeat, poverty, and dispossession; and, finally at least in the Anglophone world, as a culture that has clear resemblances with that of the American South, not least because of the remarkable twentieth-century literary achievements of both unlikely places. Ireland is to England, the argument sometimes goes, as the American South is to the United States: both places have long been the "problem," if also frequently romanticized regions, of otherwise "progressive" nations. They exist, all too really if often unwillingly, as the untamed peripheries of their respective civilized centers.

It was very much in such a vein that a half a century ago, the Irish short

3. H. L. Mencken, *Prejudices: A Selection* (New York, 1958), 76; W. J. Cash, *The Mind of the South* (New York, 1969), 15.

story writer Seán O'Faoláin remarked that in his own County Cork and William Faulkner's rural Mississippi, "There is the same passionate provincialism; the same local patriotism; the same southern nationalism . . . the same vanity of the old race; the same gnawing sense of defeat; the same capacity for intense hatred . . . the same oscillation between unbounded self-confidence and total despair; the same escape through sport and drink." In 1993, the dean of southern historians, C. Vann Woodward, following in O'Faoláin's steps, noted that James Joyce and Faulkner "were conscious of the provinciality of their culture and its subordinate relation to a dominant one."[4]

The Irish "presence" in the American South, then, is a varied and complex one. It is, as I will argue here, far more varied and more complex than either O'Faoláin or Vann Woodward recognized. It requires, among other things, a search for what a 1930s commentator referred to as "the lost Irish tribes of the South." The Irish form a part of the irregular patchwork, the "crazy quilt," of the Southern experience. Like Mississippi writer Eudora Welty's description of her long and deep friendship with Anglo-Irish author Elizabeth Bowen, there has been much "crisscross" in the association. Irish poet Seamus Heaney captures some of the complexity beautifully in describing a "little epiphany" he had when engaged in what turned out to be his enormously popular translation of *Beowulf*. When he came to the word *tholian*—meaning "to suffer"—in an Old English glossary, he gradually realized that, far from being strange, "it was the word that older and less educated people" like an aunt of his in Northern Ireland used:

> "They'll just have to learn to thole," my aunt would say about some family who had suffered an unforeseen bereavement . . . [It] remind[ed] me that my aunt's language was not just a self-enclosed family possession but an historical heritage, one that involved the journey *tholian* had made north [from England] into Scotland and then across into Ulster with the planters, and then across from the planters to the locals who had originally spoken Irish, and then farther across again when the Scots Irish emigrated to the American South in the eighteenth century. When I read in [southern poet] John Crowe Ransom the line, "Sweet ladies, long may ye bloom, and toughly I hope ye may thole," my heart lifted again, the world widened, something was furthered.

4. Seán O'Faoláin, *The Vanishing Hero: Studies in Novelists of the Twenties* (New York, 1957), 75; C. Vann Woodward, *The Burden of Southern History* (Baton Rouge, 1993), 263.

Indeed, Heaney credited this "multicultural odyssey" with opening his "right of way" to translate the Anglo-Saxon poem.[5]

There is no intention here, however, of minimizing the differences between the two regions—the one a vast (though its population for a long time was either smaller than, or the same as, Ireland's), humid, relatively new (at least in terms of its European and African populations, though Native Americans were thriving in the southeast long before settlers from the European continent had even reached the shores of Ireland), racially divided area of a mighty nation; the other a tiny, damp, old, fairly uniform country, three-quarters of which is an independent republic. At the end of *A Book of Migrations: Some Passages in Ireland*, Rebecca Solnit, a Californian of Jewish and Irish ancestry, expresses relief at leaving such a "homogeneous" society with its "wall-to-wall white faces" for a Paris "full of Africans and Asians who had reversed the colonial process and were remaking the city, making it less predictable, less conventional, more porous to other possibilities and more complicated identities—more like home for me." Such distinct demographics highlight one difference between the two places: There are few blacks and hardly any Native Americans at all in Ireland, while, as noted earlier, most white southerners identify with England and Scotland rather than with Ireland as their mother country.[6]

The American South, too, is perceived as being staunchly Protestant in an evangelical, fundamentalist tradition that is often hostile to Roman Catholicism, the faith of the majority of inhabitants of the Republic of Ireland at least. The South is, indeed, the part of the United States with which Irish people nowadays least identify and to which they hardly ever emigrate. The foremost expert on the history of southern folk music—a medium that seems especially to betray Irish and Scottish origins—warns that the Celtic influences are only part of the story, and that African American and other popular and commercial influences are so much present that it is almost impossible, and certainly misguided, to attempt to separate out its original ethnic strains.[7]

Yet there is a need for some caution in trying to disassociate the Irish

5. Quoted in William D. Griffin, *The Book of Irish Americans* (New York, 1990), 114; Ann Waldron, *Eudora Welty: A Writer's Life* (New York, 1998), 220; Seamus Heaney, "Translator's Introduction" to *Beowulf: A Verse Translation* (New York, 2002), xxxv.

6. Rebecca Solnit, *A Book of Migrations: Some Passages in Ireland* (New York, 1997), 167–68.

7. See Bill C. Malone, "Neither Anglo-Saxon nor Celtic: The Music of the Southern Plain Folk," in *Plain Folk of the South Revisited*, ed. Samuel C. Hyde Jr. (Baton Rouge, 1997), 21–45.

and southern experiences. The 1990 U.S. census, for example, has shown that about the same percentage of southerners as Americans in other parts of the country identify their primary heritage as Irish (about 18 percent). That such identification obscures the distinction between those of Irish-Irish (mainly Catholics from the southern and western parts of Ireland) and Scotch-Irish (mainly Protestants from Scotland whose ancestors migrated first to the north of Ireland in the 1600s and thence to the United States) descent only serves to highlight the complications of the comparison, challenging a too-easy perception of an Irish society that today has several, and often contesting, identities, partly, though by no means exclusively, based in traditional religious affiliations. In other words, taking the island of Ireland as a totality, its society is much more Protestant—and often of a fundamentalist variety—than is usually thought of. Northern Irish poet John Montague, for example, mentions that in attending Dr. Ian Paisley's Free Presbyterian church in Belfast seeking to understand Protestant hatred against Catholics, he has "met the old racialism of the Deep South, where [Paisley] got his theological doctorate." Montague is still referring to a fellow countryman, however oppositional their political and religious views may be. Nor have the modes of Protestant and Catholic religious sentiment over the last two centuries always been quite as distinct as popular belief assumes. New Orleans, reputedly the most Catholic, non-Anglo city in the United States, lies in the so-called Protestant South and has a large Irish community (some of it inextricably mixed with the city's Creole population); the country's best-known Catholic monastery is in Kentucky; and the third largest St. Patrick's Day celebration takes place in Savannah, Georgia, where there are relatively few Catholics.[8]

It might be kept in mind, too, that the part of Ireland that has been independent of British rule since the 1920s has also maintained extremely close economic and cultural ties with its larger neighbor. Like the South vis-à-vis the United States, the Irish Republic remains in many ways just another region of the United Kingdom. Large numbers of Irish men and women seek employment in London or Liverpool, almost as readily as a Southerner might move to New York or Los Angeles for the same purposes.

---

8. According to the 1990 census, there are 44.3 million Irish Americans in the United States, making them the second largest European ethnic group. More significantly, the percentages given for the southern states are very similar to those for other parts of the country: Arkansas 23%, Tennessee 22%, North Carolina 17.9%, Virginia 17.6%, Louisiana 14.2%, Mississippi 19%, Alabama 18%, Georgia 18%, South Carolina 18%, Kentucky 21.3%; John Montague, in *The Celtic Consciousness,* ed. Robert O'Driscoll (New York, 1981), 437.

Notwithstanding fears of erratic prejudice, the Irish emigrant to England is likely to arrive more with a sense of entitlement than of ethnic apprehension. There is no passport control between Ireland and the UK; Irish residents in Britain routinely vote in elections there; British and Irish academics operate more or less freely in the same job (or jobless) market; and the British army has long recruited in the Republic with the tacit consent of the Dublin government. There are few Irish people who don't have intimate and multigenerational family ties with Britain, ties that were kept alive by proximity in a way that, until recently, Irish-American ones of the same vintage were not.

Even the Scottish element in the counties of Ulster is more complex than might at first appear. There has certainly been more Gaelic Highland ancestry than the nineteenth-century emphasis on Lowland roots wished to acknowledge. Furthermore, those "traditions" that we now most associate with Scotland itself come largely from its Catholic Highland, once despised, heritage. Romantic Bonnie Prince Charlie, last of the Stuart dynasty, after his defeat at Culloden in 1746 ended his days in Rome (where he had also been born) under papal protection, his fate as much lamented by the Irish Gaelic poets of the eighteenth century—as well they might since a good part of his army had been recruited from Irish Brigade regiments in the service of France—as by William Faulkner in the twentieth. Meanwhile, Scottish Presbyterians, both in Northern Ireland and in the American South, were often Gaelic speakers.[9]

Part of the explanation for such cultural amnesia is that most of the Irish immigration to the American South dates from the pre–Civil War era, so that unlike the case in the Northeast or West where there has been a continuous stream of newcomers, a sense of distinctive inheritance has become muted. In confrontation with a large African American presence, Irish ancestry has frequently faded into generic whiteness. It has even been argued, a little tongue-in-cheek perhaps (though Margaret Mitchell concurred), that the Irish were so anxious to fit in that they eventually became more southern than the southerners themselves. A somewhat surprising finding of David T. Gleeson's *The Irish in the South, 1815–1877* is that, even in regard to Roman Catholic immigrants, it is the southern states that have

9. Harman Murtagh, "Irish Soldiers Abroad, 1600–1800," in *A Military History of Ireland*, ed. Thomas Bartlett and Keith Jeffery (Cambridge, 1996), 308; Roger Blaney, *Presbyterians and the Irish Language* (Belfast, 1996); Celeste Ray, *Highland Heritage: Scottish Americans in the American South* (Chapel Hill, 2001), 17–44.

always been more welcoming to the Irish (not least because they arrived in smaller numbers) than those of the Puritan Northeast; moreover, in the booming and confident South on the eve of the Civil War, it was possible for an Irish laborer to earn more in Mississippi than in Massachusetts.[10]

While for most of the last two hundred years, Irish self-identification has been almost exclusively with the South's white population, there have also been multiple, if less direct, associations and comparisons with African and Native Americans. Drawing parallels between these groups and the Irish is not unusual, as we saw in the Frederick Douglass epigraph. Apart from a measure of miscegenation (often between master or overseer and slave) common to all races in the South—and some of it quite notable—the emphasis here is on a similarity of situation and treatment. So, for example, in Mississippian Richard Wright's 1940 novel *Native Son*, an Irish maid remarks to the protagonist and southern migrant, Bigger Thomas, "My folks in the old country feel about England like the colored folks feel about this country," an observation that resonated in the nineteenth century also. Indeed, abolitionist William Lloyd Garrison, when trying to wean Irish Americans away from the Democratic Party and its support for slavery, constantly reiterated that the subjection of slave to master paralleled that of the Irish in Ireland to England. Nineteenth-century black leaders who bitterly complained about Irish-American prejudice against them often conceded that the Irish in Ireland were different and deserving of sympathy because of their subordination to British rule. On a different front, in encouraging the writers of the Harlem Renaissance in the early part of the twentieth century, black southerner James Weldon Johnson invoked what he thought of as the parallel model of John Millington Synge in Ireland.[11]

Many of the early English settlers in Virginia found that the native inhabitants reminded them of the "wilde Irish." Captain John Smith observed that the deerskin robes Indians wore in Virginia did not differ much "in fashion from the Irish mantels." In a famous speech in 1892 on the loss of the Irish Gaelic language, Douglas Hyde, future first president of the Irish Free State, commented that "our place names have been treated with about the same respect as if they were the names of a savage tribe . . . and with

10. David T. Gleeson, *The Irish in the South, 1815–1877* (Chapel Hill, 2001), 54.

11. Richard Wright, *Native Son* (New York, 1993), 58; Arnold Shankman, "Black on Green: Afro-American Editors on Irish Independence, 1840–1921," *Phylon* 41, no. 3 (1980): 293; Lauren Onkey, "Celtic Soul Brothers," *Éire-Ireland* 28, no. 3 (1993): 149. Note also Alain Locke: "Harlem has the same role to play for the New Negro as Dublin has had for the New Ireland" (ibid.).

about the same intelligence and contempt as vulgar English squatters treat the topographical nomenclature of the Red Indians."[12]

More recent examples of the Irish-Indian relationship are to be found in the poetry of southerner R. T. Smith, which celebrates his Yonosa (a North Carolina tribe) and Irish inheritances equally. Attention has also been given to the help Choctaw Indians in Oklahoma sent to the starving Irish in 1847 in memory of their own similar plight on the trail of tears from northern Mississippi in 1831. In 1996, Irish president Mary Robinson went to Oklahoma to thank them, while the Irish government commissioned a painting by Choctaw artist Gary White Deer to commemorate the 150th anniversary of Ireland's famine. The painting depicted a Choctaw woman holding an Irish child, with an Irish woman embracing a "third world" infant. A new organization for world famine relief resulted from the visit, "Celts and American Indians Together." Traditions lie buried inside one another, inextricably enmeshed.[13]

This connection between the Irish in Ireland and the Choctaws in the southern United States (driven, incidentally, from their original lands by the Scotch-Irish Andrew Jackson) is neither obvious nor simple, yet it has both significant practical and sentimental importance. It also serves in the present instance to underline that while much of what follows in this study will be indeed more obvious, no attempt is being made to find a mechanical, one-on-one relationship between Ireland and the American South. In fact, from one perspective there is a massive difference between them: Ireland, or at least Catholic Ireland, is generally seen—even by those who care little about it—as a country that has had a wrong done to it over the centuries, whereas the white American South, in spite of continuing fascination with the romance of the plantation legend, is thought of, like Germany perhaps, as a place that has done wrong to others and that has continued to do so until very recently. Some scholars have thought that the point of comparison should be between Northern Ireland and the American South since serious minority problems have persisted in both. The basic claim here, then, is not that there is a rigid sameness between the two cultures but rather that there exists a set of family and circumstantial resemblances the

12. Ronald Takaki, "*The Tempest* in the Wilderness: The Racialization of Savagery," *Journal of American History* 79, no. 3 (1992): 895; Douglas Hyde, "The Necessity for De-Anglicising Ireland," in *Language, Lore and Lyrics*, ed. Breandán Ó Conaire (Dublin, 1986), 166.

13. R. T. Smith, *The Cardinal Heart* (Livingston, Ala., 1991); this Irish–Native American association has even reached the children's book market: see Marie-Louise Fitzpatrick, *The Long March* (Dublin, 1998).

detailed exploration of which can lead to an enhanced understanding of each region separately, as well as of the larger British and American polities.[14]

What differences would there be were one to compare the American South with England or with Scotland? In the former case, of course, the narrative would be quite dissimilar, packed of necessity with background on the founding of Virginia and the other early colonies, and with subsequent English activities in the formation of the elite, as well as the dominant common, southern civilization. But in spite of the wealth of historical material, it would be very difficult, if not impossible, to draw any parallel at all between the progress of the English nation over the following three centuries and that of the South, for even keeping in mind the imperial decline and various other setbacks of the "Mother Country" during the last one hundred years, in no way has England's story been one of defeat, occupation, shame, and ambivalent recovery. Even John Keegan, the well-known British military historian (whose regularly acknowledged Irish Catholic background, incidentally, points to some relevant complexities in the construction of "Britishness") who has confessed to "being at home in Dixie" more than in any other part of the United States because of that sense of pain and defeat, as well as its class system and "the famous femininity of its women," in the end describes his identification with the South as "slight."[15]

The Scottish case offers more parallels and is expressed in southerners' celebration of their partly inherited "Highland" heritage. But even Scotland has tended to associate itself with the overall British enterprise to such an extent that its earlier defeat is one of historical fact rather than current consciousness—this in spite of periodic revivals of intense nationalism and the recent move to devolution. Moreover, it is not unfair to say that the Scottish literary production in the twentieth century has been, from an in-

14. See Christine Kinealy, "Potatoes, Providence, and Philanthropy: The Role of Private Charity during the Irish Famine," in *The Meaning of the Famine,* ed. Patrick O'Sullivan (Leicester, UK, 1997), 140–71; for a comprehensive assessment of the current literature on the famine, see James S. Donnelly Jr., *The Great Irish Potato Famine* (Stroud, UK, 2001); see, for example, Frank Wright, *Northern Ireland: A Comparative Analysis* (Totowa, N.J., 1988).

15. John Keegan, *Fields of Battle: The Wars for North America* (New York, 1996), 41. Keegan discusses his Irish background in the preface to *The Face of Battle* (New York, 1976). In *Circling Dixie: Contemporary Southern Culture through a Transatlantic Lens* (New Brunswick, 2001), Helen Taylor deals with English-southern connections in terms of music, theatre, images, etc., rather than from a historical point of view.

ternational perspective, relatively modest. It is in this sense—the existence of a tradition of defeat and denigration combined with an unexpected literary flowering—that the Irish connection, though less significant numerically than that of England, or emotionally than that of Scotland, much more closely parallels the South's historical trajectory. Indeed, it might be said that the reluctance of southern elites to be identified with the Irish is mirrored in the educated Irish hesitation to be identified with such a backward region of the United States as the South is generally perceived to be.[16]

In searching for Ireland and the Irish—or indeed for any other ethnic traditions—in the American South, one is mindful of the cautions about the dangers of "ethnic pride" offered by recent commentators as diverse as Orlando Patterson, Walter Benn Michaels, and Simon James. The constant rooting for origins can have atavistic and ugly implications, a desire for a new or renewed exclusivity. This is certainly true of the "Celtic South" thesis, which seems merely to tolerate the African American presence in the region. Eric Lott too has criticized this seeking out of "true" sources and origins, which he claims "unmask[s] nothing so much as the arguments themselves, self evident plays for rhetorical (and racial) mastery over a very confused and confusing history of cultural intermixing." Such considerations are part of my investigation, however, as I attempt to examine issues involving the definitions of ethnicity and race, stereotypes and prejudice, and colonialism and postcolonialism in the formation of a culture. More than ever, we have all become sensitive to the *constructed* nature of national identities. Twenty years ago Seamus Heaney referred empathetically to contemporary English writers as both defending and exploring "an identity which is threatened" in ways similar to what had been the lot earlier of that country's colonies, including America. Hence the ever-shifting interpretations of historical periods that until lately seemed to have their understandings set in stone. The most recent major study of the relations between England, Wales, Scotland, and Ireland, for example, calls itself simply *The*

16. Ray, 46–49, 186–88. This difference in literary achievement in the twentieth century is seen all the more readily in the many comparisons between Ireland and Scotland—as, for example, in Ray Ryan's *Ireland and Scotland: Literature and Culture, State and Nation, 1966–2000* (Oxford, 2002) and in Seamus Heaney's empathetic essays on Hugh McDiarmid, Sorley McClean, and Norman MacCaig in *Finders Keepers: Selected Prose, 1971–2001* (New York, 2002).

Isles, very consciously omitting the controversial but nevertheless traditional adjective "British."[17]

But it is also the case that we live somewhere in the interim between
the old, essentializing rigidities of identity of the past and a distant future
when we may all, as a Faulkner character speculates in *Absalom, Absalom!*,
have bleached (an interesting color assumption) out so that "I who regard
you will also have sprung from the loins of African kings." Linda Colley,
possibly the most prominent scholar on the formation of British identity
(and herself of Welsh, Irish, and English ancestry), has predicted that the
issue will, happily, have less importance in a hundred years time. But
meanwhile, neglected contributions, minor and major, still need to be temporarily acknowledged, just as the fact that the South is the *most* African
part of the United States still needs emphasizing. Only now is women's
history in Ireland, in America, in the South, and among various ethnic
groups being retrieved and written, and this effort in time is bound to alter
the landscape of our understanding, perhaps even for a time eclipsing other
approaches.[18]

So in this study I try to recreate identity even as I seek to dissolve its
tenuous foundations. I subscribe to Zora Neale Hurston's views in her short
1928 essay "How It Feels to Be Colored Me," where she describes both the
many occasions when she thinks of herself as "colored" *and* the many occasions when she does not. At times, she explains, "I have no race, I am *me*
. . . The cosmic Zora . . ." "But in the main," she concludes,

> I feel like a brown bag of miscellany propped against a wall. Against a wall
> in company with other bags, white, red and yellow. Pour out the contents,
> and there is discovered a jumble of small things priceless and worthless. A
> first-water diamond, an empty spool, bits of broken glass, lengths of string,
> a key to a door long since crumbled away, a rusty knife-blade, old shoes
> saved for a road that never was and never will be, a nail bent under the
> weight of things too heavy for any nail, a dried flower or two still a little

17. Orlando Patterson, *The Ordeal of Integration* (Washington, D.C., 1997); Walter Benn Mi-
chaels, *Our America: Nativism, Modernism, and Pluralism* (Durham, N.C., 1995); Simon James,
The Atlantic Celts: Ancient People or Modern Invention? (Madison, Wis., 1999). For a criticism
of James, see Murray G. H. Pittock, *Celtic Identity and the British Image* (New York, 1999), 6.
Norman Davis, *The Isles: A History* (New York, 1999); Eric Lott, *Love and Theft: Blackface
Minstrelsy and the American Working Class* (New York, 1993), 94; Heaney, *Finders Keepers*, 82.

18. William Faulkner, *Absalom, Absalom!* (New York, 1990), 302; Daniel Snowman, "Linda
Colley," *History Today* 53, no. 1 (2003): 18–21.

fragrant. In your hand is the brown bag. On the ground before you is the jumble it held—so much like the jumble in the bags, could they be emptied, that all might be dumped in a single heap and the bags refilled without altering the content of any greatly. A bit of colored glass more or less would not matter.

It is an arresting image, strangely prophetic too in these days of genome research. But it is also an image from a writer who confesses that in certain circumstances her "color comes" and she feels passionately "other." No longer is she "cosmic Zora." It is in addition the overly optimistic image of a woman for whom "the sobbing school of Negrohood" and the ills of slavery need to be forgotten—"I am off to a flying start and I must not halt in the stretch to look behind and weep"—in a way that Rosa Parks and the civil rights leaders of subsequent decades must have found naïve in the extreme. Origins are never simple and their contending impulses need exercise if they are to be relieved. Such is certainly the case here with the present author, and it may be too that distinctions of some kind are a necessary and constitutive part of any culture.[19]

Seamus Heaney, who was born in Northern Ireland, has elaborated on one of his motives for translating the medieval Gaelic narrative poem *Sweeney Astray (Buile Suibhne)* in the early 1980s: he wanted "to say to unionists in the North [of Ireland], 'Look! Ulster may be British but here was Sweeney, a king in County Antrim in the eighth century. The ethos of the places that you think of as Plantation places was Irish in Sweeney's day. There was and is another culture here. Listen!'" I am attracted by the defiant impulse of Heaney's claim, but, in the end, a gentler quilting metaphor from Alice Walker better reflects my intentions. In her seminal essay on Flannery O'Connor, another southern writer with Irish associations, Walker remarks that "the truth about any subject only comes when all the sides of the story are put together, and all their different meanings make one new one." Walker wanted to establish what she saw as the neglected African American contribution to southern history; I want to register the Irish input and so too make a "new" meaning for the whole. I want to reimagine Irishness in a southern context, but more to establish presence than to assert pride.[20]

---

19. Zora Neale Hurston, *I Love Myself When I Am Laughing*, ed. Alice Walker (New York, 1979), 155.

20. Seamus Heaney, interview with Mike Murphy, in *Reading the Future: Irish Writers in Conversation with Mike Murphy*, ed. Clíodhna Ní Anluain (Dublin, 2000), 94; Alice Walker, *In Search of Our Mothers' Gardens* (New York, 1983), 49.

*   *   *

This book, then, has three purposes. Its first is to gather together and broadly analyze what is known to date about those Irish who actually left their native land to come to the southern area of the United States and who, in many cases, were aware of profound similarities between the two places in spite of their significant differences. The second, and possibly more important, purpose is to explore the similarity of historical and cultural experiences between Ireland and the American South as places marginal to the predominant ethos of their respective larger societies in Britain and the United States, and the influences of the one on the other. The third, which is intertwined with the first two, is to reflect on questions of identity, race, culture, colonialism and postcolonialism, stereotypes, and prejudice that are of current and ongoing concern.

The five chapters in the section entitled "Kin" deal with the actual connections between Ireland and the South in terms of immigrants, their attitudes toward the "peculiar institution" of slavery, their participation in the Civil War, and those subsequent southern writers of immediate Irish background who were conscious of a tragic similarity between both places. The five chapters in the "Kinship" section are more concerned with making significant comparisons between the two cultures in terms of their use of religion to create sustaining nationalist mythologies in the late nineteenth century, the often similar stereotyping to which they have been subjected, their uncertain literary beginnings (at least in English) and parallel literary revivals, and their long noted—and much criticized—preoccupation with historical defeat and intimate engagement in bitter disputes as to the interpretation of their respective pasts.

The relationship between Ireland and the American South, I will argue, is a "postmodern" rather than a "modern" one in that it is made up of a patchwork of bits and pieces from the past and the present rather than forming a comforting organic unity. Even most of the historical actors in the drama, those Irishmen or sons and daughters of such who had emigrated to the South in the eighteenth and nineteenth centuries and conceived its situation as similar to what they had experienced back home, by and large did not interact with one another, however much they may have had in common. That an Irish-born soldier in a Civil War battle (and on either side) may have been thinking of his own country's plight while the American or German-born infantryman next to him was experiencing totally different historical associations does not in any way invalidate the Irishman's perceptions. So what follows is a sub (one might even hesitatingly refer to it in computerese as a "slave") narrative rather than a new "master" account. It supplements and complements rather than replaces. At the same time, the story highlights a relation that is also symptomatic of much that is going on in the world today where cultures are intertwined as never before:

> You know the passport forms
> Or even some job applications noo-a-days?
> Well, there's nowhere to write
> Celtic-Afro-Caribbean in answer to the "origin" question;
> They think that's a contradiction.

So writes Jackie Kay, a contemporary British poet (Scottish mother, Nigerian father) living in England, in lines that could equally describe much of the complexity of the South, except that one might want to add Anglo or Creole or both to the gumbo of "Celtic-Afro-Caribbean."[21]

Research for this study has led me into many byways of the Irish and southern, British and American, black and white psyches, and into contact with levels of emotion in both historical and literary writing which I would normally prefer to avoid. It is not easy to write with empathy about views on race and ethnicity that are offensive not only to contemporary sensibilities but also to the humanity of those who were their original object. But these matters too are part of what this work is all about, its shortcomings and partialities an indication of authorial imperfections. Moreover, my own approach is not without its peculiar pieties. Irish by birth and early education, I live in a southern city with no especial Irish connections, but which nevertheless is home to a fortress-like Quinlan Castle (the only one in the world that I know of) that daily flies, as all proper castles do, the Union Jack, and that is marked by a shield sporting an accurate rendering of the rather undistinguished family's coat of arms.[22] Two of my great aunts came to the state early in the twentieth century as Roman Catholic nuns and are buried in a convent cemetery in Mobile. In the 1870s, Charles Stewart Par-

---

21. Jackie Kay, personal communication, 2003; see also her *The Adoption Papers* (London, 1991).

22. The castle was the inspiration of two local doctors returned from service in France during World War I. Its name derives from an adjoining street named after John Quinlan, Mobile's bishop during the Civil War; the site was originally intended for a Catholic cathedral. Now a national historic building, Quinlan Castle has served as a hotel and apartment house, enjoying less than a salubrious reputation for much of its existence.

nell considered investing in the city's new steel industry—his older brother already being a peach farmer in the state—and only changed his plans when his train was derailed outside Birmingham, an ill omen for the superstitious future leader of the Irish Home Rule party, a man destined to be celebrated as the "uncrowned king" of his country. According to one account, it was even his brother's discontent with the indignities of Reconstruction that sharpened Parnell's own perception of English-Irish injustices. In 1908, what is believed to be the first statue erected to a female educator in America was unveiled in the city's central park; it honored Mary Cahalan, daughter of Irish Catholic immigrants. At the city's Roman Catholic cathedral in 1921, an Irish-born priest was fatally shot by an itinerant Methodist preacher because he had just performed a wedding ceremony between the preacher's rebellious daughter and a dark-skinned Puerto Rican. In the celebrated trial that followed, the defendant was successfully represented by the able Hugo Black, then a member of the Ku Klux Klan but who was to go on to become one of the most liberal members of the U.S. Supreme Court, and whose own ancestors claimed that they had fled Ireland in the 1790s because of being related to the proscribed revolutionaries Thomas Addis Emmet and his better-known brother, Robert.[23]

In more recent times, Irish connections—random, curious, sometimes significant—persist. The current Earl of Bantry in County Cork was for many years a farmer in the state and taught English at one of the local private schools. The Irish Georgian Society (of which I am not a member), a group dedicated to preserving eighteenth-century Irish architecture, has a branch in the city. A recent candidate for the Irish presidency, a popular singer of staunchly conservative outlook, resides here too, though I was not aware of that until she began to run for office and a number of Irish journalists sought out my uninformed ear. Almost the first person I met on arrival in Birmingham in 1986 was a Lebanese restaurant owner who had lived for years in Dublin and still retained his Irish passport. On my way to work during the last couple of years I have begun to notice the frequency with which a Guinness truck is parked outside a popular restaurant (nearby Atlanta being now the number one consumer of that beverage in the United States), making me fondly nostalgic for a youth spent watching that com-

23. R. F. Foster, *Charles Stewart Parnell: The Man and His Family* (London, 1976), 94; John D. Fair and Cordelia C. Humphrey, "The Alabama Dimension of the Political Thought of Charles Stewart Parnell," *Alabama Review* (January 1999): 21–50; Roger K. Newman, *Hugo Black: A Biography* (New York, 1994), 4, 71–85.

pany's barges lower their grimy red and black funnels as they passed beneath the Liffey bridges of "dear dirty Dublin" in the 1950s.[24]

My own experience, therefore, leads me to pay particular heed to Irish historian Roy Foster's admonition in *Paddy and Mr. Punch* that "Dutifully based theories of culture usually break down when posited against the variety and ambivalence of historical experience." But, he adds, "The disciplines of history and literature can . . . illuminate crooked corners and eccentric alleyways—even if the shadows around them loom more questioningly than ever." Such, then, are the mental and emotional pieties that energize, I hope, the narrative that follows.[25]

24. Rosemary Scallon, better known as "Dana." She won the European Song Contest in 1970, worked for the EWTN Catholic television station in Birmingham, and lost the Irish presidential election in 1997 but went on to become a senator in the European Parliament.

25. R. F. Foster, *Paddy and Mr. Punch: Connections in Irish and English History* (New York, 1995), 305.

{ KİΠ }

CHAPTER 1

ELUSIVE ANCESTRIES

Any serious non-racist history of the Irish in the United States should spend as much time upon the Baptists (especially the Southern Baptists), Methodists, Anglicans and Presbyterians as upon the history of the Catholic Church.

—DONALD HARMAN AKENSON, 1992

Emigration is a much more serious matter than revolution. Virtually, it is obliteration.

—JOEL CHANDLER HARRIS, 1884

On September 4, 1607, Hugh O'Neill, Earl of Tyrone, and Rory O'Donnell, Earl of Tyrconnell, having been decisively defeated by the English just six years earlier at the Battle of Kinsale and apparently unwilling to continue to rule their Ulster chiefdoms as mere representatives of the crown, secretly boarded a French ship in Lough Swilly with the intention of fleeing to their former ally, Catholic Spain. Although the immediate reasons for their hasty and unexpected departure have never been wholly clear, they were already compromised by holding both English and Irish clan titles and so were always in danger of failing to satisfy the expectations of one or other party. In any case, after many upsets, both navigational and diplomatic, they and a retinue of about a hundred followers arrived instead in Rome in April of the following year to a life of permanent exile. With their departure most of what remained of the Old Gaelic order came to an end and modern Irish history began.

Within the next hundred years about 85 percent of Irish lands would be expropriated for English and Scottish occupation, the country's political leadership becoming resolutely Protestant in the process. Sometime after the departure of O'Neill and O'Donnell, a poem attributed to the poet-priest and historian Geoffrey Keating—Séathrún Céitinn in the Gaelic language that was his usual means of expression, though he was himself a long-

assimilated scion of earlier invaders from the British mainland—bitterly
commended the wisdom of what was to be known afterward as "the flight
of the Earls":

Muna bhfóiridh Ceard na n-ardreann pobal chrích Chuirc
ar fhoirneart námhad ndána n-ullamh ndíoltach
ní mór nárbh fhearr gan chairde a bhfoscaindíolaim
's a seoladh slán i bhfán tar tonnaibh Chlíona.

[If the Craftsman of Stars protect not Ireland's people
from violent vengeful enemies, bold and ready,
better gather and winnow them now without delay
and sail them out wandering safe on the waves of Cliona.[1]]

There would be many "Irish" earls in future years but few that the general
populace could readily accept as legitimate heirs to ancient patrimonies.
The hope for another century—and even as late as Culloden in 1746—was
that a return and restoration would be possible when England was ruled
once again by a Stuart of more Catholic sympathy. Such was the hope also
of thousands more of the defeated Irish Catholic officers and soldiers who
would emigrate to join the armies of the European monarchies during the
next two centuries after O'Neill's and O'Donnell's flight.[2]

The expectation, as we know, was never to be realized, though the rising of 1641 led by Owen Roe O'Neill, Hugh O'Neill's nephew returned from
service with Spain in the Netherlands, had given temporary hope of success. Inspired by the opportunities for redress and religious concession that
the English Civil War seemed to offer, the Irish made an uneasy—on both
sides—and belated alliance with Charles I's Cavaliers against Oliver Cromwell's republican Roundheads. In the end, however, following Cromwell's
triumph, additional thousands of men, women, and children would be
transported to the West Indies as prisoners and even, according to some
historians, as slaves. Ireland, unlike England, would never see a restoration
of its lost leadership; rather, with the defeat of Catholic King James II, a

1. *An Duanaire, 1600–1900: Poems of the Dispossessed,* ed. Seán Ó Tuama, trans. Thomas
Kinsella (Dublin, 1981), 86–87.

2. It should be noted, however, that since as early as 1585, Catholic Irish mercenaries had
been recruited by the Spanish crown for its wars in the Netherlands, a country being suppressed by Spain as much as Ireland was by England, though the Dutch managed to survive
while the Irish did not. See Hiram Morgan, *Tyrone's Rebellion: The Outbreak of the Nine Years
War in Tudor Ireland* (Woodbridge, UK, 1993).

Stuart, at the Battle of the Boyne in 1690 by his son-in-law, Dutch Protestant William of Orange, a new Anglo-Irish ascendancy would come into being. This elite was all the more hostile to the Catholic masses and their former chieftains because of the constant threat of a repossession to be brought about by a Spanish or a French invasion; they were thus ready to impose draconian penal codes in order to keep control of their recent acquisitions.[3]

Earlier in 1607—the same year the old Irish order began its relentless decline to be replaced by an English Protestant hegemony fortified by its many Scottish settlers—a different native leadership on the other side of the Atlantic was also, if unwittingly, facing its eventual decimation at the hands of another "English" invasion. The process bore obvious, and frequently recognized, similarities to events in Ireland, for many of the new colonists from as early as 1594 onward—Sir Humphrey Gilbert, Sir Walter Raleigh, Ralph Lane, Sir Richard Grenville—had gained their first experiences of conquest by crossing the Irish sea and were armed even now with settlement layout plans that had already been used in Ulster. As Ronald Takaki notes, "The conquest of Ireland and the settlement of Virginia were bound so closely together that one correspondence, dated March 8, 1610, stated: 'It is hoped the plantation of Ireland may shortly be settled. The Lord Delaware . . . is preparing to depart for the plantation of Virginia.'"[4]

The original settlers in what was to become the Virginia colony occasionally noted that the American natives reminded them of that official category of Hibernians known as the "wilde Irish" because of their dress and tribal ways. The two groups were also frequently treated in the same savage manner. Moreover, Powhatan—the name given to Wahunsonacock by the English—suffered a fate that involved many of the same elements and actors as had been the case with the Irish chiefs. Driven north from Florida by the invading Spaniards, first his father and then he himself had conquered other Indian tribes along the mid-Atlantic coast. He was even "crowned" by Christopher Newport in 1609—and balked at the subordina-

3. See, for example, Seán O'Callaghan, *To Hell or Barbados: The Ethnic Cleansing of Ireland* (Dingle, IR, 2000). In *Success Is Never Final: Empire, War, and Faith in Early Modern Europe* (New York, 2002), Geoffrey Parker has argued that the Irish with their officers trained in continental warfare were well prepared for the trials of the 1600s, that their defeat was by no means preordained, and that it stemmed from "political, not military, factors" (191).

4. Ivor Noel Hume, *The Virginia Adventure: Roanoke to James Towne, An Archaeological and Historical Odyssey* (New York, 1994), 148; Ronald Takaki, "*The Tempest* in the Wilderness: The Racialization of Savagery," *Journal of American History* 79, no. 3 (1992): 895.

tion involved—as a consolation for the loss of his recently acquired territories, but he quickly declined into political irrelevance as further European depredations depleted his tenuous acquisitions.[5]

While it is tempting to extend the Irish-Indian parallel further, the important difference between the Ulster and Virginian invasions is that from the very beginning there were significant scatterings of Irishmen among the new American colonists too. The first recorded Irish immigrant to continental America, Father Richard Arthur, a native of Limerick and formerly one of those exiled Irish serving in the Spanish army, had landed in St. Augustine in Florida in June 1597 and was already dead by the founding of Jamestown. Francis Magnel, an Irishman, arrived in Virginia with Christopher Newport in May 1607 and afterward worked for Spain, which suggests that he may have been Catholic. Kerby A. Miller notes that "As early as the 1620s ships were sailing regularly from southern Irish ports such as Cork and Kinsale, laden with provisions, textiles, and Irish servants to exchange for West Indian sugar and Chesapeake tobacco. As a result of this trade, during the 1600s Irish Catholics appeared in every mainland colony, where tracts of land named 'New Ireland' and 'New Munster' were set aside for Irish settlers and their servants." In April 1636, one Thomas Anthony "hired agents to attend the markets in Cork, Bandon and Youghal, beating their drums and making their spiel about the advantages of life in Virginia."[6]

The recently defeated, dispossessed, emigrating, and exiled Irish were to arrive in the American colonies from several directions—Ireland, England, France, Spain, either directly or via the Caribbean—and in several different capacities: as adventurers, indentured servants, transported prisoners, soldiers, clergymen, administrators, or agents of contending empires. On the other side of the American continent, they were eager supporters of the Spanish missions that displaced Pueblo Indians to found Santa Fe, also in 1607. Conquered themselves, they left Ireland in the expectation of conquering others. It would have been extraordinary for the time had they intended otherwise.[7]

5. Frederic W. Gleach, *Powhatan's World and Colonial Virginia: A Conflict of Cultures* (Lincoln, Neb., 1997), 126–27.

6. Michael J. McNally, "Florida," *Encyclopedia of the Irish in America*, ed. Michael Glazier (Notre Dame, 1999), 340; David B. Quinn, *Ireland and America: Their Early Associations, 1500–1640* (Liverpool, 1991), 27; Kerby A. Miller, *Emigrants and Exiles: Ireland and the Irish Exodus to North America* (New York, 1985), 139.

7. The last Spanish viceroy on the eve of Mexican independence in the 1820s, General Juan O'Donoju, was a descendant of those Irish who had left for Spain in the sixteenth and seventeenth centuries.

A substantial number of those earliest Irish arrivals were either Catholic or of recent Catholic background, though it is suspected also that many of them either had converted to Anglicanism back in Ireland or were to do so in the colonies where they were often servants of Protestant families. Clergy of their own faith were scarce, and it was expected that Irish Catholic servants "would be amenable to reform when placed in a godly environment."[8]

There were too some individual cases that must have been quite outside the general norm. Astute political maneuvering had enabled the O'Carrolls, for example, (unlike O'Neill and O'Donnell, though some of their kinfolk too had actually connived at and profited from their departure) to hold on to their lands in counties Tipperary and Offaly through the crisis of 1607 and Cromwell's assault in the 1640s (in which, however, they forfeited three-quarters of their lands), only to be forced finally to abandon Ireland in 1688. At that point the head of the family, afterward known as Charles Carroll the Settler, emigrated to Catholic Maryland where for a very short time he served as attorney general under Lord Baltimore. Carroll succeeded in founding what is reputed to have been the wealthiest mercantile and plantation-owning dynasty in the colonies. But religion and ethnicity made the family's fortunes precarious until the American Revolution; for example, the exploits of Bonnie Prince Charlie in far away Scotland in the 1740s led to Maryland banning Catholics—especially those of Irish background—from service in its militia.[9]

The immediate descendants of the O'Mores, who had also lost their lands in Offaly, Anglicized their name and religion and went on to serve as colonial governors of South Carolina. Even some of Carroll's extended family in Maryland switched to the established Anglican Church and tried to use the courts to dispossess their Catholic relatives. Dr. Charles Carroll arrived in 1715 at age twenty-four still a Catholic. In 1738, however, he joined the Church of England—possibly in part because the papacy in its loyalty to the exiled Stuarts was unwilling to compromise on an acceptable oath to the British Crown, which would have eased the situation of propertied Catholics—removed his son from a Catholic school in Portugal to England's Eton, and roused up anti-Catholic hysteria in the Maryland Assembly. In

8. See Nicholas Canny, "The Origins of Empire: An Introduction," in *The Oxford History of the British Empire*, vol. 1, ed. Nicholas Canny (New York, 1998), 18.

9. Ronald Hoffman, *Princes of Ireland, Planters of Maryland: A Carroll Saga, 1500–1782* (Chapel Hill, 2000), 270.

1776, his son reverted to Catholicism and worked to see the laws against it removed. Other somewhat atypical Irish Catholic exiles arrived, as has been noted already, in the employ of the French and Spanish colonial administrations in Florida, Louisiana, and Texas.[10]

It was not until a few generations after 1607 that many of the descendants of the Lowland Presbyterian Scots who had been settled in Ireland in the decades following the flight of the earls would themselves immigrate to the American frontier in considerable numbers. They were driven by the pressure of religious—since they were considered "Dissenters" from Anglican orthodoxy, Presbyterians were required to have their marriages validated by an Anglican clergyman—and economic necessity, or simply by a desire to better themselves in a less hostile environment. By then they had formed an identity separate both from the Ulster Irish among whom they lived and from the inhabitants of the Scotland their ancestors had left. Self-made, or rather re-made, these "Ulster Scots" emigrated to the New World in considerably greater numbers—possibly as many as 250,000 in the 1700s alone—than did Irish Catholics. Thus future president Andrew Jackson's linen-weaving ancestors, who had left Scotland as recently as 1690 to move to Castlereagh in Ulster, emigrated once again some seventy-five years later. His widowed mother regularly regaled her young sons with tales about "the sufferings of their grandfather during the siege of Carrickfergus"—presumably a reference to the brief French occupation of the town in 1760, which had alarmed the Protestant population—"and the oppression imposed by the Irish [Anglican] nobility on the laboring poor."[11]

Jackson is undoubtedly the best-known representative of those Ulster Scots-Irish, who by the second half of the nineteenth century would call themselves the "Scotch-Irish" but who were originally satisfied in the New World at least to be designated as simply "Irish." That is the designation W. J. Cash used in his emblematic account of the rise of the backcountry southern "aristocracy":

> A stout young Irishman brought his bride into the Carolina upcountry about 1800. He cleared a bit of land, built a log cabin of two rooms, and sat down to the pioneer life . . . he drove the plow into the earth, with uptorn roots bruising his shanks at every step. Behind him came his wife with a

10. Miller, *Emigrants and Exiles*, 141; Kerby A. Miller et al., *Irish Immigrants in the Land of Canaan* (New York, 2003), 452–461.

11. Robert V. Remini, *Andrew Jackson and the Course of American Empire, 1767–1821* (New York, 1977), 15.

hoe. In a few years the land was beginning to yield cotton—richly, for the soil was fecund with the accumulated mold of centuries . . . Five years more and he had two hundred acres and ten Negroes . . . When he was fifty, he became a magistrate, acquired a carriage, and built a cotton gin and a third house—a "big house" this time . . . Tall and well-made, he grew whiskers after the Galway fashion—the well-kept whiteness of which contrasted very agreeably with the brick red of his complexion—, donned the long-tailed coat, stove-pipe hat, and string tie of the statesmen of his period, waxed innocently pompous, and, in short, became a really striking figure of a man.

But while Cash's Irishman and others like Jackson were very much the frontiersmen, individualists, and Indian fighters of traditional perception, David N. Doyle has argued that settlement patterns were most often dictated by whatever opportunities were available at the time, the particular skills the immigrants brought with them, and that, contrary to stereotype, the Scotch-Irish generally preferred settled to undeveloped lands.[12]

In all, the Irish who came to the New World in the 1600s and 1700s had varied origins, belonged to a variety of religious denominations, served diverse governments, and spoke an assortment of languages and dialects—English, Gaelic, Scots, Spanish, French. It was only following the huge Irish (largely, though not wholly, Catholic) immigration of the 1840s that the complex histories of these original settlers were often, and literally, lost in translation.

But the matter is a good deal more complicated than the above description suggests. While it is fairly certain that most (though not the earliest) of the pre–American Independence Irish settlers were of Ulster Protestant background (in other words, Scotch-Irish), and that even in pre-famine days there was a marked animosity between them and those of Irish Catholic ancestry, the exact origins of even the Protestant inhabitants of Northern Ireland have always been open to some speculation. Irish Catholics of social position not infrequently changed their religion and even their names to fit in better with the new realities and thus avoid losing their possessions under the Penal Codes, which severely restricted Catholic legal, political, and property rights to the advantage of those who converted to the Anglican faith.

Marianne Elliott has pointed out that the turncoat Gael was a not un-

---

12. W. J. Cash, *The Mind of the South* (New York, 1969), 15; David N. Doyle, "Scots Irish or Scotch-Irish," *Encyclopedia of the Irish in America*, 845.

common character in Ulster, especially in the eighteenth century, and that his former co-religionists regarded him as more heinous than any English or Scottish settler. Thus the condemnation of one Phelim O'Neill of County Tyrone, who changed his name to Felix Neel and his religion to Anglican:

> Scorning to spend his days where he was reared,
> To drag out life among the vulgar herd,
> Or trudge his way through bogs in bracks, and brogues,
> He changed his creed, and joined the Saxon rogues
> By whom his sires were robbed. He laid aside
> The arms they bore for centuries with pride—
> The ship, the salmon, and the famed Red Hand,
> And blushed when called O'Neill in his own land!
> Poor paltry skulker from thy noble race,
> Infelix felix, weep for thy disgrace!

Such switching of sides could go the other way too, as we see in the popular Protestant ballad "The Old Orange Flute" in which weaver Bob Williamson, "a stout Orange blade," changes his religion on marrying a Catholic:

> But Bob the deceiver he took us all in,
> For he married a Papish called Brigid McGinn,
> Turned Papish himself, and forsook the old cause
> That gave us our freedom, religion, and laws.

Generic though the reference may be, it surely points to a regular phenomenon in the culture, perhaps by way of warning, for the flute that Bob plays so well never conforms to Catholic practices, and even when tossed into the flames like a heretic at the hands of the Inquisition continues to whistle "The Protestant Boys."[13]

It seems likely too that many of those who were nominally Roman Catholic when they emigrated, on arrival in the New World either contentedly abandoned a religion that had hardly been theirs to begin with or readily joined whatever denominations were conveniently available to them. Even Ulster Catholics who immigrated to Scotland prior to the 1830s freely adopted the Presbyterian faith. These generations had been born and grown up before what historians refer to as the "devotional revolution" of the 1850s, a renewal and regimentation of Catholic ecclesiastical discipline

---

13. Marianne Elliott, *The Catholics of Ulster: A History* (New York, 2001), 37; *The Field Day Anthology of Irish Literature*, vol. 2, ed. Seamus Deane (New York, 1991), 107.

after Emancipation—which granted Irish and English Catholics the right to openly profess their religion and be elected to political office—that required more regular church attendance and observance.[14]

To complicate matters even more, Kerby A. Miller has found that the "Scots-Irish" designation was used even of Scottish Catholic immigrants to Ireland early on (such as the MacDonnells). His study of the Shenandoah Valley in Virginia shows that nineteenth- and twentieth-century Protestant Scotch-Irish scholars had often eliminated "O"s and "Mc"s in estimating the Catholic Irish names of settlers there. Miller argues that just as there were probably more Irish Catholics among the early immigrants than previously recognized, so too it seems likely that some of the later famine Irish were Scotch-Irish Presbyterians, a fact suggested, for example, by his study of an Antrim village that experienced a remarkable depletion in its population at this time.[15] Pride in self-sufficiency—as opposed to Catholic fecklessness—and a sense of solidarity with British interests led later generations to downplay their suffering. Miller also notes:

> The lives of numerous "ordinary" emigrants from Ireland to the Old South illustrate the variety and mutability of early Irish identities in that region: John O'Raw, for example, in 1806 a Catholic emigrant from County Antrim to South Carolina, who in the "Charleston schism" of 1815–19 defied his archbishop's threats of excommunication in order to maintain his social and political links to that city's Irish Protestant immigrants, fellow Irish nationalists, and members of the local Hibernian Society. Or Andrew Leary O'Brien, a "spoiled priest" from County Cork and a former canal worker in Pennsylvania, who in 1838 removed to Georgia, converted to Methodism, and founded a college for students of that faith. Or, most remarkably, Samuel Butler, an Irish [Gaelic]-speaker who was christened and raised in the city of Cork, who helped British officers in New York raise an Irish loyalist regiment during the American revolution and whose cultural and linguistic claims to "Irish" identity could only be mitigated by the fact that, genetically, he was an African American who had been born in Charleston and taken to Ireland in infancy.[16]

14. T. M. Devine, *The Scottish Nation: A History, 1700–2000* (New York, 1999), 488–89; Emmet Larkin, *The Historical Dimensions of Irish Catholicism* (New York, 1981).

15. Kerby A. Miller, presentation at "Ulster Roots/Southern Branches: A Symposium on the Scots-Irish Heritage in Northern Ireland and the American South," Emory University, March 2001. See also his *Emigrants and Exiles,* 147, and "'Scotch-Irish' Myths and 'Irish' Identities in Eighteenth- and Nineteenth-Century America," in *New Perspectives on the Irish Diaspora,* ed. Charles Fanning (Carbondale, Ill., 2002), 75–76.

16. Stephen Howe, *Ireland and Empire: Colonial Legacies in Irish History and Culture* (New York, 2000), 105; Miller, "'Scotch-Irish' Myths and 'Irish' Identities," 83–84.

In any case, at least some—certainly never a majority, nor probably even a very large portion—of those subsequently identified as Anglicans, Presbyterians, and Baptists in the American South had their immediate origins in a residually Roman Catholic world.[17]

To all of this should be appended the wider considerations that Ireland and Scotland had a history of intermingling long before the post-1607 plantation, that the Irish regarded the Scottish Catholic Stuarts as their legitimate rulers until well into the eighteenth century, that even Cromwell's soldiers stationed in Ireland sometimes married into Catholic families and converted, and that immigration patterns from the British Isles are notoriously difficult to follow, not least because many emigrants set out from English ports without their place of origin in England, Ireland, Wales, or Scotland being recorded. Ancestries, then, are not quite as straightforward (or straight back) as one might assume.[18]

Joel Chandler Harris—himself born of an itinerant Irish father whom he never knew—devotes the first few pages of his story "At Teague Poteet's: A Sketch of the Hog Mountain Range," to describing this process of circumstantial assimilation. The story's protagonist, of French Huguenot origin, finds himself lost in the stream of English settlers in the Carolinas and, in spite of an initial protest, the family's first names shift over the generations from Gerard to Huguenin to Hugue to Hague, finally—in the last stage of the immigrant's "obliteration"—arriving at Teague, an appellation most frequently and disdainfully associated with the Irish, though there is no explicit mention of that in Harris's story. In an even more general sense, British historian Keith Robbins, noting that much English history has been written by academics from the south of that country who have presumed more uniformity in England than there actually is, reminds us that there is

17. Kerby A. Miller adds: "By the late 1800s . . . the group designated as 'Scotch-Irish' had expanded to include not only Americans of Scots Presbyterian descent but also those of Irish Anglican, Quaker, or other Protestant antecedents . . . as well as all those of Gaelic Irish or Hiberno-Norman descent who were currently *not* Catholic. Thus, by the early twentieth century, the authors of county histories as far afield as South Carolina and South Dakota were happily rebaptizing as 'Scotch-Irish' the ancestors of respectable Methodist merchants and Baptist farmers who had embarrassingly 'native Irish' names such as O'Hara and O'Brien!" ("'Scotch-Irish' Myths and 'Irish' Identities," 80–81). Miller goes on to give a detailed account of a William Hill from County Antrim whose Irish identity underwent many transformations over the course of a long lifetime in South Carolina and even after his death (84–87).

18. See Thomas J. Archdeacon, *Becoming American* (New York, 1983), 260, 53, 74, 240.

no "monolithic" British identity opposing an Irish one since both are in constant flux.[19]

An interesting case of this multiple uncertainly of ancestry is given by a prominent historian of southern traditions, Bertram Wyatt-Brown. During what he calls "the Anglo-Saxon revival" of the late nineteenth century, one branch of the distinguished Percy family of Mississippi hired a professional genealogist in London to trace their history in the British Isles. They were surprised to find no definite link with the family of the same name that had been, and still were, the Earls (now Dukes) of Northumberland, and with which the American Percys had always assumed close affinity. They discovered rather that their earliest known ancestor was associated with County Kilkenny in Ireland, was a mere private in an undistinguished regiment of the British army of the time, and, moreover, was of no ascertainable religious denomination, Anglican or Roman Catholic.

Wyatt-Brown records that the family had anticipated English ancestry, could have lived with Scottish—after all, Northumberland is a border county—but were in no way prepared to accept a possible *Irish* origin, and Irish, moreover, of no distinguished genealogy even on its own terms. No Anglo-Irish aristocrat or even a once-lordly O'Neill or O'Donnell, Carroll or O'Carroll, seemed to lurk in their ancestor's background. True, one of the granddaughters of Charles Carroll of Carrollton, signer of the Declaration of Independence, had married an earl, the brother of the distinguished Duke of Wellington—the hero of Waterloo who famously excused his Dublin birth with the remark that being "born in a stable did not make one a horse"—in 1825, but that alliance simply absorbed her into the English aristocracy rather than bringing about a revival of her family's Irish one.[20] In the Percy case, the branch of the family that had made the troubling discovery suppressed the information, which remained hidden until the 1990s.[21]

Given the accepted English origins of much of the American South, the

19. Joel Chandler Harris, *Mingo and Other Sketches in Black and White* (Boston, 1893), 39–42; Keith Robbins, *Nineteenth-Century Britain, England, Scotland, and Wales: The Making of a Nation* (New York, 1989), 2.

20. She remained a Catholic, however, corresponding regularly with her Maryland grandfather on the religious situation in Ireland, and accompanied her husband to Dublin when he was appointed British viceroy there in the 1820s (Hoffman, 390).

21. Bertram Wyatt-Brown, *The House of Percy: Honor, Melancholy, and Imagination in a Southern Family* (New York, 1994), 33, 339–49.

Percy family response was hardly unusual at that time and place, though Wyatt-Brown points out that the "revival" of interest in Anglo-Saxon origins was often driven by anxiety concerning certainty of ancestry in the face of new waves of immigrants from the Scandinavian and southern European countries. The truth in the Percy case seems to have been that the truth could no longer be found; the destruction of Irish records in the fighting of the 1920s further eliminated the possibility of a satisfactory answer. In the meantime, in the America of the 1890s, the reputation of the "plain" (W. J. Cash's term) Irish, whether justified or not, was not one with which a distinguished family would have wished to be associated. Immediate descendants of novelist Margaret Mitchell's perfectly respectable and reasonably prosperous Irish Catholic ancestors in Georgia were to downplay the connection at about the same period, especially when they left the South to live in the Northeast. F. Scott Fitzgerald acknowledged the comparative wealth of his mother's Irish Catholic family in St. Paul but preferred to identify with his genteel paternal Maryland ancestors—though some of these too were Catholic, a hulking, unknown Irish Michael Fitzgerald among them from whom he received his surname. The actual complexity of Fitzgerald's ancestry is partly explained, but also partly obscured, in his well-known comment to the similarly doomed Frank O'Hara: "I am half black Irish and half old American stock with the usual exaggerated ancestral pretensions. The black Irish half of the family had the money and looked down upon the Maryland side of the family who had, and really had, that certain series of reticences and obligations that go under the poor old shattered word 'breeding.' "[22]

That the Irish side of Fitzgerald's family "looked down upon" his genteel southern relatives indicates a measure of confidence and security in their own social position (and even he admitted that he had known "many Irish who have not been afflicted by this intense social self-consciousness"). It is not surprising, however, that the Percys' discovery should have sounded a note of alarm in their circles and resulted in a discreet silence on the matter. But that incident, and the others alluded to above, suggests once again (despite Wyatt-Brown's judgment that the Irish materials on the original Percy are both incomplete and inconclusive and that the Percy-Northumberland claim can be justified on other grounds) that ancestral lines are often not as clear as families might hope, that earlier generations

22. Darden Asbury Pyron, *Southern Daughter: The Life of Margaret Mitchell* (New York, 1991), 251; *The Letters of F. Scott Fitzgerald,* ed. Andrew Turnbull (New York, 1963), 503.

may have glossed over rather inconvenient truths about their origins or perhaps simply have seen them in a different light in accordance with the contemporary zeitgeist. In short, things—families in this case—aren't always what they appear to be. Fitzgerald went on to write famously about plebeian Jimmy Gatz who transformed himself into patrician Jay Gatsby and whose exact origins might never have been known except for a fatal shooting.[23]

As in the case of the Joel Chandler Harris story, Canadian sociologist Donald Akenson has also drawn attention to the fact that many immigrants from every group tend to lose their consciousness of their origins over time—something that probably happened to the Catholics coming to Maryland and Virginia in the 1600s—which makes it quite difficult for sociologists and demographers to trace their subsequent movements (and explains why sociologists and others find it easier to study those who have not taken such a step). For Akenson,

> The history of any ethnic group includes not only those who shared an extroverted sense of ethnic identity, but also those who cared little, and also those who were hostile to their own ethnic group. If one cuts away from the history of any set of migrants and their descendants the personal histories of all of those whose actions do not agree with some predetermined standard of behaviour, of ideology, of religion, then one is merely tailoring the evidence to fit assumptions about who was "really" Italian, or Jewish, or Irish. That will not do. Intermarriage with other groups, rejection of familial religious beliefs, blurring of traditional values, all of these are part of the story of the Irish and it is a pluralistic history, complex and rich.

Akenson goes on to contend that by studying identifiably ethnic neighborhoods one is focusing on the "losers" in the group: "That is, those of the second, third and fourth generation who still lived in the old neighbourhood, went to the family church and belonged to the old political clubs, were probably . . . the ones least able to compete in the larger society to which their parents or grandparents had migrated." So those Irish who had a real influence were the ones that "moved freely in the larger culture and abandoned many of the traditional identifiers of their ethnic background."

23. In Fitzgerald's *The Great Gatsby* (New York, 1992), Nick Carraway is aware that Gatsby doesn't quite belong, but it is only with the appearance of Mr. Gatz, his father, at the funeral that the deceased's origins are fully clarified.

It is for this reason that Akenson asserts that a "serious non-racist history" of the Irish in America would include the Protestant, as well as the Catholic, tradition.[24]

Akenson argues extensively that the differences between Irish Catholics and Irish or Scotch-Irish Protestants in terms of economic, educational, and sociological status have been mistakenly exaggerated in much of the literature on the subject. It is worth mentioning also that while the descendants of the Irish nobility such as O'Neill and O'Donnell who emigrated to Spain joined the aristocracy and retained their family names, most of the common soldiers and the women with them "were eventually and irremediably dissolved into the general population of the peninsula . . . and in time were lost even to memory."[25]

In light of these generalizations, it is instructive to turn to a particular Irish community in the American South to examine its development. Earl F. Niehaus's 1965 study, *The Irish in New Orleans, 1800–1860,* deals with a city that in the early nineteenth century was among the largest in the nation, with one-fifth of its population born in Ireland.

Originally at least, whether the latter were Catholic-Irish, Anglo-Irish, or Scotch-Irish, they all identified themselves simply as "Irish." Many of the early Irish in New Orleans had arrived in the wake of the failed 1798 rebellion waged by the United Irishmen, the republican movement that drew its inspiration from the American and French Revolutions and marked a shift in Irish loyalties from Catholic Jacobite (supporters of a restoration of the Stuart monarchy) to Enlightened Jacobin, thus seeking to unite Catholics, Anglicans, and Dissenters (largely Presbyterians) "under the common name of Irishman." Such liberal-minded refugees intermingled freely with the city's French and Spanish residents (sometimes acquiring Latin names in the process), ran businesses, bought and sold slaves, engaged in the professions, owned newspapers, and were in general quite prosperous, having

24. Donald Harman Akenson, "The Historiography of the Irish in the United States of America," in *The Irish in the New Communities,* ed. Patrick O'Sullivan (London, 1992), 99–127, and "The Irish in North America: Catholic or Protestant?" *Irish Review* 11 (1991/92): 20–21.

25. Donald Harman Akenson, *Small Differences: Irish Catholics and Irish Protestants, 1815–1922* (Montreal, 1988). It is relevant to note here that a direct descendant of the first Charles Carroll who now lives on the original Maryland property has often told the family's latest biographer that "he knows little about and is not particularly interested in his family's Irish past" (Hoffman, xxv); R. A. Stradling, *The Spanish Monarchy and Irish Mercenaries: The Wild Geese in Spain, 1618–68* (Dublin, 1994), 158.

paid their own way over. They had their own ethnic-based militias and their own cultural center—Hibernian Hall—but avoided denominational distinction: "for the early Irish, whether Catholic or Presbyterian, the church was not a significant institution in the development of ethnic self-consciousness."[26]

These early Irish immigrants voted for Andrew Jackson in his bid for a second term in the presidential election of 1832 partly because they saw him as a fellow countryman. A "Song for St. Patrick's Day" glorified Jackson as anti-British and an Irishman's son:

> An Irishman's son our President is,
> And now, to explain it, we proudly declare,
> The foes of old Ireland are no friends of his
> By this token—he ne'er did their carcass spare!

Nor had the Scotch-Irish Jackson, himself unchurched until near the end of his life (when the main obstacle to his conversion was his sincere inability to forgive his enemies), seen anything incongruous in attending the Crescent City's Catholic Cathedral for thanksgiving services in 1815 following his celebrated victory at the Battle of New Orleans.[27]

One of these early Irish immigrants, prominent New Orleans architect James Gallier, has shown in his *Autobiography* just how complicated an ancestry—even when some of it may have been self-servingly fictionalized—can be. Gallier conceives his distant ancestors as having been driven from Gaul by the Romans, first into Wales and thence to hospitable Ireland. "There are places in the county of Limerick called Gall Baile, or Gaul's town [present-day Galbally], and Baile na Francoigh, or Frank's town," he reports accurately, "which may probably indicate where the refugees established themselves." His family name was afterward changed by the invading English "to the more guttural sound of Gallagher." Closer to the present, Gallier's paternal grandfather (Gallagher) was a cattle dealer in County Louth, his father a builder associated with work on the Mourne Park and Ravensdale country houses. Born in Ravensdale village in 1798, James went to England in 1816 and thence to the United States as an architect in 1832. In New Orleans, he obtained work from established Irish merchants (and had dealings with a Count O'Reilly from Havana about building a hotel there) but changed—or, as he thought, reverted—his name to the French "Gal-

26. Earl F. Niehaus, *The Irish in New Orleans, 1800–1860* (Baton Rouge, 1965), v, 17.
27. Ibid., 73.

lier." Somewhere along the line he also became an Episcopalian, although he designed one of the first Catholic churches in the city too.[28]

Although poorer Irish immigrants began arriving in New Orleans in the 1820s, the influx of "new" Irish did not really swell until the famine of the 1840s. Rather than paying their passages as the earlier Irish immigrants had done, some of the new arrivals came as ship's ballast, replacing the cotton bales sent to Liverpool, others with financial assistance from landlords eager to be rid of them. The arguments in the newspapers of the time indicate a distinction "between the industrious and ambitious Irish and the bogtrotters and turf-diggers."[29]

Niehaus stresses that while Irish people lived in all parts of the city, their concentrated presence in certain districts and streets was well known: "Destitute Irish, during the height of the post-famine invasion, moved into shacks abandoned by Negroes in an extremely poor section of the Third Municipality." While some of even these Irish immigrants eventually prospered, many others were canal diggers and servants; many of them replaced slaves in the more dangerous occupations since their injury or loss was of no economic consequence to the owners (a phenomenon that had also happened with English laborers in Jamestown); many more were poor, diseased, and often without motivation, unable to cope with the oppressive climate.[30]

This huge influx inevitably led to an ongoing confrontation between Irish and black laborers, one that only intensified after the Civil War. The competition also led to a tradition of blacks denigrating the Irish who had replaced them in many jobs. For these and other reasons, Niehaus judges that marriage and concubinage between Irish and blacks was rare.

The Irish in New Orleans were unlikely to have been abolitionists, since they always linked the latter cause with the anti-Catholic nativist and Know Nothing (so called because whenever outsiders asked them about their organization they claimed to "know nothing") movements. At best, they, like Thomas Jefferson, were for returning the slaves to Africa. By the 1850s, however, they had become very pro-South. Their paper, the *Catholic Standard,* argued that slavery was not against the natural law and that, besides, Ireland's condition was even worse. There was also fierce objection to the antislavery position of Daniel O'Connell, the immensely popular Irish

28. James Gallier, *Autobiography* (New York, 1973), 1, 2.

29. Niehaus, 26.

30. Ibid., 30.

leader who had won Catholic Emancipation in 1829. The sympathies of the New Orleans Irish were much more with O'Connell's opponents, the Young Irelanders, despite their abortive and even farcical insurrection in 1848, as the leaders of this movement were much more sympathetic to the southern cause. Again and again, the South's situation was compared to that of Ireland itself, so that the exiled Irishman was "willing to render every possible assistance to a land struggling for that which Ireland attempted to obtain."[31]

By the time the Civil War came, the old Irish militia of Emmet Guards, Montgomery Guards, Mitchel Rifles, and Southern Celts were ready to be incorporated into Louisiana's Confederate regiments. By the time the war was over, there was little left for new immigrants to come to. The Irish remaining in New Orleans became primarily southerners.

Who, then, *are* the Irish in the South? The answer would seem to be that they are all those who either themselves or whose ancestors have been in some way intimately connected with the island of Ireland. Some of them can still be easily identified in Scotch-Irish communities in North Carolina and Tennessee or among the Catholics of New Orleans. Some, like the Irish Travelers of Georgia (now largely settled in Murphy Village, South Carolina)—Irish tinkers who came to the South at the time of the Civil War— have maintained their unique traditions of intermarriage, work, language ("Cant," a version of the "Shelta," derived from Gaelic, spoken by the group in Ireland), and funeral rites, while also displaying most of the attitudes and prejudices of southern whites of their class. Some, like those Dennis Clark described as the "wealthy merchant cliques, successful plantation magnates, philanthropists, and distinguished leaders among the Southern Irish-Americans," or like the descendants of the Carrolls of Carrollton in Maryland, over time so blended in with the reigning Anglo elite as to become almost indistinguishable from them. Some, like the railroad workers in Nashville, the bakers and confectioners in Mobile, the blacksmiths, plasterers, druggists, and even brothel keepers have been lost with the disappearance of their trades or are no longer significantly identified with them.[32]

31. Ibid., 158.

32. Jared Vincent Harper, "The Irish Travelers of Georgia" (Ph.D. diss., University of Georgia, 1977); David T. Gleeson, *The Irish in the South, 1815–1877* (Chapel Hill, 2001), 38, 39, 43. Clark was actually criticizing the hostility toward Irish Catholics and the fact that the "cultural connection to England" among the Southern upper classes helped perpetuate traditional negative stereotypes and prejudices so that these success stories were neglected; see *Hibernia America: The Irish and Regional Culture* (New York, 1986), 100–101.

A few are the descendants of Irish immigrants to France and Spain who subsequently arrived in the American southeast as employees, soldiers, administrators, and clergy with the French and Spanish colonial powers. Or like Pierce Butler, one-time husband of English actress and antislavery campaigner Fanny Kemble, who was descended (in the illegitimate line) from the Butlers of Ormonde (from whom poet William Butler Yeats also, unverifiably, claimed origin) and was one of the largest plantation owners in Georgia. Or like John Roy Lynch, born of an unlawful marriage between a slave and a plantation overseer from Cork whose request that his wife and son be freed on his premature death wasn't honored by his closest friend. Lynch, a youth at the time of Lincoln's emancipation decree, went on to become Speaker in the Mississippi legislature during Reconstruction and then lived to see the fortunes of the black community steeply decline. Some are the offspring of the offspring of other illegal but rapacious alliances between master or overseer and slave. The descendants of perhaps most Irish are so mixed in with the Euro, African, and Native American populations that it is no longer possible to distinguish them as Irish except, on occasion and unreliably, in their surnames.[33]

It is in this sense that Bill Malone's argument that the musical heritage of the South is "neither Anglo-Saxon nor Celtic" applies equally and inevitably to the region's ethnic makeup. Even someone with as stereotypically Irish a name and religion as Flannery O'Connor seems to have given little thought to her Irishness. As her family's biographer, Sally Fitzgerald, notes: "For more than 150 years now, Hartys, Treanors, Flannerys, Clines, and O'Connors have lived and worked in, and contributed to, their adoptive society, retaining as their single difference from their neighbors in Sharon, Savannah, Augusta, Atlanta, and Milledgeville, an allegiance to the Catholic faith they brought with them at the outset." One of the few comments O'Connor made on the subject was to complain that "The Irish in America are sometimes more Irish than the Irish and I suppose some of my indifference is a reaction against that." From Donald Akenson's perspective, that response doesn't make her any less Irish, but in being understated about her Irishness, O'Connor too unwittingly—or at least unselfconsciously—

33. Malcolm Bell Jr., *Major Butler's Legacy: Five Generations of a Slaveholding Family* (Athens, Ga., 1987); Miller, "'Scotch-Irish' Myths and 'Irish' Identities," 82; John Roy Lynch, *Reminiscences of an Active Life: The Autobiography of John Roy Lynch*, ed. John Hope Franklin (Chicago, 1970). For a detailed account of sexual relations between master and slave and their consequences over the generations, see Edward Ball, *Slaves in the Family* (New York, 1998).

followed the pattern of the majority of those southerners who belonged to her ethnic group.[34]

When Eamon De Valera, the president-designate of an Irish Republic still struggling for its independence and international recognition, visited New Orleans in 1919 to a warm welcome and the freedom of the city, he laid a wreath at the monument of his "fellow-countryman," Andrew Jackson. De Valera's subsequent long career suggests that he himself, even in that small island of which he was the leader for several decades, held rather naïve views as to the common inheritance of Ulster Protestants (Jackson's immediate ancestry) and Irish Catholics. But he was also recognizing traditions that are so entangled with each other that one still has to explain their many ongoing unities and divisions.[35]

The story does not end there, however. More recently, the Irish presence in the South has been co-opted into a much larger claim about the character of the entire culture of the region. Over the last twenty years or so, the once-reigning "Anglo-Saxon" interpretation of southern origins has come under intense, and highly controversial, scrutiny from several quarters, though the shift in understanding is just now filtering down to the level of popular awareness. Most notable, or at least most provocative, among the scrutinizers have been two of the South's own historians, Grady McWhiney and Forrest McDonald, who have argued for a Celtic rather than an Anglo-Saxon South. Their point has not been to deny the English founding of Jamestown, or the similar ancestries of many of the settlers in coastal Virginia and South Carolina, but rather to argue that the pervasive culture of the southern states up until the Civil War at least was formed by immigrants from what they argue are the recognized "Celtic" regions of the British Isles: Ireland, Scotland, Wales, and much of the north and west of England, a somewhat novel—though not unprecedented—configuration that risks making many unlikely historical figures into covert, or at least unwitting, Celts.[36]

34. Sally Fitzgerald, "Root and Branch: O'Connor of Georgia," *Georgia Historical Quarterly* 64 (1980): 378. But after a visit to Ireland in 1958 and dinner with Gaelic poet Máire Mac an tSaoi, O'Connor announced, "My opinion of the Irish has gone up"; see *The Habit of Being* (New York, 1979), 262.

35. See Charles Edwards O'Neill, "Toward American Recognition of the Republic of Ireland: De Valera's Visit to New Orleans in 1920," *Louisiana History* 34, no. 3 (1993): 305.

36. Grady McWhiney, *Cracker Culture: Celtic Ways in the Old South* (Tuscaloosa, Ala., 1988). McWhiney's assertion flies in the face of the opinion of respected Southern historians such as

According to the proponents of the Celtic South thesis, it is the American northeast that has been quintessentially Anglo-Saxon, a cultural divide that helps explain the long-perceived differences between the regions. So, for example, the devastating southern losses in the Civil War can be seen to have been influenced by cultural factors: a romantic, *Celtic* South confronting a pragmatic, Anglo-Saxon North had employed "the same courageous dash and reckless abandon that had characterized their Celtic ancestors for two thousand years."[37]

Quite apart from the problem of defending such a novel interpretation of southern war casualties, establishing that those ancestors were indeed Celtic poses an even greater difficulty. Here McWhiney and McDonald point out that simple name analysis of the censuses between 1790 and 1860 suggests that "about half of the white population of the South was of Irish, Scottish, or Welsh extraction, and about half of the remainder had originated in the western and northern English uplands." Such figures leave those from the non-Celtic parts of England decisively in the minority.[38]

Uniting the inhabitants of Ireland, Scotland, Wales, and the north and west of England together as "Celts" is no easy task, however, let alone showing that such a unified culture was transported intact to the American South. Nevertheless, McWhiney and McDonald are right to point out that, as was noted earlier, there has indeed always been a close relationship between Scotland and the northern counties of Ireland, with populations going back and forth over the centuries, often rising up against English rule at the same times, and speaking a similar Gaelic language. They are probably right too to claim that it was misguided of scholars in the past to make too sharp a distinction between a Celtic Catholic Highland and a Protestant, non-Celtic Lowland in Scotland: "Not until the eighteenth century did the Lowlands come to be dominated by the dour, industrious, orderly, morally rigid, and frugal Presbyterian Scots of the stereotype."[39]

Moreover, as several other historians not quoted by McWhiney have acknowledged, the Scots who were brought over to Ulster by James I in 1610 did in fact mingle with the native Irish more often than has been thought previously. "The image of the Calvinist Scot introducing civilisa-

---

Clement Eaton and George B. Tyndall that "the South *is* the habitat of the quintessential WASP" (2).

37. Grady McWhiney and Perry D. Jamieson, *Attack and Die: Civil War Military Tactics and the Southern Heritage* (Tuscaloosa, Ala., 1982), xv.

38. McWhiney, *Cracker Culture*, xxi.

39. Forrest McDonald, "Prologue," in McWhiney, *Cracker Culture*, xxxvii.

tion and the work ethic into Ulster was a nineteenth-century fabrication to explain the *status quo* then," observes Marianne Elliott in *The Catholics of Ulster*. "In reality, the early Scots settlers were closer to their Irish counterparts, in dress, work practices and housing, than to the English." But even allowing for such intermingling, McDonald's claim that "the 'Scotch-Irish' who emigrated to America during the eighteenth century were not descendants of Lowland settlers in the Ulster plantations but members of a traditionally Gaelic (or Norse-Gaelic) society who had been moving back and forth between Ulster and the Highlands and Islands for nearly a thousand years" strikes one as, to say the least, extravagant.[40]

In further support of his argument, McWhiney has also found remarkably similar cultural and behavioral patterns between the Celts of the British Isles and the white inhabitants of the American South, causing both groups to be perceived in like ways by their English and Yankee neighbors. The comparisons are not at all complimentary. "In 1785 a foreigner insisted that most white South Carolinians were the 'ignorant, drunken descendants of the wild Irish'—'poor as rats, proud as dons . . . lazy . . . [and with] no morals.'" Indeed, argues McWhiney, adding insult to injury (though who is being insulted isn't quite clear), the Celtic lifestyles were so slow and easy that black slaves, Indians, and Cajuns had no problem adapting to them![41]

One of McWhiney's central propositions in examining these two rural societies is that their "open-range" herding practices were similar. Similar too were culinary and drinking habits, a tendency to prefer play to work, a love of violence, a "romantic sense of honour," and a general disposition toward hospitality. Even today, McWhiney observes, "The Irish disregard traffic laws; they drive and stop and park and walk anytime and anywhere they please, just as Southerners tend to do."[42]

According to McWhiney, then, the Civil War was a cultural clash between a Celtic South that was hospitable, impractical, and reckless, and an Anglo North that was shrewd, disciplined, and practical. As he concludes with dramatic flourish, given such ethnic differences, "Secession was inevitable."[43]

While McWhiney's Celtic thesis is new in its comprehensive sweep,

40. Elliott, *The Catholics of Ulster*, 128; McWhiney, *Cracker Culture*, xli.
41. McWhiney, *Cracker Culture*, 36, 21.
42. Ibid., 152, 167.
43. Ibid., 270.

many of its individual elements are not especially original or even controversial. That large numbers of peoples from the parts of the British Isles he
regards as "Celtic" immigrated to the American South is not in doubt, nor
is the fact that their ancestries were often tangled and interwoven. Even
Thomas Nelson Page, a stalwart defender of the South's Anglo-Saxon legacy, claimed in a landmark speech in 1892 that "the inhabitants of these
colonies were the strongest strains of many stocks—Saxon, Celt, and Teu-
ton." The order is different, but the Celt is quite solidly there. Even Page's
southern Cavaliers are presented as Englishmen driven out, as were the
Irish, by the terrors of Oliver Cromwell's religious wrath.[44]

W. J. Cash had basically subscribed to this view in his classic debunking
of southern pieties in *The Mind of the South,* where the quintessential southern planter is a backwoods Irishman who finally allies his progeny with
impoverished English gentry from Charleston. In *Albion's Seed: Four British
Folkways in America,* David Hackett Fischer has emphasized the regional
aspects of emigration patterns from England in ways that indirectly support
McWhiney, though Cornwall, rather than the northern shires, is usually
perceived as the "Celtic" part of England.[45]

Nevertheless, McWhiney's thesis has some obvious problems. It minimizes the immediate causes of the Civil War and makes practically no mention of slavery. It also minimizes perceived differences between Irish,
Scottish, and Welsh ethnicities and omits real consideration of northern
England. While, as we have seen, its emphasis on nominal Catholics becoming Protestants is historically accurate—as is its point that the Scotch-
Irish were not a monolithic Presbyterian group—it tends to bypass denominational differences between these communities that were very real in the
nineteenth century. One of the supporters of the thesis perhaps shows the
dangers of the position in his stunning claim that "if one wants to see the
remnants of the old culture of Cuchulain [the Irish mythical hero usually
seen as Celtic], as filtered through the 'wild Irish' of Colonial times, one
might as well visit Appalachia."[46]

McWhiney's work has received cautious but surprisingly respectful acceptance from many academic historians (including African American
scholars), though it is not without its serious critics. Northern Irish schol-

---

44. Thomas Nelson Page, "The Old South," in *A New Reader of the Old South,* ed. Ben Forkner and Patrick Samway, S.J. (Atlanta, 1986), 394.

45. David Hackett Fischer, *Albion's Seed: Four British Folkways in America* (New York, 1989).

46. Leroy V. Eid, "The Colonial Scotch-Irish: A View Accepted Too Readily," *Éire-Ireland*
21, no. 4 (1986), 104–5.

ars of the Scotch-Irish, for example, claim that all of the American work in this area is insufficiently aware of the historical complexity of the British Isles, while Donald Akenson has referred disparagingly to the entire corpus of historical literature on the Scotch-Irish as "a strange underwater kingdom."[47] Some have criticized McWhiney's static view of culture and his emphasis on open-range herding as a peculiarly Scotch-Irish method of farming.[48] McWhiney has been especially taken to task for relying far too heavily on middle-class travelers' accounts, accounts that tend to follow fixed patterns and meet audience expectations and preconceptions. His most comprehensive critic, Rowland Berthoff, in an essay aptly titled "Celtic Mist over the South," wonders why, if all the peoples in Northern Ireland today are Celtic, there has been so much conflict in the region without anyone appealing to their shared ethnic inheritance?[49] Perhaps McWhiney's most dismissive critic was one of the senior scholars of Irish-American history, the late Dennis Clark, who referred to the Celtic South thesis as a "fantasy of hyperbole." Clark added disdainfully: "The imputation of some wild élan to the South, linked by the most illusory supposition to the Celts of pre-Roman Europe, is a historical confection surpassing that of the magnolia-drenched plantation fantasies of cheap Southern novels."[50]

Meanwhile, in the wider world of academic research, a fierce debate currently rages among scholars of ancient history as to whether it is right to assume that even early Irish culture was Celtic, the far western extension of that centered at La Tène in modern-day Switzerland. Simon James, of the British Museum, has argued provocatively that the very idea of the "Celt" is a post-1700 invention. More conciliatorily, but in opposition to James, Ox-

---

47. Akenson, "The Historiography of the Irish," 122 n.8. More recently, and for similar reasons, Hendrik Booraem has noted that the literature on the Scotch-Irish, though vast, was "of little value" until the 1960s and that even James Leyburn's standard *The Scotch-Irish* (Chapel Hill, 1962) was "only a start"; see *Young Hickory: The Making of Andrew Jackson* (Dallas, 2001), 216.

48. See H. Tyler Blethen and Curtis W. Wood Jr., "Scotch-Irish Frontier Society in Southwestern North Carolina, 1780–1840," in *Ulster and North America: Transatlantic Perspectives on the Scotch-Irish,* eds. Blethen and Wood (Tuscaloosa, Ala., 1997), 221–26. For an African American perspective on McWhiney, see Charles Joyner, "African and European Roots of Southern Culture: The 'Central Theme' Revisited," in *Dixie Debates: Perspectives on Southern Cultures,* eds. Richard H. King and Helen Taylor (New York, 1996), 12–30.

49. Rowland Berthoff, "Celtic Mist over the South," *Journal of Southern History* 52 (1986): 523–46. Some Protestant extremists have, in fact, invoked the legendary Cuchulainn as a model for their own defense of Ulster.

50. Clark, 106.

ford University's Barry Cunliffe has maintained, "What is not in doubt . . . is the very strong emotional appeal which the idea of sharing a common Celtic heritage has. Perhaps the only real definition of a Celt, now as in the past, is that a Celt is a person who believes him or herself to be Celtic"—hardly a consoling thought for those in search of unambiguous origins.[51]

Such stark reminders of how contingently traditions and communities can be imagined and invented does not, unfortunately, make them any less potent.[52] The twentieth century gave rise to many invented ethnicities that had gruesome consequences while they lasted. The Celtic South thesis too has taken on a rather ugly form recently in its adoption by the Southern League, a group anxious to assert the heritage of the white South in the face of what it sees as a corrosive multiculturalism.[53] Still, even with the relative decline of traditional religion in the American South, Celtic neo-paganism is unlikely to become a major social force. It seems destined rather to dwell on the periphery among a random assortment of neo-Confederates, Country Music aficionados, New Age-ers who enjoy U2 or the Celtic soul of Enya, those perennially in pursuit of Jungian archetypes, and even among a few lonely seekers of their presumed Celtic-African roots.

The Celtic South thesis stands to one side of the present study. If I frequently employ the word "Celt" in what follows, it is mainly because it crops up so regularly in the historical record. What this chapter has attempted to show, rather, is that the ethnic composition of the southern population—largely of those who are white, though by no means exclusively so—is "softer," more porous, and a little more diverse than was claimed in the past. It is chastening to realize that the exact origins of so many people, and even of those who are famous, have been lost to history. One might well wonder too what possible differences there could be in the lives of the descendants of, say, "Scotch-Irish" Presbyterians who had arrived in America as such and those of Irish Catholic ancestry who had changed their original church affiliation shortly after landing? Without resorting to the absurd presumption of some initial genetic difference between them, it would seem that in the broadest sense—and allowing for individual circumstances—they would all belong identically to the Ameri-

---

51. Simon James, *The Atlantic Celts* (Madison, Wis., 1999); Barry Cunliffe, *The Ancient Celts* (New York, 1997), 267.

52. I am partly thinking of Benedict Anderson's work, *Imagined Communities: Reflections on the Origins and Spread of Nationalism* (New York, 1991).

53. See its web page at www.southern-heritage.com.

can Protestant tradition. At the same time, however, the recognition that some of the group had started out differently is important for an understanding of the past, as well as for present empowerment.

It is with cautions such as these in mind that I limit myself in the next four chapters to those "Irish" in the South who were strongly conscious of being such—the "unobliterated" remnant, so to speak—most often because either they or their immediate ancestors had come from the island itself. They were the ones who could least easily forget the nightmares of their ancestral history, or who chose not to. To what extent they are representative of the whole—a nineteenth-century Irish Fenian once observed that most Irish people had never belonged to any nationalist organization—will never be known.

CHAPTER 2

SLAVES AND SLAVERIES

Thy songs were made for the pure and free,
They shall never sound in slavery.

—THOMAS MOORE, "The Minstrel Boy"

It was not in Ireland that you learned this cruelty. Your mothers were gentle,
kind, and humane . . . How can your souls have become stained with a darkness
blacker than the negro's skin?

—DANIEL O'CONNELL, letter to Cincinnati Repeal Association, 1843

The British colonies of North America, and, later, the United States, to
which Irish men and women immigrated or were transported in the more
than 250 years between 1607 and 1863, were among the many areas of the
world where chattel slavery was practiced. The Ireland the immigrants left
was dominated for most of that time by members of a minority church that
excluded Catholics and Presbyterian Dissenters from the free exercise of
their religion and participation in government. Even if some of the Penal
Laws were only erratically and inconsistently applied—with the infamous
obligation of a Catholic to sell a horse for a mere £5 to any Protestant bid-
der little more than a dead letter—and even if various restrictions were
greatly relaxed from the 1770s onward, those who were not of the Anglican
persuasion remained very much second-class citizens. In 1729, a Presbyterian minister in Ulster starkly explained the departure of so many of his
flock to America: "If they Stay in Irland, their Children will be Slaves." His
description may have been exaggerated, but his perception of the situation
was hardly uncommon.[1]

While nearly all blacks had been brought as slaves from West Africa on
the horrific Middle Passage, a half or more of all white immigrants from
the British Isles arrived as indentured servants—meaning that they had

---

1. Quoted in *Irish Immigrants in the Land of Canaan*, ed. Kerby A. Miller et al. (New York,
2003), 2.

contracted to work off the price of their passage over a number of years. Indentures were sometimes auctioned off in ways similar to those of the slave markets, and huge numbers of immigrants died while still in servitude. Early on, there was some fluidity in both enterprises, and it was decades after the arrival of the first cargo of slaves in 1619 before the system was fully regularized and slavery replaced indenture as a preferred means of obtaining workers. By the time the importation of new slaves from Africa was outlawed in 1808, an estimated 600,000 had been transported to the North American colonies, about 6 percent of the total that came to the Americas. Soon thereafter, the states in the rapidly industrializing Northeast further outlawed the institution, driven as much by economic conditions as by the religiously motivated abolitionists to do so.

Slavery might have been banned, or died out, in the South too—there were several abolitionist societies, possibly the earliest ones, active in the late 1700s—except that the invention of the cotton gin in 1793 renewed its usefulness. Slavery was especially thriving in the new cotton states of Alabama and Mississippi right up to the beginning of the Civil War. Indeed, what finally provoked the war was the political threat of western, nonslave territories added to the Union. Virginia and the southern states—from which Washington, Jefferson, Madison, Henry, and many other American leaders had come—saw their power declining. Southern elites feared that northern abolitionists would finally succeed in winning emancipation for the slaves, thus causing the region severe economic loss, not to mention major social upheaval. In short, there were in America, as Irish patriot John Mitchel was to note upon his arrival in 1853, two nations that "must either peaceably separate . . . or else the one must conquer the other."[2]

What is painfully clear is that the issue of chattel slavery in the American South, to all appearances an indisputable example of the unjust oppression of others, was not of major concern to most of the "oppressed" people of Ireland. True, the great Irish "liberator" Daniel O'Connell, who won the Catholic Emancipation, which permitted members of that church to be elected to the Westminster parliament, again and again condemned slavery. True, Ireland's national poet Thomas Moore, following his 1804 visit to America, denounced the hypocrisy of the country's supposed freedom: "To think that man, thou just and gentle God! / Should stand before thee, with a tyrant's rod / O'er creatures like himself, with souls from thee, / Yet dare

2. C. Vann Woodward, *The Strange Career of Jim Crow* (New York, 1957); William Dillon, *Life of John Mitchel* (London, 1888), 2:54–55.

to boast of perfect liberty!" Moore also noted the irony of Thomas Jefferson's relationship with Sally Hemings (here identified as "Aspasia"): "The weary statesman for repose hath fled / From halls of council to his negro's shed, / Where blest he woos some black Aspasia's grace, / And dreams of freedom in his slave's embrace!" But such sentiments were not at all typical, either among the Irish in Ireland or among those in America.[3]

The most famous of the escaped American slaves, Frederick Douglass, spent several months in Ireland in 1845–46 lecturing to enthusiastic audiences and overseeing the publication of the second European edition of his autobiographical *Narrative* by a Dublin publisher, for which he wrote a special preface. Because of his easy acceptance at all levels of Irish society— Daniel O'Connell introduced him to an audience as "the black O'Connell of the United States"—Douglass described his time there as comprising "some of the happiest moments of my life": "Instead of the bright blue sky of America, I am covered with the soft grey fog of the Emerald Isle. I breathe, and lo! the chattel becomes a man." He was additionally glad to have temporarily escaped from his abolitionist mentors in America who, he felt, regarded him as their "property" and required him to behave as they commanded. Douglass considered his writing of the new Dublin preface for his *Narrative* to be an important assertion of his independence from dictatorial white patronage.[4]

But for all his enthusiasm about his Irish reception, Douglass recognized that all was not well there. As his most recent biographer notes:

> On his way through Ireland, Douglass saw what his antislavery hosts seemed blind to. Reports of famine—the grim result of the first of the rotted potato crops—were in the newspapers. Thin-armed children and their defeated mothers huddled at doorstoops, as fathers tried, often unsuccessfully, to earn passage out of the ports of Wexford, Waterford, and Cork. The

---

3. Thomas Moore, from "Epistle VI. To Lord Viscount Forbes. From Washington" and "Epistle VII. To Thomas Hume, Esq, M. D. From the City of Washington," excerpted in *Amazing Grace: An Anthology of Poems about Slavery, 1660–1810*, ed. James G. Basker (New Haven, 2002), 593, 594.

4. Frederick Douglass, *Narrative of the Life of Frederick Douglass, an American Slave, Written by Himself*, ed. William L. Andrews and William S. McFeely (New York, 1997), 96–97, quoted in Paul Giles, "Narrative Reversals and Power Exchanges: Frederick Douglass and British Culture," *American Literature* 73, no. 4 (2001): 796; Letter to William Lloyd Garrison, 1 January 1846, in "Frederick Douglass in Ireland," *Journal of Negro History* 8, no. 1 (1923): 104, 105; Patricia J. Ferreira, "Frederick Douglass in Ireland: The Dublin Edition of His *Narrative*," *New Hibernia Review* 5, no. 1 (2001): 60.

antislavery people stepped around these Irish poor as they made their way into Douglass's lectures about mistreated Africans in America. Abolitionists were generous in their concern for those who had been wronged, but in the late 1840s, a curious deafness to suffering at home accompanied their sympathetic response to what was endured across the Atlantic.

Douglass himself thought it politic not to draw too much attention to the anomaly lest it detract from the support needed by his own cause, but he wrote home to abolitionist leader William Lloyd Garrison that "I see much here to remind me of my former condition and I confess I should be ashamed to lift my voice against American slavery, but that I know the cause of humanity is one the world over." One of the texts that as a slave he had read in *The Columbian Orator* was that of a speech on behalf of Catholic Emancipation given in the Irish parliament in 1795—just five years before it was dissolved by the Act of Union that made Ireland a constituent part of the United Kingdom. What he got from it, Douglass explained joyfully in his *Narrative,* was "a bold denunciation of slavery, and a powerful vindication of human rights."[5]

Douglass's reference to slavery in the context of the movement for Catholic Emancipation serves as a reminder that the word "slavery" was in constant use in Ireland in the nineteenth century to describe local conditions in which political and religious rights were often either absent or severely limited. Belatedly and reluctantly granted in 1829—it was supposed to have been a benefit of the 1801 agreement that joined Ireland with the United Kingdom—Catholic Emancipation came accompanied by new property requirements that restricted the number of Catholics who could vote. Even decades after its passage, Irish people of that faith or Dissenters were still required to pay dues, through their landlords, for the support of the minority-established Anglican church.

It was not, of course, that the Irish in Ireland confused their own situation with that of chattel slaves in America, although there was a constant barrage of southern propaganda literature that extolled the social benefits of slavery for blacks themselves as opposed to the uncertainties of employment encountered by the "wage slaves" of the northern states and the Euro-

5. William S. McFeely, *Frederick Douglass* (New York, 1991), 126. In Belfast, however, Douglass found a different problem, for there he had to preach against the Free Church of Scotland, which had many Irish members in the city and supported the rights of slaveowners in the American South, provided they treated their human possessions in a Christian way (128). Douglass, *Narrative,* 33.

pean countries, and many of the Irish at home did live in conditions worse than those of at least *some* American slaves. Rather, they did not consider themselves to be wholly free.[6] Thus, for example, at one of O'Connell's monster meetings—so called because of the huge crowds that attended— for Repeal of the Union, the liberator's next major project, in Cork in 1843, a leading float in the procession "featured two boys, one painted black, the other white. The black figure bore the label *Free*, since Westminster had abolished slavery in the West Indies. He displayed to the crowd his broken chains. The white figure, representing the Irish, wore intact chains, and a label round his neck which proclaimed *A Slave Still!*"[7]

Unfortunately, the American abolitionists had a long history of being anti-Catholic, partly from their origins in Protestantism, partly because they (rightly) saw that church as an opponent of liberal views on most so- cial issues, a verdict reinforced by Pope Pius IX's condemnation of the kind of secular democracy that the United States represented. Recently, too, many Irish Catholics had fought in defense of the Papal States against the movement to unite Italy as a secular kingdom. This battle had made the Irish more conscious than ever of their Catholicism and the American na- tivists—most visibly represented in the Know Nothing movement—wary of all things Catholic and fearful that the papacy might have designs on their country. For these and other reasons, Irish Catholics in America had little cause to be sympathetic with the abolitionists' agenda.

The Catholic Church's position on slavery, meanwhile, was yet further justification for many of the Irish to have southern sympathies. After all, most of the slaves brought to the Americas had come under the auspices of Catholic countries: Spain, Portugal, France. Although the reigning pope had belatedly condemned the international traffic in the 1830s, the settled conditions of slavery in the American South were considered to be exempt from such censure. Irish-born Bishop John England of Charleston, South Carolina, though personally opposed to slavery, which he blamed as an un- fortunate legacy of earlier British rule, nevertheless saw it as not contradict-

6. Itinerant Gaelic poet Mícheál Óg Ó Longáin (1766–1837) referred to himself as being "*im dhubhsclábhai bheag bhocht*"—literally a "poor little black slave"—to describe his own condi- tion as a man of learning reduced to the lowest form of menial labor. This usage, of course, suggests that this was not his, much less his nation's, normal condition. See Tom Dunne, "Subaltern Voices? Poetry in Irish, Popular Insurgency and the 1798 Rebellion," *Eighteenth- Century Life* 22, no. 3 (1998): 36.

7. Thomas Keneally, *The Great Shame and the Triumph of the Irish in the English-Speaking World* (New York, 1999), 92.

ing Catholic teaching and was even "'determined' to prevent the 'mischief' of antislavery interference in the South." The founder of the first Catholic newspaper in the United States, and a relative progressive on racial matters in Charleston, where he had instituted a school for free blacks, Bishop England observed in his paper in 1835: "Those who have known the *saints* [i.e., the Puritan abolitionists] in Great Britain and Ireland, know that whilst they were petitioning for NEGRO EMANCIPATION and the BETTER OBSERVANCE OF THE SABBATH, they were disseminating tracts filled with the foulest calumnies, and straining every nerve to OPPRESS IF NOT TO EXTIRPATE THE ROMAN CATHOLICS."[8]

In the South, moreover, Catholics were anxious to be identified with southern culture. Not only were many of them slaveowners themselves, including the revered Charles Carroll in Maryland, but even the Irish-born Archbishop John Hughes of New York was himself a former overseer of slaves in Maryland and the brother-in-law of a plantation owner in the Caribbean. Regarding slavery as only comparatively evil and "infinitely better than the condition in which [Africans] would have been, had they not been seized" and transported to America, Hughes had no desire to see the "peculiar institution" brought to an abrupt end. Many of the religious orders too, male and female—Jesuits, Capuchins, Ursulines—held slaves. Randall Miller mentions the case of a Jesuit, Brother Joseph Mobberly, who "was relieved of his plantation duties after repeated complaints about his harsh treatment" as an example of how slavery corrupted clergy as well as lay people. When, in 1838, the Jesuits in Maryland sold 300 slaves to planters in Louisiana, the sole criticism of the transaction was that they had not ensured that the new owners would allow those sold to practice their Catholic faith. In 1856, just five years before the Civil War began, Father James Healy, born in Georgia of an Irish father and slave mother, directed from his home in Boston that the family's sixty-one slaves be auctioned off, separating at least one mother from her children in the process.[9]

In all, the Catholic Church of the Old South—like its Protestant counterparts and its own northern dioceses—"mirrored the racial values of its followers and reinforced planter hegemony by supplying biblical justifications for slavery and a conservative social order." Thus at least part of the

8. Randall M. Miller and Jon L. Wakelyn, *Catholics in the Old South: Essays on Church and Culture* (Macon, Ga., 1983), 15, quoted in David T. Gleeson, *The Irish in the South, 1815–1877* (Chapel Hill, 2001), 129.

9. Quoted in James M. O'Toole, *Passing for White: Race, Religion, and the Healy Family, 1820–1920* (Amherst, Ma., 2002), 33; Miller, 125; O'Toole, 78, 47–48.

Church's attitude was as much in response to its congregation as it was prescriptive of it. Randall Miller adds that this position was very much in line with a Protestantism that "subordinated ethical responsibility to personal salvation." Jewish views, as Eli N. Evans notes, were also in line with local custom.[10]

Catholics saw southern society's present organization as part of God's will. Even in New Orleans, where the Church was unusually strong, there was no conflict between it and the southern traditions of slavery. Rather, the Church was mainly concerned with developing its school system so as not to lose ground to the Protestants. The result for the Protestant side was that this "Catholic response of political and social accommodation with the southern Protestant world order, like the response of the Yankees who settled and stayed in the Old South . . . strengthened a culture of which neither Catholics nor Yankees could ever be fully a part." Such, Miller conjectures, "is the reason why southern Catholics, perhaps deservedly, passed into historical obscurity."[11]

In his provocative study *How the Irish Became White*, Noel Ignatiev has expressed surprise that the Irish, the victims of oppression in their own country, should have been so ready to oppress others in the United States. He argues that they chose to become "white"—understood as a constructed and ever-shifting, rather than an essential, identity to which several immigrant groups, Jews and Italians among them, aspired—because that was the way to achieving position and prosperity in American society. Whatever the overall merits of his argument, however—David T. Gleeson has criticized it as based exclusively on labor history, and it also downplays obvious matters of actual skin color, which, on occasion, allowed African Americans of lighter complexion to "pass" as white—in the South the Irish became so white at times that their ethnic past might be almost totally forgotten. Indeed, the Civil War would force them to forge a new local, southern identity in a way not quite true perhaps of their fellow-countrymen in the northern states.[12]

10. Miller, 21–22; Eli N. Evans, *The Provincials: A Personal History of Jews in the South* (New York, 1997), 263.

11. Miller, 129–30.

12. Noel Ignatiev, *How the Irish Became White* (New York, 1995), 1–6, 178–88; Gleeson, 224. Much of Ignatiev's work has been influenced by David R. Roediger's *The Wages of Whiteness* (1991) and Theodore W. Allen's *The Invention of the White Race* (1994), studies that have been seriously criticized for their simplistic understanding of Irish and Irish-American history.

In Ireland, meanwhile, as Joseph M. Hernon records, the Irish abolitionist Richard Allen "disapproved of the decision of the Irish Society of Friends to accept contributions from slaveholders during the [1840s] famine," a gesture hardly likely to endear either him or his cause to the starving populace. Daniel O'Connell was almost unique in being a bitter opponent of American slavery, one so prominent that Garrison quoted him in the 1845 preface to Douglass's *Narrative,* though he was well aware of the anti-Catholicism of the abolitionists both outside and within his country. When, in 1842, he told an audience of 70,000 that the Irish should "leave slave America," O'Connell knew that his comments might offend many, but he considered human freedom to be more important: "Though this be a blow against Ireland, it is a blow in favour of human liberty, and I will strike that blow. Come freedom—come oppression of Ireland—my conscience shall be clear before God. We may not get money from America after this declaration, but we do not want bloodstained money."[13]

To complicate matters for O'Connell, the national head of the Irish Repeal Association in the United States was the son of slave-owning President John Tyler. Garrison was moved to ask:

> What means this sudden interest of the slave plunderers in the cause of Irish Repeal? . . . Again, what means this sudden regard for the sacredness of "Southern institutions" on the part of the leading Irish declaimers at the Repeal meetings of the South, and in other parts of the country? I will tell you. The game is this: "You tickle me, and I will tickle you!" In other words, the bargain obviously is . . . that the South shall go for Repeal, and the Irish, as a body, shall go for Southern slavery!—Here is a "union," most unnatural and horrible! . . . And will our hard-working, liberty-loving Irish fellow-countrymen allow themselves to be bought for such a purpose? Heaven forbid!

Whatever the attitudes of the Irish in the Northeast, in the South the Repeal Associations were stressing their support of local institutions. Some time after Garrison's appeal, a leading abolitionist wrote to Allen in Dublin "asking him and O'Connell and the Irish antislavery people to 'send us a startling, scorching, bitter, unsparing, pointed rebuke . . . telling the repealers that you don't want the money or voices of slaveholders . . . laugh, hoot, scorn, hiss, spit at the recreant Irishman'"—a tactic hardly likely to endear

13. Quoted in Joseph M. Hernon Jr., *Celts, Catholics, and Copperheads: Ireland Views the American Civil War* (Columbus, Ohio, 1968), 61.

the matter to O'Connell's auditors, one would think. That O'Connell wanted to be more conciliatory shows that he had a better understanding of the fractious situation.[14]

Ignatiev points out that O'Connell accepted the risk of alienating Irish-American support at a time when he particularly needed it. Moreover, O'Connell's antislavery position was disturbingly close to that of the British government, a circumstance that caused the Irish-American papers to refuse to print some of his comments. Even in Ireland, the confrontation over the slavery issue could be quite intimate at times. Gleeson notes that a Father James McGarahan of Mobile, on a visit to Dublin with funds for the Repeal Association, "insisted that slaves were 'well-fed, well taken care of, and sleek in their appearance' [and] . . . that emancipation would bring serious disorder and violence to the South and the United States." O'Connell welcomed his financial contribution but "continued to insist that 'so long as slavery existed in any quarter of the globe, he would be found among the ranks of its bitterest and most decided enemies.'" Another Irish priest resident in the South, Father Jeremiah O'Neill Sr., "scolded O'Connell for 'going out of [his] way to cast a nettle on the grave of the father [slaveholder George Washington] of my adopted country.'" The priest advised O'Connell that he would be doing well if he brought the material existences of Irish peasants up to the "comfortable" level of southern slaves.[15]

It is worth noting that such comments on the condition of the impoverished Irish (as opposed to that of American slaves) were not merely the usual obfuscations of a self-serving complacency. After all, Douglass himself had acknowledged the parallel. In the years after the Civil War, several black authors wrote about the Irish in similar terms as people confined to a "potato plantation." A black paper in Washington in 1871 noted that the "standard of subsistence and habitation in many parts of Ireland is lower than [that] formerly upon Southern plantations." A Pennsylvania black newspaper in 1884 advised that "Every Republican, whether colored or white, should be present [to hear a speaker from Ireland], and aid the movement to emancipate the Irish people from as great a system of slavery as that which the colored race suffered under at the hands of their Southern taskmasters." Just as concerned as the Irish were about their own job prospects, many African Americans hoped that if the Irish were "freed" at

14. Ibid., 16, 19.
15. Gleeson, 130–31.

home, they might stop immigrating to the United States and thus ease the employment situation there.[16]

The strongest response to O'Connell's position on slavery came from his friend and former colleague, Bishop England. In a letter to O'Connell, which was published posthumously, England accused him of being "ignorant" of the South. Writing as "a Carolinian," the former Corkman stated that with O'Connell's attack on American slaveholders, "a more wanton piece of injustice has never been done to a brave and generous people." England concluded with a caustic admonition in the manner of Father O'Neill: "I deny your right to interfere, and I pray that you may succeed in raising the ruined population of Ireland to the level of the comforts of the Carolina slave." Later, the Repeal Association of Natchez and Charleston dissolved, the latter with what Hernon has described as "perhaps the frankest statement to come out of the whole dispute": "as the alternative has been presented to us by Mr. O'Connell, as we must choose between Ireland and South Carolina, we say South Carolina forever!" O'Connell did not waver however, and even when, in October 1843, he was imprisoned as a political agitator for his monster rallies, he wrote his most famous statement on the subject to the Cincinnati Repealers, a statement, however, colored by its own racial assumptions: "It was not in Ireland that you learned this cruelty," he declared. "Your mothers were gentle, kind, and humane . . . How can your souls have become stained with a darkness blacker than the negro's skin?"[17]

The Irish both in Ireland and in America remained largely unmoved by O'Connell's appeal. After all, as Hernon has shown again and again, Irish Americans "were under the constant derisive barrage of the abolitionist press and prominent abolitionist authors." A typical example was that of Hinton Rowan Helper, the North Carolina abolitionist, in his famous 1857 book, *The Impending Crisis of the South*, a work that didn't go unnoticed by the *Cork Examiner*: "Helper said that the Irish 'are a more brutal race and lower in civilization than the Negro . . . The Irish are coarse-grained, revengeful, unintellectual, with very few of the finer instincts of humanity.' He predicted a fusion of Irishmen and Negroes which would be of great service to the Irish and improve their character." It was this kind of remark that reinforced antiblack attitudes among the American Irish, so that Fred-

16. Quoted in Arnold Shankman, "Black on Green: Afro-American Editors on Irish Independence, 1840–1921," *Phylon* 41, no. 3 (1980): 293.

17. Gleeson, 130–31; Ignatiev, 26, 29.

erick Douglass, in spite of his acknowledged debt to O'Connell and the Catholic Emancipation movement, would reluctantly conclude that Irish Roman Catholics in America were "the enemies of human freedom, so far, at least, as our humanity is concerned."[18]

Patrick Lynch, Bishop England's Irish-born successor in Charleston, was so much of an apologist for slavery that in 1864 the Confederate government requested him to represent their cause to the Vatican. In performing this task for a European audience, Lynch composed "one of the last Southern proslavery treatises and the longest published discussion of the institution by a Confederate prelate." Lynch had grown up in a slaveholding family and was the owner, as a bishop, of ninety-five slaves. His argument in favor of the institution was fairly typical: black existence in Africa, often in slave conditions anyway, was much worse than in the American South; the king of Dahomey was rumored to have killed 5,000 of his tribesmen as a tribute on the occasion of his father's death—a barbaric deed much worse than any white southern planter could conceive of, let alone perpetrate; blacks needed guidance since the evidence was that those of them that were free had lost all sense of self-control; slavery provided material security from birth to death; disaster awaited blacks in the competitive world of the free labor market. One additional ingredient in Lynch's account was that he was very much influenced in his views by memories of the slave revolt in San Domingo (modern Haiti), which had caused many owners, most of them Catholic, to flee to Charleston bringing with them the worst horror stories about the consequences of black emancipation.[19]

Douglass's remark about Irish Catholics as "the enemies of human freedom" was largely the result of his wounding battles with the American Irish but also reflected his Methodist dislike of Catholicism and its superstitions and was not without a measure of nativist disdain. The comment came from a later time when Young Ireland, the political group that replaced O'Connell in the sympathies of the nationalist population during the 1840s, had become the representative voice in Irish political culture. Comprised,

18. While a few southerners were hanged for merely possessing Helper's book, and while the author was initially sympathetic with the slaves, his basic opposition was to slavery as an institution that was damaging the economic and cultural life of the South; he went on to become an ardent Negrophobe. See Fred Hobson, *Tell about the South: The Southern Rage to Explain* (Baton Rouge, 1983), 44–63; Hernon, 65.

19. David C. R. Heisser, "Bishop Lynch's Civil War Pamphlet on Slavery," *Catholic Historical Review* 84, no. 4 (1998): 681–97.

unlike O'Connell's movement, of an ecumenical mix of educated Protestants and Catholics, it was much more militant both in its pursuit of Irish freedom and in its support for what it felt was a similar cause: the American South's assertion of states' rights. Because the South-leaning Democratic Party was sympathetic toward immigrants and the antislavery Republicans were not, there naturally was a further reason for Young Ireland's choice of loyalties. In this regard too, the Irish were well aware that then-U.S. senator Jefferson Davis had been a stalwart supporter of their right to immigrate.[20]

Regrettable as Young Ireland's choice might appear, one can wonder also how the movement could have been expected to think otherwise? After all, its members more or less accepted the British view of race, nation, and empire and objected only to this same view being applied to the Irish. Moreover, ideas derived from German Romanticism on the organic relation between race, nation, culture, and language served only to reinforce their own sense of uniqueness and destiny. It is with them that we associate the peculiar phrase "racy of the soil"—the need for Irish culture to be of organic, home growth—even if, not insignificantly, the expression bore a striking resemblance to a phrase used by Lord Macaulay in a British context.[21]

The truth is that the Irish-English struggle over the centuries has often been wrongly interpreted as simply one of the unjustly oppressed against an immoral oppressor. Ireland's real complaint is that it has not been allowed to take its rightful place among the nations of the earth as another small European country, one that in all likelihood would have itself acted as a colonizing nation had circumstances allowed, or had its alliances with Spain or France been successful. The eighteenth-century Gaelic poet Eoghan Rua Ó Súilleabháin had something like this in mind when he wrote:

> Ní ins an ainnise is measa linn bheith síos go deo
> Ach an tarcaisne a leanas sinn i ndiaidh na leon . . .

> [The worst thing is not to be sunk forever in misery, but to face
> the insult that follows us, now that the princes have gone . . .[22]]

20. Giles, 798; Gleeson, 102.

21. See Mary Helen Thuente, *The Harp Re-strung: The United Irishmen and the Rise of Irish Literary Nationalism* (Syracuse, N.Y., 1994), 196.

22. Quoted in Declan Kiberd, *Irish Classics* (Cambridge, Mass., 2001), 269. The Irish word *leon*, which Kiberd has here translated as "princes," literally means "lions"—a perhaps unwitting, but still revelatory, association of the Irish with British emblems of empire; see *An Dua-*

Seventeenth- and eighteenth-century Irish Catholic hegemony on the tiny West Indian island of Montserrat, where they conducted a brutally repressive slaveholding regime, indicates that their racial and imperial views perfectly mirrored those of the English and that it is misleading to think of them as eternal victims "who were incapable of hard dealing" themselves: "Thousands of African slaves on Montserrat . . . were during the course of the seventeenth, eighteenth and part of the nineteenth centuries owned by Irish slaveholders, and still others experienced the fierceness of an Irish overseer . . . Oliver Cromwell at his bloodiest did not indulge in the sadistic methods of torture through which we saw errant slaves being put to death for crimes as minor as stealing an item worth a single shilling." Wolfe Tone, the father of Irish republicanism, contemplated a free Ireland that would also be a colonizing nation and was always fascinated by the Sandwich Islands—today's Hawaii—as a prospective colony.[23]

In the eighteenth century, under the Protestant ascendancy, Irish Catholics of means, such as the O'Connells in County Kerry or the Carrolls in Maryland, routinely sent their sons to colleges in France, Belgium, Spain, and Portugal, often Irish-run, to be educated as clerics and lawyers, or to forge a career in the armies of those countries. The officers-at-arms in the London government colluded in this affirmation of monarchy by supplying them with the proofs of pedigree needed for advancement in these institutions.[24] It was only with the elimination of the monarchy in France after 1789, and with the possibility now open for Catholics to join the British military, that the scene began to change. Irish service at all levels of the British imperial administration—such positions abroad were intended to be one of the enticements to educated Catholics to accept the union—however frustrating at times it may have been to the individuals themselves since their "Irishness" was necessarily subordinated to British interests, was a concrete enactment of their ideological outlook. The Young Ireland founder of the revolutionary *Nation* newspaper in the 1840s, Charles Gavan Duffy, went on to receive a knighthood as an Australian governor; deported rebel

naire, 1600–1900: Poems of the Dispossessed, ed. Seán Ó Tuama, trans. Thomas Kinsella (Dublin, 1981), 196–97.

23. Donald Harman Akenson, *If the Irish Ran the World, 1630–1730* (Montreal, 1997), 174–75; Marianne Elliott, *Wolfe Tone: Prophet of Irish Independence* (New Haven, 1989), 55–58.

24. See R. Dudley Edwards, *Daniel O'Connell and His World* (London, 1975). This information was supplied until the middle of the eighteenth century "by surviving officers-of-arms of the exiled Stuarts . . . [Then] the Hanoverian officers-at-arms regularly facilitated exiles seeking substantiation for their claims" (18).

and convict Thomas Darcy Magee became a cabinet minister in the Canadian government; while fellow-convict and Union Civil War veteran Thomas Francis Meagher peremptorily requested the government in Washington to "Give me Idaho!" and was sent out instead as the interim governor of Montana where he subdued the Flathead Indians. Even the less administratively oriented John Mitchel expressed an interest in owning a slave plantation in Alabama, and the biography of William Smith O'Brien, a Harrow and Cambridge-educated leader of the abortive rebellion of 1848, is titled *Revolutionary Imperialist*. It is hardly too much to say that the Irish were monarchists when God's anointed kings and queens ruled the earth, that they were imperialists when imperialism was in vogue, and that they have only shifted to the postcolonial mode now that the acceptability of empire has declined and fallen. It might be kept in mind also that the recent, and proper, celebration of the financial help the displaced Choctaws in Oklahoma (some of whom were probably part Irish through intermarriage in the South before their resettlement) gave to the starving Irish in 1847 was immediately preceded by a long period of neglect, and before that, in the nineteenth century, interpreted as "repaying the Christian world a consideration for bringing them out of benighted ignorance and heathen barbarism."[25]

One story that encapsulates many of the issues dealt with earlier in this chapter is that of the nineteenth-century Healy family in Georgia, from which the "slave," and slave-owning, Father James Healy came.

In 1818, County Roscommon–born Michael Morris Healy moved to the small town of Clinton, Georgia, where his brother was already settled. Acquiring in a lottery some of the land that had recently been "ceded" by the local Indians—a passing reference to the Indian removal policies that were to find their strongest advocate and executor in Andrew Jackson—he, like both Cash's "stout young [Scotch] Irishman" and Faulkner's Thomas Sutpen in *Absalom, Absalom!*, purchased slaves and set out to establish a plantation. By 1831, according to the Jesuit biographer of his two most famous sons, he had "more than sixteen hundred acres and held seventeen slaves." His holdings in both land and slaves were to become substantially greater

25. See the essays in *An Irish Empire? Aspects of Ireland and the British Empire*, ed. Keith Jeffrey (Manchester, 1995); Richard Davis, *Revolutionary Imperialist: William Smith O'Brien, 1803–1864* (Dublin, 1998); and Christine Kinealy, "Potatoes, Providence and Philanthropy: The Role of Private Charity during the Irish Famine," in *The Meaning of the Famine*, ed. Patrick O'Sullivan (Leicester, UK, 1997), 163.

within the next few years. More importantly, Healy obtained a "consort," Mary Eliza Smith, a light-skinned slave of uncertain origin but likely enough born on a neighboring plantation. Father Albert S. Foley explains the matter in the following way: "Eliza was taken to wife by the immigrant Irishman, in spite of the fact that it was technically against the laws of the State of Georgia. There was no official record of the ceremony, but whether it was a common law union or not, the marriage was recognized by Michael Healy as his only one, and in the seclusion of the remote plantation, few neighbors ventured to pry into his personal affairs." Healy treated the nine surviving children born to this union as his own, even though the law regarded them as slaves. He made a point of never letting them accompany him to town, but it seems to have been several years before he fully realized the consequences of their status under the increasingly restrictive Georgia laws, which prohibited him from freeing his slaves even on the occasion of his death.[26]

Confronted with this dilemma, a very prosperous Healy decided to have all of his children attend schools in the North. The oldest boys were sent first to liberal Quaker institutions in New York, which nevertheless continuously embarrassed them by drawing attention to their racial origins and which were also less than sympathetic to the Irish side of their inheritance. They then went to the Jesuits for their formation. In some ways, this was a surprising choice since Michael Healy himself seems to have fallen into the category of pre-devotional revolution Irish Catholics in that he was never very exercised about matters of religion, nor did he ever attend the little Catholic church that had opened in Macon in the 1840s.

The sequence of events that followed was stranger still. In the first place, Healy's oldest children were in their teens when they were baptized as Catholics, thus accepting, as Foley puts it, "the faith that was theirs by their Irish inheritance." Then, while there was some adverse commentary on their origins while they were at the Jesuit Holy Cross College, their main concern seems to have been their faith rather than their race, Irish or African. Three of the six boys aspired to become priests, two of the three girls to be nuns. Anxiety about race was never far away, however, and not unlike Frederick Douglass in Massachusetts and Harriet Jacobs in New York, they always lived in fear of the fugitive slave laws. Furthermore, as there were no papers attesting their father's marriage, the boys were likely to have difficulty in receiving ordination without the intervention of powerful ecclesi-

26. Albert Foley, *Bishop Healy: Beloved Outcaste* (New York, 1954), 5, 7.

astical allies on their behalf. Even with that, two of them had to go to France for their later studies and final ordination, which took place, however, in the rather privileged space of Notre Dame cathedral.[27]

Mary Eliza Healy died in 1849, Michael in 1850 as he was about to leave Georgia permanently for New York. His substantial property, which included sixty-one slaves, was sold and the money divided among his children. The most distinguished among them were James, who went on to become chancellor of the Boston diocese and later the bishop of Maine, and Patrick, the second "founder" of Georgetown University. There were always rumors about their origins, of course, ranging from the derogatory— "The Bishop Is a Nee-Gar"—to the presumption that they were of a semi-aristocratic French Creole inheritance, a rumor the Healys did not discourage, and while the Healys were supportive of black parishioners and clergy, they never identified with those of their mother's race.

It is almost as fascinating as the saga itself that Foley waited from 1954 until 1976 to publish his second slim volume on the Healy family, *Dream of an Outcaste.* In an appendix titled "The Meaning of the Healys," the priest explained that he had wanted to provide a similar commentary in his earlier book but had decided to await the "range of reactions" to it. Most of the reviews had been positive, seeing the bishop's story in particular as a sign of Roman Catholic tolerance, the working out of Divine Providence, a demonstration of the "unconquerable spirit of born leaders." Not everyone was so benign, however. Foley speculates as to why a portrait at Georgetown of Patrick Healy was defaced sometime after the appearance of his first book, suggesting that this act of vandalism may have been the work of outraged white students. A black Roman Catholic priest, meanwhile, noted that while Bishop Healy should not necessarily be blamed for failing to identify with the black part of his inheritance, neither could he be regarded as a hero.[28]

Foley's response reflected liberal Catholic views as late as the 1970s. He saw the issue as not just a question of black and white, but—in terms that call to mind the dilemma of Joe Christmas in Faulkner's 1932 novel, *Light in August*—as "the perennial problem of the 'outcaste,' the 'marginal man,' the person of mixed background who has relations with each of two opposing groups." The "half-caste," according to Everett Stonequist's *The Marginal Man*, has to fear prejudice from either ancestral group. Foley, who

27. Ibid., 20.
28. Albert Foley, *Dream of an Outcaste* (Tuscaloosa, Ala., 1989), 289.

campaigned on behalf of civil rights long before the cause was popular among his fellow southern Catholic clergymen, finally justified the Healys' identification with their white Irish heritage by posing the question thus: "Does [such a person] not share the higher culture in common with the white Americans?" He argued that it was quite natural for the Healys to identify with their white peers since they had spent most of their lives in white communities. Appealing indirectly to the existentialist thinking of the day, Foley subtly shifted the question itself: "The essence of the problem faced by both Bishop Healy and his brother Patrick is simply put: can a man, coming from a marginal or outcaste position, actually realize achievements that stand up as being comparable to those expected of fellow human beings who are characterized by the cultural and external traits of the dominant majority group?" Foley answered that the questionable background of both the bishop and the Jesuit was widely known, and that they still performed remarkably well. So too with another brother, who was also a priest and vice-president of a New England seminary, even though he failed to gain the rectorship of the North American College in Rome because his "African blood," which showed "distinctly in his exterior," was expected to be a hindrance to his effective rule over his white American students. Furthermore, a sister, Eliza Healy, joined an order of nuns where she became a mother superior in several houses.[29]

Foley concluded his second book with some remarkable observations on Patrick Healy's epilepsy, arguing that this was much more significant than any anxiety about race. He had been reluctant to write the original biography because of the epilepsy factor, normally an impediment to ordination, and something that many might have attributed to Healy's interracial background rather than to certain physical injuries he had sustained as a youth.

Overall, Foley's accounts give the impression of having been written by a Jesuit properly sensitive to the reactions of older members of his order, as well as to Georgetown alumni, and at the same time confident that the emphasis of the story ought to be on religion more than on race. A more recent biography of the entire family, based on wider access to the materials and written in a less racially constrained era, offers much the same general picture but nevertheless adds several important details. The author, James M. O'Toole, notes, for example, that Foley had been advised against researching the family at all. Descendants of the married Healys were fear-

29. Ibid., 290, 291, 292.

ful of what might result from such exposure in 1950s America, one family member dreading the possibility that his wife might divorce him as a result of learning about his racial "taint."[30]

O'Toole cautions that there is no reason to think that Michael Healy, however loving his relationship with his "trusty woman" Eliza may have been, was ideologically opposed to slavery as such. Moreover, the journal that eldest son James kept at Holy Cross shows that even early on he too was no abolitionist: James refers to William Lloyd Garrison as a "fool," uses derogatory terms for blacks, and reports his enjoyment of blackface minstrel shows. Intellectually and administratively gifted, as were his two priestly brothers, James was a shrewd manager of the family's considerable fortune derived from the sale of their father's property. Unable to return to Georgia in 1850, where, if discovered, it was not impossible that he would be reduced to the condition of a chattel slave, he nevertheless took a careful business approach to the sale of the family's slaves, hiring them out to neighboring plantations for three years before finally putting them up for auction and receiving unexpectedly good prices for them. While there were small numbers of free blacks in the South who were themselves slaveowners—and not merely, as was once thought, because they had purchased their enslaved relatives from white plantation owners to ensure their "freedom," but sometimes for the same kind of profit that white owners sought to achieve—Bishop Healy would not have seen himself as among them.[31]

O'Toole stresses that all the members of the family saw themselves as white and that even the final auctioning of the slaves of their father's estate only served to reinforce that notion. Their Irish name—*pace* Ignatiev—and clerical status clinched the matter, though at least James and one other brother were described on their passports as having "dark" complexions. From the very beginning, clerical patrons—admirable men in every way by all accounts—had become their surrogate parents, a Jesuit from an old southern planter family being affectionately addressed as "Dad." Bishop Healy was a conscientious and effective prelate whose battles were with nativists, labor unions (a man of property, he feared socialism), Irish secret societies such as the Fenians, and liberal "Americanists" within his own church. Nativists in particular were a serious threat to Catholics in the

30. O'Toole, *Passing for White*, 2. O'Toole found no evidence of Father Patrick Healy having epilepsy (253 n.31).

31. See Larry Koger, *Black Slaveowners: Free Black Slave Masters in South Carolina, 1790–1860* (Columbia, S.C., 1985).

Northeast, who also had to fight to have their chaplains allowed to visit prisons and asylums, and even to serve in non-Irish regiments of the Union army during the Civil War. In remote Maine, the bishop's struggles were not at all about race, at least in the usual sense of the term. Patrick Healy's career as a Jesuit was much the same, though O'Toole thinks he may have received some satisfaction from changing Georgetown from a college for the sons of southern planters—many of them not Catholic—to an institution catering mainly to the children of socially aspiring Irish immigrants from the Northeast.[32]

It is easy now to be critical of the Healys and to want more pained awareness, even agony and divided consciousness, from them than they seem able to deliver. Both Foley and O'Toole resolutely refuse to present such an interpretation, though the latter acknowledges the feeling that, from our perspective, there was something "wrong" about their choice of identity. For the most part, however, the Healys, whether celibate or married, led successful lives and were at ease with their whiteness. When a brother intended for the business world died prematurely at twenty-one, the family's main thought was that he had been spared the temptations of commerce that might have endangered his eternal salvation. The Healys had gone, as the eldest of them liked to say, from being "nothing" to being Catholic.[33]

The choice the Healys made was emblematically that followed by millions of their lighter-skinned Irish fellow-countrymen in constructing a viable identity in a white-dominated world. At worst, they "passed" (in both senses of that word). But for the Irish in general, it is doubtful that the issue was a real one—persons of Asian origin, for example, were classified differently in different states—and they were likely puzzled that others should think that a choice was involved at all. Racial comparisons were predictable insults rather than exploratory challenges.

From a religious perspective, the Irish saw the race issue as being of relatively little concern in light of a Pauline eternity in which there would be no gender, or race, or giving in marriage, or other such earthly distinctions. Simply put, religion—religion in the sense of ensuring one's personal salvation—was deemed far more important than race. In the meantime, they felt no urgency in solving the question of slavery; after all, doing so would only create greater competition for the least well-paid jobs. The Hea-

32. O'Toole, 164.
33. Ibid., 224.

lys seem not even to have recognized any incongruity in the benefit they and their respective religious orders received from monies acquired from the sale of their father's human property. While recent African American histories have begun to claim Patrick Healy of Georgetown as the first black Ph.D. in America—O'Toole thinks that in light of our current understanding of the Healys this is misguided—the entry on African American/Irish relations in the South in the 1999 *Encyclopedia of the Irish in America* devotes itself almost exclusively to the history and needs of pastoral care for a disadvantaged, but distinctly separate, minority.[34]

No wonder that Joseph Hernon asserts that "by the early 1850's the main body of Irish nationalists had no use for American abolitionism. For them, now, the dour Yankee reformers were the re-emergence of that Puritan fanaticism that had historically warred upon the Irish people, and that remained alien to the more richly expressive spirit of the church." "The saints of CROMWELL rise again / In sanctimonious hordes," wrote Young Irelander Joseph Brenan, a refugee from the insurrection of '48 who had escaped capture to settle in New Orleans as a journalist, in "A Ballad for the Young South" in 1856. Brenan also condemned radical abolitionist Senator Charles Sumner, who was to become one of the leading architects of Reconstruction in the post–Civil War era, as the "snarling poodle pet / Of virgins past their prime." Back in Ireland, while (Protestant) Unionists were mildly abolitionist for a while, they too largely became pro-South when the war broke out, even lauding the "moral superiority of the Confederacy." Most tellingly of all, Hernon points out that not one of the three churches in Ireland—Anglican, Presbyterian, Catholic—was abolitionist.[35]

John Mitchel, a major figure in the pantheon of Irish nationalists, was undoubtedly the most famous of the Young Irelanders to show southern sympathies. He was also the most ardent among them in his approval of slavery. Born in Ulster in 1815, the grandson of a United Irishman (the American/French-influenced movement that brought about the 1798 rebellion) and the son of a liberal, "New Light" Presbyterian minister, Mitchel was technically Scotch-Irish. If that identification tends to subvert a too-rigid interpretation of the ideologies of that ethnic category, Mitchel's sympathetic 1888

34. See the entry on "Ethnic Relations: The African-Americans and the Irish," *Encyclopedia of the Irish in America*, ed. Michael Glazier (Notre Dame, 1999), 275–78.

35. Hernon, 67; Joseph Brenan, "A Ballad for the Young South," in *War Songs of the South* (Richmond, 1862), 26; Hernon, 71.

biographer's judgment that since he was Ulster Irish he could not be a Celt subverts yet another.

Trained as a lawyer, Mitchel began his nationalist career as a defender of Catholics arrested for violence against Orange loyalist marchers. Then, as a regular contributor to Duffy's widely circulated *Nation*, he attacked the "act of God theory" of the famine, insisting that English administrators were responsible, rather than divine retribution. He viewed the ordeal as a crime of mass murder. But Mitchel's analysis was more than merely anti-British. In fact, it anticipated much of current postcolonial criticism. He made the point that "the English are not more sanguinary and atrocious than any other people would be in like case, and under like exigencies," so that "the disarmament, degradation, extermination and periodical destruction of the Irish people, are measures of policy dictated, not by pure malignity, but by the imperious requirements of the system of empire administered in London." Of course, Mitchel also, or as a consequence, called for the "dismemberment of that empire."[36]

One of the most formative influences on Mitchel was the Scottish sage Thomas Carlyle, a prominent figure in nineteenth-century British thought. Carlyle was suspicious of modern progress in an industrialized society, accepting of slavery, and unsympathetic with the American abolitionists. Mitchel even went to London to visit his hero, and when the latter came to Ireland, he remarked of his protégé: "Poor Mitchel. I told him he would most likely be hanged, but I told him, too, that they could not hang the immortal part of him." Mitchel trusted Carlyle on almost everything except his mentor's fondness for Cromwell and his judgment that Ireland needed to remain a part of the United Kingdom.[37]

In 1848, the year of revolutions in several European countries, most notably France, the London and Dublin authorities had good reason to fear that the same might happen in Ireland (when the revolt did come, it was a pathetic affair at a farmhouse in Tipperary, but it might have been different had the local clergy not dissuaded their parishioners from taking part). They arrested Mitchel and other prominent Young Irelanders who were recommending violence. Following a hasty and rigged trial, Mitchel was sentenced to fourteen years of servitude in a penal colony. The authorities—a classically minded Mitchel regularly referred to them as the Carthaginians—seem to have been uncertain about where to send him, so after

36. Quoted in Dillon, 1:250.
37. Dillon, 2:58, 1:127.

a few days in a prison on Spike Island, off the coast of Cork, Mitchel was transferred to a convict ship bound for Bermuda. There he spent almost a year, his ship anchored near a small island called "Ireland," then the government base. Concern for his health, or at least the desire not to create another Irish martyr, together with fears and rumors that the American Irish might chart a boat in an attempt to rescue Mitchel soon caused him to be sent on his way. His final destination was Van Diemen's Land, modern Tasmania, a penal colony south of the Australian mainland.[38]

In spite of its hardships, Mitchel was relatively free in Australia, and his family soon was able to join him there. Five years from the date of his conviction, he escaped. Mitchel set out for the United States—a felon, he couldn't return to Ireland—there to be greeted by an astonishing and eclectic array of governors and mayors and Irish societies that hoped to win his approval and "use" him to their political advantage. After the huge influx from the famine, the Irish, even if often disliked, could not be ignored, and their exiled patriots, especially those as well educated as Mitchel, Thomas Francis Meagher, and William Smith O'Brien were, were widely courted.

The Young Ireland escapees from Australia arrived in America months apart, each of them to be subjected to a ritual of patriotic celebrations. At one of his, at the Broadway Theater in New York with Horace Greeley in attendance, Mitchel unwittingly reversed Frederick Douglass's speeches in Ireland and England, declaring: "The Monarchical East casts me out—the Republican West welcomes and embraces me. One slave the less in Europe—one free man more, America, to Thee!"[39]

After the round of "escape celebrations," as they were known, Mitchel set about publishing his account of his ordeal, *Jail Journal*, a classic of Irish nationalist literature. It was in these intense, but urbane and even humorous, pages that Mitchel first expressed what Malcolm Brown has referred to as his "fondness for Negro slavery." Observing some Brazilian slaves in Pernambuco, Mitchel confessed that while he "would not himself like to own slaves, yet they did have their charm, 'fat and merry, obviously not overworked or underfed,' and it pleased him to watch the 'lazy rogues, lolling in their boats, sucking a pot of green sugar cane.' " When he realized that there were "two nations" emerging in the United States, one of which

38. John Mitchel, *Jail Journal* (Dublin, 1982), 34–35, 45. See Rebecca Ann Bach's *Colonial Transformations: The Cultural Production of the New Atlantic World, 1580–1640* (New York, 2000), 110–12, for an account of the possible significance of the original mapping and naming of the island.

39. Quoted in Keneally, 270.

espoused slavery, it was all too clear to him to which of them he ought to belong.[40]

Like Carlyle, Mitchel was suspicious of progress and genuinely skeptical—as were John C. Calhoun and George Fitzhugh in the American South—that the institution of slavery that had served civilization for thousands of years could become obsolete overnight without negative consequences. A religious liberal, he was a social conservative and always imprudently honest, though with the self-deprecating awareness that others frequently saw him as "a very bright and intelligent maniac." Thus, on his arrival in New York in 1854, Mitchel started a proslavery newspaper, *The Citizen.* When James Haughton, a well-known philanthropist in Dublin who had supported both O'Connell's repeal movement and Young Ireland, wrote asking him and other Irish patriots to join the abolitionist cause, Mitchel replied with an open letter in the *Citizen:* "But what *right* has this gentleman to expect . . . [Irish patriots now in America] . . . to take up his wearisome song—which they always refused to sing at home? . . . We are not abolitionists; no more abolitionists than Moses, or Socrates, or Jesus Christ." Mitchel stated that he saw no crime in owning, selling, or flogging slaves, concluding with a remark that would haunt him long afterward: "and as for being a participator in the wrongs [of slavery], we, for our part, wish we had a good plantation, well-stocked with healthy negroes, in Alabama."[41]

Mitchel's nineteenth-century biographer judges that what really drove him to align himself with the pro-slavery South was his astonishment at the fury of Henry Ward Beecher's attack on him for the Alabama comment, in which Beecher—brother of Harriet Beecher Stowe, author of *Uncle Tom's Cabin*—pointed out that Mitchel was for freedom in Ireland but against it in the United States. It is clear, however, from his references in *Jail Journal* to "Sambo" leaders, his distaste for Negro music, and especially his condemnation by contrast of the British exploitation of India that Mitchel had been moving in that direction long beforehand. Mitchel described Beecher condescendingly as "a very popular clergyman in Brooklyn, of the sect of people called 'Congregationalists'; an eloquent, powerful, and rowdy preacher, of no great cultivation," adding with malicious wit that Beecher "pronounced me a dead man, and thereupon proceeded to mangle my corpse and suck my bones . . . this reverend man minced me extremely

---

40. Malcolm Brown, *The Politics of Irish Literature* (Seattle, 1972), 138; Mitchel, 154.
41. Brown, 139; Dillon, 2:44.

small." Addressing Beecher as "most learned clerk," Mitchel went on to explain that the golden rule is not "Masters, discharge your slaves" but rather that "if you are a slaveholder, use your slave with gentleness, humanity, and kindness . . . just as you could reasonably wish, were you the slave and he the master, that he would behave towards you."[42]

It was not Mitchel's views on slavery, however, that caused his highly successful paper (it peaked at a circulation of fifty thousand) to fold within a year. Mitchel's opinions were well tolerated, if not always embraced, in that regard. Fugitive slave Harriet Jacobs, living in New York in fear of being captured and sent back to her owner, complained later: "John Mitchell [sic] was free to proclaim in the City Hall his desire for 'a plantation well stocked with slaves;' but there I sat, an oppressed American, not daring to show my face." Rather, Mitchel managed the impressive feat of antagonizing the abolitionists and the Roman Catholic clergy, the latter, in the circumstances, a fatal error. He informed Archbishop Hughes that "your Grace, and the whole hierarchy of your Church, and the priesthood of it, too . . . is an enemy of . . . the manhood, and the very rights of Irishmen . . . the Irish here will be good and loyal citizens of this Republic in the exact proportion that they cut themselves off, not from Religion, but from the political corporation which you call the Church of God." This objection to another form of slavery (one from which James Joyce would also try to escape) was probably the only one of Mitchel's views with which Henry Ward Beecher, and even Frederick Douglass, would have heartily concurred.[43]

Mitchel's prominence as an unexpected defender of slavery and an able anti-abolitionist in the Beecher affair led to his being invited to give the commencement speech at the University of Virginia. His own summary of the Carlyle-style address, "Progress in the Nineteenth Century," is revealing: "the drift of it was to show that there is no *progress* at all; that is, no progress making men wiser, happier, or better than they were thirty centuries ago; but admitting, also, that they are no worse, no foolisher, no more wretched than they were at that period and ever since. Of course, gas, steam, printing press, upholstering, and magnetic telegraphs could not be denied, but they were put aside as altogether irrelevant to the inquiry."

42. Quoted in Dillon, 2:46, 45, 47.

43. Harriet Jacobs, *Incidents in the Life of a Slave Girl* (New York, 2001), 154; *Citizen*, 9 September 1854, 568. See Bryan McGovern, "John Mitchel: Ecumenical Nationalist in the Old South," *New Hibernia Review* 5, no. 2 (2001): 99–110.

Sagely, Mitchel adds: "I could see that those around, how courteously so-ever they listened, and even sometimes applauded, did not in their own hearts assent to my conclusions." He had not devoted his speech directly to the topic of slavery as the audience may have expected, and his views on a lack of progress could not have sat well with even conservative southerners. The general tenor of his argument, however, explains why he would not be in sympathy with abolishing the institutions of the past, slavery among them.[44]

Mitchel's Virginia speech was the prelude to his journey southward. There he reported seeing the "luckiest, jolliest, *and* freest negroes on the face of the earth," a remark that reinforces the suspicion that his actual contact with slavery—unlike that of another foreigner, English actress Fanny Kemble, who had received a rude awakening on her husband's plan-tation in Georgia in the 1830s—was always marginal. Settling in Tucka-leechee Cove, near Knoxville, Tennessee, because it reminded him of his own County Down and in the expectation that the new railway lines would increase the value of his property—Mitchel sounded a Thoreauvian note with "I desired . . . to try whether life might be possible for us amongst the woods"—he began another proslavery paper, this time called the *Southern Citizen*. But, as DeeGee Lester observes, "Charleston, Savannah, New Or-leans, and even nearby Memphis, with their large Irish populations and enthusiasm for slavery would seem natural power bases for the Irish martyr and advocate of slavery"; instead, he settled in "an area of few Irishmen and a hotbed of Southern antislavery sentiment." Although he described the people in Tuckaleechee as consisting of "40 or 50 families all original Tennessee 'Hoosiers,' lately neighbors to the Cherokies [*sic*] who have but 15 years ago been removed from these mountains" and as "excessively igno-rant and cunning, but civil and otherwise not intolerable," they were pre-sumably Scotch-Irish of an earlier era who simply did not recognize a new, educated immigrant, who, tangentially at least, was one of their own.[45]

John Mitchel's life in Tennessee was far removed from that of a south-ern planter: "We have no help as yet, male or female. As to field work, I can get, and do get, such help as I want from the neighbouring 'mean whites' of these parts; but James and I milk the cows, drive them out, drive them in,

44. Quoted in Dillon, 2:6.

45. DeeGee Lester, "John Mitchel's Wilderness Years in Tennessee," *Éire-Ireland* 25, no. 2 (1990): 8; Mitchel papers, 1 November 1855 (Public Record Office of Northern Ireland, Bel-fast, D.1078).

separate them twice a day from their calves, a task of much labour and sweat, feed horses, drive nails, light fires, make up fences." He adds: "The 'mean whites' of these parts admire my conduct, costume, and manners much, and have hopes that I will become in time as good a citizen and as mean a white as any of themselves."[46]

Being a Protestant, Mitchel was befriended by the city's mayor, the district attorney, and other local noteworthies—causing him to abandon the isolation of his farm for a house in Knoxville. But he was also suspected of being a Catholic spy (indicating that the Protestant-Catholic distinction was very much alive in the area), an accusation provoked by the building "of the new Roman Catholic church where, rumor said, vaults beneath the church would hold the gunpowder to be used by the Jesuits when they 'took over the country.' "[47]

As usual, Mitchel got himself involved in a number of feuds, even with those who held views similar to his own. One such controversial view was that the international slave trade, prohibited since 1808, should be reopened; he supported plans to raid the Caribbean islands for this purpose. It is hardly surprising that he got along well with Edmund Ruffin, the agriculturalist and southern fire-eater, when they met in 1859: both were mavericks too extreme for their constituencies. Mitchel too had been led to the brink of suicide during his deportation to Australia, a resolution that Ruffin succeeded in at war's end.[48]

Mitchel wrote so frequently about Irish affairs that he had to defend his newspaper being "southern." But, since he always regarded the South as the "Ireland of this continent," making a sharp separation between the two probably did not seem to him to be a real necessity. When the longed-for war finally came, Mitchel, even more the most plantation owners, had no difficulty in identifying himself with its purposes. After all, Carlyle too favored the South since it seemed to him "that the industrial North wanted to make agricultural slaves into industrial slaves; and that, from all reports, the slaves in the South were treated with reasonable justice and compassion by a basically benevolent ruling class."[49]

* * *

46. Dillon, 2:72, 73.

47. Lester, 8.

48. Gleeson, 132; *The Diary of Edmund Ruffin*, ed. William Kauffman Scarborough (Baton Rouge, 1972), 2:265–66.

49. Fred Kaplan, *Thomas Carlyle* (New York, 1983), 490.

Tempting as it is to conclude that the attitudes of O'Connell, the Healys, and Mitchel toward slavery offer a fair representation of the nineteenth-century Irish mind on the issue, it would seem that O'Connell's active opposition to the institution left him very much in the minority. It is therefore of more than passing interest to find that Arthur Griffith, founder of the Sinn Féin party in 1906 and leader of the new Irish Free State in 1922—he died unexpectedly at the moment of its inauguration—was particularly sympathetic with Mitchel's extreme views. Griffith was a former resident of South Africa's Transvaal region and had been a strong sympathizer with the Boers in their turn-of-the-century war with Britain, a significant episode for Irish nationalists, including socialist James Connolly and W. B. Yeats, but one that was certainly not fought in the interests of black Africans. In his extended preface to the 1913 edition of *Jail Journal* he praised Mitchel for "introducing the element of reality into the Irish politics of his time," and for arousing fierce enemies because of his opposition to "humbug." He also commented starkly on the Young Irelander's southern episode:

> Later, when Mitchel avowed his approval of slave-holding and the Northern States which had but a few months before banqueted, bouquetted and brass-banded him to weariness, shrieked threat and insult, he was genuinely astonished to find that in a "land of liberty" a man was supposed to conceal unpopular opinions . . . Had humanity not enough crimes already to its charge, he inquired, that the benevolists and human-progress people should invent another? Were they to write "criminal" across the civilizations and the wise and noble men of all ages because some benevolists at the end of the eighteenth century had decided for the first time that slave-holding was immoral?

Griffith commended Mitchel for invoking the example of Moses, the ancient Greeks, Jesus, and the American founding fathers in their acceptance of slavery.[50]

In Griffith's view, Mitchel did not need any apology. His "essential work" had been that of "dissevering the case for Irish independence from theories of humanitarianism and universalism." Griffith added: "Even his views on negro-slavery have been deprecatingly excused, as if excuse were needed for an Irish nationalist declining to hold the negro his peer in right." For Griffith, Mitchel was "a sane Nietzsche in his view of man, but

50. Arthur Griffith, "Preface to 1913 Edition," in Mitchel, 369.

his sanity was a century out of date back and forward." He concluded with the bold assertion that "The right of the Irish to political independence never was, is not and never can be dependent upon the admission of equal right in all other peoples. It is based on no theory of, and dependable in nowise for its existence or justification on the 'Rights of Man'; it is independent of theories of government and doctrines of philanthropy and universalism."[51]

Griffith's view is harsh and jarring, but apart from the vehemence of its expression, it is not atypical. Charles Stewart Parnell always entertained a romantic sympathy with the southern cause, one shared by Oscar Wilde, who considered his visit to the defeated Jefferson Davis in 1882 a pilgrimage and was not unduly troubled when his train stopped for a lynching on the tracks; W. B. Yeats was proud that one of his family's trading ships had been designed to break the Union blockade of the Confederate states. For better or worse, and without apparent moral strain, Irish patriots tended to see the white southern struggle as parallel to their own, ignoring in the process the cries of the African American slaves in their bondage. Even much of the subsequent positive Irish American involvement with the black community was to be understood in terms of religious mission, helping the needy, providing separate schools, hospitals, and even churches for an eventual equality that was only likely to come about in the next world.[52]

After the war, when the South had been destroyed, there was relatively little reason for more than a handful of impoverished Irish people to immigrate there. Almost the only ones that did come were Catholic missionaries. The recent discovery of the diaries of two Irish Dominican nuns from comfortable families—but who had probably been sent to America because they didn't have the dowries necessary to support them in their convents at home—who made the journey, first-class, to New Orleans in October 1889, casts a revealing light on contemporary Irish attitudes toward race.[53]

Suellen Hoy describes the passages in which the nuns discuss blacks as

51. Ibid., 371.

52. See R. F. Foster, *Charles Stewart Parnell* (London, 1976), 94; Yeats, *The Autobiography of William Butler Yeats* (New York, 1965), 32; Mary Louise Ellis, "Improbable Visitor: Oscar Wilde in Alabama, 1882," *Alabama Review* (October 1986): 248. Ellis comments simply: "As shocking and raw as Southern violence was, Wilde understood it in terms of the violent history of his native Ireland."

53. Suellen Hoy and Margaret MacCurtain, eds., *From Dublin to New Orleans: The Journey of Nora and Alice* (Dublin, 1994).

the "most startling." Their first sight of such people was a totally new experience for them, and they sought the opinion of the congenial Devonshire captain of their ship (surely a fellow Celt by Grady McWhiney's reckoning). His views were not positive, however, nor did the sisters disagree with him. In fact, Hoy finds it necessary to remind the reader that the nuns were living in the period "before Franz Boas at Columbia [University] began to question such scientific racism." Despite Hoy's caveat, it seems highly unlikely that their views would have been radically different even decades later.[54]

Sister Nora feels "amusement" on first encountering blacks at a distance, though she soon finds them "disagreeable in the extreme," admitting that "their appearance alone excites disgust." When the captain tells her that the natives of the Caribbean islands "are little more than cannibals, those with whose presence we are now blessed included," she notes for her sister nuns in Dublin that "if you happen to hear of my mysterious disappearance some fine morning, you may rightly conjecture what has become of me. However it is to be hoped we shall be soon rid of them."[55]

Sister Alice, on the other hand, seems somewhat more discerning, though she perceives much coarseness and laziness even among affluent blacks. Finally, even she declares, "I can't endure them, notwithstanding all the fun they create." Hoy thinks that the two nuns probably had very little contact with blacks afterward in carrying out their duties as teachers in all-white Irish Catholic schools in New Orleans. There is certainly no reason to suppose that they ever changed their opinions on the subject of race.[56]

In any case, such were the views of even good people who were dedicating their lives to the service of others. Such were probably the views of most of the Irish in America at the time. In the early twentieth century, black leader W. E. B. Du Bois strongly supported the movement for Irish independence as shown in a brief article in Crisis magazine for March 1921, titled "Bleeding Ireland": "No people can more exactly interpret the inmost meaning of the present situation in Ireland than the American Negro." But, he added, "No people in the world have in the past gone with blither spirit to 'kill niggers' from Kingston to Delhi and from Kumasi to Fiji" than the Irish—presumably as soldiers of the British army invading and controlling these places—while Irish Americans "provided the backbone for the AFL's

54. Ibid., 34–35.
55. Ibid., 78–79, 80.
56. Ibid., 115.

[American Federation of Labor] policies excluding Negro workers." Although the accuracy of Du Bois's wholesale condemnation might be questioned, it seems fair to say that like many others among the downtrodden, the Irish sense of their own unjustified dispossession and exile had served to harden them rather than make them more empathetic with the plight of others. As Du Bois was to lament: "In this world it is the Oppressed who have continually been used to cow and kill the Oppressed in the interest of the Universal Oppressor."[57]

57. *Crisis* (March 1921): 200; David Levering Lewis, *W. E. B. Du Bois* (New York, 2000), 2:61.

CHAPTER 3

"AΠ UΠHOLY & CRUEL WAR"

As the alternative has been presented to us by Mr. O'Connell, as we must choose between Ireland and South Carolina, we say South Carolina forever!
—THE (IRISH) REPEAL ASSOCIATION OF CHARLESTON, 1842

I must admit that I grudge [the South] what it has cost us—the lives of our two sons in defence of a country which, after all, was not their own.
—JOHN MITCHEL, letter to an Irish friend, 1865

Comedian Harry Macarthy was performing in Jackson, Mississippi, in January 1861, when the delegates to the state's secession convention voted to break from the Union. He quickly composed what was to become one of the most popular southern songs of the war, "The Bonnie Blue Flag," setting it to the air of "The Irish Jaunting Car." Macarthy has been variously described as both English and Irish (of a Scotch-Irish father). Famous for his singing and "dialect impersonations" of Yankee, Irish, English, Dutch, French, and Negro characters—he was often billed as "the Irish comedian"—he was but one of the many white entertainers of the period, several of them Irish, who at times employed blackface and performed minstrel routines. According to E. Lawrence Abel, "One of the few existing descriptions of him says he was 'a small, handsome man, and brimful of the humor and the pathos and impulsive generosity of the Celtic race.'" When Macarthy sang his composition a few months later in New Orleans dressed in a newly designed Confederate uniform and with his wife by his side, the enthusiasm of the audience of soldiers on their way to the front led to a near riot in the theater:

> Hurrah! Hurrah! For Southern rights, hurrah!
> Hurrah for the Bonnie Blue Flag that bears a single star.

Macarthy spent the war years repeating his success and became, as Abel notes, "the most popular performer in his country, the Confederate States of America." Even his desertion to the North near the end of the conflict didn't prevent him from being well-received on his return in 1867.[1]

South Carolina had been the first state to secede, doing so in December 1860. Ten others followed. By April 1861, the war had begun. It was of enormous interest in Ireland, becoming, as Joseph M. Hernon observes in his 1968 study, *Celts, Catholics, and Copperheads*, "the principal topic of public interest . . . from 1861 to 1865." Irish histories focused as they generally are on the ups and downs of the national struggle for repeal of the 1801 Act of Union that had made Ireland a constituent part of the United Kingdom—adding the cross of St. Patrick to those of St. George and St. Andrew in the hope of circumventing the possibility of another colonial revolution on the model of America in 1776 or Ireland in 1798—never mention the preoccupation with the American war.[2]

There was very good reason for such an unusual degree of popular concern about a war thousands of miles away. Money from Irish workers in America—an important component in the Irish economy of the Victorian era—was not reaching its destination, while jobs in English factories dependent on the importation of southern cotton were also drying up. Then, the challenge to the Union in the United States called into question the more recent union between Great Britain and Ireland. Most important of all, not only were many Irish-born immigrants fighting in this war, but they were doing so on both sides—150,000 in the Union army, at the very least 20,000 with the Confederates. Even more surprisingly, perhaps, the evidence leads overwhelmingly to the conclusion that Irish sympathies—despite that far more Irish fought for the Union army—were with the southern cause.[3]

By the time the Civil War began, John Mitchel was living in Paris, nursing the hope that hostilities would break out between France and England and thus provide Ireland with yet another opportunity for insurrection. If

1. E. Lawrence Abel, *Singing the New Nation: How Music Shaped the Confederacy, 1861–1865* (Mechanicsburg, Pa., 1999), 59–63.

2. Joseph M. Hernon, *Celts, Catholics, and Copperheads: Ireland Views the American Civil War* (Columbus, Ohio, 1968), 1.

3. The usual number cited for the Confederates is 40,000, which was the number claimed by John Mitchel, three of whose sons fought in the war. Another frequent figure is 30,000. In the absence of hard data, I am conservatively opting for David Gleeson's "plausible 20,000"—still a very substantial participation of native-born Irishmen; see *The Irish in the South, 1815–1877* (Chapel Hill, 2001), 154.

the turmoil of his year in New York had driven him to seek seclusion in Tennessee—he had expressed the wish to go to *la belle France,* then as later a haven for exiled revolutionaries, but needed the fees that his semiannual American lecture tours provided ("a loathsome business")—by 1857 his desire for greater intellectual stimulation had driven him out again, first to Washington, and then to France in 1859.[4]

What led Mitchel to leave France to return to the warring South—now the Confederate States of America—in the early part of 1862 was that two of his sons had joined the army there. His eldest was the only foreigner to receive an officer's commission in South Carolina (partly because of his father's reputation). Indeed, Captain John C. Mitchel was present when Edmund Ruffin fired the first shot on Union-held Fort Sumter. Moreover, he was paying court to the seventeen-year-old Miss Claudine Rhett, daughter of "the father of secession," former U.S. senator Robert Barnwell Rhett. Like Ruffin, Rhett was known as a "fire-eater" because of his radical pro-slavery and pro-states' rights views, which placed him far to the right of Jefferson Davis, a reluctant convert to secession and a believer in southern federalism. Rhett had also aspired to the Confederate presidency, was ever fearful that the South would seek a compromise with the North, and, in general, was Mitchel-like in being a thorn even in the side of the Confederacy. From Paris, Mitchel too had contributed to Rhett's son's newspaper, the diehard *Charleston Mercury.*[5]

Mitchel and his youngest son returned incognito to America by way of New York. From there, as if reenacting his Australian escape, the two were ferried by night past the Union gunboats that patrolled the Potomac River, arriving finally in Richmond, Virginia, now the capital of the Confederacy. There, having been rejected for military service on the basis of his near-sightedness, the forty-seven-year-old Mitchel began his official Confederate career as an editor at the *Enquirer,* a pro-government, moderate newspaper. At war's end, three bloody years later, he was still in Richmond, though now as an editor at the much more radical *Examiner* and a consistent critic of Davis's caution in his conduct of the war. Nelson Lankford describes the ambiance of the paper:

> The *Examiner*'s editor and proprietor, John Moncure Daniel, a former diplomat, led the field for violent, acidulous invective. He counted nine duels to

4. Dillon, 2:115.
5. Ibid., 160.

his credit and egged on the radicals who demanded secession in 1861. Earlier he had declined a challenge from Edgar Allan Poe, whose work he afterward rated highly . . . When the conflict that he helped bring on finally erupted, the highly strung journalist tortured Jefferson Davis with fine editorial cruelty. Daniel surrounded himself with a coterie of editors known for their brilliance and sarcasm. John Mitchel, an Irish nationalist who had escaped a British jail, quixotically embraced the Confederacy and found a congenial home with the *Examiner*.

Another editor, Edward Pollard, was to achieve fame after the war as the herald of the "Lost Cause" movement. Once again, Mitchel had managed to position himself as a rebel among rebels.[6]

In spite of their strong southern sympathies, not all of the Young Irelanders took Mitchel's position on the conflict. Since the southern cause was subservient to that of Ireland's, there was some debate as to what strategy it would be best to adopt in the crisis. The general opinion was that supporting the South seemed to be the right thing to do because its struggle for self-determinacy was very much like Ireland's. However, the Young Irelanders also realized that by opposing the U.S. federal government they were helping to weaken an ally of Ireland, one that had recently pressed Britain for pardons for the convicted Young Irelanders. There was also something suspicious in the fact that the British government seemed to be leaning toward the Confederate side.[7]

In late 1863, prominent Young Irelander William Smith O'Brien, whose statue now graces O'Connell Street in Dublin, gave his reasons for supporting the South: since Ireland, Poland, and Canada had a right to legislative independence, then why not the individual states of America, "which never for a moment, relinquished the title of sovereignty that belongs to them individually." For the Union side, Thomas Francis Meagher, who had earlier shown southern sympathies, cautioned that:

> The identification of the Irish people at home with the Orangemen and Tories of England in their avowed sympathy and active connivance with the rebels . . . will not be forgotten by the jealous exclusionists [the Know Nothings] of this country when the war is over . . . when they remember how, even in the very season when the Loyal States were pouring their grain and

6. Nelson Lankford, *Richmond Burning: The Last Days of the Confederate Capital* (New York, 2002), 18.

7. See R. J. M. Blackett's *Divided Hearts: Britain and the American Civil War* (Baton Rouge, 2001) for an analysis of British responses to the war.

gold into Ireland to relieve the starving poor [during the crop failures from 1860 to 1863], the public opinion of Ireland . . . went forth to condemn the action of the national government, and approve the infidelity and usurpation of its enemies.

Mitchel, writing from Richmond, disagreed—and southern militia units that had earlier been called after Meagher changed their name—complaining about the pro-Northern sympathies of some Irish in Ireland who "seem to have got themselves persuaded that . . . repeal of one union in Europe depends on the enforcement of another union in America."[8]

It was in 1863 also that Mitchel, as if giving prior assent to Grady Mc-Whiney's "Celtic-South" thesis, asserted that the Confederates had "universally repudiated Anglo-Saxonism" and that separation from the Yankees was necessary "by reason of the difference of *race*. We consider ourselves here rather to belong to the 'Latin races' and claim kindred with the Celts." By any standard, this was surely a strange and astonishingly fluid definition of race, although Mitchel was by no means the only one to suggest a racial difference between North and South.[9]

In practice, however, persons of Irish birth, like almost everyone else, ended up fighting for whatever region of the country they happened to live in. This meant that numerically more of them were in the Union army—often unwillingly, it appears—though, proportionate to their numbers in the South, there was a higher representation of the Irish in the Confederate ranks. Once the war had begun, the northern blockade of southern ports meant that the Confederates, unlike the Union army, would be unable to receive new recruits from Ireland. Initially at least, those Irish in the Confederate forces fought for their cause with fewer hesitations, greater enthusiasm, and less sense of coercion.

As the war dragged on, there were many reasons for Irish people to be unhappy with its conduct. The Union side, for example, illegally and aggressively recruited soldiers in Ireland, often under the false pretense that they would be employed as civilians rather than in the army. There was a sense too that the Irish, most of whom were in non-Irish regiments, were not well regarded or well treated within the military due to reigning nativist sentiment. Then, of course, there were the tremendous losses. An editorial from a Dublin nationalist paper, *The Irishman*, after the Battle of

8. Hernon, 90.

9. Ibid., 93; Bertram Wyatt-Brown, *The Shaping of Southern Cultures: Honor, Grace, and War, 1760s–1880s* (Chapel Hill, 2001), 180.

Bull Run remarked that Irish soldiers were "fighting with desperate brav-ery, under 'Native American' generals of astounding incompetency, for that very people who, a year or two before, burned their convents, insulted their priests, and threatened to rob themselves of all lawful rights of citizenship." Even the decimation of Irish Union troops at the battle of Fredericksburg in December 1862, the most significant Irish engagement in the entire war, rather than inspiring sympathy with the northern cause, made the people at home yet "more hostile toward the Union war effort."[10]

It now appears that one of the most famous and poignant legends of that encounter—that Thomas Francis Meagher's Irish Union Brigade was cut down by Irish Confederates from Georgia who sadly recognized their fellow-countrymen's approach and cried out "Oh, God, what a pity! Here comes Meagher's fellows!"—is a later fabrication based on questionable evi-dence. Be that as it may, Meagher and Mitchel, mutual friends, former Young Irelanders, and fellow escapees from Australian imprisonment, were within a mile of one another but on opposite sides, one as a Union major general, the other as a Confederate journalist. Their proximity demon-strates the poignancy of the situation and its alienating effect on Irish sensi-bilities.[11]

The final blow to Irish sympathies for the Union came with the New York draft riots in July 1863, during which about eleven blacks were lynched and over a hundred rioters, mainly Irish, killed. The riots were bitterly xenophobic—though Irish policemen were prominent among those deployed to quell them—but their provocation derived from a deep sense of unfairness in the conscription process for the army whereby a $300 pay-ment could purchase a waiver, a sum wholly out of reach of new immi-grants. More importantly, the shift in focus from a war being waged to preserve the union to one aimed at freeing the slaves further alienated the newly arrived and likely to be conscripted Irish, who, unlike their fellow countrymen who had arrived some years earlier, had as yet no sentimental or economic stake, much less a political one, in American society.[12]

10. Hernon, 17, 18.

11. See Kevin O'Neill, "The Star-Spangled Shamrock: Meaning and Memory in Irish America," in *History and Memory in Modern Ireland*, ed. Ian McBride (New York, 2001), 130, for the received account; see Craig A. Warren, "'Oh, God, What a Pity!': The Irish Brigade at Fredericksburg and the Creation of Myth," *Civil War History* 47, no. 3 (2000), for how the legend was intentionally constructed.

12. Hernon claims that "an estimated 85 per cent of the twelve hundred to fifteen hundred whites killed by policemen and soldiers came from Ireland" (19). The far lower number of-fered here comes from Iver Bernstein, *The New York City Draft Riots* (New York, 1990).

At home, meanwhile, Sir William Wills Wilde, father of Oscar Wilde, in a lecture in 1864 "regretted that so many Celtic-Irishmen were 'shedding their blood for hire in an alien cause, in which they feel neither interest nor sympathy.'" The *Cork Examiner* described southerners as an "innocent and unoffending people" and protested that some Irish (in the Union army) sought "to conquer, subjugate and devastate a country whose citizens are fighting for their independence, and defending their homes and altars." Irish members of the Westminster parliament were especially prominent in the effort to recognize the Confederacy, William Henry Gregory, MP for County Galway, subsequently governor of Ceylon (now Sri Lanka), and husband of the later famous dramatist Lady Gregory, being the first member of parliament to do so.[13]

Thomas Conolly, owner of one of Ireland's largest estates and an MP for Donegal, was the last notable foreigner to visit the Confederacy in late 1864. After a failed attempt at running his own blockade ship to the southern coast—a highly profitable enterprise if successful (Conolly's aborted effort was laden with complimentary horse saddles for Lee and his entourage, as well as other saleable goods, both necessities and luxury items)—he employed the famed (or notorious) Captain John Newland Maffitt, "the prince of privateers," to land him on the coast of North Carolina. Conolly then wined and dined his way through what remained of the Confederacy, meeting Davis, Lee, and Fanny Kemble's ex-husband Pierce Butler along the way. He was in church with Davis on the Sunday morning when the call came to evacuate Richmond, and he made his way rather adventurously through the fires, fleeing crowds, and looters.[14]

Nor was this interest wholly one-sided. Union recruitment efforts in Ireland were an ongoing worry, especially since the blockade prevented the South from doing likewise. Informed Southerners also were troubled by the frequent and even positively intended comparison being made between Stonewall Jackson and Oliver Cromwell because they perceived themselves rather as Cavaliers fighting *against* New England Puritans. Henry E. R. Jackson editorialized about "a war of invasion . . . inflicted by a people of the same race with ourselves," adding that "Cromwell's invasion of Ireland was conducted on precisely the same plans, and with identically the same purposes which actuate our foes."[15]

13. Hernon, 33, 34.

14. Nelson D. Lankford, ed., *An Irishman in Dixie: Thomas Conolly's Diary of the Fall of the Confederacy* (Columbia, 1988).

15. Mark E. Neely Jr. et al., *The Confederate Image: Prints of the Lost Cause* (Chapel Hill, 1987), 115.

"At any rate," Hernon concludes, "the evidence is overwhelming that majority sentiment in Ireland was against the northern prosecution of the war." He notes that Father John Bannon—whom he describes as "a prejudiced commentator"—would nevertheless likely "be close to the truth in identifying Irish opinion with the words of a 'labouring peasant' in 1864 who said: 'We, who were all praying for the North at the opening of the war, would now willingly go to fight for the South if we could get there.'"[16] All three of John Mitchel's sons fought in the Confederate army. Even as a journalist, Mitchel himself had come under close fire on the first day of the Battle of Fredericksburg and was also serving in Richmond's Ambulance Committee. His youngest son, who had accompanied him on the journey from France, was to be killed in Pickett's division at Gettysburg in 1863. The sad intimacy that still bound the Irish on both sides of the conflict is illustrated in the report that an Irish Union officer was assigned to try to find Willy Mitchel's body for suitable burial as the son of a famous—albeit now enemy—Irish patriot. Mitchel's son Jack, Claudine Rhett's suitor, was killed a year later as commander of Fort Sumter where the war had begun. His third son lost an arm in battle.[17]

In the midst of all this chaos and tragedy, Mitchel's devoted, resilient, and long-suffering wife and two daughters left Ireland to run the blockade in even more daring fashion than Mitchel and his son had done. Chased and fired on for several hours by federal patrols, they landed safely on the Outer Banks of North Carolina only to witness the drunken sailors burn the ship with all the passengers' possessions in it and then abandon them. An Englishman helped the Mitchels on the rest of their journey. "No more destitute refugees ever came to Richmond, even in these days of *refugeeing*, than my wife and two little girls," observed Mitchel when he finally greeted them several days later.[18]

As we saw in the previous chapter, the Roman Catholic Church's position on slavery was one that made it possible for its adherents to take either side in the war in all good conscience. A small, and grossly inadequate, number of Catholic chaplains, including members of religious orders, served both sides. The most famous Confederate chaplain was the "prejudiced" Father Bannon referred to by Hernon. This extraordinarily capable and energetic

16. Hernon, 108.
17. Thomas Keneally, *The Great Shame* (New York, 1999), 385.
18. Dillon, 2:189.

priest was even to serve as a kind of "spy" for the southern cause both in Rome and in Ireland.[19]

We have a direct record of Bannon's exploits from his own short account, "Experiences of a Confederate Army Chaplain," which was published in, of all places, *Letters and Notes of the English Jesuit Province* in 1867. Born in County Roscommon in 1829, Bannon came to St. Louis, Missouri, as a priest in 1853. There he built a church that later became the pro-Cathedral for the city. Serving a pre-famine Irish community, he was also chaplain to the local militia, which blended "Irish nationalism, militarism, and religion," and which in Missouri as elsewhere was designed to protect Catholics against nativist attack from members of the Know Nothing movement. He also got caught in the Kansas-Missouri conflict that immediately preceded the Civil War and in which "Some pro-Southerners were shot and hanged during a raid common to both factions."[20]

Bannon had been influenced by the Young Ireland movement and its abortive rebellion in 1848. His biographer, Phillip Thomas Tucker, points out that "Self determination for the South was linked to Irish nationalism," so that Bannon "thought that the Southern people and the Irish people both had the natural right to choose their own leaders, systems of government, and destinies." Again, there was a strong perception that abolitionism equaled anti-Catholicism. Still, as Tucker notes, "the majority of the St. Louis Irish in 1861 overlooked the historic antagonisms, the analogy of the plight of Ireland with the South, . . . the discrimination, and their life as second-class citizens. Most would side with the Union in large part because the Northern army provided an avenue by which they could obtain instant equality." John Bannon was among the minority that chose the southern side. A "zealot," his pro-South sympathies were so strong in fact that some of his parishioners objected to his constantly declaring them in sermons and prayers.[21]

19. Randall M. Miller, in "Catholic Religion, Irish Ethnicity, and the Civil War," in *Religion and the American Civil War,* ed. Miller et al. (New York, 1988), explains that only forty chaplains served the 200,000 Catholics in the Union forces (265). This deficit was the result of local shortages, bishops unwilling to release clergy badly needed for diocesan work, and, at the other end, of Know-Nothing prejudice that refused to accept these ministers.

20. *Letters and Notes of the English Jesuit Province* 34 (1866–1868): 201–10. This document is more readily accessible as Appendix A of W. B. Faherty's *The Fourth Career of John B. Bannon* (Portland, Ore., 1994), 83–92. Phillip Thomas Tucker, *Father John B. Bannon: The Confederacy's Fighting Chaplain* (Tuscaloosa, Ala., 1994), 7, 10.

21. Tucker, 13, 16.

When the war began, Bannon fled the divided city to serve the rebel forces by acting as unofficial chaplain to the First Missouri Confederate Brigade. From the very start, the priest identified with the soldiers, who "ragged and starving, were fighting for the protection of their homes." He even wore the regular uniform together with a slouch hat, and stood side by side with them in battle, believing that such chaplains "were much respected by all the men, whether Catholic or not; for they saw that [I] did not shrink from danger or labour to assist them." In the account he wrote after the war when he had become a Jesuit in Ireland, Bannon added a polemical comment for his clerical audience: "the Protestant Chaplains were frequently objects of derision, always disappearing on the eve of an action, when they would stay behind in some farm house till all was quiet, and then overtake us in a day or two, riding up on their mules with their precious saddle-bags." Bannon, on the other hand, went into the thick of the fighting armed only with viaticum, a tourniquet, and whiskey. On occasion, as at the battles of Elkhorn Tavern and Vicksburg, he even helped the Irish gunners "maintain a continuous rate of fire," since he "knew each cannoneer's duties on the gun team as well as he knew the Bible."[22]

For Bannon, the war was a matter of "good versus evil, the forces of lightness against darkness." In his sermons, he emphasized that southerners were God's chosen people, while the Unionists were the Egyptians or Philistines. The conflict was one between "the cross and the crescent for which last the Yankee substitutes the dollar; a war between [the] materialism and infidelity of the North, and the remnant of Christian civilization yet dominant in the South." Nationalism and religion blended together in the southern experience as they had in the Irish. The matter of slavery did not seem to be part of the picture at all. Instead, "the conflict had been caused by one region of the country trying to dominate the other economically and politically," resulting in what he felt was "an UNHOLY AND CRUEL WAR." In his view, the North was trying to turn the South into a political and economic dependency, as England had already done to Ireland.[23]

In spite of its unholiness, however—reflected not only in the slaughter of battle but also in the "recreational" activities of some of the soldiers as they wallowed "in the slave whorehouses and drinking and gambling dens"—the war itself was a kind of godsend for someone of Bannon's way

22. Ibid., 39, 42; Bannon, "Experiences of a Confederate Chaplain," in Faherty, 83; Tucker, 52, 128.

23. Tucker, 65.

of thinking. There were so many conversions in the hospitals run by the Sisters of Mercy that the priest commented later, "The four years' civil war has done more to advance the cause of Catholicity in the States, both North and South, than the hundred years that preceded." Patriotism too seemed to require a level of endurance and self-denial that needed a religious foundation. Still, warrior though he was—and perhaps inappropriately so—one senses that Bannon saw his main goal (and this is almost the exclusive emphasis of his account in *Letters and Notes*) as saving souls, even when those souls were reluctant to be saved, rather than saving the Confederacy.[24]

After years as an unpaid and unofficial pastor, Bannon was finally made a regular chaplain. So crucial was he that President Davis offered him generous financial aid to go to Ireland to persuade the young men there not to enlist in the Union army. Secretary of State Judah P. Benjamin provided him with an official letter for such a mission in September 1863: "At my solicitation, [the Reverend John Bannon] has consented to proceed to Ireland and there endeavor to enlighten his fellow-countrymen as to the true nature of our struggle, and to satisfy them, if possible, how shocking to all the dictates of justice and humanity is the conduct of those who leave a distant country for the purpose of imbruing their hands in the blood of a people that has ever received the Irish emigrant with kindness and hospitality." Concerned that the U.S. government was about "to make fresh efforts to induce the Irish laborers to emigrate to New York, the ostensible purpose being to employ them in railroad works, but the real object to get them as recruits for the Federal Army," Benjamin even granted Bannon permission to visit the pope if such endorsement would "secure him a welcome among the Catholic clergy and laity of Ireland."[25]

Successfully running the Union blockade the following month, Bannon did visit Rome first, possibly carrying a personal letter from Davis. During long audiences with Pope Pius IX, himself under siege from the forces of the Italian nationalists since 1860, Bannon argued for "the righteousness of the Confederate experiment in rebellion" and spoke out against "the unscrupulous recruiting methods of the North."[26]

---

24. Ibid., 107, 149; see a similar view in James M. McPherson's *What They Fought For, 1861–1865* (Baton Rouge, 1994), in which the author examines letters written by thousands of Union and Confederate soldiers: "A Louisiana cavalryman believed that a Yankee triumph would be 'more galling in its tyranny than the darkest horror under which Ireland or Poland has ever groaned'" (25); Tucker, 64–65.

25. Ibid., 165.

26. Ibid., 167.

Bannon appears to have received some support from the pope. In any case, when he arrived in Ireland, where he joined Bishop Lynch of Charleston on the same mission, he was quite successful in discouraging young men from joining the Union army. In association with John Martin, former Young Ireland deportee to Australia and John Mitchel's closest friend, Bannon composed several broadsheets for this campaign, many of which were distributed at church services on Sundays. In the most effective of these, Bannon "emphasized the historic analogies to the American Revolution of the Confederacy's struggle. He stressed how the last 'remnant of Christian civilization [was] yet dominant in the South,' for in his view, true Christianity had disappeared throughout the remainder of America." He also mentioned the nativist riots and how Union troops had colluded with them in attacking Catholics and burning their churches. Finally, Bannon expressed confidence that "no Catholic will persevere in the advocacy of an aggression condemned by his Holiness." The significant result was that the number of Union recruits dropped by two-thirds. Henry Hotze, then acting as a representative of the Confederate States in London, commended Bannon for his success in Ireland, and the Confederate government voted him $3,000 in thanks.[27]

The Union's naval blockade, however, prevented a still young and vigorous Bannon from returning to the American South. Tucker's final comments on the priest seem a little extreme: the war years and the Confederacy were "an obsession as sacred as Christianity" and "had an even greater impact on him than his religious experience." Had the war turned out otherwise, Tucker concludes, Bannon "might have been among the founding fathers of a democratic and independent South." This judgment is very doubtful. As a fellow Jesuit has recently observed, the geographical limitations of Bannon's southern experience probably made him think of the region as more Catholic than was actually the case. But what remains significant, perhaps troubling, about his reaction to events is that he could see the issues quite differently from a religious Garrison, or Douglass, or O'Connell, a perception that hadn't in the least changed by the time of his 1867 recollection, and one that does not appear to have done so during the remainder of his long life.[28]

Bannon's Civil War contribution may have been relatively unknown except to those who had immediate contact with him, but Major General Patrick

27. Ibid., 175–76.
28. Ibid., 182, 184.

Ronayne Cleburne in contrast was the most famous Irish participant in the Confederate forces during his own lifetime. Born in 1828, a scion of minor Anglo-Irish gentry from County Cork that had roots in old Protestant and Catholic family alliances—some of his relatives were still Catholic in the 1840s—Cleburne had come to America as a result of declining fortunes in Ireland rather than from any political or religious motive. He brought with him several years of service in the British army, in which he had reluctantly enlisted as a private to save his family the expense of his upkeep.

The Cleburnes appear to have been good landlords, but without any unusual interest in the movements of the day—especially O'Connell's Catholic emancipation drive—beyond being generally sympathetic toward their neighbors and tenants and voting for reform. Nevertheless, as a soldier in Ireland in the turbulent 1840s when revolution was in the air, Cleburne witnessed the force of repression on a starving, frequently evicted, and intermittently rebellious population. Indeed, his regiment was kept at home rather than being sent to its regular assignment in India precisely to be available should a Young Ireland–inspired rebellion break out. Thus, in the early part of 1849, Cleburne served for a time at the prison on Spike Island, off the coast of Cork, where John Mitchel had been held for a few days the previous year. His family, unable to pay the new levies imposed by the government on landowners for the relief of famine Ireland, was eventually forced to emigrate. They came to Helena, Arkansas, at the end of 1849, where Cleburne at first used the training his physician father had given him to work as a pharmacist; later, after study, he became a lawyer.[29]

Never very politically minded, and reserved by nature, Pat Cleburne, unlike Mitchel and Bannon, does not appear to have been especially concerned with the parallel between Ireland and the American South. Rather, once he had left Ireland, he seems to have identified himself totally with his new homeland. He wrote to his favorite sister that he considered Ireland's future "a lost cause." Still, he may have belonged to the local Helena branch of the Fenian movement, the secret Irish nationalist organization that succeeded the Young Irelanders but that, in practice, often served as more of a social than a political venue. He did publicly attack the Know

29. There are two standard biographies of Cleburne: Howell and Elizabeth Purdue's *Pat Cleburne: Confederate General* (Hillsboro, Tex., 1973) and Craig L. Symonds, *Stonewall of the West* (Kansas City, 1997). Symonds remarks that Cleburne's father, a medical doctor, seems to have supported Catholic emancipation but also notes that "if the notion of national independence as a political birthright touched a chord in the young Patrick Cleburne, he left no record of it" (19).

Nothing party for its anti-immigrant and anti-Catholic policies, receiving a near-fatal bullet wound for his efforts. Cleburne was always identified as Irish, teased about his brogue (which he later tried to get rid of for effective military command), and referred to affectionately by his troops as "Old Pat" (although he was only in his early thirties). Certainly, too, as we shall see, Cleburne was to become more of an iconic Irishman in death than he probably had been in life.[30]

When the war began, Cleburne was immediately elected as a leader by the local militia. Then, in the restructured army of the Confederacy, he rose in less than two years to the rank of major general, one of only twelve, in command of a division in the Army of Tennessee. Although his British military training was responsible for his initial selection—and he was always concerned that his troops learn to drill and obey in those traditional ways to which they as a free citizenry were relatively unaccustomed—his steadiness and fairness were what led to his popularity. Beginning as a rather wooden commander at the Battle of Shiloh, where he lost three quarters of his unit, he quickly learned from his mistakes and reorganized his training methods accordingly. So outstanding was he that Jefferson Davis referred to him as the "Stonewall Jackson of the West."[31]

A pattern of rebellious—or at least injudicious—behavior was to mar Cleburne's subsequent progress within the military establishment, however. Commended for his valor in the Battle of Shiloh, one of the bloodiest of the war, he was bitter that so many of his men had been killed through inept leadership at higher levels, remarking that the encounter was "gallantly won and as stupidly lost."[32] Although he led his troops to victory at the Battle of Chickamauga in September 1863, and, later that same year, successfully defended Missionary Ridge against General Sherman until the Confederates were eventually defeated at other points in the field, further promotion continued to elude him. Some of this was undoubtedly due to his earlier criticism of his commander, General Braxton Bragg, but it may also have been, as Craig L. Symonds suggests, because he was better at carrying out orders efficiently and creatively than at inventing grand strategies.[33]

Yet there was one major innovation Cleburne did suggest, one that re-

30. Mauriel Phillips Joslyn, "Irish Beginnings," in *A Meteor Shining Brightly: Essays on Maj. Gen. Patrick R. Cleburne*, ed. Joslyn (Atlanta, 2000), 21.

31. Symonds, 158.

32. Wiley Sword, "The Other Stonewall," *Civil War Times Illustrated* (February 1998): 39.

33. Symonds, 223.

veals something of both his pragmatic and excessively idealistic character. In January 1864, Cleburne made a surprising, radical, and ultimately self-defeating, proposal, arguing that since the South was suffering a severe loss in manpower, it was time to free black slaves to fight for the cause. In doing so, he very consciously took the risk of being court-martialed.

Cleburne composed the proposal himself. He began with noting that the Confederate soldiers, seeing no hope of success against numerically superior forces, were beginning to show signs of apathy and restlessness. Then, he starkly outlined the consequences of failure in phrases that, surprisingly, *may* have been informed by his Irish experience:

> If this state continues much longer we must be subjugated. Every man should endeavor to understand the meaning of subjugation before it is too late. We can give but a faint idea when we say it means the loss of all we now hold most sacred—slaves and all other personal property, lands, homesteads, liberty, justice, safety, pride, manhood. It means that the history of this heroic struggle will be written by the enemy; that our youth will be trained by Northern school teachers; will learn from Northern school books their version of the war; will be impressed by all the influences of history and education to regard our gallant dead as traitors, our maimed veterans as fit objects of derision.

The only way to prevent this and correct the present disparity in numbers was to recruit southern slaves as soldiers, just as the Union army was doing.[34]

Ever practical even with such a novel proposal, Cleburne pointed out first of all that former slaves were already a kind of "spy system" for the North, more and more of them being recruited by the day as the Union army advanced. The problem as he saw it was that "slavery, from being one of our chief sources of strength at the commencement of the war, has now become, in a military point of view, one of our chief sources of weakness." Even the Europeans recruited by the Union army, he contended, had hearts that were "fired into a crusade against us by fictitious pictures of the atrocities of slavery." Moreover, as Union forces continued to advance, southern planters were living in fear of a slave revolt and could "no longer with safety to their property openly sympathize with our cause."[35]

---

34. Robert F. Durden, *The Gray and the Black: The Confederate Debate on Emancipation* (Baton Rouge, 1972), 55. The entire proposal is given on 54–62.

35. Ibid., 55, 56.

Having laid this groundwork, Cleburne elaborated on the most radical part of his recommendation: that "we immediately commence training a large reserve of the most courageous of our slaves, and further that we guarantee freedom within a reasonable time to every slave . . . who shall remain true to the Confederacy in this war. As between the loss of independence and the loss of slavery, we assume that every patriot will freely give up the latter—give up the negro slave rather than be a slave himself." England and France in particular were likely to respond to this gesture and support the southern fight for independence.[36]

Cleburne strikes one, however, as being a little over-optimistic in the expected response from blacks: "It will leave the enemy's negro army no motive to fight for, and will exhaust the source from which it has been recruited"; "The measure we propose will strike dead all John Brown fanaticism"; "[it] will probably cause much of it [the Negro Union Army] to desert over to us." He concluded his analysis here with a flourish: "The chronic irritation of hope deferred would be joyfully ended with the negro, and the sympathies of the whole race would be due to his native South."[37]

The painful reality of the situation is conveyed in Cleburne's final comments, a curious but typical blend of shrewd judgment and humanitarian idealism, however faint:

> The slaves are dangerous now, but armed, trained and collected in an army they would be a thousandfold more dangerous; therefore when we make soldiers of them we must make free men of them beyond all question, and thus enlist their sympathies also. We can do this more effectively than the North can now do, for we can give the negro not only his own freedom, but that of his wife and child, and can secure it to him in his old home. To do this we must immediately make his marriage and parental relations sacred in the eyes of the law and forbid their sale.

Cleburne's radical proposal was, as one would expect, rejected by his superiors—including President Davis—only to be attempted in a somewhat different form a year later when the southern cause was already lost. In several of the military promotions for which he was the obvious choice, he was passed over in favor of less accomplished officers (though there is still the argument that he may not have been suitable for higher command). The

36. Ibid., 58.
37. Ibid., 59.

controversial proposal was not published until 1890, twenty-five years after the war had ended.[38]

Afterward, Cleburne continued to be as loyal as ever, distinguishing himself in particular in the defense of Atlanta on the famous Jonesboro Road. He made his last stand in Franklin, Tennessee, where he was ordered—almost in the precise terms that McWhiney uses of Celtic fighting practices—to attack the enemy frontally "where the fortifications were strongest and the concentrated enemy fire would be heaviest."[39] Cleburne was killed in this mindless offense, so that, as Wiley Sword comments: "The man who was perhaps the South's most brilliant major general . . . had died leading a suicidal frontal attack in the manner of some captain of infantry." When his body was discovered after the battle, "His boots, diary, watch, wallet, sword-belt, and pistol had been stolen."[40]

News of Cleburne's death devastated the Confederate troops. Indeed, the response to it and the continuing interest in his exploits even down to the present—at a sentimental as well as a scholarly level—are remarkable. A Cleburne Circle still meets annually in Nashville. Nor were the Irish in Ireland unaware of his life and valor. In the *Nation,* the Young Ireland paper for which Mitchel had once written, the following lines appeared in a poem entitled simply "Cleburne":

> There were eyes afar that watched your star
> *As* it rose with the "Southern Cross,"
> There were hearts that bled when its course was sped,
> And Old Ireland felt your loss!

As recently as 1994, Cleburne was commemorated by a plaque at Cobh, where he and so many other emigrants had embarked for a new life in America, North and South.[41]

With defeat imminent, John Mitchel continued to soldier on in his ambulance work and in his articles in the *Examiner:* "I point out diligently and conscientiously what is the condition of a nation which suffers itself to be conquered; draw pictures of disarmings, and disfranchisements, and civil disabilities, such as we have experienced in Ireland, and endeavour to keep

38. Ibid., 60–61.
39. Sword, 42.
40. Ibid., 45; Purdue and Purdue, 429.
41. Quoted in Purdue and Purdue, 430.

our good Confederate people up to the fighting point. Then I have most freely criticized Mr. Davis for his failure to practice retaliation sternly." When, in a last desperate attempt to turn the tide in the early part of 1865, Robert E. Lee, in the footsteps of Cleburne and others, requested that black slaves be conscripted for the fighting and freed as a reward, Mitchel was appalled:

> The general [Lee] further urged that the Government should hold out emancipation as a reward [for slaves fighting as Confederate soldiers]. Now, if freedom be a reward for negroes—that is, if freedom be a good thing for negroes—why, then it is, and always was, a grievous wrong and crime to hold them in slavery at all. If it be true that the state of slavery keeps these people depressed below the condition to which they could develop their nature, their intelligence, and their capacity for enjoyment, and what we call "progress," then every hour of their bondage for generations is a black stain upon the white race.

One wonders what Mitchel thought of free blacks, not to mention those among them who were slaveowners themselves. Paradoxically, his comment also points to the possibility of his own views on slavery being revised were he to be convinced that racial differences were not absolute. On this occasion, however, "Mitchel went so far as to raise the blasphemous doubt as to whether Lee was a 'good Southerner'; that is, whether he is thoroughly satisfied of the justice and beneficence of negro slavery."[42]

To the very end, the Young Irelander remained defiant, even possibly enjoying his finest hour:

> There is, of course, a great deal of sadness, for every family almost has lost its flower, and bands playing some dead march pass often through these bowery streets, escorting some officer to the cemetery. But no sadness shows itself; above all, no cowardice. No doubt there are people whose hearts quake within them as they hear the roll of artillery, but public opinion requires an outward cheerfulness and courage. This people has arrived at such a point of passionate daring and defiance that cowards must pretend to be brave, and traitors in their hearts (for such there are) must act like patriots. I confess that I delight in the spectacle of a people roused in this way to a full display of all its manhood, feeling itself indeed isolated from all other people, and without a friend in the world, but planting itself firmly in its own ground, stripped for battle, and defying fate.

42. Dillon, 2:109.

The war that in Ireland he had never had a chance to wage had come to him in all its "terrible beauty"—Mitchel would not have disdained Yeats's phrase—in the American South.[43]

The story of some friends of John Mitchel and his family during their time in America casts a kind of summary light on Irish attitudes in the southern states toward the Civil War, not only at the time it was taking place but almost a century afterward. The Dooleys, a Catholic couple from Limerick, arrived in America in 1832 with rather modest means. They fairly quickly became wealthy as furriers and hatters in Richmond, and, according to the account written in 1945 by their son's sympathetic Jesuit biographer, "Their home was the recognized center of a social group whose importance has never been sufficiently appreciated—the Irish-Americans of the pre-war South." Dooley senior "typified neatly the fusion of two distinct but mutually complementary national loyalties when in April 1861, at the head of his Company, the Montgomery Guards, he marched out of Richmond in a uniform of vivid bottle-green with gorgeous gold stars and bars." Once again, Irish and southern nationalisms neatly coincided.[44]

The Dooleys' son, also named John, who was later to become a Jesuit himself, has left a war diary of his experience in the Confederate army, a diary that when it was published in 1945 bore a foreword by Robert E. Lee biographer Douglas Southall Freeman. At one point John Dooley reports meeting a captured "Yanko-Irish soldier" who had served under Mitchel in the 1848 rebellion in Ireland—technically an impossibility since Mitchel was deported in May, while the revolt took place in July, but the sense of Dooley's comment is that the enemy Irish soldier was a follower of the great man. Dooley informed him that Mitchel's three sons were now in the Confederate army. "I began . . . asking him how it was possible for him who had in '48 fought or intended to fight for the same cause for which we were contending . . . [to] turn his back on his principles and for the pitiful hire of a few dollars do all in his power to crush a brave people asserting their right of self government; and now that he was engaged in the cause of tyranny, fighting against honesty, justice and right . . . what, we asked, would Mr. Mitchel think of him?" A discussion of the defeat of the Union army's Irish Brigade at Fredericksburg follows, in which it is pointed out that the

43. Quoted in Keneally, 396; Dillon, 2:205.

44. Joseph T. Durkin, S.J., *John Dooley, Confederate Soldier: His War Journal* (Georgetown, 1945), xiv–xv.

crop from the field where the battle took place had been sold by its owner years earlier to help the famine Irish—an argument, incidentally, that had previously been used by Irish supporters of the Union side. With the onset of the war, however, the Irish people, "invigorated and under infamous leadership, have now done far more than the envenomed *puritan* to rob us of our property, devastate our lands, starve the pleading orphan and the broken hearted widow, trample in the dust every principle of right, and crush out completely our identity as a free people."[45]

Whichever side the Irish were on in the war, it is hard not to think that it was indeed an "unholy and cruel" enterprise for most of them. If it were a crusade at all, it was such because for the Confederate Irish it represented a parallel with their own struggle at home, while for the Union Irish it gave promise of future support from a grateful federal government. For the Irish on both sides, it was in a strange way less an American war than an Irish one fought reluctantly in America for their own advancement. No sooner was the war over than Irish American patriots, North and South, vigorously set out to shape the interpretation of their participation in it.

45. Ibid., 115, 116–17.

CHAPTER 4

DEFEAT AND DEFIANCE

The muffled drum's sad roll has beat
    The soldier's last tattoo;
No more on Life's parade shall meet
    The brave and daring few.

—THEODORE O'HARA, "The Bivouac of the Dead"

Aye, this very hand that trembles thro' this very line,
Lay hid, ages gone, in the hand of some forefather Celt.

—FATHER ABRAM RYAN, "The Song of the Deathless Voice"

White southerners believed they had lost the war because of the superior military and economic strength of the North rather than from any moral failure or lack of will on their part. Far from feeling guilty over slavery, or finally acknowledging the constitutional rights of the U.S. government or seeking immediate reconciliation with the rest of the country, most southerners remained convinced of the righteousness of their cause. "Northern soldiers frequently commented about the insolence and animosity they perceived among former Confederates," notes Civil War historian Gary W. Gallagher. This defiance became even stronger with the punitive treatment the South received after the assassination of the conciliatory President Lincoln on April 14, 1865, and the subsequent dominance of radical and revengeful Republicans in the Washington government. Having shown their recalcitrance by voting for members of the defeated Confederate political and military establishments—more than forty former Richmond Congressmen and five Confederate generals, for example—and opposing the extension of the franchise to former slaves, it was clear to Washington that sterner measures were needed to bring about change. The Louisiana legislature had declared in 1865 that "this is a Government of white people, made and to be perpetuated for the exclusive benefit of the white race." So, in 1867, the eleven rebellious states of the Confederacy were divided into five military zones for hostile occupation by federal troops, a situation that was not to end until 1877.[1]

The recently emancipated slaves did not see things that way, of course, though many of them no longer had homes, couldn't find work as freedmen or were forced to sign unfair labor contracts, and above all were subject to the bitter hostility of a defeated people. A race riot in Memphis, Tennessee, a year after the war's end between Irish policemen and demobbed black Union soldiers led to a death toll of forty-eight, mostly black. A federal investigation found the police responsible, but local sentiment was overwhelmingly on their side. It was a pattern that would repeat itself again and again during the years of Reconstruction, years in which whites awaited their political redemption from what they felt was their undeserved dishonor.[2]

Toward the end of the war, dispirited Irish Confederate troops deserted in unusually large numbers. However, John Mitchel kept up his belief in the southern cause long after it seemed hopeless to almost everyone else. Following Lee's surrender at Appomattox in April 1865, Mitchel left Richmond for New York, "the freest, and, at present, the most southern city on the continent," to continue his pro-South writing activities as editor of yet another paper, the *Daily News*. He was presciently aware that his adventure as a Confederate might not yet be over and, in fact, after a friendly warning from the local authorities, typically unheeded, he was arrested in June 1865, and taken to Fortress Monroe, Virginia, where Jefferson Davis was also confined. The well-known New York lawyer Charles O'Conor had already offered his services *gratis* to Davis. Though O'Conor denied that he had been prompted to do so by anyone who ever had a connection "with any of the Southern States," it is difficult to believe that the man who had hosted Mitchel's Broadway "escape celebration" in 1854 had not been encouraged in some way by his Young Ireland hero.[3]

1. Gary W. Gallagher, *The Confederate War* (Cambridge, Mass., 1997), 167, quoted in James Gill, *Lords of Misrule: Mardi Gras and the Politics of Race in New Orleans* (Jackson, Miss., 1997), 76.

2. DeeGee Lester, "Memphis Riots (1866)," in *Encyclopedia of the Irish in America,* ed. Michael Glazier (Notre Dame, 1999), 603–4.

3. David T. Gleeson, *The Irish in the South, 1815–1877* (Chapel Hill, 2001), 170; William Dillon, *Life of John Mitchel* (London, 1888), 2:215, 37; Hudson Strode, *Jefferson Davis, Tragic Hero: The Last Twenty-Five Years, 1864–1889* (New York, 1964), 241. Strode makes no mention of O'Conor's Irish Catholic origins and presents John Mitchel as simply another political prisoner

The first two months of his imprisonment permanently damaged Mitchel's health. Under a regimen of rough, minimal food, no company, no exercise, and no books, his American confinement was probably harsher than anything he had experienced as a prisoner of Britain, where he had generally been treated as a "gentleman." When the pressure of influential Irish-Americans brought about his release after another two months of somewhat better conditions, the fifty-year-old patriot was in marked physical, if not mental, decline.

Despite his sacrifices for the Confederate cause—or rather *because* of them, since few Irishmen, probably few southerners, can have given as much for the Confederacy as he did—when Mitchel's surviving son wanted him to provide "a vindication of the defeated South," the old patriot confided to an Irish friend, Miss Thompson, "I must admit that I grudge it what it has cost us . . . the lives of our two sons in defence of a country which, after all, was not their own." He didn't want his remaining son to make "a martyr of himself." In later years, Mitchel appears to have tried to excuse his extremism on the war, which was certainly an embarrassment to Irish nationalists and a cause for English celebration, as it showed the errors of the revolutionary movement. Nevertheless, Mitchel and his wife were happy that their remaining son had married a Virginian and that their daughter was wedded to a former Confederate colonel, also a Virginian.[4]

In exile in Paris once again, Mitchel reluctantly acted as a representative of the new Fenian movement, which had by now replaced Young Ireland and was plotting to use the military experience gained by Irishmen in both the Union and Confederate armies, as well as by those in Britain's army, to free their homeland from British rule. Although some of them entertained the quite fantastic hope that the Irish-born Union general Phil Sheridan might lead them on such a campaign, the only outcome of all their plotting were several abortive raids into British Canada.

Unsympathetic with the kind of secrecy the Fenians practiced, Mitchel resigned his position in Paris and returned yet again to the United States in 1867 where his remaining son, James, had fathered a future mayor of New York. His thoughts now turned almost exclusively to Irish affairs—his new paper being called the *Irish Citizen* rather than the *Citizen* or the *Southern Citizen*—and he declined an offer to write about the effects of Reconstruc-

---

at Fortress Monroe (266). A subsequent reference to Oscar Wilde as "the British poet" pretty much elides, if inadvertently, all things Irish from at least this southern narrative (459).

4. Dillon, 2:235, 264–65.

tion in New Orleans. Risking a visit to Ireland in 1874, he returned there again the following year as a newly elected MP for Tipperary, though the Westminster government refused to accept the result and required that the election be held again. In the meantime, Mitchel stayed in Cork for a few days with one of the Ronaynes, also an MP, from the maternal side of Patrick Cleburne's family. Mitchel had just been re-elected to parliament when he died in 1875 in his Ulster home, just a few feet, after all his adventures, from where had had been born some sixty years earlier. Both Davis and Lee sent tributes. "Together we struggled for states rights, for the supremacy of the Constitution, for community independence, and, after defeat, we were imprisoned together," Davis wrote to Mitchel's widow.[5]

John Bannon, following his successful anti-recruitment efforts in Ireland and his inability to return to the American South, took on another kind of military discipline when he joined the Jesuit order and made a new career for himself as an enormously popular preacher of missions throughout the country. He also served as rector at the main Jesuit church in Dublin, in Lower Gardiner Street, where he had particular success with retreats for businessmen. William B. Faherty, S.J., even speculates that Bannon, rather than the noted English Jesuit preacher Father Bernard Vaughn, may have been the model for James Joyce's Father Purdon in his short story "Grace," part of which takes place in the Gardiner Street Church, because the meticulous and practical style of the sermon is similar to that of the former Confederate chaplain.[6]

Nor was his southern experience wholly irrelevant to Bannon's later life. Contacts from his days in St. Louis influenced the progress of his ecclesiastical career in Ireland. Many of his old military comrades would visit him to reminisce about the "lost cause," while he at one point had to be restrained by his superiors from regaling the young Irish Jesuit novices with his war exploits. Like Mitchel, he could hardly have been said to have been "reconstructed" or to have come to doubt the righteousness of the southern cause.[7]

---

5. DeeGee Lester, "John Mitchel's Wilderness Years in Tennessee," *Éire-Ireland* 25, no. 2 (1990): 8; Thomas Keneally, *The Great Shame* (New York, 1999), 528–29.

6. W. B. Faherty, S.J., *The Fourth Career of John B. Bannon* (Portland, Ore., 1994), 65–66. Vaughn, however, still seems the more likely source.

7. Phillip Thomas Tucker, *Father John B. Bannon: The Confederacy's Fighting Chaplain* (Tuscaloosa, 1992), 181.

In 1870, five years after the war had ended, it was decided to remove the remains of Patrick Cleburne from their temporary resting place in Tennessee and rebury them in his hometown of Helena, Arkansas. The mourners on the occasion included ex-president Davis, several generals, and more than a hundred Confederate veterans. In addition, as if representing all shades of Irish opinion, there were "the Cleburne Circle of the Fenian Brotherhood, two other Irish societies, and the St. Andrew's Society."[8] Huge crowds assembled in Memphis; church bells tolled; flags were at half mast. The Emmet Guards escorted the bier on the journey down the Mississippi to the cemetery. The leading newspaper compared Cleburne's significance in the states of the Old Southwest to that of Stonewall Jackson in Virginia, though with the notable proviso that while Cleburne "possessed the loftiest, sublimest courage of man," Jackson's was "that of a god."[9]

Twenty-one years later, a monument in Cleburne's honor was erected in Helena. Paid for in part by his immigrant Irish family, in part by a Father O'Reilly who lectured for the cause, but in the main by contributions from local people—a bale of cotton, road carts, plows, crazy quilts, pigs, and sheep—that were sold by the ladies of the local Confederate Memorial Association. A former slave sent $2.50, writing that "General Cleburne's 'Kindness to me when a little boy peddling apples upon the streets of Helena will never be forgotten.'" A plaster replica of the Confederate seal—the original of which, incidentally, had been designed in London by the Dublin sculptor John Henry Foley, who was later responsible for the Daniel O'Connell monument in Ireland's capital—along with various Irish memorabilia sent by a Catholic priest in Cleveland, a Union veteran, were incorporated into the monument.[10]

On a Sunday in May 1891, a large crowd that included veterans and family relatives gathered for the unveiling of the monument. Father O'Reilly gave the invocation; a poem, "The Death of Cleburne," was read; and five young ladies, all daughters of Confederate veterans, unveiled the monument. The sixteen-foot marble memorial with its inscription "*Dulce et decorum est pro patria mori*"—Horace's assertion that it "is sweet and right to die for one's country"—and the names of Cleburne's battles, stands on

---

8. Howell Purdue and Elizabeth Purdue, *Pat Cleburne: Confederate General* (Hillsboro, Texas, 1973), 431.

9. Ibid., 435.

10. Ibid., 443; Benedict Read, "John Henry Foley," *The Connoisseur* 186 (1974): 262–71. Best known for his sculpture of Queen Victoria's husband for the Albert Memorial, Foley was also commissioned to produce a statue of Stonewall Jackson shortly after he was killed in 1863.

the summit of Confederate Hill, overlooking the Mississippi. "In winter," the Purdues movingly conclude their biography of Cleburne, "when trees were bare, the tall marble shaft was visible from the Mississippi. Whenever men who had followed Cleburne traveled on the river past the monument, they stood at attention."[11]

The postwar ceremonies for Major General Patrick Cleburne, with all their pageantry and display of popular enthusiasm, were typical of the white southern Lost Cause movement of the late nineteenth and early twentieth centuries. Lines from Theodore O'Hara's "The Bivouac of the Dead" were used so often on headstones—and approved by the federal government— that the poem soon became associated with the Civil War rather than with the occasion for which it was originally composed in 1847, the Battle of Buena Vista in the Mexican-American conflict. The confusion wasn't totally inappropriate, however, for O'Hara, the son of an Irish-Catholic Kentucky schoolteacher who had fled to America in the wake of the 1798 rebellion, was a strong advocate of the Confederate cause:

> On Fame's eternal camping-ground
> Their silent tents are spread,
> And Glory guards, with solemn round,
> The bivouac of the dead.

In fact, O'Hara's poem achieved worldwide fame among diverse groups, celebrated not least by Ulster Unionists to commemorate their compatriots who were killed as British soldiers at the Battle of the Somme in World War I. Even in 2004 there are frequent authorship inquiries to websites from seekers who have come across the lines in some lonely military cemetery in the United States or in England, and there is often confusion still as to the particular war for which the poem was composed.[12]

Claudine Rhett was one of the many female memorialists of the time. She was still single when she wrote a "sketch" of the Mitchel family in 1882 for the *Southern Historical Society Papers*. There, she retraced all its ups and downs, from the father's trial and unjust deportation in 1848 to his son's death and burial in 1864. Her account of the Mitchels having their property

11. Purdue and Purdue, 445.

12. See Nathaniel Cheairs Hughes Jr. and Thomas Clayton Ware, *Theodore O'Hara: Poet-Soldier of the Old South* (Knoxville, 1998), and Norman Vance, *Irish Literature: A Social History* (Oxford, 1990), 191.

confiscated and auctioned off by the British government in 1848—"the vulgar gaze and careless touch of strangers desecrated the most personal possessions of the family"—has the strong inflection of her own family's losses after the war, when her father hoped that what remained from several properties could all be put together to furnish a small town house. According to her, "of all the hallowed spots at Magnolia [Cemetery], none is so well known, or is ever heaped so high with roses, as the Irish officer's grave, which, for fourteen years, was utterly unmarked, save by this touching tribute of honor to his memory."[13]

After the war, both Lincoln and Lee—a committee of southern veterans decided to champion him rather than the one-time more celebrated Stonewall Jackson—were painstakingly "marble-ized" as the noble, if opposing, heroes of a noble conflict. After all, Lincoln had once offered Lee the command of the Union army. In the somewhat smaller world of Irish-American affairs, there was a deliberate attempt to erase the stigma of the New York draft riots and associate the Irish unambiguously with the defense of the Union through their various military achievements. Randall M. Miller notes that "As part of the general trend late in the nineteenth century in which particular veterans' groups staked off a share of the hallowed ground at Gettysburg, Irish Catholic veterans and clergymen, led by [Irish-born General St. Clair] Mulholland, pushed hard to erect a statue of [Fr. William] Corby on the spot where he delivered his absolution. The effort succeeded . . . with the unveiling of the bronze Corby statue, its hand upraised in blessing of all who would walk before it, in October 1910. With that statue, Catholics entered American sacred space and memory." Forgotten were the hesitations, discrimination, and ambiguities that had bedeviled the actual participants. In the South, the final rites for Cleburne satisfied a similar urge, associating him with a wider variety of Irish causes than had been his in his lifetime, but thereby vindicating all the Irish Confederates who had fought and allowing them to enter southern "sacred space and memory."[14]

Even without Cleburne, however, the Irish in the American South had another upholder of their "belongingness." Surprisingly, perhaps, the prin-

13. William C. Davis, *Rhett: The Turbulent Life and Times of a Fire-Eater* (Columbia, S.C., 2001), 545–6; Claudine Rhett, "Sketch of John C. Mitchel, of Ireland, killed whilst in Command of Fort Sumter," *Southern Historical Society Papers* 10, no. 6 (1882): 272.

14. Randall M. Miller, "Catholic Religion, Irish Ethnicity, and the Civil War," in *Religion and the American Civil War*, ed. Miller et al. (New York, 1988), 285.

cipal celebrant of the quasi-religious rites of the Lost Cause was a Roman Catholic priest of immediate Irish background, Father Abram Ryan. Charles Reagan Wilson has described Ryan as "a melancholy, morose figure. A sad-eyed man with stooped shoulders and curly, unruly hair that hung down his back, he was given to legend-making, and he fostered the legend of himself as a man of mystery. He cultivated his unusual appearance by wearing a faded black coat that reached to his feet."[15] Indeed, a story goes that sometime in the 1970s, in a school named after the priest in Nashville, Tennessee, an irreverent student summoned to explain some misdemeanor or other identified the priest's portrait as that of singer Johnny Cash. Apart from the difference in height, the attribution was not merely provocative or wholly frivolous, for, take away the Roman collar and cloak, and substitute jeans and a denim shirt, Ryan's face might be seen in many a honky-tonk lounge in Music City. As a child, Margaret Mitchell too heard about a less lugubrious priest: she wrote to a friend about "how much fried chicken Father Ryan could put away."[16]

The actual place of Ryan's birth has long been uncertain. This "man of mystery" himself offered different accounts on different occasions. Because of the confusion, as recently as 1987 an Irish scholar gave Ryan's birthplace as Limerick, Ireland, in April 1840. He drew his information from a nineteenth-century volume published in San Francisco with the wonderfully meandering title of *Irish Poets and Novelists: Profusely Illustrated and Embracing Complete Biographical Sketches of Those Who at Home and Abroad Have Sustained the Reputation of Ireland as the Land of Song and Story with Copious Selections from Their Writing*. In fact, Oscar H. Lipscomb, the present archbishop of the Mobile diocese in which Ryan once worked, had resolved the matter in 1972: Ryan was born in Hagerstown, Washington County, Maryland, February 5, 1838, of recently immigrant Irish parents. He grew up in St. Louis—where he may have heard Father Bannon preach—and went to seminary at Niagara, New York. He was a pastor in Peoria, Illinois, when he received word that his brother, David, had been killed as a Confederate

---

15. Charles Reagan Wilson, *Baptized in Blood: The Religion of the Lost Cause, 1865–1920* (Athens, Ga., 1980), 59. Gaines M. Foster describes him as an unlikely laureate: "In a society that celebrated virility, he was a scraggly-haired, enfeebled, almost effeminate man whose appearance underscored the despair of his poetry"; see *Ghosts of the Confederacy: Defeat, the Lost Cause, and the Emergence of the New South, 1865 to 1913* (New York, 1987), 36. He adds that Ryan seemed to have "some deep grief weighing him down."

16. Darden Asbury Pyron, *Southern Daughter: The Life of Margaret Mitchell* (New York, 1992), 35.

soldier. It appears that this incident, coupled with his inability to find his brother's grave, made him into a memorialist of the southern cause.[17]

Like Bannon, Ryan seems—though this matter is not at all clear either—to have served as an unofficial chaplain to the Confederate army. After the war, he was a pastor in Nashville, Mobile, and Augusta. It was during his five years in Georgia that he founded the rabidly pro-South *Banner of the South*. David T. Gleeson describes its contents:

> Ryan used his columns to attack Reconstruction. Virulently opposed to any compromise with the Radicals, he believed that the "fungus" of "negro equality" would not "survive" in the South. Although Ryan aimed the *Banner of the South* at southern readers, he also published it for Irish Catholics throughout the nation. . . . In his editorials, Father Ryan defended attacks against the faith, especially ones emanating from northern churches.
>
> *The Banner* contained copious coverage of events in Ireland as well as news of Fenian meetings in the South . . . On one occasion, he reprinted the remarks that former Young Irelander Richard O'Gorman [a friend of John Mitchel's] made at a meeting in New York City. O'Gorman had stated that the southern states had become like Ireland because they were fighting for control of their "local concerns." On the other hand, the Republicans were like the British government—purveyors of "Empire" and "occupation." . . . Ryan's ultimate aim with the *Banner* was to rally Irish and native southerners to oppose Radical Reconstruction by supporting the Democrats.

Ryan also edited another newspaper for a short while, the New Orleans *Morning Star*. In Mobile, he was pastor of St. Mary's Church from 1870 to 1883, though he often traveled to lecture on behalf of Confederate widows and their children.[18]

Reputed to have been a man of "broad human sympathies"—surely a rather commonplace encomium of the time—Ryan obviously retained his prejudices against "Yankees" and was very reluctant to reconcile himself

17. See the entry by T. P. Foley of University College, Galway, in *Notes and Queries* 34 (1987): 46, in which he refers to the correspondence between Ryan and Longfellow. The compiler of *Irish Poets and Novelists: Profusely Illustrated . . .* was the Reverend D. O. Crowley, who brought out a second edition in 1892. For the correct place and date, see Rev. Oscar H. Lipscomb, "Some Unpublished Poems of Abram J. Ryan," *Alabama Review* 25 (July 1972): 164; see also Benjamin Buford Williams, *A Literary History of Alabama: The Nineteenth Century* (Rutherford, N.J., 1979), 129.

18. Gleeson, 182.

with the South's defeat. The priest was described in his lifetime as "A Southerner of the most pronounced kind," one "unwilling to make any concession to his victorious opponents of the North which could be withheld from them." A famous story told about him—though it has sometimes been attributed to another clergyman—comes from the period of the war: "Father Ryan was once summoned to appear before the notorious General Ben Butler [in New Orleans] to answer the charge that he had refused to bury a dead soldier because he was a Yankee. He defended himself by saying: 'Why, I was never asked to bury him and never refused. The fact is, General, it would give me great pleasure to bury the whole lot of you.'" This hostile attitude persisted until after Reconstruction when northern help was offered during an outbreak of yellow fever in Memphis in 1878.[19]

According to Civil War historian Drew Gilpin Faust, "The centrality of religion to Confederate nationalism gave the clergy extraordinary power in shaping the South's wartime ideology." This was true, as we have seen, in regard to Father Bannon. It was all the more true after the war in the case of Father Ryan. He was at a parish in Knoxville in April 1865, when news came of Lee's surrender. Ryan wrote "The Conquered Banner" in response while the choir in the next room was preparing for Holy Week. It was this single, typically hasty effort that made him the poet of the lost cause almost overnight.[20]

> Furl that Banner, for 'tis weary;
> Round its staff 'tis drooping dreary;
>   Furl it, fold it, it is best;
> For there's not a man to wave it,
> And there's not a sword to save it,
>
> . . . .
>
>   Furl it, hide it—let it rest!

So successful was Ryan's poem that an English baronet, Sir Henry Houghton, composed a verse reply, not by way of criticism but rather in vigorous support of the cause, only expressing regret that his own nation

---

19. *Library of Southern Literature* (New Orleans, Atlanta, Dallas, 1909), 10:xxxi, quoted in Jay B. Hubbell, *The South in American Literature, 1607–1900* (Durham, N.C., 1954), 477. In *Lords of Misrule*, James Gill attributes the story to a "notably turbulent" Father James Ignatius Mullon, pastor of St. Patrick's (66).

20. Drew Gilpin Faust, *The Creation of Confederate Nationalism* (Baton Rouge, 1988), 81.

had not come to the aid of the Confederacy: "Shame, alas! for England's glory, / Freedom called, and called in vain!"[21]

We now tend to think of this kind of verse as perpetuating a romantic image of the South that, indirectly at least, results in the justification of a respectable racism and societal complacency about it. It is not certain that Ryan would have disapproved of either attitude, but he would probably have seen them from a different perspective. However, we should not discount the genuine emotive force of such writing for its original audience. At the time, it offered a moving and appropriate response to feelings of devastation, loss, and humiliation already shared by a large group of people, feelings that even W. E. B. Du Bois acknowledged with reluctant empathy. A friend of Ryan's, Hannis Taylor, suggests the poem's significance for his contemporaries:

> At the end of the Civil War, when the people of the South, draped in mourning for their warrior dead, stood as mourners might stand in some dim Cathedral at the bier of their own and only one, a funeral dirge was chanted by an unknown voice from an unseen shrine . . . Only those who lived in the South in that day, and passed under the spell of that mighty song, can properly estimate its power as it fell upon the victims of a fallen cause. The fact that this dirge was not destined to immortality because the state of soul to which it was addressed was ephemeral did not at all impair its effect at the moment it was uttered.

This last observation is important also because Ryan's verse, in purely aesthetic terms, is not of a kind that would readily appeal to modern—much less to modernist—sensibilities. It is also very prescient because it anticipates the kind of justification that Jane Tompkins, among others, has offered in recent years for the "sentimental" tradition in American writing.[22]

In a notable 1985 essay, Tompkins tried to justify what she called the "sentimental power" of Harriet Beecher Stowe's Uncle Tom's Cabin, the most influential novel of the nineteenth century in America, despite the fact that literary critics have not held it in high esteem since. Her aim was

---

21. Houghton's poem is available on several websites. The baronet lived from 1809 to 1885 and was a friend of Tennyson and Thackeray. His, and Father Ryan's, position still has some ardent—and unexpected—followers; see "Chaplain's Comments" by Father Alister C. Anderson, Chaplain in Chief, Sons of Confederate Veterans, reprinted from the Confederate Veteran 1 (2000), www.tennessee-scv.org/camp87/comments.

22. W. E. B. Du Bois, Black Reconstruction in America (New York, 1956), 725; Hannis Taylor, "Abram J. Ryan," Library of Southern Literature, 10:4623.

to try and restore the cultural context of the evangelical piety that Stowe's novel assumes. In Tompkins's view, *Uncle Tom's Cabin*—and all such literature (she mentioned Augusta Evans Wilson in passing, the author of a pro-South novel directly contradictory to Stowe's)—"is the *summa theologica* of nineteenth-century America's religion of domesticity, a brilliant redaction of the culture's favorite story about itself—the story of salvation through motherly love."[23]

Tompkins asked the modern-day reader to see such work less in our familiar psychological terms and more as "a political enterprise, halfway between sermon and social theory, that both codifies and attempts to mold the values of its time." Above all, she wrote, these texts presume "a set of religious beliefs that organizes and sustains the rest."[24]

In particular, Tompkins sought to show that the death of little Eva in Stowe's novel was not merely sentimental but that against a background of religious belief, such stories "are compelling for the same reason that the story of Christ's death is compelling; they enact a philosophy, as much political as religious, in which the pure and powerless die to save the powerful and corrupt, and thereby show themselves more powerful than those they save." She added by way of further explanation: "The power of the dead or the dying to redeem the unregenerate is a major theme of nineteenth-century popular fiction and religious literature." Tompkins concluded therefore that "rather than making the enduring success of *Uncle Tom's Cabin* inexplicable, these popular elements . . . —melodrama, pathos, Sunday-school fiction—are the *only* terms in which the book's success can be explained."[25]

One might also approach the problem of Ryan's kind of verse with a slight variation on Tompkins's argument. Thus, while one is tempted to think at times that much of his writing deserves the censure that Mark Twain offers for Emmeline Grangerford's efforts in *Huckleberry Finn*—"she could rattle off poetry like nothing. She didn't ever have to stop to think. . . . she would slap down a line, and if she couldn't find anything to rhyme with it she would just scratch it out and slap down another one, and go ahead. She warn't particular, she could write about anything you choose to give her to write about, just so it was sadful"—this is a very secular and

23. Jane Tompkins, "Sentimental Power: *Uncle Tom's Cabin* and the Politics of Literary History," in *Sensational Designs: The Cultural Work of American Fiction, 1790–1860* (New York, 1985), 125.

24. Ibid., 126, 127.

25. Tompkins mentions evangelist Dwight Lyman Moody's preaching in Great Britain and Ireland in 1875 on the theme of "The Child Angel" (128); 135.

narrowly aesthetic, not to say cynical, judgment of such work. However amusingly lugubrious, the religious tone of Ryan's writing was such that it appealed to several generations of southerners as an expression of their deepest sentiments about their sacred cause and its tragic defeat. It is hard, in any case, not to be impressed that forty-seven editions of his poems were published between 1879 and 1930, even if many of these were likely purchased as gift items similar to the contemporary *Rubaiyat of Omar Khayyam* or, later, Khalil Gibran's *The Prophet*. Perhaps Ryan himself best explained their appeal in "Sentinel Songs": "The grandest songs depart, / While the gentle, humble and low-toned rhymes / Will echo from heart to heart."[26]

Still, understanding the context that once made Ryan's poetry so popular does not make it appealing for even the least discerning reader today. Seamus Deane has pointed to exactly the same problem with much Irish poetry of the period—epitomized by Thomas Davis's hugely popular verses in the *Nation*—and has similarly suggested that we read it in its own political and religious terms rather than imposing what he calls an "aesthetic ideology" on it. After all, when the fastidious Oscar Wilde, brought up on such patriotic Irish poetry in the pages of the *Nation*—with which Father Ryan was quite familiar—and having long endured more of it in his mother's very similar verse, came to New Orleans during his 1882 lecture tour of the United States, he declared that he "admired" the southern priest's poems. He probably felt compelled to say so, but neither was he being totally insincere.[27]

But "sadful" is certainly the dominant note in Ryan, and, despite his enormous success, even as early as the end of the nineteenth century Rev. John Talbot Smith in his introduction to the thirteenth edition of *Poems: Patriotic, Religious, Miscellaneous* felt a need to defend Ryan against the criticism of those who considered that his work showed the same weaknesses as were to be found in Tennyson, Poe, Longfellow, and Lowell (hardly the worst company to be in, one might think): "The reader seems to be moving about in cathedral glooms, by dimly-lighted altars, with sad processions of ghostly penitents and mourners fading into the darkness to the sad music

26. Mark Twain, *The Adventures of Huckleberry Finn* (New York, 1995), 114; Father Abram Ryan, *Poems: Patriotic, Religious, Miscellaneous* (New York, 1895), 179.

27. According to Deane, "some of the best-known poems [of nineteenth-century Ireland] are, to present-day taste, among the worst . . . they are propagandistic, full of standard clichés and rhythmic vulgarities . . . But it is not necessary or wise to replace hostility to a political ideology with an aesthetic ideology"; see *The Field Day Anthology of Irish Literature* (New York, 1991), 2:1. Richard Ellmann, *Oscar Wilde* (New York, 1988), 198.

of lamenting choirs." Another apologist, John Moran, acknowledged that some of the priest's efforts "did not bear evidence of deep thought or careful and exhaustive preparation," but also claimed that the Christian poet is better than Homer and Virgil since "the Biblical narratives furnish the highest and best models and the richest sources of poetic inspiration." In spite of such justifications, the twenty-first-century critic is unlikely to be impressed by most of the commendation that Moran offers—the poems' "simple sublimity," the "grandeur" of the priest's thoughts," the "refined elegance and captivating force of the terms he employs"—though the same critic would probably be inclined to assent to Moran's comment on their "weird fancy."[28]

Although Father Ryan's name is forever linked to the Lost Cause, most of his poetry is generically religious. In the 1895 edition of his work, fewer than twenty of over one hundred poems obviously relate to the Civil War and Reconstruction. Yet it is for a couple of these that Ryan is remembered at all. What is of particular interest for the present study is that four of the remaining poems are specifically concerned with Ireland and that, moreover, the attitudes and word usage in them is very similar to the southern poems—though, strangely, the Irish poems seem to be more hopeful.

In this 1895 collection, a poem titled "Erin's Flag" (accompanied by an illustration) commands its readers to "Unroll Erin's flag! Fling its folds to the breeze!" and to "Lift it out of the dust—let it wave as of yore." The green and gold of the flag remain unstained, "Tho' the woes and the wrongs of three hundred long years / Have drenched Erin's Sunburst with blood and with tears!" For some reason—perhaps the success of Parnell's Land League in the 1880s or the beginnings of the Home Rule movement?—Ryan believes that all this is about to change: "Erin's dark night is waning, her day-dawn is nigh!" Even the country's suffering has ennobled its people, a constant theme in Ryan's poetry: "The blood of its sons has but brightened its sheen." There are specific references to Ireland's traumas in some of the lines that follow, especially to the famine:

> And we'll swear by the thousands who, famished, unfed,
> Died down in the ditches, wild-howling for bread,
> And we'll vow by our heroes, whose spirits have fled,

28. Rev. John Talbot Smith's introduction to thirteenth edition of *Poems: Patriotic, Religious, Miscellaneous*, xiii; Moran, ibid., xxxvii, xxxiv–xxxv.

And we'll swear by the bones in each coffinless bed,
That we'll battle the Briton through danger and dread.

Ryan also appears to have held the view—common among the Young Irelanders themselves—that after the Civil War, Irish soldiers would return
home to liberate their own country. Among them would be those Irish who
had fought for the Confederacy, a group possibly being referred to in the
allusion to the flag following "the fate of its sons o'er the world, / But its
folds, like their hopes, are not faded nor furled."[29]

In the poem that immediately follows, "The Sword of Robert Lee," one
of Ryan's most famous and one that he recited when that hero's monument
was unveiled in the 1880s at Washington and Lee College, he emphasizes
the nobility and rightness of the southern cause:

Forth from its scabbard, pure and bright,
    Flashed the sword of Lee!
Far in the front of the deadly fight,
High o'er the brave in the cause of Right,
Its stainless sheen, like a beacon light,
    Led us to Victory.

Bertram Wyatt-Brown gives a sense of the poem's emotional appeal when
he recalls that these were the first lines of poetry he ever committed to
memory as a child of southern parents in 1940s Pennsylvania. In Thomas
Connelly's 1977 study of Lee's iconography, *The Marble Man*, he explains
that "No element of the image [of Lee] was overlooked. One author even
wrote a manual of instructions for pantomiming and reciting Father Ryan's
poem. The student was told, for example, that when the phrase 'Flashed
the Sword of Lee!' was recited, he should: 'Sway weight of body forward to
R[ight]. foot as R. arm swings out to R. oblique at shoulder-level, then
swing straight above head; head tilted back; face up. Pleased expression.'"[30]

In "The Prayer of the South," kneeling "'mid ruin, wreck, and grave— /
A desert waste, where all was erst so fair," Ryan manages, uncharacteristi-
cally, to forgive his enemies, while in "The Land We Love," he sees the

---

29. Ryan, 61.

30. Ryan, 63; Bertram Wyatt-Brown, *Southern Honor: Ethics and Behavior in the Old South*
(New York, 1982), ix; Thomas Connelly, *The Marble Man: Robert E. Lee and His Image in American Society* (New York, 1977), 115; the instructions are from Cozette Keller, *Sword of Robert E.
Lee: Poses and Directions for Pantomiming and Reciting* (n.p., 1911), in Lee Papers, Washington
and Lee University.

South's suffering as leading to a more intense religious feeling: "Land where the victor's flag waves, / Where only the dead are the free! / Each link of the chain that enslaves, / But binds us to them and to thee." Indeed, this linking of the South and Christianity—"waiting an Easter-day" as we read in "Sentinel Songs"—was to be a constant theme with him, as, later, it dominated the imaginations of the poet-leaders of the 1916 Easter rebellion in Dublin.[31]

It is in "Sentinel Songs" also that one finds a kind of litany of the South's righteousness and its present sufferings. Thus, "the men were right who wore the gray, / And Right can never die." It is through the poet's verse, meanwhile, that there is an outlet for "the orphan's cry— / / And the father's curse and the mother's sigh, / And the desolate young wife's moan." In another poem about Lee that reflects the style of Henry Timrod, a more accomplished memorialist of the Lost Cause, Ryan laments:

> All lost! But by the graves
>   Where martyred heroes rest,
> He wins the most who honor saves—
>   Success is not the test.[32]

Here indeed is Ryan's essential theme, best expressed on an occasion in Nashville in 1878 where he spoke of "A Land without Ruins":

> A land without ruins is a land without memories . . . A land that wears a laurel crown may be fair to see; but twine a few sad cypress leaves around the brow of any land, and be that land barren, beautiless and bleak, it becomes lovely in its consecrated coronet of sorrow . . . Crowns of roses fade—crowns of thorns endure. Calvaries and crucifixions take deepest hold of humanity—the triumphs of might are transient—they pass and are forgotten—the sufferings of right are graven deepest on the chronicle of nations.
>
> Yes, give me the land where the ruins are spread,
>   And the living tread light on the hearts of the dead;
> Yes, give me a land that is blest by the dust,
>   And bright with the deeds of the down-trodden just.[33]

---

31. Ryan, 93; see William Irwin Thompson, *The Imagination of an Insurrection: Dublin, Easter 1916* (New York, 1967).

32. Ryan, 175, 181.

33. Ibid., 90. Conor Cruise O'Brien quotes a similar sentiment from Arthur Griffith's 1919 essay "Nationality": "In the martyrology of history, among crucified nations, Ireland occupies the foremost place"; see *Ancestral Voices: Religion and Nationalism in Ireland* (Chicago, 1995), 9. Notice James M. McPherson's claim in *For Causes and Comrades: Why Men Fought in the*

The seamless associating of the South's cause with that of Christianity here is remarkable. It is also shown in an anecdote told by Ryan's contemporaries: "He saw his young niece standing before a painting of the death of Christ, and he asked her if she knew who the evil men were who had crucified her Lord. Instantly she replied, 'O yes I know,' she said, 'the Yankees.' "[34]

Some of Ryan's Irish interest—and his persistent linking of nationalism with Christianity—is evident in "The Poet's Child," a poem addressed to the daughter of Richard Dalton Williams, an Irish poet who had published in the *Nation* under the pen name "Shamrock" and been imprisoned in Dublin in the 1840s as a consequence of his incendiary writings. In *Jail Journal*, John Mitchel expressed concern that "poor Williams, with his fragile frame and sensitive poetic temperament" might be made "a martyr felon." Emigrating to America, Williams taught for several years at the Jesuit Spring Hill College in Mobile before resuming his medical studies in Louisiana, where he died in 1862 at age forty. He was sufficiently well known that when Irish Union soldiers from New Hampshire discovered his grave during the Civil War, they erected a marble memorial to him as a great patriot. It was the patriotic poems of Dalton Williams that had inspired Oscar Wilde's mother, Lady Wilde (then Jane Francesca Elgee), to defy her family to become an ardent Irish nationalist, and a poet to boot. In Father Ryan's poem, the tragic Williams "moaned o'er Erin's ev'ry wrong!" and "swept with purest hand / The octaves of all agonies," his lament finally reaching the priest himself "Like a shadow song from some Gethsemane."[35]

While some of Ryan's writing on Irish themes was no more than occasional—his "St. Bridget," for example ("Thou art in light— / They are in night")—the second to last poem in his 1895 anthology is quite remarkable and shows clearly the relationship between Ireland and the South as he conceived it. "The Song of the Deathless Voice" runs to several pages. The setting is Halloween. A voice comes to the narrator from "far away" and is "weak-sung"—almost like his own distant memory of Ireland, or, not unlikely, the echo of a more Freudian impulse. The song opens:

Civil War (New York, 1997) that the words most used in letters by Confederates were "subjugated" and "enslaved" (12).

34. Wilson, 25.

35. John Mitchel, *Jail Journal* (Dublin, 1982), 58; Ellmann, 7. Ellmann comments a little cruelly: "She did manage a rhetoric close to her master's." Ryan, 410–11.

How long! Alas, how long!
How long shall the Celt chant the sad song of hope,
That a sunrise may break on the long starless night of our past?
How long shall we wander and wait on the desolate slope
Of Tabors that promise our Transfiguration at last?
How long, O Lord! How long!

In the third stanza, in the tradition of "The Conquered Banner," he asks how long shall "our banner . . . droop furled?"

Ireland is still a Golgotha awaiting the close of its Good Friday. Stanza five inquires "How long ere the dawn of the day in the ages to be, / When the Celt will forgive, or else tread on the heart of his foe?" Then, rather amazingly, in stanza six the narrator wonders who the singer is and suspects it is himself, his "heart athrill with some deathless old cry." He explains that this is so because "blood forgets not in its flowing its forefathers' / wrongs— / They are the heart's trust, from which we may ne'er / be released" (a sentiment that doesn't seem all that different from Tom Hayden's twenty-first-century belief in the "invisible ancestral influences" of his Irish forbears, though the consequences for him generally take a more socially progressive turn).[36]

The song goes on a few lines later: "Am I not in my blood as old as the race whence I sprung? / In the cells of my heart feel I not all its ebb and its flow?" Soon afterward, we find the following (almost in the manner of Seamus Heaney's "Digging"): "Aye, this very hand that trembles thro' this very line, / Lay hid, ages gone, in the hand of some forefather Celt." While the latter, however, may be "stronger," it is "not truer than mine, / And I feel, with my pen, what the old hero's sworded hand felt." Even more clearly expressive is:

Our dead are not dead who have gone, long ago,
    to their rest;
They are living in us whose glorious race will not die—

Their "brave buried hearts" continue on in "the child of each Celt" wherever he or she may be.[37]

Like Father John Bannon, though in the postwar era, Ryan took the South's cause to the embattled pope, Pius IX. The pontiff gave him an auto-

36. See Tom Hayden, *Irish on the Inside: In Search of the Soul of Irish America* (New York, 2001), 69.

37. Ryan, 461–62.

graphed photo to present to Jefferson Davis, causing the latter to tell Ryan that he saw the pope's and his own situation as similar, the one "the prisoner of the Vatican," the other the prisoner of Reconstruction.[38]

As Ryan was a frequent visitor to Davis's home in Mississippi, even offering at one stage to help the former president with his memoirs, it is tempting to wonder how he might have reacted when Oscar Wilde spent the night of June 27, 1882, with the Davises—to the delight of Mrs. Davis and the chagrin, or at least barely suppressed distaste, of Davis himself. A twenty-seven-year-old, modestly accomplished Wilde was on his hugely successful American lecture tour, decked out in cloak and knee-breeches, carrying his emblematic sunflower and promoting his aesthetic approach to life—very popular then in a re-United States temporarily alienated from the hypermasculinity of the Civil War era—and rediscovering enough of the Irishness he had abandoned at Oxford a few years earlier to compose a supplementary talk on "The Irish Poets of '48" and to proclaim his country's affinity with the South.[39]

As usual, Wilde charmed the ladies present on the occasion. Mrs. Davis even made a pencil sketch of him. For Davis, however, "Wilde's thick, sensual lips gave him a slightly gross look. At dinner Davis let his wife and Wilde carry on most of the conversation; he remained courteous, but aloof. Pleading doctor's orders for some temporary indisposition, he excused himself early." Davis's biographer adds, with a nod to the as yet unwritten *Picture of Dorian Gray*: "Wilde had felt restrained in the presence of this sincere man. By simply being himself, Davis had held up to Wilde a mirror which reflected an image that was not flattering." A few days after the Davis visit, however, Wilde wrote to Julia Ward Howe, author of "The Battle Hymn of the Republic," from Augusta, Georgia:

> I write to you from the beautiful, passionate, ruined South, the land of magnolias and music, of roses and romance: picturesque too in her failure to keep pace with your keen northern pushing intellect; living chiefly on credit, and on the memory of some crushing defeats. And I have been to Texas, right to the heart of it, and stayed with Jeff Davis at his plantation (how fascinating all failures are!) and seen Savannah, and the Georgia forests, and bathed in the Gulf of Mexico, and engaged in Voodoo rites with the Negroes.

38. This anecdote comes from H. J. Heagney, *Chaplain in Gray: Abram Ryan, Poet-Priest of the Confederacy* (New York, 1958), a story account of Ryan's life (with index) aimed at juveniles.

39. See Mary Warner Blanchard, *Oscar Wilde's America: Counterculture in the Gilded Age* (New Haven, 1998).

Although their views on most things were almost certainly very different—one can only imagine Ryan's likely reaction to the mention of Voodoo rites in Wilde's letter to Howe, or to his comment, quoted in the New Orleans *Daily Picayune,* on the need for portraiture and poetry about blacks: "I saw them everywhere, happy and carefree, basking in the sunshine or dancing in the shade, their half naked bodies gleaming like bronze and their lithe and active movements reminding one of the lizards that were seen flashing along the banks and trunks of the trees"— and although Ryan might have shared some of Davis's instinctive distaste for the "sensual" visitor, there is a strange symbiotic relationship between the two long-haired, exotically dressed figures, not least in their mutual Irish and southern sympathies. After all, Ryan would have been meeting a self-declared admirer of his poems, a Catholic-leaning writer who had also held private audience with the pope. More importantly for Ryan, he would have been meeting the son of "Speranza," Lady Wilde's pen name as a poet in the *Nation,* who almost forty years earlier had been so moved by the writings of their mutual inspiration, Richard Dalton Williams. John Mitchel too, after his return to Ireland in the 1870s from his volatile period in America, had been entertained by the Wildes, as Oscar noted proudly in a lecture given in San Francisco shortly before his arrival in New Orleans, in which he referred to Mitchel's "eagle eye and impassioned manner." Wilde's own final poetic work in 1897, *The Ballad of Reading Gaol,* would bear many of the hallmarks of his mother's, and the *Nation's*—and, by implication, Father Ryan's—kind of immediately appealing, less aestheticized verse. Seamus Heaney explains that in his imprisonment, Wilde "became like other men. He became one of the chain-gang poets, a broken shadow of the brilliant littérateur." Rebels, defeated defiers of convention, Wilde in his aesthetic cloak—and described in an Alabama newspaper as an "utter Celt"—Ryan in his ecclesiastical cassock and similar floor-length cape, might not have made such strange bedfellows after all.[40]

Six years later, in 1888, President Davis's daughter Varina Anne would publish the first of her three books, *An Irish Knight of the 19th Century; Sketch of the Life of Robert Emmet,* a work that bears the distinct influence of Father Ryan not merely in subject matter but also in tone. Emmet, a

40. Strode, 460; *The Complete Letters of Oscar Wilde,* ed. Merlin Holland and Rupert Hart-Davis (New York, 2000), 175–76, quoted in Blanchard, 19; Ellmann, 7, 198; see Seamus Heaney's essay on Wilde, "Speranza in Reading: On 'The Ballad of Reading Gaol,'" in *The Redress of Poetry* (New York, 1995), 83–102, esp. 97.

Protestant—and by far the most romantic of Irish heroes—was executed in 1803 after leading an unsuccessful rebellion, and was especially famous for his speech from the dock requesting that his epitaph not be written until Ireland was free. While Varina Anne Davis provides a fairly conventional and mildly nationalist account of Irish history—Celts, Christians, invasion, oppression, revolt—her tone is somewhat surprising in its marked sympathies with the Catholic cause. In any case, the inflection of Father Ryan's poetry is clear: "In the deserted churchyard of St. Michins [sic] there is a slab on which no name is traced. Beneath this stone rest the ashes of Robert Emmet. How long, oh, Ireland, how long will it remain without an epitaph!" Nor was she unaware of the parallel with the defeated South: "Thus died Ireland's true knight, sinking into the grave clothed in all the bright promise of his youth; never to put on the sad livery of age; never to feel the hopelessness of those who live to see the principles for which they suffered trampled and forgotten by the onward march of new interests and new men."[41]

But a grimmer "Celtic" note was also being sounded in the years immediately following the Civil War. Relations between whites and blacks—their numbers were almost equal in the southern states at about four million each—had become more and more antagonistic as the freedmen acquired the vote and positions in state and federal government and whites sought to reestablish their earlier dominance. The Lost Cause movement was a part of this reassertion, though in its preoccupation with commemoration it shied away from the past of slavery and the present of emancipation. The newly founded, militant Ku Klux Klan—to which, in spite of its incipient anti-Catholicism, Father Ryan (described at one point as a kind of "honorary Protestant") may have acted as a chaplain—borrowed much of its lore and symbolism from Scottish and Irish (and, sartorially, Catholic) tradition as recycled through Sir Walter Scott's novels. Though banned by 1871, it survived into the twentieth century to blaze forth in the pages of former Baptist minister Thomas Dixon's 1905 novel, The Clansman, a work dedicated "To the Memory of a Scotch-Irish Leader of the South, My Uncle, Colonel Leroy McAfee, Grand Titan of the Invisible Empire Ku Klux Klan."[42]

41. Varina Anne Davis, An Irish Knight of the 19th Century; Sketch of the Life of Robert Emmet (New York, 1888), 89.
42. Thomas Dixon, The Clansman (New York, 1905).

The second novel in a trilogy, the first of which offered a "historical outline of the conditions from the enfranchisement of the Negro to his disfranchisement," *The Clansman* eclectically, and sometimes contradictorily, invoked Scottish and Irish history in its establishing of southern rights: "The old club-footed Puritan, in his mad scheme of vengeance and party power, had overlooked the Covenanter; the backbone of the South . . . His race had defied the Crown of Great Britain a hundred years from the caves and wilds of Scotland and Ireland, taught the English people how to slay a king and build a commonwealth." In an era when lynching had become common in the Southern states—carried out without apology or guilt—Dixon's message emerged even more vengefully in 1915 in the movie version of his novel, *Birth of a Nation*, a landmark in motion picture history and the inspiration for the spread of a reborn KKK—this time antiblack, anti-Catholic, and anti-Jewish—on a national level. It would inspire too what is arguably the best-known novel of the twentieth century, a work much more deeply inflected with Irishness and even KKK-proscribed Catholicism, in the pages of which the defiant southern poet Father Abram Ryan would not be forgotten.[43]

43. Ibid., 347; Tom Watson, the populist, racist, and anti-Catholic political leader in early-twentieth-century Georgia, wrote a defiant reply to Father Ryan's "Conquered Banner": "Keep that glorious flag that slumbers, / One day to avenge your dead," quoted in Bertram Wyatt-Brown, *The Shaping of Southern Culture* (Chapel Hill, 2001), 270.

CHAPTER 5

ṪARA ṪRAṄSPLAṄṪED

The only Latin he knew was the responses of the Mass and the only history the manifold wrongs of Ireland. He knew no poetry save that of Moore.

—MARGARET MITCHELL, *Gone with the Wind*

The Harp that once through Tara's halls,
The soul of Music shed,
Now hangs as mute on Tara's walls
As if that soul were fled.
So sleeps the pride of former days.

—THOMAS MOORE, *Irish Melodies*

The popularity of Abram Ryan's verse and outlook—the priest himself died in 1886—was at its height during the 1890–1920 period when aesthetic interest had wilted, masculine heroism come back into fashion, and the Lost Cause movement was in full swing. As a girl, Margaret Mitchell, born in 1900, was still hearing stories about him from her Irish Catholic relatives in Augusta. Years later, in *Gone with the Wind*, Mitchell would write of a postwar, impoverished Melanie Hamilton entertaining such notables as "General John B. Gordon, Georgia's great hero," and "Father Ryan, the poet-priest of the Confederacy." The latter "never failed to call when passing through Atlanta. He charmed gatherings there with his wit and seldom needed much urging to recite his 'Sword of Lee' or his deathless 'Conquered Banner,' which never failed to make the ladies cry." Charming, witty, a self-conscious performer and a noted putter-away of fried chicken, perhaps, after all, the priest was not quite as chronically morose as legend claims.[1]

One side of Mitchell's maternal ancestors had migrated from the British Isles to Catholic Maryland in the seventeenth century as part of the same movement that also brought the Carrolls of Carrollton to that religiously

---

1. Margaret Mitchell, *Gone with the Wind* (New York, 1973), 730; Darden Asbury Pyron, *Southern Daughter: The Life of Margaret Mitchell* (New York, 1992), 35.

tolerant state. Taking care always to marry other Catholics—not an easy choice in the areas in which they lived—they still retained their denominational identification when they moved to Taliaferro County, Georgia, at the beginning of the 1800s. Then, in the 1820s, Mitchell's American Catholic line was revitalized by a Phillip Fitzgerald, whose family had fled Tipperary for France after the 1798 uprising, and, later, by a John Stephens in the Civil War era, also of Irish birth. Both of these, notes Mitchell's most recent biographer, "brought with them a vigorous ethnic identity" and an "Irishness that added a new source of peculiarity to the family legacy. It set them apart from the Southern norm, but it also exaggerated the family's clannish self-consciousness, sense of its own distinction, and the feeling of being at odds with the world."[2]

Fitzgerald was the owner of a large plantation in "the isolated settlement at Locust Grove in Taliaferro County," the same Locust Grove community from which Flannery O'Connor's ancestors also came, and which was to have a Catholic offshoot in Mississippi. Darden Asbury Pyron comments that with "his ambition, enterprise, intelligence, Irish heritage, puritanical Catholicism, and devotion to the Southern way of life," Phillip Fitzgerald seems to have been unique in the area—except that his daughter married a similar Irish-born immigrant, John Stephens. "Indeed, the pious rationality and systematic thought of St. Thomas Aquinas offer the key to his temper and to the ideas he pressed upon his family," Pyron somewhat idealistically suggests.[3]

Herself the daughter of an ardent Catholic mother in this line, who was both a defender of her church against the attacks of the anti-Catholic Senator Tom Watson, and, rather surprisingly perhaps, a very active suffragette, Margaret Mitchell was to reject her religious inheritance in her first year at Smith, become an Episcopalian, and generally identify herself with her father's Methodism, though she never lost a deep consciousness of her ethnic background. Her only brother remained a Catholic, and even in the twenty-first century, the ongoing disputes about Mitchell's estate and the uses to which her legacy can be put frequently take place within the context of the conservative Catholic outlook of his offspring.[4]

Whether one thinks of *Gone with the Wind* as no more than a remark-

2. Pyron, 17.

3. Ibid., 20.

4. See, for example, "Mitchell Estate Settles 'Gone with the Wind' Suit," *New York Times*, 10 May 2002, C6.

ably successful popular romance novel, even a cheap "magnolia-drenched plantation fantasy" as Dennis Clark described it, or as an epic representation of southern culture of its period—and one can use Jane Tompkins's argument discussed in the previous chapter to give depth to such a response—there can be no doubt that it has had a tremendous impact throughout the world, though in diverse and often contradictory ways. The movie version inspired endurance and hope in both Britain and Japan—mutual enemies—during and after World War II. Welcomed at first in Germany in the 1930s when Adolf Hitler was in power as an affirmation of white racial superiority, *Gone with the Wind* was afterward banned—and people were hanged for possessing a copy of it—for its emphasis on rebellion and survival. The French Resistance too circulated it clandestinely among their fighters. The response in the South, even today, often bears elements of a "religious fervor."[5]

Once academics outside of media studies and history got over their professional disdain for the novel—based on the awareness, and perhaps troubled prejudice, that such a nonprofound and shamelessly marketed work could have such serious cultural impact—and began commenting on it systematically, it has furnished material for a surprising array of analyses: as a deeply gendered, racist, revolutionary, or debunking text, depending on the orientation of the commentator or even the decade of the commentary. In this regard, Jacquelyn Dowd Hall's caution that *Gone with the Wind* is very much a book of the Jazz Age and that its original intentions are distorted when we look back at them from a post–civil rights and second wave feminist perspective is well taken.[6]

At all events, a book that has been so successful—it still sells almost a half-million copies a year—must in some way touch deep-seated human desires and fears. Amused and frustrated that Mitchell was considered as "the Writer" in the Georgia of the 1950s, Flannery O'Connor mocked such attachment in her short story "A Late Encounter with the Enemy," where the one-hundred-and-four-year-old "General"—who had only been a foot soldier in the war—remembers most of all the "preemy [premiere] they had in Atlanta" for the movie at which he was feted by visiting Hollywood celebrities and even obtained from them his "Confederate" uniform. Alice

5. Dennis Clark, *Hibernia America: The Irish and Regional Cultures* (New York, 1986), 106; James P. Cantrell, "Irish Culture and the War between the States: *Paddy McGann* and *Gone with the Wind,*" *Éire-Ireland* 27, no. 2 (1992): 7–15.

6. Jacquelyn Dowd Hall, "The Prong of Love," *Southern Cultures* 5, no. 1 (1999): 46.

Walker has presented Mitchell's book as the site of division between black and white female friends in her didactic story, "A Letter of the Times, or Should This Sado-Masochism Be Saved?" But neither of these "serious" writers could or would have attacked the work had *Gone with the Wind* not been so well known. O'Connor didn't even have to mention it or its author by name.

Walker's short story, in the form of a letter from a black woman to her white female friend, registers not only the shock of seeing the latter attend a costume ball dressed as Scarlett O'Hara but also her disturbance with the lesbian couples appearing as masters and slaves in enactments of their supposedly harmless fantasies. For Walker's letter writer, such charades are harmful indeed. In Mitchell's case, we know that she herself as a young girl dramatized Dixon's *The Clansman* and that he wrote to commend her for her novel as a continuation of his own defense of the Confederacy. Given her interest in sexually transgressive fiction, it is possible to see the Rhett Butler who "rapes" Scarlett as a transferred fantasy of the black rapist in Dixon's story. Elizabeth Young has commented that Rhett Butler is "a white character who is drawn from fantasies of black masculinity, as mediated through the 'brown' skins of Arab sheik and Latin lover. The 'white imagination' at work in Rhett's case is that of a woman, Margaret Mitchell, whose investments in reviving white masculinity were at once personal and historical. Eating the cake of blackness without having to have it, she conjured her own ideal man within the historical space of the Confederacy." Reading Young's not-unconvincing analysis, one is inclined to agree with a recent critic's observation on *Gone with the Wind* that "After countless debates and exhaustive deconstructions, it is hard to tell what we are left with."[7]

When Catherine Clinton of the W. E. B. Du Bois Institute at Harvard, who made that last remark, had concluded her wonderfully detailed account of the real lives of women, black and white, under the Confederacy, she still found herself needing to explain the continuing power of Mitchell's novel and movie. Her honest amazement and frustration are evident in her carefully placed italics in a sentence about the unexpected consequences of the sequel that was published in 1991: "Mitchell's own novel proceeded to reappear on the national bestseller list, *over fifty years* after it was pub-

7. Alice Walker, *You Can't Keep a Good Woman Down: Stories* (New York, 1981); Elizabeth Young, *Disarming the Nation: Women's Writing and the American Civil War* (Chicago, 1999), 262–63; Catherine Clinton, *Tara Revisited: Women, War, and the Plantation Legend* (New York, 1995), 208–11.

lished." Nevertheless, Clinton adds, "If we dismiss widespread affection for Selznick's film, its characters, and its settings, and see the story and its impact as mere nostalgia for slavery, we are reducing a complex formula of art, commerce, hype, and history to its lowest common—and most divisive—denominator." In her view, we need to come to terms with the disturbing fact that the first Oscar received by an African American was Hattie MacDaniel's for her performance in *Gone with the Wind*, a significant milestone in the country's history of race relations. For Clinton, some of the story's appeal derives from its depiction of an immigrant—she doesn't specify his Irishness at all—who succeeded, then lost his gains, only to triumph once again in the success of his daughter. In other words, it is, through and through, an American story. Clinton concludes, though with a note of hollowness: "Our stake in America's plantation heritage continues to haunt as we wrangle over its meanings, its sentimentalism and sins, its legacy today. After countless debates and exhaustive deconstructions, it is hard to tell what we are left with. Yet certain legends endure. Tara remains contested yet transcendent—bewildering, unbending, and beguiling. And its distinctive, compelling image prods us to re-examine a fascinating crossroads of history and memory, beckoning us to revisit, yet again, another day."[8]

In the end, in the face of all objections, and for better or worse, *Gone with the Wind* stands as much a signifier for the American South as Big Ben for England or the Eiffel Tower for France. When the German automobile company Daimler-Benz wanted to register its presence in America in the 1990s, it did so by restoring—indeed recreating—Margaret Mitchell's home in Atlanta. Southerners, for more than one reason, couldn't afford to do so.

Only a few critics have commented on *Gone with the Wind*'s pervasive Irish provenance, though it was precisely this aspect of the story that was emphasized when Vivien Leigh's Irish heritage was advertised at the time of the movie version in 1939 (she was also marketed as an "English rose"). Perhaps, though there are certainly many indicators to the contrary, by then the Irish—even Irish Catholics—had so much blended into southern culture that their difference was barely noticed. That's what Mitchell thought when she wrote to a fan about "the part the Irish played in the building up of our Southern section and in the Civil War . . . our Southern Irish became more Southern than the Southerners. When the trouble in

8. Clinton, 208–11.

the 'sixties began they went out with the Confederate troops and did great deeds for their new land."[9]

Not only is much of the characterization here Irish—and the central terms of the story too—but we also know from the author's own biography that she drew substantially on her family's Irish-American experience, and especially on her colorful but hated maternal grandmother, for her fictional narrative. At many points the novel expresses the central Irish conflict between the Green, the Red, and the Orange: the heroine's Catholic father fled Ireland to escape the British authorities after he had killed an Orangeman who had insulted him; mentally disoriented after the war, Gerald O'Hara only refuses to sign the federally required oath to the Union when he hears that his Orange neighbor has done so. James P. Cantrell, in the tradition of Grady McWhiney, even sees the novel as presenting a fundamental contest between Celtic and Anglo-Saxon cultures—a conflict Mitchell embodies in Scarlett's love for Ashley Wilkes—in which the Celtic side, for once, wins.[10]

Cantrell claims that "as an epic protagonist, Scarlett O'Hara is to some degree a symbol of the South." Both Ireland and the South, unlike England (John Bull) and the United States (Uncle Sam), are "always seen as female. Scarlett's story, then, is not merely a personal love tragedy; it reflects a larger cultural tragedy." The tragedy is that the South's "Celtic hardheadedness did not prevent it from choosing the pretty illusions of cavalier gentility, which include a cavalier defense of chattel slavery and the caste system that goes with it. The South, like Scarlett, blinded itself to reality, and thereby lost what was most precious to it." By returning to Tara at the end of the novel, then, Scarlett is symbolically declaring the need for this Irish element.[11]

Cantrell's interesting, though not wholly convincing, argument assumes that Mitchell is fully approving of Scarlett and is presenting her as a role model. The text is much more ambivalent on the matter. It is obvious on many occasions that the position that Scarlett adopts—her almost total focus on the commercial aspects of life, for example—is not as admirable as that of those less willing to make peace with the former enemy or even to exploit the opportunities of a new situation. Still, however extravagant Cantrell's argument may be, there seems no debating the Irish character of

9. Quoted in Young, 256.
10. Cantrell, 11–15.
11. Ibid., 15.

the South's best-known work of fiction. Pyron's 1991 biography of Mitchell only adds to and complicates that profile. He stresses Mitchell's use of family material in the construction of her narrative but also points out that Mitchell exchanged her actual family's Irish history—that of the Fitzgeralds and Stephenses—for one that would conform more to type (even bordering on stereotype), at least in certain of its features. Paradoxically, she would do this in order to give a "realistic" picture of the Old South—in the manner that W. J. Cash was also attempting—rather than perpetuate the mythological one presented in so much southern fiction. So, in Pyron's view, Mitchell was as much a debunker as a celebrant of the Old South. If it is well known that Mitchell herself criticized the film version of the plantation homes for their being much "grander" than the novel's, it is less familiar that the author detested the opening caption by scriptwriter and dramatist Ben Hecht, in which he refers sentimentally to a land of cavaliers and ladies that has passed away, never to be found again.[12]

According to Pyron, Mitchell "delighted in deflating what she deemed the Stephens women's inflated notions of the past. When she visited her rich Aunt Edythe in Connecticut, her snobby relative trembled, the niece wrote, lest 'I'd say her father was born in Ireland and even her husband didn't know that—. Or that I'd let out that the farm at Jonesboro was just a plain Georgia farm and not a plantation home with white columns, gravelled walks and magnolias such as she had described.'" Mitchell's grandmother was the main culprit here: after her husband's death, she sent the younger girls up north "to finishing schools where they were taught that it was shameful to be the daughters of an Irishman born in the old Country."[13]

Mitchell not only dramatically revalidated her suppressed Irish background, she also reinvented it. Pyron argues that she "took her own ancestors, roughed them up considerably, and projected them, thus transformed, into her epic."

Actually, of course, the real-life Fitzgeralds and Stephenses bore little resemblance to the fictional O'Haras except in religion, place of birth, and economic status. Where she depicted Gerald as rough, semi-literate, and uncultured, Phillip Fitzgerald and his son-in-law were actually members of the Irish gentry and fit naturally into the planter order. Her forebears' knowledge and intelligence set them apart, and even Protestant locals valued their learning and subsidized the schools these immigrant gentlemen

12. Pyron, 389.
13. Ibid., 251.

founded. Her own ancestors possessed good connections and cultivated better ones in the antebellum South. Unlike the O'Haras, they turned political
activity and Democratic party loyalties to good account. They also tied up
with local communities of well-established, non-Irish Catholics in the back
country and married among them. By such methods outsiders had traditionally won entry into the Southern ruling class since its seventeenth-
century origins.

Almost wholly Irish and certainly wholly Catholic, Mitchell's maternal ancestors were unlike most of those perceived as belonging to the race. Pyron
explains that there were few Irish Catholic planters in the South and even
few Irish Catholic farmers. Rather, the Irish "remained mostly in the large
coastal cities like Charleston and Savannah; they lived mostly as single men
rather than with families; and they came as close to representing a regional
underclass as any category in the entire population." A disproportionate
number of them were prison inmates. While Pyron's is a view that has been
called into question by recent work such as David T. Gleeson's, which suggests a greater variety of class and occupation among the Irish in the South
than was recognized heretofore, it is not in its broad outline inaccurate.[14]

In any case, the novelist, attacking especially the pretensions of women
both in the South in general and in her own family,

> effectively took elements of the real Irish in Georgia and tacked them onto
> her own ancestors to produce Gerald O'Hara. At the same time, she made
> her fictional Gerald something like a standard for her own genealogy, too.
> In unmasking the plantation South, she debunked her own family. She
> downplayed her own ancestors and their influence. Rural Home, she in-
> sisted, was no great plantation but rather an ordinary farm. Phillip Fitzger-
> ald and John Stephens were ordinary. "They were both Irishmen born and
> proud of it and prouder still of being Southerners and would have withered
> any relative that tried to put on dog," she continued. ". . . they left that to
> the post war nouveau riche who had to carry a lot of dog because they had
> nothing else to carry." This down-to-earth portrait of her own ancestors
> resonates nicely with her depiction of the fictional Gerald O'Hara.

Pyron adds that Mitchell "specifically spared her immigrant patriarchs from
this characterization and isolated the evil completely in the women." Thus,
in the novel, Scarlett, far from being the ideal heroine (as Cantrell and the

14. Pyron, 249, 250; David T. Gleeson, *The Irish in the South, 1815–1877* (Chapel Hill, 2001),
38, 39.

world at large suppose), is full of "splurge, and swagger": Scarlett is, in fact, ultimately "vulgar" and "mindless." Nevertheless, even in this revised form, the lesson still seems to be that Scarlett, both like and because of her resilient Irish ancestors, survived when others of more accepted pedigree did not.[15]

Indeed, in this critical tradition—which is also that of Cantrell—Eliza Russi Lowen McGraw has recently argued that Scarlett's Irish identity "complicates" a gender-centered model of her survival offered by feminist critics. For them, Scarlett thrives not because she is a Southern belle but rather an independent new woman. McGraw's point, by contrast, is that "Even if family history explains how Irishness entered Mitchell's consciousness, Scarlett's ethnic identity goes beyond authorial happenstance to a revision of Southernness." For her, Mitchell's novel argues that "the survivors of the New South must have blood other than that of the defeated Anglicized planters idealized by plantation legend. Within the economy of the text, Scarlett's Irishness accounts for her transgressive nature, and ensures she will thrive in post-bellum Atlanta."[16]

McGraw also argues that within the economy of the text, Scarlett cannot be anything other than a pretender to aristocracy because her Irishness necessarily excludes her from the caste and that Mitchell equates Irishness with commonness. In this vein too, Patricia Yaeger sees Ashley's use of the Episcopal burial service at Gerald's funeral as "bringing us back, with a start, to Gerald's initial status as an underclass, immigrant outsider and setting up the equivalence between the Wilkes's nameless slaves and the dead Mr. O'Hara." For McGraw, then, Scarlett's "desire" is vulgar and Irish, though it helps her survive. Making an even more controversial point, McGraw claims that Scarlett can be seen as a kind of "tragic mulatta" figure, with "green" as her color marker, who needs to "pass" in white, Anglo society. This is so even if, again, it is this very mixture of coastal aristocracy with Irish peasantry that, according to Mitchell's novel, "provides strength for the brutal world of the post-bellum South." My own reading, however, brings me to a rather different conclusion, or at least to one with a different emphasis.[17]

15. Pyron, 251.

16. Eliza Russi Lowen McGraw, "A 'Southern Belle with Her Irish Up': Scarlett O'Hara and Ethnic Identity," *South Atlantic Review* 65, no. 1 (2000): 123, 124.

17. McGraw, 128, 130. By this time, historian Joel Williamson had raised an even more controversial question in his essay "How Black Was Rhett Butler?" in *The Evolution of Southern Culture,* ed. Numan V. Bartley (Athens, 1988), 187–207. Patricia Yaeger, "Race and the Cloud of Unknowing in *Gone with the Wind,*" *Southern Cultures* 5, no. 1 (1999): 25.

One of the noteworthy developments in recent examinations of *Gone with the Wind* is that critics now tend to foreground their personal biases before discussing the work itself. In the past, when the novel was dealt with at all, the purpose was to lament that, appearing in the same year as Faulkner's masterpiece *Absalom, Absalom!*, Mitchell's work had unfairly eclipsed the genius of southern letters. In contrast to Faulkner's multilayered depictions, his willingness to show the brute sexual reality of master-slave relations—though even with him not quite as brutal as the reality in which, as Mary Chesnutt lamented, the plantation was all too often a whorehouse for the master and his lusty sons—Mitchell's characterizations and plot were superficial, the light her novel threw on the complexities of Southern race minimal at best. Richard Dwyer has commented that "the academics resorted to a variety of rhetorical strategies that serve, in hindsight, to reveal nothing so much as their elitist ideological biases against the nonacademic majority of the American public as consumers of convenience, comfort, and mindless diversion."[18]

Now, however—or at least since Leslie Fiedler in 1978 confessed his secret love for the work despite his previous dismissals of it—even an African American parodist of Mitchell's book, Alice Randall, admits to a love-hate relationship with the text. Patricia Yaeger acknowledges finding her immediate sympathies when she rereads Mitchell's novel "completely at odds with my own position as a liberal academic—empathizing with the Klan after they've brutalized the inhabitants of shantytown, identifying with Scarlett as she abuses convict labor," and all this for "a story whose politics (and, for that matter, whose writing style) drives me over the brink." Yaeger and other feminist critics, however, now find fascinating instabilities of race and gender in the book which are socially revealing even if they never quite redeem the narrative itself. In other words, Mitchell throws light where she herself didn't intend to, or didn't even see clearly enough to do so.[19]

In this tradition, then, I openly confess that I feel no particular attach-

18. See, for example, Louis D. Rubin Jr., "Scarlett O'Hara and the Two Quentin Compsons," in *A Gallery of Southerners* (Baton Rouge, 1982), 26–48, or Floyd C. Watkins, "*Gone with the Wind* as Vulgar Literature," in *Gone with the Wind as Book and Film*, ed. Richard Harwell (New York, 1987), 198–210; Richard Dwyer, "The Case of the Cool Reception," in *Recasting:* Gone with the Wind *in American Culture*, ed. Darden Asbury Pyron (Miami, 1983), 29.

19. Alice Randall, *The Wind Done Gone* (New York, 2002). See Leslie Fiedler, "The Anti-Tom Novel and the Depression," in Harwell, 244–51; Yaeger, 21.

ment to Mitchell's novel as such, though I regard it as a reasonably well-told tale of its kind (but with lots of clotted prose, a text not nearly as transparent as explainers of its popularity have assumed). The movie version, or rather moments in it, does have a certain "sentimental power" for me—the silhouette of Gerald and Scarlett O'Hara standing against the darkening sky looking toward Tara, the emotion amplified by the swelling score (I admit this with some embarrassment)—but not much different from my ambivalent attachment to a random assortment of similar moments from the silver screen: the end of *Casablanca,* Lawrence Olivier's Heathcliff delivering the line "I'm master here now" in *Wuthering Heights,* Salieri in *Amadeus* stunned by the realization of Mozart's divine genius as he jealously gazes at the composer's uncorrected original notations. As an Irishman brought up in a less Hollywoodized culture, I've been slow to recognize the importance of popular media and am awkwardly aware of how dismissive Irish academics can be of this kind of Americanness in particular, even while the Irish population at large has traditionally had higher than usual cinema attendance. But neither do I regard Mitchell's work as a mere obscenity, and I can understand how it had, and has, genuine appeal for readers in ways that are not to be explained fully by meticulously analytical accounts of the forces behind its production and consumption. It appeals in ways that many chauvinistic anthems—Irish, white southern, African American, English, labor, Ulster Unionist, Jewish, Christian, Islamic—do, even though their message is often xenophobic and exclusionary in various degrees. It salves the wounds of those who, for whatever reason, feel they have been crucified.[20]

Drew Gilpin Faust's less radical view that Scarlett O'Hara is a kind of female Thomas Sutpen, the protagonist of Faulkner's *Absalom, Absalom!,* anxious to succeed and similarly oblivious of the travesties of slavery, seems to me to be more in line with actual Irish attitudes in the South at the time of the Civil War. Whether her claim that Mitchell's "ambivalence about the foundations of her own identity translated into contradictions and confusions in the novel's narrative and depictions of character" is true, however,

20. A popular Atlanta reporter wrote that after the premiere in December 1939, "Men and women who had never understood quite rightly what the old folks meant when they told in trembling voices their passionate stories of those days knew at last what their grandfathers fought for, what their grandmothers suffered for"; see Harold Martin, "Atlanta's Most Brilliant Event," in Harwell, 148.

is another matter. I would suggest rather that in light of Irish-Southern social realities, there is a good deal less "confusion" than Faust supposes.[21]

I want to argue, then, that *Gone with the Wind* is far more Irish—and far more Catholic in its references also—than has generally been acknowledged. In seeking to expose Mitchell's "misrecognitions," misrecognitions of a different kind have been imposed on her text. Mitchell does call into question an excessively romantic view of the Old South—Rhett Butler, for example, sometimes sounds like the disillusioned protagonist of Ernest Hemingway's *A Farewell to Arms*—but she also affirms much of it in her implied criticism of Scarlett. Certainly, the view that it is the strong that survive—and those also who forget or know least about the past—is stressed, and there is even some sense in which peasant virtues can triumph where more aristocratic ones lead to downfall. But it is always implied that Scarlett needs both to know more and to feel more. Most unnoticed of all is that although the Irish and Catholic themes are strongly present, there is much variation—as one should expect—in their representation and meaning; in other words, there are several Irishnesses here.

While Scarlett is again and again identified as being like her father— "There was something vital and earthy and coarse about him that appealed to her"; "she possessed in some degree these same qualities"—in fact she wishes to be more like her mother. At least the matter is not as simple as some critics have suggested. Even at the very beginning of the novel she is described equivocally as having "the delicate features of her mother, a Coast aristocrat of French descent, and the heavy ones of her florid Irish father."[22]

From their names, it would seem that several families in the novel must be of Irish descent—both the "trash" Slatterys and the more bourgeois Kennedys, for example—but their ethnicity isn't referred to at all. Gerald, with his brogue and his "short sturdy legs," apparently described by his prospective Charleston in-laws as a "bandy-legged little Irishman," is stereotypically Irish—"His was as Irish a face as could be found in the length and breadth of the homeland he had left so long ago—round, high colored, short nosed, wide mouthed and belligerent"—but his two immigrant brothers in Savannah are said to be tall and wide-shouldered.[23]

21. Drew Gilpin Faust, "Clutching the Chains That Bind: Margaret Mitchell and *Gone With the Wind*," *Southern Cultures* 5, no. 1 (1999):17.

22. Mitchell, 33, 5.

23. Ibid., 44, 32.

The Irish references, then, are far more than merely token; they are also more nuanced than has been generally acknowledged. They point to Mitchell's awareness of such lore in her family and to her research for the novel. Pyron confirms that she worked hard at getting things right, even if some of the authorities she relied on—noted Columbia University historian Charles Beard in particular (who was to have an important influence on the reorientation of Irish historical writing in the late 1930s also)—are now deemed to have been wrong about southern history, especially about the era of Reconstruction.[24]

While the Irish historical asides are sentimental in some ways—and don't quite have the authentic ring of the southern historical pieces—yet they seem very true to how people actually remember and speak about such matters. "The Battle of the Boyne had been fought more than a hundred years before, but, to the O'Haras and their neighbors, it might have been yesterday when their hopes and their dreams, as well as their lands and wealth, went off in the same cloud of dust that enveloped a frightened and fleeing Stuart prince, leaving William of Orange and his hated troops with their orange cockades to cut down the Irish adherents of the Stuarts." The description here, incidentally, of Irish "lands and wealth" that "went off" in a "cloud of dust" with Stuart hopes is surely parallel to the South's fortunes being "gone with the wind." The reference to the Stuarts also shows that the author was familiar with that element as it affected the Irish situation.[25]

A jumbled—but not thereby unconvincing—version of Irish history is on Scarlett's mind when Atlanta is under attack and she refers to the situation as a siege such as she had heard about from her father. "What siege?" asks a puzzled Rhett. "The siege at Drogheda when Cromwell had the Irish, and they didn't have anything to eat and Pa said they starved and died in the streets and finally they ate all the cats and rats and even things like cockroaches. And he said they ate each other too, before they surrendered . . . And when Cromwell took the town all the women were—." Surely Rhett's interjection here that she knows nothing and that her father wasn't alive then, is much sillier than Scarlett's original invocation of the incident, even if his pointing out that "Sherman isn't Cromwell" is saner than her response, "No, but he's worse!"[26]

24. Pyron, 311.

25. Mitchell, 45.

26. Ibid., 303; for what it's worth, recent historians have revised the identity of who was slaughtered by Cromwell's forces at Drogheda, not the fact of the slaughter itself.

A reference to Gerald being irritated at the "blackguardery of the Irish who were being enticed into the Yankee army by bounty money" points to Mitchell's awareness of those same problems that concerned Father Bannon. When a temporarily returned Ashley discusses his possible death, Scarlett "was Irish enough to believe in second sight, especially where death premonitions were concerned, and in his wide gray eyes she saw some deep sadness which she could only interpret as that of a man who has felt the cold finger on his shoulder, has heard the wail of the Banshee"—sentimental and even embarrassing, certainly, but not thereby in any way invalid, and a superstition possibly more common among the Irish than one would like to acknowledge.[27]

When Gerald defies the Yankees who have invaded Tara, the reader is informed about the reasons for his rebellion: "There were too many Irish ancestors crowding behind Gerald's shoulders, men who had died on scant acres, fighting to the end rather than leave the homes where they had lived, plowed, loved, begotten sons." For a postwar Scarlett hearing this: "Of a sudden, the oft-told family tales to which she had listened since babyhood, listened half-bored, impatient and but partly comprehending, were crystal clear. Gerald, penniless, had raised Tara; Ellen had risen above some mysterious sorrow . . . There were the Scarletts who had fought with the Irish volunteers for a free Ireland and been hanged for their pains and the O'Haras who died at the Boyne, battling to the end for what was theirs." When Tony Fontaine has to flee after killing Wilkerson because the latter had urged a black man to woo his sister-in-law, Scarlett "felt herself akin to him, for she remembered the old story how her father had left Ireland, left hastily and by night, after a murder which was no murder to him or to his family. Gerald's blood was in her, violent blood."[28]

Gerald O'Hara is presented as much more than a stock Irish character. He is accurately seen locally as both an outsider and an insider—a "new man" but also a gentleman. Mitchell shows again and again how relative these matters are, how the lower classes can become gentle folk, and how the former aristocracy can fall into decline—as in the cases of several families whose position was built on nothing but "money and darkies" so that after the war, they "will be Cracker in another generation." In fact, her

27. Ibid., 202, 271; for a vivid example of the persistence of superstition in the Ireland of the 1890s, see Angela Bourke's *The Burning of Bridget Cleary* (New York, 2001).

28. Mitchell, 404, 414, 640.

emphasis on the power of economic relations would almost place her in the Marxist school![29]

While Gerald's brogue is both mocked (by Mrs. Tarleton) and affectionately imitated, he himself is happily unwilling to change it for the "lazy, blurred voices" he hears all around him. He does not aspire to a "drawling voice," that elaborate concoction that some southern journalists were to ascribe later to Oscar Wilde's speech during his 1882 visit to the South. In Charleston, meanwhile, irritated by the overly pretentious southern accents of her relatives, Scarlett apes her father's brogue "to her aunt's distress." But Gerald is also described as being vital and as having an unbefuddled Irish head. Although it took him almost ten years to "arrive," the really significant comment is that "he didn't notice it"—not out of ignorance, but rather because his own hierarchies were different than those that prevailed, contingently, in the society of the time.[30]

Somewhat similarly, we are told that "He liked the South, and he soon became, in his own opinion, a Southerner," even if "There was much about the South—and Southerners—that he would never comprehend." Like the Carrolls of Maryland, if far less grandly, Gerald is presented as being anxious to restore the fortunes of the dispossessed O'Haras and conscious—more than others around, one would think—of the *arriviste* position of his Scotch-Irish neighbors, the MacIntoshs, who had been there for seventy years and were earlier in the Carolinas. Hence Scarlett's response on hearing that the MacIntoshs were receiving Union compensation for damaged property: "They never gave aid and comfort to anybody," snapped Scarlett. "Scotch-Irish!"[31]

Mitchell is quite good too at conveying Gerald's not wanting to be rejected by the local families—the reason he goes to Charleston to find a bride—and yet not having any sense of inferiority either. He marches to a different drummer, but one no less real for being inaudible to the ears of most of the social hierarchy of the day. Readers who interpret his consciousness of past dispossessions and loss of social position as merely nostalgic and ethereal surely align themselves with the narrow outlook of those among his contemporaries who didn't know better, and are even more politically regressive than Mitchell herself ever was. O'Hara's is but another instance of the Gaelic poet Eoghan Rua Ó Súilleabháin's sentiment that was quoted earlier:

29. Ibid., 710.
30. Ellis, 254; Mitchell, 139.
31. Mitchell, 46–47, 692.

Ní ins an ainnise is measa linn bheith síos go deo
Ach an tarcaisne a leanas sinn i ndiaidh na leon . . .

[The worst thing is not to be sunk forever in misery, but to face
the insult that follows us, now that the princes have gone . . .]

Scarlett and Gerald are alike, then, in defying convention and in wanting
to make a new beginning free from "the insult that follows us."[32]

Gerald is much more aware of the past than Scarlett is, however. While
on several occasions he is described as being ready to sing a "lugubrious
lament for Robert Emmet: 'She is far from the land where her young hero
sleeps,'" or "The Wearin' o' the Green," one senses that he really does know
something about that whereof he sings. Scarlett "was proud of Gerald and
what he had accomplished unaided except by his shrewd Irish brain," but
she does not realize that he too was engaged in an act of restoration rather
than one of mere creation. Gerald's attachment to the Confederate cause
stems from his Irishness in a way that perhaps Scarlett's pragmatism does
not.[33]

The truth, then, is that there are many kinds of Irish men and women
in the pages of Gone with the Wind. Ashley notes that the new Yankee soldiers include "wild Irishmen who talk Gaelic." After the war, some of these
settle in Atlanta. When Tommy Wellburn has an Irish labor crew building
the new hotel in the city, René Picard comments: "Tommy, you weel own
ze Irish slaves instead of the darky slaves." There is the cruel, prisoner-
driving Johnnie Gallegher, who is fully understood by Scarlett—and she by
him. Gallegher even puts the proverbial curse of Cromwell on her when he
is crossed. And when Scarlett states that there are no Irish servants in Atlanta for nursing babies, she is not merely asserting her own pride in her
ancestry but likely making a factual statement too.[34]

The Irish do not escape "from the insult that follows us," of course.
When Scarlett objects to Rhett's discussion of kissing with "I'd just as soon
kiss a pig," his brusque reply is the old canard that he'd "always heard that
the Irish were partial to pigs—kept them under their beds, in fact." Jonas
Wilkerson attacks Scarlett—rather strangely since he himself is married to
the very Irish-sounding Emmie Slattery—as "highflying, bogtrotting Irish."
During Rhett's reversion to his Charlestonian gentility, he retorts: "Do you

32. Declan Kiberd, Irish Classics (Cambridge, Mass., 2001), 269.
33. Mitchell, 84, 138, 238–39.
34. Ibid., 272, 595.

think I'd let [our daughter] marry any of this runagate gang you spend your time with? Irishmen on the make, Yankees, white trash . . . My Bonnie with her Butler blood and her Robillard strain—." And when Scarlett tries to defend the O'Haras, she is cut off with the rebuttal that they "might have been kings of Ireland once but your father was nothing but a smart Mick on the make. And you are no better—." Had Scarlett cared enough, she might have replied that the only difference between them was that his Butler family had been "on the make" a few generations earlier.[35]

The Catholic theme is present again and again and also in more than token ways. While divorce is not permissible for Catholics, Scarlett would condone it to have Ashley and so she can't pray the rosary. Though it has been months since Scarlett went to church, she tries, vainly as it happens, to find comfort in saying the rosary: "For some time she had felt that God was not watching out for her, the Confederates or the South, in spite of the millions of prayers ascending to Him daily." Scarlett is annoyed to see Carreen praying—"the time for prayer had passed"; God had failed her and therefore she owed Him nothing. Scarlett will even fornicate if it will save Tara, whatever the Church may say, but she is also afraid of dying and going to hell for deceiving Frank Kennedy. Although she neglects her son's Catholic upbringing, we are told that she has an "active Catholic conscience." And there can be few southern belles also who have a sister preparing to enter a convent in Charleston to become a nun.[36]

In the end, at least in the context of this kind of popular romance novel, perhaps we should accept Will Benteen's judgment—the Will who had no class, though Scarlett didn't care since he was in practice a good match for her sister—on Gerald (and, tangentially, on the Irish): "He was a fightin' Irishman and a Southern gentleman and as loyal a Confederate as ever lived. You can't get no better combination than that." At the burial service too, the ancestry-conscious Grandma Fontaine, who recognizes that Scarlett is only part "aristocratic" Robillard—although the nuances of the French social hierarchy aren't explored anywhere in the novel—also states that Will, who is about to take over Tara, will always be a cracker so that "even if he makes a mint of money, he'll never lend any shine and sparkle to Tara, like your father did."[37]

35. Ibid., 304, 528, 891; if one wanted to take the matter to an extreme, one could even argue that the "Butler" name was suggested by Mitchell's interest in English actress Fanny Kemble and her American husband Pierce Butler, about whom she had written an essay earlier. Butler's family was Anglo-Irish, *arrivistes* of another time.

36. Ibid., 280, 329, 502, 935.

37. Ibid., 702, 707–8.

In a way—though one is reluctant to say this and though most Irish commentators would probably be appalled by the suggestion—Margaret Mitchell did indeed revise the concept of southernness, giving the Irish, and especially the Catholic Irish, a natural and emblematic place within it.[38]

In the 1970s, when Alice Walker went with her mother to visit Flannery O'Connor's well-preserved home, Andalusia, in rural Georgia near where Walker herself grew up—a home not very different from what Margaret Mitchell had been familiar with—she did not see it as the remnant of specifically English, Scottish, or much less of Irish rule but simply as a typical dwelling of a middle-to-upper-class white family of a century earlier, an ensemble made complete by the standard, decaying black cabin in the back. Much as she had admired O'Connor's writing and empathized with her illness and early death, at that point Walker was conscious only of the fact that:

> There are rich people who own houses to live in and poor people who do not. What I feel at the moment of knocking is fury that someone is paid to take care of her house, though no one lives in it, and that her house still, in fact, stands, while mine—which of course we never owned anyway—is slowly rotting to dust. Her house becomes—in an instant—the symbol of my own disinheritance, and for that instant I hate her guts. All that she has meant to me is diminished, though her diminishment within me is against my will.

Walker here registers a dismay and protest against the structure of things that in a strange, tangential way, may not have been very different from Gerald O'Hara's when he first came to his Georgia county. But the circumstances of the time had also allowed him to have more hope of reconstructing his lost Irish fortunes and of holding on to them in the face of all opposition—Creek, white, or even black. In a revisioning of southernness, this Irishman had simply become part of the planter landscape.[39]

Put differently: it was understandable that those first Scotch-Irish immigrants to what would become the American South should have seen a

---

38. A few years ago when I was invited to give a talk about the subject of the present book to an Irish studies group at a University of California campus, my inviter, an Irish-born academic, balked when I said that I would probably be mentioning *Gone with the Wind* in passing.

39. Alice Walker, *In Search of Our Mothers' Gardens* (New York, 1983), 58, 57.

similarity between their situation in the old country and that in the new. Not only was colonial America, whatever the freedoms it offered, dominated by an English ruling class of largely Anglican persuasion, but even after independence it was easy to imagine Andrew Jackson's war with Britain as a prolongation of earlier confrontations at home. It was understandable too that later generations of Scotch-Irish, firmly settled in a new, largely Protestant, country, should have seen themselves as southerners first and been less aware of where they had come from—especially since there had been relatively few additions to their numbers from Ireland in the preceding decades—the more ambitious among them blending into the generic, white, Anglo culture.

Likewise even with those significantly smaller numbers of Irish Catholic background, whether they had immigrated earlier or later, who saw Southern nationalism as replicating their own—to the extent of playing down or ignoring the plight of the slaves—and then, after the traumatic demise of their short-lived new country, joined the party of the lost cause and became less concerned with Ireland. A fresh new defeat had inscribed itself over a cragged old one.

The sense of a shared *southern* identity had only been strengthened by a war that had begun with the piecemeal secession of individual states, and even if there were serious tensions between Scotch-Irish and Irish-Irish from time to time—as we see from Margaret Mitchell's novel and as she herself witnessed in the Klan-controlled Atlanta of her youth, with its outbreaks of militant anti-Catholicism—in a more basic sense they were all *white* southerners now. In a way, one might say that they were lost to Ireland, and that Ireland was lost to them. "Tara," "Shamrock," "Connemara," or whatever they chose to call their southern homes, would now be in Georgia and Louisiana and South Carolina, not in the glens of Antrim or on the plains of County Meath or in the bogs of Connaught. A new era had begun, an era in which the active remembrance of kin would give way at best to a faint and intermittent consciousness of kinship.[40]

40. Pyron, 6.

{ KINSHIP }

{CHAPTER 6}

CAUSES LOST, REDEMPTIONS FOUND

[The Catholic writer] will feel a good deal more kinship with backwoods prophets and shouting fundamentalists than he will with those politer elements for whom the supernatural is an embarrassment.

—FLANNERY O'CONNOR, "The Catholic Writer in the Protestant South"

The [Irish] people who wept in Gethsemane, who trod the sorrowful way, who died naked on a cross, who went down into hell, will rise again glorious and immortal, will sit on the right hand of God.

—PATRICK PEARSE, *The Sovereign People*

The war changed everything, including the relation between Ireland and the American South. Defeated, poor, and traumatized afterward—Mississippi had to spend a fifth of its first budget on prosthetic limbs—the states of the former Confederacy were no longer an attractive place for the aspiring and hopeful, though individual states did make efforts to recruit European immigrants to augment their own numbers over against the emancipated black, and voting, population. In general, however, when able, both white and black southerners were as eager to leave their region as were the still numerous Irish immigrants to the American Northeast and Midwest to leave their own native country. Besides, competition for wages from the new freedmen meant that it would have been harder than ever for the unskilled Irish to find work in the South. They did not want to pick cotton. Rather, Ireland and the South now were both areas from which there would be a "great migration" out to an America dominated by true blue Yankees.[1]

In Ireland, meanwhile, it was in the interest of the always-struggling nationalist movement to seek to mend its fences with the U.S. government,

1. Wolfgang Schivelbusch, *The Culture of Defeat: On National Trauma, Mourning, and Recovery* (New York, 2003), 38; David T. Gleeson, *The Irish in the South, 1815–1877* (Chapel Hill, 2001), 183.

especially in the aftermath of the New York draft riots, several failed forays of Fenian U.S. army veterans into British Canada in the late 1860s in the cause of Irish independence, and the recent efforts of agitator John Mitchel on behalf of the Confederacy. For a time, a nostalgic attachment to the South continued, but after a few decades with little direct contact through new immigrants, the region was largely forgotten, except by a few Catholic seminaries and religious orders dedicated to staffing what was generally designated as "mission" territory. From then on any similarity between the two places was to be found in comparable historical experiences rather than in direct and ongoing ethnic influence; it was, it might be said, to be a matter of detected affinities rather than of indisputable consanguinities. Nevertheless, it was precisely the number and extent of those affinities that struck several commentators, even if, for a variety of reasons, they also remained unfamiliar to most people on both sides of the Atlantic who did not have the kind of immediate contact that would have made the similarity apparent or, indeed, especially significant.

It should be noted too that many of the things that Ireland and the American South now shared unintentionally in common would have been so even in the absence of any historical connection between them: comparable economic and social conditions, rather than ethnicity, bred comparable experiences. Thus, the white South's semi-colonial status within the Union—exemplified in federal troops' occupation of the rebellious states for a decade, former Confederates who refused to take a loyalty oath being disenfranchised, and the imposition of punitive tariffs on exports to other parts of the country—was very similar to Ireland's within the United Kingdom, a situation of technical legislative equality but where some were less equal than others.

Of course, they were *not* colonies—Ireland was a constituent part of the United Kingdom, the South a constituent part of the United States—and in some ways they each received more positive attention and support from their respective governments than did other parts of the British Isles or America. But Ireland and the American South *were* considered to be outside the mainstream, to be in some way "other." Even certain aspects of the black experience after the war were not unlike those of the Irish at home, though it should be said too that many, and even most, were not. In addition, such distinctions and divisions were made within an Anglophone world, making the comparison between Ireland and the American South all the more applicable.

For a multitude of reasons, then, Ireland within the United Kingdom and the South within the United States have stood out as places of cultural difference, peculiarity, potential, and active rebelliousness, not infrequently too as benighted and impoverished departures from the metropolitan, and supposedly more civilized, norm. Franklin Roosevelt in 1931 famously referred to the South as "the nation's number one economic problem," and the "Irish Question" was to bedevil the Westminster parliament for over a century. Inevitably, there is an element of stereotyping (a process that will be examined in detail in the next chapter) even in sympathetic efforts at understanding why this has been so. Suffice to say for the moment that some of the characterizations in this mode do represent a genuine and not totally inaccurate description of the unique conditions of these two cultures. None more so than the trait with which Ireland and the American South are invariably associated: their unusually strong, even possibly excessive, religious ethos.

Religion has been a recourse among all these groups—Irish Catholic, Irish Protestant, southern black, southern white—for the injustices of history: dispossession, persecution, siege, famine, slavery, occupation, loss, mockery. Religion was there prior to these events, but reinforced by each successive trauma, and even adapted in a variety of ways to secular purposes as a form of what has come to be called "civil religion." No doubt England and the American Northeast also invoked religious sanctions for their own political agendas and military successes; after all, Christianity had been a driving force in the abolitionist movement, while members of the British government during the Irish famine invoked "Providentialism" to explain, or explain away, the disaster. As victors, however, America and Britain were never forced to rely on religion as their only succor to the extent to which the defeated Irish and southerners, or black slaves, were; besides, even the religious viewpoints in Washington and Westminster coexisted with strong secular interpretations of national destinies.

Yet it is in terms of excess, repression, anti-intellectualism, and even bigotry that the Irish and southern versions of religion are best known to the worlds of debate and editorializing that find their centers in New York and London, rather than in those of their respective, if modest, successes in education, medicine, positive missionary ventures abroad, and even as providers of genuine consolation at home. Perhaps this is partly the case because, with some notable exceptions, neither Irish nor southern religion has fared well with writers and intellectuals from the regions themselves. W. J. Cash, Thomas Wolfe, and Richard Wright on the southern side; James Joyce, Seán O'Casey, and Seán O'Faoláin on the Irish, were all—belatedly by general British and American standards—hostile toward their region's religiousness. Joyce's *A Portrait of the Artist as a Young Man* is the classic statement in the genre; its protagonist, Stephen Dedalus, boldly declares: "I will not serve that in which I no longer believe whether it call itself my home, my fatherland or my church." This sense of an overall hostility to religion remains even when we see that Stephen's rejection is bound by the parameters of his early religious formation: asked if he is about to become a Protestant, he retorts "What kind of liberation would that be to forsake an absurdity which is logical and coherent and to embrace one which is illogical and incoherent?" For these and other writers, the worlds immediately beyond their native boundaries represented less those of their traditional oppressors, British or Yankee, than centers of artistic possibility and openness, places free of "absurdity" whether Catholic or Protestant. They left the darkness for the light, even if in later years many of them were to become skeptical that the world could be so neatly rendered in such black and white terms.[2]

It is noteworthy that the religion that such southern and Irish writers abandoned was seen on both sides as originating in the Celtic imagination. Following this vein in his study of the development of the Irish mind, Seán O'Faoláin has argued that the Irish Celt's religion, "as opposed to those of the Greeks and Hebrews," was "basically imaginative rather than intellectual." O'Faoláin implies that this element survived even after the advent of Christianity in the fifth century. When American commentators such as H. L. Mencken and W. J. Cash came to explain what was wrong with the postwar South, especially its excessive preoccupation with religion, they too attributed this unfortunate aberration to the region's being essentially Celtic. Cash was aware of his own Scotch-Irish ancestry when he remarked that the people there were Celtic and that the Celtic blood strain is "of all Western strains the most susceptible to suggestions of the supernatural. Even when he was a sort of native pagan, knowing little of the Bible and hooting contemptuously at parsons, he was nevertheless at bottom religious. Ancestral phobias grappled him toward the old center, and immemorial awes, drawn in with his mother's milk, whispered imperative warning in his ears." However much this magnificently evocative passage aspires to objective analysis, there is, of course, an edge to Cash's comments: southerners might like to think of themselves as Anglo-Saxons, he implies, but

2. James Joyce, *A Portrait of the Artist as a Young Man* (New York, 1977), 246–47, 244.

they are really Celts and thereby, unfortunately, overly superstitious and religious.[3]

In case any smug complacency in the matter might linger among upper-class southerners not readily identified with such superstitions, Cash went into some detail on the subject. He pointed out, for example, that southern religion, even among most of the planters, was not high-toned Anglicanism: "What our Southerner required . . . was a faith as simple and emotional as himself. A faith to draw men together in hordes, to terrify them with Apocalyptic rhetoric, to cast them into the pit, rescue them, and at last bring them shouting into the fold of grace. A faith not of liturgy and prayer book, but of primitive frenzy and the blood sacrifice." What they wanted, Cash concluded dismissively, "was the God and the faith of the Methodists and the Baptists, and the Presbyterians."[4]

Whatever their degree of disdain and hostility, however, what all of these commentaries establish beyond doubt is that both places have been exceptionally religious. Precisely because of their bias, however, it remains to detail some of this religiousness more clearly, and more sympathetically. It is particularly necessary to further illustrate the underlying similarity because of an apparent opposition between a Protestant South and a Catholic Ireland, between a faith of supposedly raw emotion and one of supposedly restrained, if exotic, ritualism.

Even allowing for their mutual antagonisms, one tends to think of the different groups of people in Ireland and the American South—Presbyterians, Roman Catholics, Methodists, Baptists (black and white), even Anglicans and Episcopalians—as all being more overtly religious than the general society of England or the Northeast. This is not just a matter of perception: statistics bear out the conclusion. There is a greater degree of church attendance, a more frequent invocation of the divinity, and, at least in the public mind, a greater measure of prejudice and intolerance than elsewhere. It is reported that black slaves on Catholic-owned plantations frequently abandoned that church because they were not allowed to "shout" at the services, but it is the intense concern of all of the denominational services with personal salvation that gives them an unusual degree of unity. There is an echo of this phenomenon too in W. E. B. Du Bois's concept of a "double-

---

3. Seán O'Faoláin, *The Irish* (London, 1972), 22, 32; W. J. Cash, *The Mind of the South* (New York, 1969), 56.

4. Cash, 58.

consciousness" in African Americans, the sense that their heritage from Africa is basically—and positively—spiritual, that from America, materialistic. The trope of industrialized England's materialism versus agricultural Ireland's spirituality has long been a commonplace in Irish people's understanding of their political and economic situation. In all, there is less evidence of a secular consciousness, more acceptance of an ultimate purpose in things.[5]

This leads too to the assertion that the institutions of Protestantism and Catholicism have more in common than is often realized, their descriptions at times being almost interchangeable. After all, the "logic" that Joyce claimed for Catholicism has just as often been attributed to a rational Protestantism, the "incoherence" he noted in the latter regarded as the hallmark superstition of the Roman faith. So it is fairly clear that the historically opposing traditions of Protestantism and Catholicism come together in the recent southern and Irish experiences, at least in the sense of shaping overarching world views that are very similar.

Looking for a way to identify and describe this similarity, one might turn to Flannery O'Connor, who was very conscious of the apparently anomalous, and yet strangely not so, situation of the Catholic writer in the Protestant South, giving that title to one of her essays. On the positive side, this similarity comes from sharing the same "skeleton" of beliefs: in spite of the ignorance of the Bible found among her fellow Catholics in Georgia and throughout the South, "When the poor hold sacred history in common [as Catholics and Protestants certainly do], they have ties to the universal and the holy, which allows the meaning of their every action to be heightened and seen under the aspect of eternity." She confesses that she herself had felt "forced to follow the spirit into strange places and to recognize it in many forms not totally congenial" to her. The Catholic writer, she judged:

> will feel a good deal more kinship with backwoods prophets and shouting fundamentalists than he will with those politer elements for whom the supernatural is an embarrassment and for whom religion has become a department of sociology or culture or personality development. His interest and sympathy may very well go—as I know my own does—directly to those aspects of Southern life where the religious feeling is most intense and where its outward forms are farthest from the Catholic . . . The result of

5. W. E. B. Du Bois, *The Souls of Black Folk* (New York, 1999), 16. There are several meanings in Du Bois's use of the term "double-consciousness."

these underground religious affinities will be a strange and, to many, perverse fiction, one which . . . gives us no picture of Catholic life, or the religious experiences that are usual with us, but I believe that it will be Catholic fiction.

It was certainly a position that O'Connor herself succeeded in embodying, for it is hard today to think of another writer more Catholic, or more southern, than she.[6]

Seamus Heaney, who is also of Catholic background, reports a similar awareness, if in a less assertively religious way, in his poem "The Other Side." Here, the narrator—presumably Heaney himself—comes upon a Protestant neighbor pausing outside the door of the Heaneys' Catholic home in 1950s Northern Ireland until he is sure the family has completed the nightly saying of the rosary. The neighbor is shy about interrupting a religious practice that he neither understands nor approves of. "Your side of the house, I believe, / hardly rule by the Book at all," is his mildly critical comment. The Catholic Heaneys, in turn, among themselves at least, gently mock his patriarchal references to "Lazarus, the Pharaoh, Solomon // and David and Goliath," references that, the poet confesses, were "like loads of hay / too big for our small lanes." While the poem gestures toward the domination of Protestants ("big"), even those of goodwill, over Catholics ("small") in the province, more important is its pointing to the shared religiousness of the peoples of Northern Ireland.[7]

Less apparent, however, but of importance for the present study, is the wider context of Heaney's poem: Ireland, often conceived of as almost an entirely Catholic country, is, when taken as a whole, significantly Protestant, about one-fifth of its five million people professing some form of that faith. Its nationalist pantheon is full of Protestants, even if some of them were only culturally such: Wolfe Tone, leader of the 1798 rebellion and the father of Irish Republicanism; doomed romantic Robert Emmet, who has a statue and a park named after him in Savannah; Thomas Davis, Young Ireland poet and editor of the *Nation*; William Smith O'Brien of the '48 rebellion; John Mitchel; Irish Home Rule leader Charles Stewart Parnell; and Roger Casement, who won a knighthood for exposing Belgium's mistreatment of blacks in the Congo and went on to be hanged as an Irish martyr for his part in the 1916 rebellion, to name just a few. In turn, the suppos-

6. Flannery O'Connor, *Mystery and Manners* (New York, 1977), 203, 207.
7. Seamus Heaney, *Poems, 1965–1975* (New York, 1981), 112–14.

edly Protestant South has significant pockets of Catholicism in Kentucky, Louisiana, and Alabama, while the region itself has produced a surprising number of Catholic writers in the twentieth century: O'Connor, Allen Tate, Caroline Gordon, Katherine Anne Porter, and Walker Percy among them. Moreover, the religious minister most frequently associated with Northern Irish Protestantism (though he doesn't represent a majority of his co-religionists within it), the Reverend Ian Paisley, holds his highest theological qualification from Bob Jones University in South Carolina, a fact not lost on his critics who accuse him of showing the same narrow-mindedness and bigotry that they believe are endemic to the American South. In any case, the sentiment of American southern Protestantism is not totally alien, for good and for bad, to the Irish experience.

The idea that there is an underlying Celtic propensity in both groups—rather than the pressure of particular historical, economic and social forces—to be "religious" is suspect, however. What is most surprising about religion in the South is that originally there was not that much of it. A city like Charleston may have had lots of churches of various denominations, but many parts of the rural South were sometimes without any church at all. As Christine Leigh Heyrman has observed, "By 1790, [only] about 14 percent of southern whites and nearly 4 percent of blacks belonged to Baptist, Methodist, or Presbyterian churches." With so many unchurched in the region, even Thomas Jefferson was of the opinion that "Unitarianism would triumph among his countrymen within a generation." As Heyrman points out, "There was . . . nothing inevitable about the triumph of evangelicalism in the South." The *saints* resided in the New England states.[8]

Here too, rather surprisingly perhaps, we find that Ireland also in the late eighteenth and early part of the nineteenth century appears to have been a highly unchurched society. A vastly increased population—likely the result of the nutritional benefits of the potato tuber originally brought there from South America—as well as a shortage of priests as a consequence of the Penal Laws were part of the problem. The early and mid-nineteenth century was a time of religious renewal, however—just as the Great Revival at the end of the eighteenth century had been in the South—when what is now termed the "devotional revolution" took place. Both the Anglican and Catholic churches in Ireland were in need of reform—the Catholic partly because, as Seán Connolly indicates, "Up to 1766 the exiled Stuarts were

8. Christine Leigh Heyrman, *Southern Cross: The Beginnings of the Bible Belt* (New York, 1997), 23.

permitted to nominate [bishops] to all vacant Irish sees." The devotional revolution that Cardinal Paul Cullen strengthened, if not quite initiated, was a kind of mirror image of the evangelicalism of the Protestant churches, Anglican, Presbyterian, and Methodist. Cullen was anxious to curtail Catholic attendance at popular Protestant revival services. So, although these movements were very different from each other in many ways, they were alike in stressing religious devotion and in encouraging aggressive missionary efforts, some Presbyterians and Methodists in Ulster even using the Gaelic language to try to convert Catholics. As a result of this activity, by the 1860s levels of religious practice for both Catholics and Protestants were unusually high by general European standards.[9]

Notions of apocalypse also pervaded both Catholic and Protestant mindsets of the time. Protestants were frightened by the Irish Catholic millenarian ideas of Pastorini, the pseudonym for an English Catholic bishop, Charles Walmesley, which prophesized the second coming of Christ. Such ideas, especially popular during the typhus epidemic of 1817 and the near famine of the early 1820s, provided the poor and powerless with "the prospect of a divinely-ordained overthrow of the existing social and political order." Their emphasis on sectarian conflict also coincided with Daniel O'Connell's efforts to win Catholic emancipation. In the end, "militant Protestantism and militant Catholicism, products of the same general religious revival, were also mutually reinforcing movements."[10]

There were other features in common too, even in the methods of arousing religious enthusiasm. While evangelical religion was very much different from the rituals of Roman Catholicism, there were elements in Catholic practice that bore some resemblance to Protestant "enthusiasm" and that affected not only those Irish workers who moved to England but even the people at home through missions led by ardent Redemptorist and Jesuit preachers such as Father Bannon. Capuchin Father Theobald Mathew's temperance movement of the 1840s consciously borrowed from its evangelical counterparts. Again, according to Roger Finke, "The kind of Catholic Church the Irish brought with them to America had much more in common with the upstart Protestant sects than it did with the Catholicism of the 'Catholic' nations of Europe." But even the latter had a device

9. Seán Connolly, *Religion and Society in Nineteenth-Century Ireland* (Dublin, 1987), 11–12; Janice Holmes, *Religious Revivals in Britain and Ireland, 1859–1905* (Portland, Ore., 2000), 82. Cardinal Cullen was contemptuous of the American revivalists Moody and Sankey but also aware of their attractiveness to the less educated members of his flock.

10. Connolly, 24.

called *svegliarini,* described as "emotional preaching in the streets, Italian-style," which Catholic preachers in England and Ireland adopted as a model for their revivals. "One such mission to the men of dockland [in London]," notes Sheridan Gilley, "concluded in a chapel crowded to suffocation with a wild masculine outpouring of emotion as all 'burst forth into one long continued wail and lament' for their sins during the closing sermon." Gilley admits that "This kind of service bore many of the marks of Protestant re-vivalism, for Evangelicals and Ultramontanes [Catholics who stressed the authority of the pope as opposed to that of the local bishops] touched at a number of points, in their call of the agonized conscience to repentance in the midst of scenes of mass fervour, cathartically relieved in the ecstasy of promised forgiveness through the all-atoning Blood of the Lamb."[11]

Father Frederick W. Faber in particular, a power in both England and Ireland after his conversion from various evangelical forms of Christianity to Catholicism, "was glad to confess his debt to Nonconformity, explicitly preferring 'the pattern of the Wesleyans and Whitfieldians to the calm so-briety and subdued enthusiasm of the Protestant Establishment.'" He judged "the English poor instinctively right for honouring 'the coarse tyr-anny' of an unprepossessing Methodism above 'the mild, considerate and good-natured rule of Anglicans.'" Instead of obscure Latin hymns, Faber wanted "the vernacular hymn set to the tune of a drinking song." It was the duty of the Catholic missionary "to get the masses to gather, to bring them within earshot of his vulgar sermons, to excite them to a feverish sorrow for sin by any spiritual claptrap he can hit upon." The English Faber went on to write "Faith of Our Fathers," a hymn that would be sung with great gusto at·major Irish Gaelic sporting events well past the middle of the twen-tieth century, the Irish leaving out (and generally being unaware of) the verses devoted to the hope of a restoration of *English* Catholicism. It is amusing, if not surprising, now to find unbelieving Irish journalist and nov-elist Colm Tóibín confess that he had always thought "Faith of Our Fathers" an Irish hymn until an equally unbelieving Terry Eagleton recited the com-plete version for him in a pub in Oxford in the 1990s.[12]

All of this emphasis on the underlying similarities—O'Connor's "under-

11. Finke, in *Acts of Faith: Explaining the Human Side of Religion,* ed. Rodney Stark and Roger Finke (Berkeley, 2000), 136; Sheridan Gilley, "Catholic Faith of the Irish Slums: London, 1840–70," in *The Victorian City: Images and Realities,* ed. H. J. Dyos and Michael Wolff (Lon-don, 1973), 2:838, 839.

12. Gilley, 840; Colm Tóibín, *The Sign of the Cross: Travels in Catholic Europe* (New York, 1994), 255.

ground religious affinities"—between nineteenth-century Protestantism and Catholicism is not to deny or ignore the sometimes fierce opposition between Protestants and Catholics, or the proscription of the latter by organizations such as the KKK as un-American and un-southern, but to stress a shared commitment to supernatural values, even if the participants lost sight of the overall kinship by focusing on the minutiae of their denominational differences. As a further token of this interrelatedness of seemingly disparate religious practices, it has been noted, for example, in the twentieth-century South that mountain homes and churches often display Catholic pictures of the Sacred Heart, a popular motif with them "given their heart-centered religion," but that they "do not identify it as Roman Catholic."[13]

These similar religious beliefs have made it possible for Irish people and southerners of all stripes to find a meaningful interpretation of their experiences as dispossessed, unfree, starved, disenfranchised, to feel, in short— and however unjustifiably at times—that they were ultimately superior to those who proclaimed them inferior. This was the true "sentimental power" of their religion. Whether they claimed *"extra ecclesia nulla salus"* ("no salvation outside the Church"), as Catholics did, or thought of themselves as a "chosen" group, as was the case with most Protestants, they all knew— white *and* black—that they were indeed the people of God. This is an aspect of their experience that a wholly secular approach often misses. In the next section of this chapter, then, I explore how these various developments are represented in the black, southern white Protestant, and Irish Roman Catholic and Protestant experiences, respectively. Even when considered simply as expressions of ideology that mask deeper social tensions—or what Anglo-Irish writer Elizabeth Bowen described in a more jaundiced phrase as symptoms of an "incontinence of the soul"—they are, nevertheless, significant.[14]

Although both Frederick Douglass and Harriet Jacobs in their respective narratives stress how negative an impact religious conversion often had on white slave owners—making them much crueler once they had discovered

13. Deborah Vansau McCauley, *Appalachian Mountain Religion: A History* (Urbana, Ill., 1995), 168.

14. See, for example, Niall Ó Ciosáin's similar criticisms of David Lloyd's explanation of the Irish religious perception of the famine as "a form of amnesia or complicity in catastrophe by its victims": "Famine Memory and the Popular Representation of Scarcity," in *History and Memory in Modern Ireland,* ed. Ian McBride (New York, 2001), 114; Victoria Glendinning, *Elizabeth Bowen* (New York, 1979), 19.

biblical justification for their practices—it is also the case that religion (in this instance, the Christian religion almost exclusively) provided emotional and psychic comfort for most of the slaves themselves in their confinement. White historians have been commenting on this circumstance for several decades now, beginning, surprisingly, with then-Marxist Eugene Genovese in *Roll, Jordan, Roll* in 1974. Lawrence W. Levine too—opposing the previously reigning idea that black bondage was total, physically and psychologically—stresses this "sentimental power" (not his term) of religion among the slaves, showing at one point how it was in continuity with their African culture and how it could even be reinforced by a not-necessarily-sympathetic white preacher.[15]

Levine quotes an ex-slave's account of how a spiritual might come into being:

> We'd all be at the 'prayer house' de Lord's day, and de white preacher he's splain the word and read whar Esekial done say—*Dry bones gwine ter lib ergin*—And, honey, de Lord would come a-shinin' thoo dem pages and revive dis ole nigger's heart, and I'd jump up dar and den and holler and shout and sing and pat, and dey would all cotch de words and I'd sing it to some ole shout song I'd heard 'em sing from Africa, and dey'd all take it up and keep at it, and keep a-addin' to it, and den it would be a spiritual.

The message had a power that was independent of the social agendas and personal inadequacies of the messenger.[16]

Levine goes on to stress that "the single most persistent image the slave songs contain . . . is that of the chosen people." The singers were convinced that "To the promised land I'm bound to go." Whites believed this about their own destinies, of course, but the message in the case of the slaves "offers an insight into the kinds of barriers the slaves had available to them against the internalization of the stereotyped images their masters held and attempted consciously and unconsciously to foist upon them." Their spiri-

---

15. In his excellent chapter on "The Discovery of Southern Religious History," in *Interpreting Southern History*, ed. Boles and Evelyn Thomas Nolen (Baton Rouge, 1987), John B. Boles observes that while "Genovese made no use of church records, underestimated the extent to which blacks and whites worshiped together, and revealed a simplistic understanding of the white evangelical religion with which he compared slave religion . . . never again after his book would slave Christianity be dismissed as unimportant or as merely an 'opiate' for hapless black masses" (518–19).

16. Lawrence W. Levine, *The Unpredictable Past: Explorations in American Cultural History* (New York, 1993), 40–41.

tuals, according to Levine, offered the slaves a world view similar to that which they had had in Africa, "and afforded them the possibility of both adapting to and transcending their situation." Moreover, although their songs "were characterized more by a feeling of confidence than of despair," this focus was not totally on the next world. Indeed, they didn't make an absolute distinction between sacred and secular. They preferred the triumphant figures of the bible—Daniel, David, Joshua, Moses, King Jesus—to those admonitions in it (from St. Paul, in particular) to be submissive.[17]

White historians like Genovese and Levine, however, have in part been picking up on a theme long present in black scholars' accounts of their own tradition. The earliest black American historians tended to see the painful experience of the race in a providential way. They believed that all history was directed by God and that "the Negroes' achievement in the United States was part of a providential system: to elevate the race in America and Africa. God in his mysterious way was using the Negro for beneficial ends, and the blacks' passage from slavery to freedom was the clearest evidence of this progress." Historian Clarence Walker explains that:

> No black spokesperson or intellectual in the nineteenth century thought that God had willed Negroes to be slaves for white Americans, but even slavery and the slave trade could be interpreted as part of a providential design. "God seeing the African standing in need of civilization, sanctioned for a while the slave trade," Henry M. Turner told an Emancipation Day celebration in 1866, "not that it was in harmony with his fundamental laws for one man to rule another, nor did he ever contemplate that the Negro was to be reduced to the status of a vassal, but as a subject for moral and intellectual culture. So God winked, or lidded his eyeballs, at the institution of slavery as a test of the white man's obedience, and elevation of the negro." Despite human cupidity, God's purpose for blacks would be realized. In short, God would bring good out of evil.

Why God had allowed slavery to occur in the first place remained a problem, however. Walker cites a number of what appear to be rather ad hoc explanations offered by early black historians, ranging from punishment for their abandoning monotheism for polytheism and idolatry to "gross sins and abominations." Even Booker T. Washington was to argue that slavery had some mysterious part in God's providential plan for the betterment of the race.[18]

17. Ibid., 45, 46, 48, 52.
18. Clarence Walker, *Deromanticizing Black History: Critical Essays and Reappraisals* (Knoxville, 1991), 89–90, 91; Booker T. Washington, *Up from Slavery* (New York, 1986), 16–17.

Furthermore—and this is a point that reinforces those of Genovese and Levine—these early histories show black people not as passive victims, but rather as "shapers of their own destiny . . . They resist slavery, become free, acquire property, build institutions, and fight in America's wars." And even their revolts, from Nat Turner's violent rebellion in the early 1800s to the struggle for civil rights in the 1960s with its nonviolent philosophy, had their roots deep in religious belief. Today in the United States, African Americans remain the single group allowed to have themselves represented by openly religious ministers without provoking the hostile censure of the liberal or even conservative political establishment.[19]

The religious experiences of southern whites bore many resemblances to those of blacks: after all, until the end of the Civil War, both populations often attended the same churches and heard the same sermons. In radically different yet also intimately related ways, each felt that they were a "chosen" people. For example, Levine notes that "many of those whites who flocked to the camp meetings of the Methodists and Baptists were themselves on the social and economic margins of their society, and had psychic and emotional needs which, qualitatively, may not have been vastly different from those of black slaves." Or as W. E. B. Du Bois put the matter in a slightly different context: "the religion of the poor whites is a plain copy of Negro thought and methods."[20]

While it has been argued that one of the attractions of evangelical revivalism was that it assuaged a feeling of guilt that slaveowners felt, it was more often the case that the early Baptist and Methodist missionaries' opposition to slavery on biblical grounds was what made it difficult for them to win converts among the unchurched. Only when they slowly and reluctantly compromised their positions in the interests of winning over the slaveholding classes did their numbers grow. As John Boles notes, the churches were "Essentially subservient to the slaveholding interests . . . even when they were unwilling to defend slavery in the abstract." Many of them found biblical justification for the institution, even seeing it as God's providential way of offering the benefits of salvation to the people of Africa (a concept not very different from the one previously ascribed to black leaders). Making an observation that Frederick Douglass and Harriet Jacobs would have had difficulty agreeing with, Boles argues, however, that the

19. Walker, 91–92.
20. Levine, 38; Du Bois, 121.

evangelical ministers "did not always accept abuses of the ideals of the system. They worked to regularize marriage relations between slaves, used moral pressure to minimize physical and sexual mistreatment, and exhorted masters to care for the spiritual needs of the slaves long before the rise of modern abolitionism." But he admits that they also "criticized northern abolitionists for harming the cause of slave religion by making slave owners suspicious of ministers." Their own main concern was with converting the slaves because they believed "one's otherworldly destination more important than one's status in this world."[21]

In general, the main emphasis of all of the churches was on individual holiness rather than on social reform. Individual unholiness, not social injustice, had brought about the crisis that led to the war. Meanwhile, the biblical and theological debates that were exercising some of the best minds in the North, in England, and in Germany, and that would eventually alter the twentieth-century religious landscape, were hardly of any interest to southerners at all.

In the case of the Irish, the 1840s famine obviously posed serious problems for religious belief in a way very similar to those of slavery (for blacks) and the Civil War (for whites). The historical record shows that the people saw the famine largely in religious terms—as a form of punishment for not making the best use of previous harvests—rather than in political ones. According to Graham Davis in his examination of peasant folklore, there is a significant "gap" between their perceptions of the disaster and academic history, a gap that "appears to qualify [John] Mitchel's popular thesis that the Famine was the fault of the British government." Thus, as Davis notes, "The surviving evidence . . . points to a predominantly religious explanation of the potato blight. Contemporaries believed that the very abundance of the crops in good years had made people careless of their good fortune and wasteful of the Lord's bounty." From this point of view, the famine "was assumed to be a scourge from God, a punishment for the abuse of plenty." In other words, individual unholiness again.[22]

In a broader sense, much of the discourse of Irish Catholicism at the time was one of chosenness and religious election to a degree that even believers today would probably find offensive. Take, for example, the obser-

---

21. Boles, 532.

22. Graham Davis, "The Historiography of the Irish Famine," in *The Meaning of the Famine*, ed. Patrick O'Sullivan (Leicester, UK, 1997), 15–39.

vations that the first prior of Mount Melleray, the noted Trappist monastery prominently featured in Joyce's "The Dead," wrote in 1832 when Irish monks had been driven out of France by that country's aggressively secular government:

> Oh, happy Ireland! Whose faith, unconquered by ages of persecution, shines brilliantly on this never-to-be-forgotten day! That faith which in the past rendered thee supereminent among the countries of Catholic Europe, purified and strengthened by centuries of suffering, burns now more beautifully bright amid the environing darkness of apostate nations . . . Unhappy France! Behold the contrast, as discreditable to thee as it is honourable to Ireland. Those religious men whom thou didst so lately treat with contempt and refined cruelty, whom thou didst imprison as criminals and expel as traitors, because they were loyal to their Lord and to their religion, are now cherished and revered by the faithful Irish, the chosen people of the latter ages.

In the light of a profusion of recent commentary, much of it legitimate, on the degradation of the Irish during the nineteenth century, one might be struck both by the internationalism and the confidence of this assessment rather than depressed by its quaint language and overweening pride. Terry Eagleton has described the same phenomenon in twentieth-century England: "We Catholics were of course a minority in England; but we did not value the marginal or minoritarian, in the manner of a later postmodernism. On the contrary, it was we who had a monopoly of truth, and the majority who were out of line."[23]

Studies of Ulster Protestantism too have argued that such a religious identity cannot be reduced to a mere ideology whose only function is to maintain the status quo. Rather, it is a belief system that has been deeply influenced by American Fundamentalism and one that sees the threat of Catholicism as most dangerous when the Catholics preach ecumenism, not when they are being intransigent. There is a strong belief that, as the Reverend Ian Paisley has claimed, "God has a purpose for this province, and this plant of Protestantism sown here in the north-eastern part of this island." Terence Brown further complicates things by pointing out that the Presbyterian Church in Northern Ireland with its "theories of Calvinist destiny, of Calvinist soul histories" has produced a "mind different from that of the

---

23. Ailbe J. Luddy, *The Story of Mount Melleray* (Dublin, 1932), 77–78; Terry Eagleton, *The Gatekeeper: A Memoir* (New York, 2002), 37.

nationalists." He refers too to the popularity of the Scofield Bible, "a Bible that lists beside its text a whole series of dispensations, within which many Ulster Protestants have seen their own human destiny working itself out before the divine light of God."[24]

In short, southern whites and blacks, and Irish Protestants and Catholics, all believed that it was their religious faith that helped them endure slavery, defeat, attack, and starvation. On the evidence, it would be hard to disagree with them, however illusory and unfounded a more philosophical or materialistic understanding might argue their hopes to have been.

But religion was, of course, deeply implicated in the politics and social workings of Irish and southern cultures. It was the foundation of the "cultural nationalism" of both places. We saw this to some extent in the case of Father Bannon, but it was only after the South's defeat in 1865 that such religion-based cultural or civic nationalism was to become all-pervasive in the region. Its existence in Ireland had a much longer gestation.

White southerners had felt God was on their side during the war and so were puzzled by their defeat. Southern ministers argued that "the Crusading Christian Confederates had enacted the Christian drama, but without a resurrection and redemption to complete the myth." The Lost Cause movement, therefore, promised the needed "resurrection and redemption." It was a movement infused, as Boles notes, "with Protestant evangelical values," and it "became an authentic expression of religion, celebrated with and perpetuated by its own rituals, mythology, and theology, and complete with its own heroes, evangelists, and promotional institutions." The placing of a statue of Robert E. Lee in the company of John Wesley, Savonarola, and Martin Luther, at the main entrance to the Duke University chapel is a prime example of this intimate association between religion and sectional piety. Charles Reagan Wilson has pointed out that in the period before official Lost Cause organizations came into being (around 1875), "the individual who best captured the mood of the South" was Father Abram Ryan. It was Ryan, along with others, who "particularly expressed their public anguish and concern on the special days appointed for humiliation, fasting, prayer, or thanksgiving."[25]

24. Quoted in Ronald A. Wells, "A Fearful People: Religion and the Ulster Conflict," Éire-Ireland 28, no. 1 (1993): 68; Brown, in Styles of Belonging: The Cultural Identities of Ulster, ed. Jean Lundy and Aodán Mac Póilin (Belfast, 1992), 44, 43.

25. Boles, 532; Charles Reagan Wilson, Baptized in Blood: The Religion of the Lost Cause, 1865–1920 (Athens, Ga., 1980), 61.

Richmond, the former capital of the Confederacy, became the Mecca of the Lost Cause with its many statues to the defeated leaders—Jackson and Lee among the most notable—along Monument Boulevard. In sermons and revivals that called for moral reform, southerners were recommended to imitate the virtuous lives of these heroes. Well past the mid-twentieth century, the Episcopal diocese of Alabama at its annual convention honored Robert E. Lee as "a sterling example of Christian virtue," while in the 1960s, Eli N. Evans interviewed an elderly Jewish dowager in Virginia who claimed to find "inspiration" by looking at Lee's portrait. Various schools and colleges throughout the South—the University of the South in Sewanee, Tennessee, being the most prominent among them—acted as propagators of this Christian Confederate ethos, which they passed on to generations of future political, professional, and business leaders. In this manner a new southern identity was created from the wreckage of war and defeat.[26]

From such a perspective, the institution of slavery was seen not as a reason for feeling guilty but rather as God's providential way of civilizing and saving blacks. The very growth of black churches after the war—Du Bois commented that "practically every American Negro is a church member"—only confirmed the white view in the righteousness of their cause. The original Ku Klux Klan too arose out of this mentality. It was, Wilson argues, "a vital organization of the religion of the Lost Cause." Reflecting "the mystical Celtic roots of early Scotch, Irish, and Scotch-Irish Southern settlers," the semi-religious nature of the Klan was expressed in the "mysterious appearance" of its members who dressed themselves "like medieval penitents in robes, usually ghostly white or demonic black." Meanwhile, Protestant religious leaders were among the main supporters of the Klan, seeing its violent activities as a necessary defense "of our rights and homes." A Klan ceremony would end, Wilson notes, "with the singing of the hymn 'How Firm a Foundation.'"[27]

A similar unification of religion and national cause had long thrived in Ireland, though it was not without its periodic ups and downs. Marianne Elliott has argued in *The Catholics of Ulster* that the dispossessed Irish nobility

26. J. Barry Vaughn, "The Pilgrim Way: A Short History of the Episcopal Church in Alabama," in *Our Church*, ed. Caleb Dawson and Jesse Hamner (Tuscaloosa, Ala., 1995), 18; Eli N. Evans, *The Provincials: A Personal History of Jews in the South* (New York, 1997), 91.

27. Du Bois, 122; Wilson, 111, 113.

of the 1600s—the O'Neills and O'Donnells and similar families—kept the memory of their misfortunes very much alive in the community over the next 200 years mainly through having family members enter the church as priests and missionaries who stressed the need to right ancient wrongs that were as much religious as they were political. With the anti-religious French Revolution in 1789, however, the Church became wary of nationalist movements, a wariness only exacerbated by the anti-papal drive toward Italian unification in the nineteenth century. A young Daniel O'Connell, whose monarchist uncle had fled France for England in 1789, had not been at all sympathetic with the French and American-inspired birth of Irish republicanism in the 1798 rebellion. The prominence of ecumenically minded Protestants in the popular Young Ireland movement of the 1840s was further reason for caution, and it was Catholic clerical opposition to the 1848 rebellion that brought about its total collapse. The advent of the secretly organized Fenians in the 1860s provoked a notorious condemnation from the Bishop of Kerry that "hell wasn't hot enough nor eternity long enough" for them. In general, the Roman Catholic Church felt that it had more to gain from piecemeal negotiations with an overwhelmingly Protestant, but also pragmatic and pro-religious, Westminster government. When the southern part of Ireland became independent in 1922, the Church excommunicated those republican extremists—including De Valera—who were unwilling to accept the compromise made with the British government.[28]

Throughout even this period, however, individual clerics kept alive the long-standing perception that the Irish cause was the Catholic cause—the romantic, but nonetheless deeply felt, idea that the status quo before the 1607 flight of the earls, or the 1601 Battle of Kinsale, needed to be restored. Thus was sustained a symbiotic, if still often tense, alliance between the concepts of nation and faith. As recently as the 1980s, Seamus Heaney could meaningfully criticize this view of history in the work of Irish-language poet Seán Ó Riordáin: "If he [as a nationalist] would obliterate history since Kinsale, the loyalist imagination at its most enthusiastic would obliterate history before Kinsale."[29]

The Irish Christian Brothers, an order founded in the 1820s to educate the poor and lower-middle classes, were instrumental in the creation of such a religion-based nationalist ideology through their teaching of a particular version of Irish history in their many schools—this at a time when the

28. Marianne Elliott, *The Catholics of Ulster: A History* (London, 2001), 76.
29. Quoted in Frank Sewell, *Modern Irish Poetry: A New Alhambra* (New York, 2000), 32.

government-sponsored national schools were focused on a history that tended to exclude things Irish. After the fall of Parnell in the 1890s—brought about by a complex combination of his own arrogance and indiscretion and the forces of British evangelicalism allied with the Irish Catholic hierarchy—religion and nationalism came together in a way that has close resemblances to the Lost Cause situation in the American South at the same time. Thus, in Ireland too, as in the states of the former Confederacy, religious religion, so to speak, easily passed over into civil religion.[30]

This symbiosis is exemplified in the success of D. P. Moran's *The Leader,* a radically Catholic and nationalist publication, which first appeared in September 1900. The paper noted ominously that "There is something very distinctive about the face of the average [Protestant] loyalist, it is characteristic in its way as that of a Jew." Protestants would be accepted into a new, independent Ireland, but their "proper place" was "behind the Gael" until they became "absorbed." The paper used the words "shoneen" and "West Briton" to denigrate those Irish people who showed any sympathy with England, much as southerners referred to northern sympathizers and transplantees in their midst as "scalawags" and "carpetbaggers." It commended the boycotting of "soupers"—those whose families had surrendered their religion for soup during the famine—much as southerners who had favored the Union during the Civil War were ostracized after the surrender. In a 1901 essay entitled "Protestants and the Irish Nation," the case was stated plainly: "We desire to realise an Irish Ireland and let the non-Catholics help in the work or get out of the system. Their kin have robbed us and enslaved us and interrupted our development as a nation. They owe us restitution."[31]

Patrick Pearse, future leader of the 1916 Easter Rebellion, a product of a Christian Brothers' education and a deeply religious man himself—though a very independent one where nationalist belief conflicted with Catholic faith—was a master of uniting the spiritual and the political. At

30. See Barry M. Coldrey, *Faith and Fatherland: The Christian Brothers and the Development of Irish Nationalism, 1838–1921* (Dublin, 1988).

31. Conor Cruise O'Brien, *Ancestral Voices: Religion and Nationalism in Ireland* (Chicago, 1995), 39, 41, 59. It is true that O'Brien can be an erratic commentator—witness his anti-Jeffersonian *The Long Affair: Thomas Jefferson and the French Revolution, 1785–1800* (Chicago, 1996)—and he does have a running vendetta with what he sees as the all-too-cozy alliance between religion and nationalism in Irish history, but it is still possible to tease out a generally accepted narrative from his trenchant criticisms.

Wolfe Tone's grave in 1913, Pearse declared: "We have come to the holiest place in Ireland; holier even than the place where [St.] Patrick sleeps in Down. Patrick brought us life, but this man died for us. He was the greatest of Irish Nationalists . . . This man's soul was a burning flame, so ardent so generous so pure, that to come into communion with it is to come unto a new baptism, into a new regeneration and cleansing." Pearse transformed Tone from the Enlightened, Jefferson-like religious skeptic that he actually was almost into the figure of a traditional Catholic martyr.[32]

Like the Lost Cause, this nationalist movement of the late nineteenth and early twentieth centuries also had its sacred shrines, most notably Pearse's St. Enda's, officially described as "An Irish-Ireland School for Catholic Boys." St. Enda's, where the presence of the mythical Irish hero Cuchulainn was so strongly felt as to make him appear almost a member of the faculty, functioned much as Sewanee and Virginia Episcopal did for the American South, where too it must have seemed at times that Robert E. Lee and Stonewall Jackson were constituent members of their respective boards.[33]

Sometimes the correlation made between faith and fatherland could reach dizzying, and disturbing, heights. In an address delivered at the Emmet Commemoration in the Academy of Music in Brooklyn in March 1914, Pearse referred to patriotism as "a faith which is of the same nature as religious faith." Thus, Robert Emmet's execution in 1803 was "a sacrifice Christ-like in its perfection" and "such a death always means a redemption." John Mitchel joined Tone and Emmet in the Pearsean pantheon. Mitchel's *Jail Journal* was "the last Gospel of the New Testament of Irish nationalism as Wolfe Tone's *Autobiography* is the first." Pearse's nationalism, declares Conor Cruise O'Brien in a statement that makes the Irish patriot sound very similar to Father Ryan, "is thoroughly permeated by Catholic devotional feeling." Not only is there the liturgical connection between the 1916 Rising and Easter, but there is also the claim in *The Sovereign People* that "The [Irish] people who wept in Gethsemane, who trod the sorrowful way, who died naked on a cross, who went down into hell, will rise again glorious and immortal, will sit on the right hand of God, who will come in the end to give judgment, a judge just and terrible." The sentiment could hardly have sounded foreign, or unacceptably Catholic, to a southern lost causer: after all, Thomas Nelson Page had spoken of the

32. Ibid., 99.
33. Ibid., 98.

South as "crucified; bound hand and foot; wrapped in the cerements of the grave . . . sealed with the seal of [the federal] government . . . dead, and buried, and yet she rose again."[34]

This fusion of religion and politics was by no means solely an Irish Catholic phenomenon. It was also a part of the Protestant Unionist outlook, a conclusion that the development of the American southern Protestant ethos, of course, only confirms. As Alvin Jackson notes, for both Irish nationalists and Ulster Unionists, "Their historical inheritance, though different in content, shares the same form: Derry besieged or Limerick besieged, 1641 or Drogheda, 1916 on the banks of the Liffey or on the banks of the Somme. History for all the Irish is a mantra of sacred dates, an invocation of secular saints." The Orange Order, founded in 1795 to protect Protestants from growing Catholic militancy, has an iconography derived from religion that is very much like the American South's (and the Klan has seen itself as being in alliance with the Orange Order in defense of Protestantism), while at the same time it mirrors aspects of the Catholic nationalist mindset. According to Jackson, "The blood sacrifice called for by Pearse had been offered, but by different loyalties and on different altars." Panegyrical biographies of Edward Carson and James Craig presented them as the "Founding Fathers" of the northern statelet. He even notes the irony that "the evangelical tone of these [historical] works should recall the zeal of Gaelic revivalist literature no less than the apologetic of Victorian loyalism." What all of this produced was summed up by James Craig, prime minister of Northern Ireland in the 1930s, in his notorious remark—not "notorious," of course, to the bulk of the people in the province—about a "Protestant state for a Protestant people." The Irish Free State, meanwhile, with its 1937 constitutional recognition of Catholicism as the religion of the majority of its population, became almost a mirror image of its northern counterpart, even if its minority Protestant population remained privileged in a way not at all true of the Catholic minority in Ulster.[35]

There is a related similarity too between the Ireland and the American South of the pre–World War II years in that, while they both recognized themselves as less prosperous than their British or northeastern counter-

---

34. Ibid., 101, 102, 104. This quotation comes from the 1892 version of Page's famous speech on "The Old South"; see Fred Hobson, *Tell about the South: The Southern Rage to Explain* (Baton Rouge, 1983), 140.

35. Alvin Jackson, "Unionist History," in *Interpreting Irish History: The Debate on Historical Revisionism,* ed. Ciarán Brady (Dublin, 1994), 253, 258, 264. Blood sacrifice and baptism of blood were also, of course, major themes of the southern Lost Cause movement; see Wilson, 5.

parts, they often tried to make that defect into a virtue. Both stressed the advantages of an agricultural, stable, modest way of life over against an industrial, dislocated, materialistic model. While Eamon De Valera, the Irish prime minister, was recommending the virtues of a rural, faith-nurtured existence, the southern Agrarians were promoting a similar return to a land-centered way of life, one that would remind man of his dependence on a provident but inscrutable deity. The southern poet and critic John Crowe Ransom wrote a book along such lines, though he ended up defending a God of imaginative usefulness rather than of actual existence. To what extent such thinking affected the actual development of the southern and Irish economies is, of course, open to speculation, but it did tend to create an ethos of material-inferiority combined with spiritual-superiority that lasted at least until more prosperous times arrived in both places in the second half of the twentieth century.[36]

Relatively dormant among most whites, both Irish and southern, by the mid-twentieth century, that long tradition of a coming together of religion and civic cause has been most potent in the southern black community in its campaign for civil and political rights, which found its powerful inspiration and sustenance in the Christian churches and under the leadership of Baptist pastors such as Martin Luther King Jr. and Fred Shuttlesworth. It was an alliance further strengthened when opponents of the movement chose to bomb a Baptist church in Birmingham, Alabama, in 1963, killing four small girls in the process.

   This civil rights movement in the American South, however, served as a model for the Northern Irish Civil Rights Association in the 1960s, thus fortuitously bringing together the two traditions we've been examining in this narrative. The latter was inspired by the campaigns of Dr. King, even if Ulster Catholics didn't always understand what was going on in the South and in spite of the fact that their leaders never visited there. The parallel they saw between the situation of African Americans in the Deep South and Catholics in Northern Ireland did inspire them to use many of the same songs such as "We Shall Overcome" and "We Shall Not Be Moved." The leader of the Catholic moderates, John Hume, claimed that his party's philosophy came directly from the U.S. civil rights movement: "The dream which Dr. King proclaimed of a glorious opportunity for a new America, transformed by the moral energy of its minorities, was for me and others of

36. See Kieran Quinlan, *John Crowe Ransom's Secular Faith* (Baton Rouge, 1989), 46–64.

my generation in Northern Ireland the inspiration for our search for justice and equality. The American civil rights movement gave birth to ours. The songs of your movement were also ours. Your successes were for us a cause of hope. We *also* believed that we would overcome. Most importantly, the philosophy of non-violence, which sustained your struggle, was also part of ours."[37]

Even more militant activists like Bernadette Devlin have acknowledged this southern influence and have drawn attention to the parallel not only between the Selma to Montgomery march of 1965 and the Belfast to Derry trek of some four years later but also to the way the participants were attacked by the police and hecklers in both instances: "I think the impact on public opinion was something like what happened after Dr. King's people were beaten by 'Bull' Connor's cops in Alabama [in 1963]. Suddenly fair minded people everywhere could see us being treated like animals." It was a parallel reinforced in the media at the time. Chet Huntley, reporting for NBC, claimed rather simplistically that "The Catholics in Ulster are the same as the Blacks in the United States; they've been deprived of their rights, harried into slums, and denied jobs, hurt and slashed, ever since the Battle of the Boyne. And like Blacks they've revolted . . . and like Blacks they've been shot down." The racism of the Protestant extremists too was compared to that of poor whites in the Deep South, while the Orange Order was presented as an organization similar to the Ku Klux Klan.[38]

Whatever the historical inaccuracies, the false analogies, the too-easy drawing of similarities, there is no doubt that all of these cultures had their remote and even more recent origin in a peculiar blending of religion and secular hopes and expectations that now is so often the lot of marginalized peoples, though it was once part of the civic mainstream. Over the last twenty years, in both Ireland and the American South, there has been a great waning of this self-identification between national cause and religious belief; this even though the South serves as the home of some of the most-widely broadcast evangelical shows—the *700 Club*, for example—which have political as well as religious clout. (Ironically, it also is the home of the most reactionary Catholic broadcasting television station, EWTN.) It is hard to imagine that such a profoundly felt alliance—whether conceived by

37. Andrew J. Wilson, *Irish America and the Ulster Conflict, 1968–1995* (Washington, D.C., 1995), 19.

38. Ibid., 20, 21.

a Stonewall Jackson, a Patrick Pearse, or a Martin Luther King Jr.—will ever again be a widespread sustaining motivation for bravery, resistance, intolerance, or suffering. Even if no current invocation of faith and fatherland has the extended resonance and genuine force that it once had, however, a not-insignificant remnant still exists in the genuine Paisleyite fear of popery in Northern Ireland, or among several Protestant denominations in the American South, meaning that an end is not yet in sight. Depending on one's own position, the weakened forces of darkness still linger, or the work of redemption still struggles slowly forward.

CHAPTER 7

CRACKERS, CELTS, AND CALIBANS

"Irish on *both* sides! *Gracious!* And doesn't drink?"
—TENNESSEE WILLIAMS, *The Glass Menagerie*

A Montserrat Law of 1668 . . . "forbade the inhabitants to call each other
'English Dog, Scottish Dog, Tory, Irish Dog, Cavalier, and Roundhead.'"
—FROM DONALD HARMAN AKENSON, *If the Irish Ran the World*

Even trumping, perhaps, the perception of the Irishman or southerner
(black or white) as being excessively religious is the image of him as a figure
of fun and oddity, deviously servile or mindlessly violent according to circumstance. In a 1907 lecture in Trieste, James Joyce referred to Ireland as
"a country destined by God to be the everlasting caricature of the serious
world," while William Faulkner's 1948 novel *Intruder in the Dust* noted "a
volitionless, almost helpless capacity and eagerness [on the part of north-
erners] to believe anything about the South not even provided it be derogatory but merely bizarre enough and strange enough." Stereotype rather
than "reality" seems to prevail in these cases, however problematic a notion
the latter may be.[1]

That these two groups seem to provoke such stereotyping more readily
than do others, at least in the Anglophone world, may indicate no more
than that they themselves are *present* in greater numbers, or are more
widely dispersed, than others are. Polish jokes have less currency in Atlanta
than in Chicago; until the advent of Garrison Keillor on national radio, it is
unlikely that humor about Americans of Scandinavian ancestry went much
beyond the Midwest; Thomas Hardy's Dorset may well have been "a by-
word for rural misery and squalor" in nineteenth-century England, but
most of the world probably didn't know it then and certainly doesn't re-

---

1. *The Critical Writings of James Joyce*, ed. Ellsworth Mason and Richard Ellmann (Ithaca,
N.Y., 1989), 168; William Faulkner, *Intruder in the Dust* (New York, 1948), 153.

member it now. In contrast, the Irish in a British context, and southerners in an American one, have been and still are more available objects of both scorn and qualified romance.[2]

No person, nation, region, gender, class, group, or organization, however powerful, of course, can escape being stereotyped. The fact too that some stereotypes have wider currency and distribution than have those held reciprocally by their victims only indicates that the oppressed have less access to the media, not that their own prejudices are any less myopic or dehumanizing. Nevertheless, even if English-born residents of the United States, for example, sometimes complain about being locked into a stereotype of more elite background and behavior than are actually theirs, or about the fact that so many villains in Hollywood movies have upper-class British accents, their situation seems much less burdensome: the accent is, after all, on privilege, to quote the title of a recent book on the subject. In the civilized world of middle-class social intercourse, they do not live with the mild anxiety that waits in irritable anticipation of the possibly well-meant remark—the presumptuous imitation of accent; the condescending response to mention of W. J. Cash's *The Mind of the South:* "Hm. But isn't *that* an oxymoron?"; the overeffusive commendation of the novels of Toni Morrison or of the ballcourt prowess of Michael Jordan. The need to laugh politely so as not to show ill-humor, or make others feel uncomfortable, and indeed in a probably wise attempt to retain one's own equanimity for the remainder of the evening. There are always too the predictable jokes when it is announced that a major German or Japanese auto manufacturer is opening a plant in a southern state—"Would you actually buy a *Mercedes* assembled in *Alabama?*"—or when an American computer company transfers some of its operations to the west of Ireland.[3]

Meanwhile, white southerners often protest that they are the one group in America that it is not politically incorrect to ridicule, and in the United Kingdom it has taken years for mockery of the Irish to be recognized, in its more extreme cases at least, as a form of proscribed racial defamation. On the national level, African Americans daily tread their way through a minefield of stereotypes—of themselves as rappers, drug-dealers, potential rapists, welfare junkies, student athletes rather than students, unwarranted

2. Kathryn R. King, introduction to Thomas Hardy's *Wessex Tales* (New York, 1991), xii.

3. Katherine W. Jones, *Accent on Privilege: English Identities and Anglophilia in the U.S.* (Philadelphia, 2001). One English interviewee, however, thought that the Irish also benefited from unfair positive discrimination in the immigration process (73–74).

beneficiaries of affirmative action, employees rather than executives—all the more insidious for often being unspoken. Blacks from the South in addition are regularly condescended to by those from the northeastern states. The most frequent response on the part of all these groups is the internalization of a defensive or even siege mentality. Several studies have pointed to more serious consequences of such stereotyping on the health and mental stability of both blacks in the United States and Irish immigrants in Great Britain.[4]

In spite of an abundance of serious regional analyses, then, caricature and stereotype of both areas prevail, caricature that is neither pure nor simple but responsive to the preoccupations and ideologies and events of the age. As Patrick Gerster notes in his entry on "Stereotypes" in the *Encyclopedia of Southern Culture*, the South is viewed by northerners as:

> America at its extreme and as "Uncle Sam's Other Province" . . . as a land populated by a succession of predictable stock characters—formerly a land of happy darkies with watermelon or banjo, sadistic overseers, coquettish belles, chivalrous cavaliers, vengeful Klansmen, and more recently a land of rambunctious good old boys, demagogic politicians, corrupt sheriffs . . . nubile cheerleaders, football All Americans with three names, neurotic vixens with affinities for the demon rum, Bible-thumping preachers haunted by God, sugary Miss America candidates of unquestioned patriotism, toothless grizzled "po' white trash," and military "lifers" of considerable spit but little polish.

Perhaps the author has been a little carried away here by the sonority of his own southern rhetoric, but the list is still recognizable for the element of veracity it strikes in anyone who pays attention to the region's ratings. Within the white South, Appalachia fares even worse—a source of concern to southerners themselves—and images from *Deliverance* dwell indelibly in the national mind.[5]

There is the romantic image too, of course, though that also quickly passes into stereotype. Here the South is seen as a land of white columned mansions and gracious planters, the only real civilization that America has known, a frequent image still being presented, for example, in Hartnett T.

4. See Mícheál D. Roe, "Contemporary Catholic and Protestant Irish America: Social Identities, Forgiveness, and Attitudes toward The Troubles," *Éire-Ireland* 36, no. 1–2 (2002), 157–58.

5. *Encyclopedia of Southern Culture*, ed. Charles Reagan Wilson and William Ferris (Chapel Hill, 1989), 1126; see, for example, Bill Bryson, *The Lost Continent: Travels in Small-Town America* (New York, 1990), 99–104.

Kane's *The Romantic South* in 1961 (a book, incidentally, dedicated to the author's "great-grandfather, of County Cork, Ireland, and New Orleans, Louisiana, a Confederate who . . . belonged to a small, select group—one of the few privates who ever served in the Southern armies"). Even as recently as 1997, Fodor's *The South* advises: "Virtually every Southern city, country crossroads, and sleepy creek was touched by the war, and even now the memories linger, preserved for all time in yet more colorful stories, passed along from generation to generation in the rooms of antebellum mansions throughout the South." Blacks, of course, disappear almost entirely from such pictures, or are to be found segregated on other pages of the same guide. While Southern folkways and speech are glorified, it is obvious too that the commentators often have an attitude of condescension toward those they seem to admire so nostalgically and uncritically.[6]

In turning to the Irish case, we find some of the same ambiguity, the sense that the good qualities of the race are also those that elicit mockery. As the authors of *The Story of English* noted in 1986, for example, while the Irish are "envied for their eloquence, they are almost in the same breath scorned for their 'stupidity.'" Or, as Thomas Cahill put the matter in his highly successful *How the Irish Saved Civilization* (a title that itself suggests a degree of defensiveness, not to say belligerence), "The word *Irish* is seldom coupled with the word *civilization*." So much for Douglas Hyde's claim in 1892 that Ireland "was once, as everyone admits, one of the most classically learned and cultured nations in Europe."[7]

No doubt, few thoughtful observers would accept that either the Irish or southerners can be justly characterized by a handful of clichéd representations, or that these cultures themselves, or the perception of them, are unchanging over time. As Jack Temple Kirby has shown in considerable detail in his 1978 study, *Media-Made Dixie*, the image of the southern states has shifted over the decades from a preoccupation with the grandeur of the Old South in the Shirley Temple movies of the 1930s and especially, of course, with *Gone with the Wind* in 1939, to the impoverished sharecropper and racist South of Erskine Caldwell and William Faulkner, to the even

6. Hartnett T. Kane, *The Romantic South* (New York, 1961); Fodor's *The South* (New York, 1997), 3.

7. Robert McCrum, William Cran, and Robert MacNeil, eds., *The Story of English* (New York, 1986), 163; Thomas Cahill, *How the Irish Saved Civilization* (New York, 1995), 1; Douglas Hyde, "The Necessity for De-Anglicising Ireland," in *Language, Lore, and Lyrics* (Dublin, 1986), 153.

more visceral region depicted in *In the Heat of the Night*, to the engaging family values of *The Waltons* television series in the 1970s.[8]

Ireland's media image too, though less frequently present than the South's, has tended to oscillate between the romanticism of *The Quiet Man*, the ominous terrorism of *Patriot Games*, and the engaging poverty and hopefulness of *My Left Foot*, or even the seductive transgressiveness of *The Crying Game*. But all too often, complex realities are subsumed in embarrassingly popular successes like *My Cousin Vinny* and *Angela's Ashes*. Perhaps all that is going on is an oscillation between bad and good stereotypes, but stereotypes nevertheless. In addition to the movies mentioned above, there are the unforgettable images of rural deprivation rendered by photographers such as Walker Evans and Dorothea Lange (who worked in both the American South and Ireland), and also the more nuanced, if still somewhat romantic, portrayal of Heinrich Böll in his *Irish Journal* or of V. S. Naipaul in *A Turn in the South*. Whatever way one looks at the matter, then, there seems no escape from this prison-house of stereotype.

One might well wonder why this situation appears to be more prevalent in the Irish-southern scenario than in others? Is it simply that every nation, region, city, town, even family has a structural need for some such contrast? In any case, stereotypes of the Irish and of blacks—whether southern or not—as they exist now are for the most part rather benign versions of those from a more vicious past. Images of Irishness and images of Africanness, false or otherwise, go back much farther of course than those of southernness, white or black, as the latter designation is little more than a couple hundred years old. It is clear that the originals were broadly created in the context of colonial projects designed to delegitimize and render barbaric those whom the colonizers sought to subdue in the name of civilization. There is a trajectory of this kind of rhetoric from the twelfth-century Welsh chronicler Giraldus Cambrensis, who saw the Irish as "a people descended from the ancient Scythians, who in many districts were wholly pagan," through Edmund Spenser's sixteenth-century depiction of them as "Papists by their profession, but in the same so blindly and brutishly informed for the most part that you would rather think them atheists or infidels," to nineteenth-century Charles Kingsley's classic judgment of them as "human chimpanzees." Ben Jonson's *Irish Masque*, first performed at the English

---

8. Jack Temple Kirby, *Media-Made Dixie: The South in the American Imagination*, rev. ed. (Athens, Ga., 1986).

court in 1613, has the rude Irish renounce their course manners and customs and come forth "as newborn creatures all," the Irish bard now singing in polite English: "So breaks the Sun earth's rugged chains / Wherein rude winter bound her veins."[9]

As we shall see below, such negative rendering of the Irish reached its most intense development during the Victorian era when the added ingredient of social Darwinism could be called upon to justify continued subjugation of the ever unruly. Hence L. Perry Curtis Jr.'s reading of the Irish case:

> English constructions of the Irish and Irishness became increasingly appropriative over the course of Queen Victoria's reign. Examples of this form of cultural imperialism range from contempt for Irish manners and customs in the Tudor and Stuart eras to the emergence of a bestialized or demonized Paddy, bent on murder and mayhem, in cartoons after the rather farcical rebellion of 1848. The gorilla-like guerrillas found in the pages of *Punch*, *Judy*, and *Fun* may have been splendid examples of graphic satire and animalistic allegory; but they also served to remind British readers that militant Irish nationalism contained no lofty ideals or legitimate goals and reflected instead the base instincts of degenerate . . . beasts.

The Irish were thus presented as a race that "belonged in zoos if not prison."[10]

The sub-Saharan African, meanwhile, has also been seen as "other" from the earliest encounters in the sixteenth century and understanding of his alien condition sought in whatever the current anthropology offered: a biblical son of Ham, a lesser development in the Darwinian scheme of evolution, a genetic mishap with lower IQ and limited potential. Winthrop D. Jordan has pointed out that while some early English commentators were aware that whites must seem as strange to blacks as the other way around, "the hideous tortures, the cannibalism, the rapacious warfare, the revolting diet . . . seemed somehow to place the Negro among the beasts," a perception only reinforced by the tragic "happenstance of nature that the Negro's homeland was the habitat of the animal which in appearance most resembles man." Much later, in his 1785 *Notes on the State of Virginia*, an enlight-

9. David Cairns, *Writing Ireland: Colonialism, Nationalism and Culture* (Manchester, 1988), 11; Kieran Quinlan, "Their Language, So Familiar and So Foreign: The English Tongue and Its Irish Voice," in *Postscript: Publication of the Philological Association of the Carolinas* (March 1985), ed. William F. Naufftus, 115–21.

10. L. Perry Curtis Jr., *Apes and Angels: The Irishman in Victorian Caricature*, rev. ed. (Washington, D.C., 1997), xxii–xxiv.

ened Thomas Jefferson "speculated that blacks are sweaty and smelly, imaginatively dull, and lacking in reason but with a talent for music and religion, while being benevolent, grateful, and loyal."[11]

It was in the nineteenth century, at all events, as both the questions of Catholic emancipation and Home Rule were disrupting British control in Ireland and the enormous influx of impoverished famine victims was threatening to destabilize English society itself, that at least the racialized cartoon representation of the Irish reached its most extreme, even if precedents had been set by depictions of the rebellious Scots in the previous century. Similarly, in the South, the threat of northern abolitionism and federal intervention to end slavery, exacerbated the need to argue that the black slave was both happy with his lot and incapable of living as a free man in a democratic society. Darwinian evolutionary theory, together with what seemed at the time to be a more scientific understanding of the hierarchy among human races, only served to lend a note of false authority to such prejudices.[12]

A perceived racial difference obviously lay at the heart of the white-black divide in the American South. It has been suggested that it also lay at the heart of the English-Irish split. What is abundantly clear in both cases is that questions about differences in culture and race were blended and separated in confusing ways, and the definition of "race" by those who most often used the term was, for the most part, neither precise nor consistent. Because this is an important issue in the construction of stereotypes, it needs to be examined in some detail. Nevertheless, before doing so, it should be said that while current thinking inclines to see race as a cultural fiction without biological foundation, the *idea* that there are distinct races is one that has been potent over the centuries so that its past—and present—force is not to be dismissed by simple explanation of its dubious premise.

One of the questions that has preoccupied scholars of Irish affairs for the last several decades has been the extent to which it is legitimate to claim that the Irish have been perceived by the English as a *race* apart—the proverbial "Other," England's unconscious, as servant-monster Caliban

---

11. Winthrop D. Jordan, *White over Black: American Attitudes toward the Negro, 1550–1812* (New York, 1969), 28–29; *Oxford Companion to African American Literature*, ed. William L. Andrews, Francis Smith Foster, and Trudier Harris (New York, 1997), 698.

12. Murray G. H. Pittock, *Celtic Identity and the British Image* (New York, 2000), 32.

from Shakespeare's *The Tempest*—and treated accordingly, both in the actual administration of the country and in journalistic depictions of it, or simply as recalcitrant but ultimately assimilable members of a different *culture*. Such work has been influenced not only by the study of original documents from the sixteenth and seventeenth centuries, but ideologically by Frantz Fanon's thinking about colonialism in the 1960s and by the publication of Edward Said's *Orientalism* in 1978. Said argues that the West has rendered the East "exotic" and "mysterious" and in a host of other demeaning ways in order to justify exploiting it and subjecting it to different norms from those applied to inhabitants of the West.[13]

The most prominent scholar to argue that the Irish-English difference was broadly understood in the nineteenth century as a racial one is L. Perry Curtis Jr., although he allows that educated English people were sometimes aware of the degree of miscegenation between all the peoples of the British Isles. After all, Curtis reminds his readers, Thomas Davis, John Mitchel, and other Irish nationalists had said that the Irish *were* a separate race. Douglas Hyde was quite explicit in his famous essay on de-Anglicizing the nation: "In a word, we must strive to cultivate everything that is most racial, most smacking of the soil, most Gaelic, most Irish, because in spite of the little admixture of Saxon blood in the northeast corner [i.e., Ulster], this island *is* and will *ever* remain Celtic at the core, far more Celtic than most people imagine." In insisting on a perceived racial rather than merely cultural difference, Curtis is not, of course, agreeing with it. He quotes Henry Louis Gates Jr., on the dangers of using a word such as "race" that has no basis in science with the purpose of "lending the sanction of God, biology, or the natural order to even presumably unbiased descriptions of cultural tendencies and differences."[14]

Curtis's position rests largely on his remarkably detailed catalogues of the variety of Irish types that were presented by *Punch* cartoonists, from "the tall and muscular image of the Northern Irish Protestant" who resembled "however faintly, a respectable or honest Englishman," through the "reasonably good-looking rustic male of the small farmer or laborer variety," to "orthognathous Pat . . . [the] politically innocent peasant, who delivered Irish bulls with feckless abandon" but who was also "harmless" because not a nationalist and so "cartoonists treated him as fully human."

13. Frantz Fanon, *Black Skin, White Masks* (New York, 1952); Edward Said, *Orientalism* (New York, 1978).

14. Hyde, 169; Curtis, 190 n.180.

The list declines all the way down until it comes, finally, to the worst type of all: "simian Paddy, who longed to use physical force to free his country from British rule . . . this truly 'dangerous' creature looked like a cross between monstrous ape and primitive man owing to his high and hairy upper lip or muzzle, concave nose, low facial angle, and sharp teeth."[15]

While acknowledging that English cartoonists also used animal imagery for politicians and Methodist preachers, Curtis argues that their depictions of the Irish were "ideologically charged images of a people or a 'race' deemed inferior," the purpose of which was to justify the "dire need of British imperial rule." If we compare the presentation of the Irish with that of "*other* Others"—enemies such as the Ashantis, Kaffirs, and Zulus—the Irish come off quite poorly because, Curtis thinks, the Fenian was seen as a "much more serious threat to civilization and the integrity of the empire." Or, as Joseph Boskin has noted in a similar American context: "Blacks were clearly satirized, but they were also permitted a clever foolishness. They were, after all, controllable, whereas the Irish could get downright nasty and posed the larger threat."[16]

Even accepting the general thrust of Curtis's argument, however, it is noteworthy—and troubling—that he pushes his interpretations so far that he sometimes seems disappointed when a particular image fails to be as horrific as its ideologically charged purposes demand. For him, even Seamus Heaney's poem "Act of Union" is about an Ireland that is "the victim of brutal rape by an 'imperially male'" Britain, rather than a pained acknowledgement of sympathy and even collusion between the two neighboring countries in which the dominating British male admits that "Conquest is a lie" and is at least partly repentant for his frustrated crime, which he is unable now to correct: "No treaty / I foresee will salve completely your tracked / And stretchmarked body."[17]

Critics of Curtis have argued that religion and class were more relevant

15. Curtis, xxi–xxii.

16. Ibid., 146–55; Joseph Boskin, *Sambo: The Rise and Demise of an American Jester* (New York, 1986), 99.

17. Curtis, 200; Seamus Heaney, *Poems, 1965–1975* (New York, 1980), 204–5. Curtis's influence may be seen in, for example, Neil R. Davison's *James Joyce, Ulysses, and the Construction of Jewish Identity: Culture, Biography, and "The Jew" in Modernist Europe* (New York, 1996): "The darkened complexion in O'Hea's [interesting name!] cartoon . . . further yokes the 'simian Celt' to the era's racialist preconceptions: within the taxonomy of humankind, all non-Caucasians—Blacks, Asians, Indians, Arabs, Jews (whose identity as Caucasians was continuously challenged)—represent lesser types of homosapiens" (98).

issues between the Irish and the English than race. Roy Foster, the most trenchant among them, has objected not only to the theoretical underpinnings of Curtis's thesis (which Foster sees as mere fashionable Marxism with a postcolonial twist) but also to the simplistic contextualization of many of its claims. Foster points out, for example, that an early editor of *Punch* was himself Irish (as were many of the cartoonists), that the Irish were caricatured early on much like other groups, and—though he is less convincing here—that "representations of the Irish [weren't] very pro-́ nouncedly different in physiognomy from the representations of English plebeians." One is reminded of Indian viceroy Lord Curzon's remark when he saw some of his soldiers bathing: "I never knew the working class had such white bodies."[18]

Foster grants, however, that the Mitchel-inspired rebellion of 1848 undoubtedly increased English-Irish animosities. "From now on," he observes, "Ireland was presented in the classic colonial paradigm: an idealized family." But Foster's quotations from *Punch*, even if highly patronizing, are less "othering" than those that have shaped Curtis's views: "Ireland strikes us as being the Prodigal Son of England, always going astray, then coming back, repenting and being forgiven. JOHN BULL may occasionally have been a harsh parent, but we are sure the old fellow means well."[19]

Punch certainly saw a close relationship between "The lazy West Indian Negro—the contented pumpkin-consumer, hateful to gods and Thomas Carlyle" and Paddy (which would not have surprised John Mitchel, as he agreed with Carlyle on almost everything except Ireland). Foster concedes that the advent of Darwinism led to cartooning and satire of a more "chilling" kind: "A creature manifestly between the Gorilla and the Negro is to be met with in some of the lowest districts of London and Liverpool by adventurous explorers . . . it belongs in fact to a tribe of Irish savages; the lowest species of the Irish Yahoo . . . it talks a sort of gibberish . . . The somewhat superior ability of the Irish Yahoo to utter articulate sounds, may suffice to prove that it is a development, and not, as some imagine, a degeneration of the Gorilla." Nevertheless, Foster emphasizes that *Punch* could be sympathetic also and that the periodical was far more ruthless against Ibsen than against the Irish. After all, *Punch* itself asserted that it was "the

18. See Sheridan Gilley, "English Attitudes to the Irish in England, 1789–1900," in *Immigrants and Minorities in British Society*, ed. Colin Holmes (London, 1978), 81–110; R. F. Foster, *Paddy and Mr. Punch* (New York, 1993), 174; Byron Farwell, *Mr. Kipling's Army: All the Queen's Men* (New York, 1981), 132.

19. Foster, 180.

true friend of Ireland; not of Orangemen" and "even reminded its readers that . . . 'Punch' was an Irish name."[20]

Foster notes too that the *London Illustrated News*, which employed many ex-*Punch* cartoonists, presented Irishmen as "handsome, well formed and physically varied." He excuses the matter by pointing out that "the *News* was not in the business of caricature; and *Punch* was." He argues, moreover, that the same was done to the English working class and to the French, while Irish nationalist publications in turn represented the English as "grasping, prognathous, subhuman bogeymen." Foster's conclusion is that one cannot easily generalize that all of this was "simple racial prejudice against the Irish." For example, "intermarriage . . . was not counted misceg-enation but rather a valuable conversion process." According to him, "the whole process may relate more to . . . resentment against Irish resentment of the Union."[21]

Which account is more accurate? Undoubtedly, Curtis displays far more knowledge about the technicalities of the cartoons in *Punch* and elsewhere than does Foster. Yet the latter's nuanced approach will probably be more convincing to anyone who has an intimate acquaintance with the infinitely varied day-to-day interactions between the English and the Irish, an ac-quaintance, one might add, that allows for the put-down routines of all so-cial exchanges in the British Isles, and one which more upbeat Americans sometimes find disconcerting and hence misinterpret. After all, Lord By-ron's Catholic Irish friend Thomas Moore and his *Melodies* were as well known to English drawing rooms of the nineteenth century as were the *Punch* cartoons, while Moore was himself an intimate of the prime minister Lord John Russell. The radical workingmen's Chartist movement in En-gland in the 1830s had as its leader an Irish politician, former O'Connellite Feargus O'Connor. Anthony Trollope, who lived and worked in nineteenth-century Ireland for almost a decade, judged the people there to be "good-humoured, clever—the working classes very much more intelligent than those of England—economical, and hospitable," if also "perverse, irrational, and but little bound by the love of truth." In her study of the stage Irish-man, Maureen Waters questions some of the simplistic conclusions that have been drawn about his significance by those anxious to see an absolute English-Irish dichotomy. Edward Said too has been taken to task for failing

20. Ibid., 182, 184, 191.
21. Ibid., 192, 193.

to understand Ireland's place in a European context and for his chronically reductive analysis of British-Irish relations.[22]

Those scholars who stress an absolute opposition between the Irish and the English seem to have studied a very limited number of texts, and, unintentionally, they have assumed that people are seen *only* through their stereotype rather than it being just one of several evaluative strategies that negotiate with and often contradict one another. Those on the Left tend to be preoccupied with matters of exploitation and opposition, even to the extent of reinforcing for a new generation the very divisions they genuinely decry; those of more traditional liberal persuasion are inclined at times to minimize the presence of prejudice and exclusion.[23]

Some of the complexity of the situation in the twentieth century is presented by Iona Opie in her classic book on children's lore, *The People in the Playground,* where she remarks, with perhaps a touch of naiveté, though also with what would be the perception of many in the British Isles, that "The 'Englishman, Irishman, and Scotsman' stories of the 1920s and 1930s . . . are still popular and are sometimes used to ridicule Irishmen. However nowadays, more often than not, the significance of the men being of different nationalities has been lost—they might just as well be called Mr. White, Mr. Brown, and Mr. Green." Then she adds in a separate paragraph that the increase in Irish jokes in the early 1970s was due to the tensions in Northern Ireland: "Children relished them not through any anti-Irish feeling but because they always enjoy hearing about ninnies to whom they can feel superior. In fact the foolish Irishmen were part of a long tradition of folktales about simpletons."[24]

What Opie would see as a rather benign history, of course, historians and cultural anthropologists like Curtis have found to exemplify a much

22. J. J. Lee, in *Ireland, 1912–1985: Politics and Society* (New York, 1989), thinks that some "Irish" jokes are rather good and that, besides, the natives are much too sensitive about them, possibly because they have lost their Gaelic language (669). Anthony Trollope, *An Autobiography* (New York, 1993), 58–59; Maureen Waters, *The Comic Irishman* (Albany, N.Y., 1984); see, for example, Stephen Howe, *Ireland and Empire: Colonial Legacies in Irish History and Culture* (New York, 2000), 134–35, and Richard English, "Shakespeare and the Definition of the Irish Nation," in *Shakespeare and Ireland: History, Politics, Culture,* ed. Mark Thornton Burnett and Ramona Way (New York, 1997), 145–46.

23. In regard to considering more texts, one might, for example, look at the depictions of various Irish Jesuits in English writer and anti–Home Ruler Dennis Meadows's autobiography, *Obedient Men* (London, 1956).

24. Iona Opie, *The People in the Playground* (New York, 1994), 14.

more vicious pattern. According to Mary Hickman, for example, while there was a far greater number of inclusive references to Ireland and the Irish in the British media in the 1990s, and while prominent political figures acknowledged past prejudices, nevertheless: "the narrative of the dramatisations [on television] frequently relies on the regeneration of old British stereotypes about the Irish: the troublesome family in a soap is Irish; when relatives seek roots in Ireland, everyone over there is drunk, duplicitous, etc.; rural Ireland is a timeless phenomenon; and British relatives solve problems caused by warring factions among their Irish relations. The binary oppositions of Irishness and Britishness are present in these characterisations even as the extent of the ties between the two islands is being emphasised."[25]

For Hickman, the problem, at least on the British mainland, continues to be that there is no way for those of Irish origin or background—13 million, 23 percent of the population according to some government estimates—to assert their multiethnic identity without seeming to be anti-British. Paradoxically, while "Britishness" is being slowly—and painfully—redefined to include "those of African Caribbean, African and Asian origin," the Irish are not seen as different enough to require attention, yet at the same time they suffer as a consequence of their unacknowledged (and seemingly desirable) inclusion: "In a multitude of everyday encounters, some of them overtly discriminatory or prejudiced, others more in the category of cultural reminders, Irish people are constantly reminded that they can only 'pass' as British/English under particular circumscribed conditions (laughing at anti-Irish jokes, anglicising pronunciation and vocabulary, maintaining a low profile for all things Irish which stray outside the acceptable boundaries of amusing, entertaining, successful)." Thus, Hickman argues, "belonging can never be achieved," though "failure to belong is individualised and culturally pathologised." The only solution in her view is that "The myriad official and informal ways in which the superiority of being English/British is transmitted will have to become unacceptable."[26]

There is a level of particularity to Hickman's observations that cannot be ignored. Anecdotal evidence too would tend to bear out many of her claims. English writer Blake Morrison's memoir of his mother, a doctor

25. Mary Hickman, "'Binary Opposites' or 'Unique Neighbors'? The Irish in Multi-Ethnic Britain," *Political Quarterly* 71, no. 1 (2002): 53. For criticism of Hickman, see Howe, 51.
26. Hickman, 56, 59.

from a large family in County Kerry, which shows in great detail how she slowly and reluctantly elided both her ethnic identity and her Catholic religion over the decades, with her children hardly noticing the transformation at the time, would seem to support Hickman's analysis.[27]

Yet Hickman's findings still need to be balanced with the more benign perceptions of both Opie and Foster. This in spite of the IQ analysis to which the Irish were subjected in the early 1970s in the work of H. J. Eysenck, who argued, on the basis of widely disputed statistics, that "London and South-East England have the highest mean IQ score (102), and the Republic of Ireland the lowest (96)." After all, areas of the British Isles other than Ireland could justly take offense at such claims.[28]

Class and culture—regional or national—are deeply embedded in all English (and Irish) perceptions, and there is much self-construction going on at all levels and by all groups in their myriad attempts at "passing" without being ridiculed. Tyneside Newcastle is likely to be less intelligible to London than is Liffeyside Dublin. The experience of the Irish dentist in Kidlington is likely to be different from that of the "Paddy" on the building site. Moreover, the government statistic that 23 percent of the British population is of at least remote Irish origin should not be seen, as Hickman tends to do, as simple stigmatization of the "You can never become English" variety but rather as a reminder of a common inheritance with the neighboring island. Accent rather than ancestry very often defines perceived "Englishness," and it is hard to think that a politician such as former Chancellor of the Exchequer Denis Healey, grandson of a Catholic Fenian immigrant and son of an Irish nationalist schoolteacher, whose head was filled early on with "stories of Napper Tandy, Wolfe Tone, and . . . the leg-

---

27. Blake Morrison, *Things My Mother Never Told Me* (New York, 2002).

28. See a recent summary in Ciarán Benson, "Ireland's 'Low' IQ: A Critique," in *The Bell Curve: History, Documents, Opinions*, ed. Russell Jacoby and Naomi Glauberman (New York, 1995), 222–33. The quotation here is from p. 223. Benson, an Irish psychologist, reports that "even amongst relatively well-informed groups in Ireland, such as University students, there lingers the belief that it has been 'scientifically' shown that the Irish have an unusually low IQ" (222). He quotes Eysenck as holding it as quite accepted that "certain national, racial and cultural groups are more intelligent than others"; for Benson, following Curtis, this is a "myth" that derives its "vitality from the nature of the political relationship between Ireland and its larger neighbor" (222–23). Benson argues cogently that these kinds of results derive from invalidly collating diverse studies from different periods and population groups. What may be more important, however, is that the false interpretation received much more publicity than its belated rebuttal.

end of Cuchulain," would be regarded as anything other than English, even if he would not be totally free—nor seems to have cared much—to "promote" his Irish origins.[29]

It has always been the case too that many of the Irishmen and white southerners who left for London and New York, respectively, have by easy ventriloquism become indistinguishable from—or "passed" as—the native inhabitants, a choice surely not available to those who would be considered significantly different. Sir Arthur Conan Doyle, creator of Sherlock Holmes, had grandparents who were immigrant Irish Catholics in the nineteenth century and an uncle, a prominent *Punch* cartoonist, resigned from the magazine because of its antipapal bias; Brendan Bracken, scion of a Catholic nationalist family and Christian Brothers education, went on to transform himself through Australian exile and the British public school system into one of Winston Churchill's most influential government ministers and his right hand man during World War II (sometimes assumed to be Churchill's illegitimate son, Bracken was once described as being like "a Polynesian with dyed hair, for he had a large red mop that stood out like a kind of halo; his features, almost Negroid, were like those of a Papuan," proving, incidentally, that wildly imaginative stereotyping wasn't limited to those *known* to be Irish!); Peter O'Toole and Richard Harris have played English kings and overlords, while Ray McAnally ended his acting career in the role of a very convincing British prime minister; the latest incarnation of 007 is Pierce Brosnan (who confesses that he "had a hard battle" when he first went to England at eleven years of age: "They don't let you forget who you are, that you're a Mick, you're a Paddy, you're Irish"), while England wakes up daily to the lilt of Terry Wogan on morning radio. Then there are the cases of Albert Finney, and the late Charles Laughton and Vivian Leigh. . . . Irish figures, or persons of Irish background, populate the worlds of sport, racing, the arts, academia—and, most recently, business—often only an inflection away (if even that) from their ancestry. This is not to argue that tensions do not exist, or to mitigate their import, but rather to question their unintended essentialization in some postcolonial discussions. The Irish presence in England is multivalent, its various discourses submitting

29. Denis Healey, *The Time of My Life* (New York, 1997), 7. Healey does not appear to have been very exercised about such matters of identity later in life. In an election campaign, he was astonished that the Roman Catholic Bishop of Leeds "was able to tell me the date on which my grandfather had lapsed from the Roman Catholic church in Todmorden half a century before." Healey adds: "I found this a little too reminiscent of the Communist Party" (132).

to, harmonizing with, contesting, and above all reshaping that island's evolving cultures.[30]

Perhaps Terry Eagleton's work on Irish stereotypes best demonstrates the persistence of some of the ambiguities dealt with above. Of Irish ancestry himself, Eagleton has long been a staunch critic of English cultural assumptions, a writer intimate with most aspects of Irish life and literature, and a castigator of those Irish academics—such as Roy Foster—who would tend to play down the trauma of the Irish historical experience at the hands of British imperialism. Yet he has argued convincingly that from a purely *materialist* point of view:

> it would be remarkable if men and women who had for a lengthy period shared roughly the same conditions of material life revealed no psychological traits in common . . . Stereotypes are not to be confused with reality, and many of them are simply baseless; but they may occasionally provide clues to specific social conditions. The image of the immigrant Irish labourer as powerful but feckless, careless of tomorrow and much given to festivity, has some basis in the fact that small-farming in Ireland did indeed demand sustained bouts of muscular work, but in a sporadic, non-industrial rhythm which allowed for a fair degree of leisure time.

When, however, Eagleton turns from high theory to a more popular style of presentation as he does in his recent *The Truth about the Irish,* it is surprising to see him recycle many of the stereotypes that one would have thought his own previous work had intellectually outlawed. Eagleton's book does at times present a thoughtful and deconstructive view of the current Irish scene, but a good many of his comments are "caustic" in the extreme. Thus, the 1916 rebels "dashed around the city to stick up copies of the proclamation, but discovered that they had forgotten the paste"; Parnell's Land League "bequeathed to history the word 'boycott'" though "some cynics claim that this was because the Irish were unable to pronounce the world 'ostracism'"; "For a long time, confessing that you were Irish was like announcing that you were a cross between a clown and a mental defective"; and, a persistent theme of the book, "The most popular pursuit in Ireland has always been how to get out of the place."[31]

Eagleton's book invites a good many acerbic observations of its own,

30. Pierce Brosnan, quoted in *Hollywood Irish,* ed. Áine O'Connor (Dublin, 1997), 123.

31. Terry Eagleton, *Crazy John and the Bishop and Other Essays on Irish Culture* (Notre Dame, 1998), 68–69, and *The Truth about the Irish* (New York, 2000), 63, 103, 42, 70.

not least in terms of its place within his own political evolution and in his cultural and professional interactions, as a British academic, with Irish friends and associates. For now, however, I would simply suggest that it points forcefully to the complexity of British-Irish involvement in which even good friends can say what seem to be the most outrageous things about one another.

In 1991, in the United States, meanwhile, when popular fiction writer Alexandra Ripley's officially sponsored sequel to *Gone with the Wind* appeared, there was some discomfort among certain members of the Irish-American community because of her negative portrayal of nineteenth-century Catholic Ireland. Noticing the strong Irish element in the original, and in an apparent attempt to avoid recourse to nineteenth-century stereotypes of blacks—a revealing comment in itself—Ripley set a major portion of *Scarlett* in Ireland during the heroine's visit to her ancestral home. A writer in the New York-based *Irish Echo* accused Ripley of presenting the Irish as "a fickle, ignorant and violent race, prone to treachery and the most outrageous superstitions." In Ripley's account, Scarlett prefers the Anglo-Irish Protestant gentry to her peasant ancestors and at one point refers to voices of the ungrateful villagers near her estate as "so inhuman, so like the howling of wild beasts." As though adding insult to injury, the few blacks in *Scarlett* don't speak in the slave dialect that had offended some readers of Mitchell's original tale, whereas the Irish brogue is pervasive. The book, however, was a best-seller in both Ireland and the United States, the Irish at home more amused and bemused than insulted, suggesting either that everyone lived in a world little concerned with such once-provocative stereotypes or, more likely, that their reappearance in such a medium and from such a source rendered them relatively innocuous.[32]

The racialization of Irish and African stereotypes dates largely, as we have seen, from the sixteenth and seventeenth centuries. In America, there is a long tradition also of Irish and black stereotypes imitating, crossing, and sometimes opposing one another. This is clear from the varieties of simian imagery alluded to earlier. In the nineteenth-century American minstrel show too—more common in the North than in the South— Irish players often performed blackface roles, while the songs and dances intermixed Irish with African American lyrics and music. This was not, of course, a happy conjunction. The Irish frequently expressed bitter animos-

32. See the report by Associated Press writer Rick Hampson, "Critics Say Scarlett's Author Isn't Kind to the Irish," *Birmingham News*, 14 November 1991, 1C, 3C.

ity toward their black competitors at the bottom of the social scale, while, in New Orleans at least, blacks had a tradition of mocking the newly arrived Irish who had displaced them from their employments. It has been argued too that some of the fascination with blackface performances reflects hidden desire rather than obvious contempt for those imitated, and it is certainly not hard to see how such imitation provided an opportunity for Irish workers to show themselves superior to blacks and, at the same time—as rural immigrants forced to adapt to the demands of an industrial economy—envious of the apparently more carefree ways of African American culture.[33]

In any case, the southern black has regularly been portrayed as either mindlessly happy—in *Gone with the Wind* the black characters are most often like children—or incorrigibly vicious. In the former tradition of infantilizing representations, one finds such phenomenally popular portrayals as the fat bandannaed "Mammy," advertisements for Aunt Jemima pancake batter, an assortment of ceramic figurines, and the happy-go-lucky "Sambo" of numerous stage shows, with his comical dialect and dim wit. Joseph Boskin's description of Sambo is not unlike that of his Irish counterpart: "The essential features of Sambo consisted of two principal parts. He was childish and comical, employed outlandish gestures, and wore tattered clothes. Irresponsibility was a cardinal characteristic and buffoonery an inherent trait." At another point, Boskin describes Sambo as a "saucer-eyed, thick-lipped, round-faced, kinky-haired, grinningly toothed figure clad in plantation clothing or foppishly attired in formal dress." There is also the image of the black male as rapist, an image powerfully reinforced in both Dixon's *The Clansman* and the major motion picture made from it in 1915, *Birth of a Nation*. The many ritualistic lynchings of blacks in the South in the post-Reconstruction era only served to strengthen this image.[34]

That is not the whole story, of course: there has, after all, been jazz and blues and spirituals and sports, while even the reviled minstrel show when performed by blacks themselves sometimes implied a subtext that was a deconstruction of its overt clowning. Still, these much-admired cultural

33. Eric Lott, *Love and Theft: Blackface Minstrelsy and the American Working Class* (New York, 1993), 148–49.

34. Joseph Boskin, "Stereotypes," in *Encyclopedia of African-American Culture and History*, ed. Jack Salzman, David Lionel Smith, and Cornell West (New York, 1996), 2567, 2568; but, apart perhaps from the leprechaun figure, there is no parallel in the Irish case to the lawn jockeys, placemats, etc. "Irish joke" bric-a-brac such as mugs with the handle inside belong in a rather different, if still offensive, category.

manifestations haven't always changed the general white public's views of blacks, and indeed there is a long tradition of whites "slumming" with blacks without in any way altering their prejudices against them in the process. Some form of demeaning stereotype has remained the predominant image in the white mind brought about, it has been suggested, by a white need to repress its own fear of black revolution and control, much as Curtis and Said suggested was the motive for English stereotyping of the Irish.

Typical of the "milder" forms of southern white paternalism toward blacks is plantation-owner William Alexander Percy's comment in his 1941 autobiography *Lanterns on the Levee:* "How is it possible for the white man to communicate with people of this sort, people whom imagination kills and fantasy makes impotent, who thrive like children and murder ungrudgingly as small boys fight?" The entry on the "Negro" in the classic eleventh edition of the *Encyclopedia Britannica* published early in the twentieth century contained the following description by a professor of social science at Cornell:

> Mentally the Negro is inferior to the white . . . We must necessarily suppose that the development of the negro and white proceeds on different lines. While with the latter the volume of the brain grows with the expansion of the brainpan, in the former the growth of the brain is on the contrary arrested by the premature closing of the cranial sutures and lateral pressure of the frontal bone . . . but evidence is lacking on the subject and the arrest or even deterioration in mental development is no doubt very largely due to the fact that after puberty sexual matters take the first place in the negro's life and thoughts . . . For the rest, the mental constitution of the negro is very similar to that of a child, normally good-natured and cheerful, but subject to sudden fits of emotion and passion during which he is capable of performing acts of singular atrocity, impressionable, vain, but often exhibiting in the capacity of servant a dog-like fidelity which has stood the supreme test.

Even blacks themselves interiorized some of these views on IQ and did not encourage the younger generation to strive for serious betterment. On the other hand, such investigations of IQ—as in Richard J. Herrenstein and Charles Murray's *The Bell Curve*—have been viewed frequently as not-so-covert exercises in ideological racism rather than as true science, something that the oppressors impose on the oppressed to legitimize their own continuing hegemony. In this matter, it is of interest to note that Henry Hotze from Mobile, Alabama, who acted as a representative of the Confederate States in London during the Civil War, and who commended Father Bannon for his success in Ireland in discouraging Union recruiting efforts, was himself one of the two American translators of the Comte de Gobineau's *The Moral and Intellectual Diversity of Races,* which argued for Nordic racial superiority.[35]

Overall, the white southerner seems to have fared a little better than his Irish or African American counterpart. At least the portrayal hasn't descended to the same simian depictions. Fairly typical is John Mitchel's nineteenth-century account—probably not altogether untrue—of a night at Tuckaleechee Cove with his rustic neighbors:

> Sitting around our fire, of course we talk; and my worthy friends of the 'Cove' have many questions to ask. 'We're but ignorant fellers up in here,' my next neighbor, Cotter, would say; 'and you have seen a [great] many countries, and they say you have sailed over the sea.' This being a fact, and not denied, curious interrogatories would follow. 'Was it true, as we have *hearn,* that the water of the sea is all salted?' Yes, this was actually true; whereupon they exclaimed all around the fire, 'Wall, I do wonder!' this being the usual remark elicited by any singular intelligence.

The stereotype of the white southerner has by no means been excessively mild or merely bantering, however. Journalist Shirley Abbott painfully recalls leaving Arkansas about 1940 to live in California: "Southerners were Arkies, Okies, clay eaters, hicks, tramps—creatures straight out of *Grapes of Wrath* and *God's Little Acre,* novels accursed under my father's roof . . . To the tearful astonishment of my mother, landladies refused to rent to us. 'Don't want any cracker folks around here,' one said, and others shut the door as soon as we opened our mouths."[36]

Irish-American, black, and southern stereotypes were united in the work of nineteenth-century cartoonist Thomas Nast, himself of German origin. In a famous cartoon in *Harper's* in 1868, he lampooned the Democratic

35. William Alexander Percy, *Lanterns on the Levee: Recollections of a Planter's Son* (Baton Rouge, 1973), 303; *Encyclopedia Brittanica* (Cambridge, 1911), 19:344; Robert J. C. Young, *Colonial Desire: Hybridity in Theory, Culture, and Race* (New York, 1995), 140. He was also a founding member of the Anthropological Society in England, whose *Review* once pondered "The Race Question in Ireland."

36. William Dillon, *Life of John Mitchel* (London, 1888), 2:79; Shirley Abbott, *Womenfolks: Growing Up Down South* (New York, 1983), 180. See also David Bertelson, *The Lazy South* (New York, 1980).

Party's conjunction of Irish, white Southern (the figure has a knife bearing the phrase "The Lost Cause"), and northern capital against Reconstruction. These three are depicted standing on a black figure. Even though Nast was opposed to southerners as well as to Irish Catholics, in terms of representation, the white southerner, the black, and the northern banker, all look "normal," while the Irishman has a distinctly simian appearance. Presumably the greatest threat was coming from Irish labor, for in another famous cartoon in 1876, drawn at a time when Nast himself was less sympathetic with blacks—here both Irish and black represent the "ignorant vote"— while Paddy is still the vicious simian, the black figure has been reduced to a grinning Sambo.[37]

Strangely enough, the opposition between "Celt" and "Saxon" also falls within such a stereotypical framework, even if it is generally less comic or overtly hostile. Indeed, both sides tend to see it as having a real historical basis. For those disposed to such a way of thinking, then, the distinction in the Irish-English case was frequently presented—and sometimes so in the South-North case also—as that between a Celtic Ireland and a Saxon England. The former was imaginative but feckless, the latter dull but rational. Inherently superior to the Celt, the Saxon needed to give him political guidance; the Celt, meanwhile, could contribute emotion to the inhibited Saxon. Such was the thrust of Matthew Arnold's highly influential series of lectures at Oxford in 1867, subsequently published as *On the Study of Celtic Literature*. Richard Fallis summarizes what Arnold found basic to the Celtic imagination: "a sense of natural magic and the mystery of life, melancholy titanism coupled with a love for lightness and brightness, generosity, and a continuing rebellion against the despotism of fact." In its more extreme, post-Arnoldian form, as in the case of the *Punch* cartoons, the Celt was a mere child or even belonged to a more primitive race not too unlike, even possibly inferior to, that of the native African.[38]

Arnold's was the judgment of an Englishman addressing other Englishmen, though he claimed that he was grateful for his own Celtic inheritance from his Cornish ancestors. It was certainly a representation that was to have enormous inspirational force for the Irish Literary Revival and one that, however much it was subsequently criticized, many Irish commentators, Yeats and Joyce included, freely adopted. It was also, as has been noted

---

37. Morton Keller, *The Art and Politics of Thomas Nast* (New York, 1968), 27, 155.

38. See Richard Fallis, *The Irish Renaissance* (Syracuse, 1977), 60.

by several observers, relatively courageous for its time, given the degree of animosity toward the Irish then prevalent in Britain: overall, Arnold's comments elevated rather than demoted the Celt. But the Irish *adapted* the Celtic stereotype as well as adopted it, transforming it from female to male, making its powers of imagination vigorously creative rather than weakly impressionable, and so unconsciously—or willingly and unconcernedly— participating in the gender hierarchy of the age.

This Celt-Saxon opposition also appears in one of the most famous caricatures of the South, H. L. Mencken's 1920 essay, "The Sahara of the Bozart," which too was to exert a powerful influence on writers from the region as varied as W. J. Cash, the Nashville Fugitives (John Crowe Ransom and Allen Tate among them), and Richard Wright. Indeed, Wright was liberated simply by seeing that the white South could be criticized at all and took the considerable risk of borrowing the library card of an Irish Catholic co-worker in Memphis—a "Pope lover . . . who was hated by the white Southerners"—to obtain access to the Baltimore debunker's work.[39]

In his essay, Mencken lampoons the region mercilessly, though it is often forgotten that he does so because he thinks, romantically, that the South once had a great civilization, or at least the potential for such under Thomas Jefferson and his like. His most notorious passage runs thus:

> Down there a poet is now almost as rare as an oboe-player, a dry-point etcher or a metaphysician. It is, indeed, amazing to contemplate so vast a vacuity. One thinks of the interstellar spaces, of the colossal reaches of the now mythical ether. Nearly the whole of Europe could be lost in that stupendous region of fat farms, shoddy cities and paralyzed cerebrums: one could throw in France, Germany and Italy, and still have room for the British Isles. And yet, for all its size and all its wealth and all the "progress" it babbles of, it is almost as sterile, artistically, intellectually, culturally, as the Sahara Desert . . . If the whole of the late Confederacy were to be engulfed by a tidal wave tomorrow, the effect upon the civilized minority of men in the world would be little greater than that of a flood on the Yang-tse-kiang. It would be impossible in all history to match so complete a drying-up of a civilization.

In attempting to explain this dearth of culture, Mencken recommends that we turn to the ethnologists to make a study of the origins of the peoples in the region. They are wrongly believed, he argues, to be of Anglo-Saxon

---

39. Richard Wright, *Black Boy* (New York, 1993), 289.

stock. While acknowledging the French, German, Spanish, and black ("a good many of the plebeian whites have negro blood") contributions, he states that "The chief strain down there, I believe, is Celtic rather than Saxon." The Celtic strain "not only makes itself visible in physical stigmata—*e.g.*, leanness and dark coloring—but also in mental traits. For example, the religious thought of the south is almost precisely identical with the religious thought of Wales. There is . . . the same submission to an ignorant and impudent sacerdotal tyranny, and there is the same sharp contrast between doctrinal orthodoxy and private ethics."[40]

Whether encouraged or provoked by Mencken's criticisms—and both responses were widespread—there was still enough mind in the South, of whatever kind it was, to produce a rebirth and so partially free itself from the stereotypes that for so long had confined it. As in the Irish case, even the Celtic stereotype was to lead the way to positive change.

That southerners, white and black, and Irish people, have often provoked similar stereotypes—irregular and never wholly overlapping—would suggest that their real character traits may also have something in common. After all, as Eagleton has pointed out, stereotypes are not completely arbitrary but represent exaggerations and simplifications of genuine behavioral tendencies. Can we, then, find a true substratum of likeness between them? Can we see *through* the stereotypes to such an underlying similarity? Diverse ethnicities, diverse belief systems, under pressure from similar social and economic forces can dissolve into cultures that have significant commonalities.

As we saw at the outset, Seán O'Faoláin in comparing his own County Cork with William Faulkner's rural Mississippi has offered as it were a short list of presumed characteristics for comparative examination: "There is the same passionate provincialism; the same local patriotism; the same southern nationalism . . . the same vanity of the old race; the same gnawing sense of defeat; the same capacity for intense hatred; a good deal of the same harsh folk-humor; the same acidity; the same oscillation between unbounded self-confidence and total despair; the same escape through sport and drink." Grady McWhiney too found remarkably similar cultural and behavioral patterns between the Celts of the British Isles and the white inhabitants of the American South, laziness, violence, and dueling among them. "The published *Irish Code of Honor* was the model for South Caroli-

40. H. L. Mencken, *Prejudices* (New York, 1958), 69–70, 76.

na's own dueling code," he observed. Since, however, many of these non-stereotypical traits seem more suited for treatment in later chapters on comparatively similar literary developments and attitudes toward history—and some are dubious—here I choose my own list, based partly on O'Faoláin's with borrowings from other commentators, and offer some support for its various items.[41]

First, then, is the love of talk for talk's sake. In the Irish case, this characteristic can quickly dissolve into a sentimental celebration of "Blarney" and Irish "bulls," or, from a contrary point of view, into a condemnation of such speech for its insincerity and deviousness. All too often it is represented as that combination of eloquence and stupidity noted by the writer in *The Story of English*. It is, however, part of what O'Faoláin thought of as peculiarly Irish: the emphasis on the personal as opposed to the abstract—seeing life in terms of its associated human interactions rather than as a set of issues that require rational solution.

W. J. Cash considered that the white Southerner's similar love of talk derived from his exposure to "the example of the Negro, concerning whom nothing is so certain as his remarkable tendency to seize on lovely words, to roll them in his throat, to heap them in redundant profusion one upon another until meaning vanishes and there is nothing left but the sweet, canorous drunkenness of sound, nothing but the play of primitive rhythm upon the secret springs of emotion." Of course, certain words and phrases here—"until meaning vanishes," "primitive rhythm"—should make one wary of uncritically accepting his analysis. But Allen Tate offered a more convincing—albeit whiter—spin on the same phenomenon when he observed that "The traditional Southern mode of discourse . . . is the rhetorical mode." "The Southerner," he explained,

> always talks to somebody else, and this somebody else, after varying intervals, is given his turn; but the conversation is always among rhetoricians;

41. Seán O'Faoláin, *The Vanishing Hero: Studies in Novelists of the Twenties* (Freeport, N.Y., 1957), 75; Grady McWhiney, *Cracker Culture* (Tuscaloosa, Ala., 1988), 36, 153. However, in 'That Damn'd Thing Called Honour': Duelling in Ireland, 1570–1860 (Cork, 1995), James Kelly argues that the "established image Ireland possessed as a duellist's Olympus" cannot be substantiated (279). Even with Ireland's famous rural faction fighting in the nineteenth century, it isn't clear that it had a higher rate of violence than England; and in the late twentieth century with the turmoil in Northern Ireland, the number of fatalities has been far lower than in many American cities. See also Carolyn Conley, *Melancholy Accidents: The Meaning of Violence in Post-Famine Ireland* (New York, 1999).

that is to say, the typical Southern conversation is not going anywhere; it is not about anything. *It is about the people who are talking,* even if they never refer to themselves, which they usually don't, since conversation is only an expression of manners, the purpose of which is to make everybody happy. This may be the reason why Northerners and other uninitiated persons find the alternating, or contrapuntal, conversation of Southerners fatiguing. Educated Northerners like their conversation to be about ideas.

In a very similar way, British journalist John Ardagh (yet another of those seemingly all-pervasive Englishmen of Irish ancestry) in his study of *Ireland and the Irish* reports a complaint about Southern Irish loquacity as being less sincere than Northern Irish taciturnity.[42]

O'Faoláin's sense of rural Ireland and the rural South being provincial in outlook is also accurate and perhaps only to be expected. Ardagh noticed that even Irish academics seemed interested in other countries only insofar as they had some connection with Ireland. The South too, of course, perhaps partly because of its traditionally poor educational system, often seems turned in on itself without much interest in or knowledge of the rest of even the United States. Whether such provincialism is the result of having a strong sense of place is open to question, but it too is a commonly observed characteristic of both Irishmen and southerners. As O'Faoláin has claimed, the Celt's "idea of Heaven is free of Time but it is rooted in Place," while the tradition of *dinnseanachas*—naming places in accordance with their characteristics—is deeply set in Irish Gaelic poetry. Eudora Welty has devoted an entire essay to the subject in regard to the South and has subsequently related it to a similar sentiment in the works of Elizabeth Bowen from Cork. Tate too has remarked of his youth in "backward" Kentucky that "This preindustrial society meant, for people living in it, that one's identity had everything to do with land and material property, at a definite place, and very little to do with money."[43]

As Frank O'Connor has observed of Irish culture, W. J. Cash has noted

---

42. W. J. Cash, *The Mind of the South* (New York, 1969), 53; Allen Tate, *Essays of Four Decades* (Chicago, 1968), 593, 584; it is W. B. Yeats whom Tate invokes in attempting to explain the appearance of the new southern literature at the beginning of the twentieth century: "The Southern legend . . . of defeat and heroic frustration was taken over by a dozen or more first-rate writers and converted into a universal myth of the human condition. W. B. Yeats's great epigram points to the nature of the shift from melodramatic rhetoric to the dialectic of tragedy: 'Out of the quarrel with others we make rhetoric; out of the quarrel with ourselves, poetry'" (592); see John Ardagh, *Ireland and the Irish* (London, 1994).

43. Seán O'Faoláin, *The Irish* (New York, 1967), 32; Tate, 581.

too that the South lacked complexity because, in its world of small farms and large plantations, there were hardly any towns. He adds, in a remark similar to that made by the young W. B. Yeats about the Anglo-Irish gentry, that people's interest was in horses, dogs, and guns rather than in books: the culture's satisfactions were in the immediacies of speech rather than in the remoteness of writing. It was not a culture of detachment, but rather, and "before all else, personal."[44]

It was the narrow-mindedness that such provinciality inevitably led to that drove so many Southern and Irish writers and thinkers to leave for the very England or Northeast that they professed despising—and in some ways did. It could be said too that they had to go because what they were saying about the society still mattered in a personal way (painfully, perhaps, rather than deeply), whereas in London or New York it had been aestheticized into the culture of "art."

One conclusion to be drawn from all of this is that negative stereotyping is at its most intense when there is a threat to the dominant society and when there is no obvious way of containing that disturbance. Another follows: stereotypes can change over time. So, with the easing of tensions in Northern Ireland and the economic boom in the south of the country—the so-called Celtic Tiger, a figure of almost hyperaggressive masculinity—English hostile cartooning of the Irish seems to have temporarily abated. Likewise, in some ways, with the general American representation of a less racist white South, or with white southern representations of blacks where public officials and social commentators tread very carefully indeed, even if the realities on the ground remain troubling. Societies too that were once lampooned for their easygoing and even lazy ways are now sometimes criticized for their new-found efficiencies. Here again some sense of the constructed nature of all identities and of the shaping power of economic forces seems to have seeped through to popular awareness, leading to greater self-consciousness and self-criticism in the use of pejorative imagery and more objective analyses of cultural developments. Of course, there are no guarantees that rationality in this area will prevail should new tensions arise in the future.

If one is inclined to be critical of the British and northeasterners in such cases, however, it is probably well to keep in mind that neither Irish Protestant nor Irish Catholic, southern black nor southern white, would

44. Cash, 100–101.

necessarily object to racist depictions of other outside forces or nations threatening them. The stereotypical perceptions of the Irish held by southerners white and black, and of southerners white and black by the Irish, are practically identical with those found among northeasterners and British people, respectively. It is perhaps unrealistic too to expect that in times of crisis, balance and empathy should find anything more than short shrift. The self-deprecating (rather than self-accusatory) admission of past wrongs is nearly always conducted from the safe haven of a present in which there are likely to be minimal or no material consequences for the speaker. But the current enemy, it would seem, must ever be profiled; Caliban must ever be reinvented and re-repressed. While within the British Isles and within the United States, it seems unlikely that Irish (and, to a lesser extent, Scottish) and southern stereotypes are going to disappear anytime soon—and there is a large trove ever available for lazy recycling—their viciousness will continue to be modified as their perpetrators increase in their own critical self-awareness and as poverty and poor education recede in these areas. At least one can take some consolation from the fact—as did Atticus Finch in *To Kill a Mockingbird*—that the biased jury is deliberating longer than it was inclined to do in the past. While semi-simpleton Seamus Finnigan explodes his way through the pages of the *Harry Potter* stories, in the 2002 revision of *The Story of English* the phrase about the Irish being "envied for their eloquence . . . [and] almost in the same breath scorned for their 'stupidity' " has been surgically excised from its offending paragraph. And tomorrow will be another day.[45]

45. McCrum, Cran, and MacNeil, 163, and *The Story of English*, 3rd rev. ed. (New York, 2002), 170.

CHAPTER 8

WRITING WITH AN ACCENT

The language of our people has been for centuries, and is up to the present day, in a transition state. The English tongue is gradually superseding the Irish.

—WILLIAM CARLETON, *Traits and Stories of the Irish Peasantry*, 1833

The famous Southern *you-all* is a Scots-Irish translation of *yous*. The use of *all* in this context . . . is typical both of Ulster and of the (largely southern) states of America.

—*The Story of English*, 1986

Because some of his ancestors came from Ulster, Edgar Allan Poe has on at least one occasion found himself confined within the strange and eerie precincts of an anthology of Anglo-Irish literature. However, the Irish patriot Thomas MacDonagh, a college lecturer in English until executed for his part in the 1916 Easter Rising (his last classroom presentation was on the novels of Jane Austen), quite rightly considered Poe's association with Ireland to be far too "slender" to merit such inclusion. That honor belongs rather to Richard Henry Wilde, an Irish-born immigrant to Georgia whose poetry was, in fact, condemned by the fastidious Poe (though praised by Byron). Indeed, Wilde has the unique, if perhaps dubious, distinction of being represented in both the multivolume *Irish Literature* of 1904 and the corresponding *Library of Southern Literature* of 1907.[1]

Wilde's family left Dublin for Baltimore in 1797 when he was eight years old. Although hard times followed his father's death a few years later, the young immigrant succeeded in becoming a lawyer and subsequently a representative for Georgia in the U.S. Congress. He was also a noted translator of Italian literature and an accomplished man of letters in his own right. Wilde is best remembered, however, for a single poem, "The Lament of the Captive" (also known as "My Life Is Like the Summer Rose"), a ro-

1. *The Field Day Anthology of Irish Literature*, vol. 2, ed. Seamus Deane (Dublin, 1991), 990.

mantic expression of the sadness felt by a Spanish nobleman held prisoner by Indians in coastal Georgia in the 1600s:

> My life is like the summer rose,
>   That opens to the morning sky,
> But, ere the shades of evening close,
>   Is scattered on the ground—to die!

The poem enjoyed enormous popularity in the early part of the nineteenth century and survived in southern literature anthologies as late as the 1970s.[2]

Amusingly—at least now—in 1834, twenty years after its first publication, Wilde was accused of plagiarism in the pages of *The New-York Weekly Register and Catholic Diary*, where it was argued that the poem was actually the work of another Irishman, one Patrick O'Kelly, author also of the famed "Curse of Doneraile" (neither poet nor poem appears in *Irish Literature*). For Georgians, however, the manner of the accusation smacked of "arrogant discourtesy," as one might well agree on consulting the *Diary*: "We wish," declared Wilde's accuser, "to pluck the stolen laurels from the honorable plagiarist of Georgia, and replace those offerings of the Irish muse on the literary shrine of Innisfallen, to which the poetic genius, O'Kelly, the esteemed and popular bard of passion and patriotism, originally consecrated them. The white feathers of the Singing Swan of Killarney, thanks to the detection of our correspondent, have not been long suffered to remain as felonious ornaments in the black wings of the Georgian Gander." Here—with perhaps a touch of Catholic-Protestant rivalry and a total elision of Wilde's Irish origins—was grand rhetoric indeed! The only change that Wilde had added, it was alleged, was to substitute a reference to the beach at Lahinch in County Clare with one to that at Tampa in Florida.

> My life is like the prints, which feet
>   Have left on Tampa's desert strand;
> Soon as the rising tide shall beat,
>   All trace will vanish from the sand.

For a while, it even seemed as if both Irishmen had plagiarized an original Greek poem by Alcaeus.[3]

---

2. Louis D. Rubin Jr., ed., *The Literary South* (Baton Rouge, 1979), 170–71.

3. Anthony Barclay, *Wilde's Summer Rose; or, The Lament of the Captive. An authentic account of the origin, mystery and explanation of Hon. R. H. Wilde's alleged plagiarism* (Savannah, Ga., 1871), 40.

Wilde was finally vindicated, however—and the Georgia Historical Society saw fit to issue an impressive monograph on the controversy as late as 1871—one of the clinching arguments being about the difference between the life-cycles of southern and Irish roses:

> The allusion to the rose . . . could only apply, even with poetical justice, to the Florida rose, which, as Wilde states in the note, "opens, fades, and perishes during the summer in less than twelve hours." It would be false and forced in relation to any other species of rose, and could only naturally present itself to the imagination of a southern poet, who alone would be likely to be familiar with its touching poetical associations. The probability of its occurring to an Irish bard of the character of O'Kelly is in our opinion to amount to a complete bar to his pretensions.

So much for Irish-southern mutual esteem, though the incident does also show that it was not impossible for a "Wilde" Irishman to acquire "the imagination of a southern poet."[4]

Another, less controversial, poem by Wilde, "America Too Young for Poetry," laments, Hawthorne-like, that though his adopted country's "woods are as green, the skies as clear" as those in the Old World, yet there is wanting "the memories that endear / Spots haunted by the good or wise or brave." It was a common complaint in a new country and one, it could be argued, that with the exception of such problematically southern writers as Poe and Twain, authors in the region did little to remedy.[5]

In rural Ireland too, with the mass of the people in the early nineteenth century finally making the transition from Gaelic to English—English was spoken in the cities and towns centuries before that—William Carleton observed a similar sense of coming into a "new" country, of literally renaming the landscape, as indeed the British mapmakers were doing at the time. Declan Kiberd has remarked that in Carleton's stories "the enfeebled culture of Ireland after the Penal Laws, already in English, is revealed in all its poverty. Because he came from Irish-speaking parents, he was more acutely aware of the scale of that degeneration, about which he seems to have heard almost daily." Rawness, amateurism, even clumsiness prevailed in both cases, if not quite in the writers themselves, then in the culture which they were setting out to describe. Moreover, all too many talented writers

4. Ibid., 38–39.
5. Richard Henry Wilde, *Library of Southern Literature*, 13:5794–95.

in both nineteenth-century Ireland and in the American South were drawn
to composing a literature of openly political propaganda—which was what
the times demanded—rather than one primarily focused on aesthetic or
sociopsychological considerations. In all, the nineteenth century was not
the high point of literary culture in either place, a fact, of course, that in
itself points to a similarity between them.[6]

It is true that there has recently been a more sympathetic reexamina-
tion of nineteenth-century literary production in Ireland and the South,
calling into question whether they can accurately be regarded as vast waste-
lands of the fictive imagination. Rather, their very confusion and incoherence can be seen to represent a Bakhtinian dialogue of competing voices
and social uncertainties. Nevertheless, overall there is no doubt but that
the southern writers of the nineteenth century cannot match Emerson,
Thoreau, Hawthorne, Melville, Dickinson, and Whitman in the Northeast,
any more than Ireland's Thomas Moore, Gerald Griffin, James Clarence
Mangan, William Carleton, or even Maria Edgeworth are a match for England's Austen, Wordsworth, Brontë, Tennyson, Dickens, and Eliot. A
writer such as Anthony Trollope, who spanned both Irish and English culture, proves the point: his overwhelming success was with English subjects,
suggesting that the works he had composed in Ireland were not as engaging, or, more critically, that the culture simply eluded him. In any case, in
comparison with the major writers of the period in England and America,
the Irish and southern productions are distinctly minor. One has to wait
for the twentieth century to find a situation in which the balance might be
said to swing the opposite way—or a least to *balance*—with the onset of the
movements that have come to be known as the Irish Literary Revival and
Southern Literary Renascence.

But again, while the twentieth century is where the Irish-South literary
parallel and influence hold most strongly, the nineteenth century also offers, as I hinted above, a similarity that is not without significance. The
pervasive influence of Sir Walter Scott's border novels in both Ireland—
where John Mitchel was a great admirer, especially of *Rob Roy*—and the
South led to a highly romantic and unrealistic engagement with the past,
one not counterbalanced by a critical perspective. As W. B. Yeats was to
put the matter much later, Scott "gave Highland legends and Highland ex-

6. See John H. Andrews, *A Paper Landscape: The Ordnance Survey in Nineteenth-Century Ireland* (Dublin, 2002); also Brian Friel's play *Translations* (London, 1981); Declan Kiberd, *Irish
Classics* (Cambridge, Mass., 2001), 280.

citability so great a mastery over all romance that they seem romance it-self." It might not be too much of an exaggeration to say that just as Scott's novels have been held responsible for the Civil War (at least on the south-ern side), they may also be held responsible for rehistoricizing and thus for indirectly reinforcing traditional Irish-English tensions. Scott too was indebted to the international interest in all things Celtic that resulted from his fellow-countryman James Macpherson's creative translations of original Irish legends.[7]

Poe's Gothicism, influenced in part by Irish writer Charles Maturin's *Melmoth the Wanderer,* affected later Irish Gothic writers in turn. Both Sheridan Le Fanu and James Clarence Mangan have been described sepa-rately as the "Irish Poe," though, unlike him, the Irish writers tended to set their tales in recognizable historical contexts. As Kiberd has observed: "Gothic, with its aura of feudal grandeur and ruined glories, may have ap-pealed to a once-proud, now-marginal, [Irish] Protestant elite—much as it would appeal to decayed landowners of the American South." The "Big House" novel, too, dominates Irish literature as the plantation novel be-comes characteristic of the South. Augustus Baldwin Longstreet's *Georgia Scenes,* which appeared in 1835 and sought to preserve the fast-disappearing customs and speech of frontier people, have their parallel in Carleton's *Traits and Stories of the Irish Peasantry* in 1830, which also sought to preserve the manners and customs among the riotous peasantry of the pre-famine years. And, at mid-century, entrepreneur and master of the melodrama, Dublin's Dion Bouccicault, with his *Coleen Bawn* and *The Octoroon* (in which he criticized slavery openly in the European staging, more circum-spectly in the American), as well as a stint at theater management in New Orleans, seems to have functioned as an Irish and southern impresario and playwright almost equally.[8]

However, it was the voice of another kind of Irish writer that was to have the most effect in the nineteenth-century American South, perhaps because he had a covert political message. He too was the author of a "rose" poem, this time an Irish one, "The Last Rose of Summer." According to some estimates, the circulation of Thomas Moore's *Irish Melodies* was even greater than that of Scott's novels or of Moore's friend Lord Byron's poems. "The *Irish Melodies* were the most popular songs in America in the second

7. *Yeats's Poetry, Drama, and Prose,* ed. James Pethica (New York, 2000), 265.

8. Kiberd, 383. See comments on Boucicault in Elizabeth Cullingford, *Ireland's Others: Gen-der and Ethnicity in Irish Literature and Popular Culture* (Notre Dame, 2001), 173–74.

and third decades of the nineteenth century," notes Charles Hamm. On his deathbed, Thomas Jefferson—whom Moore had mocked for his relationship with Sally Hemings—quoted from the *Melodies* in his last letter to his daughter. A "dour, laconic" Jefferson Davis liked to sing "The Minstrel Boy."[9]

In the Jefferson-Hemings poem, Moore had also poked fun at the American fantasy that their capital was the new Rome:

> In fancy now, beneath the twilight gloom,
> Come, let me lead thee o'er this modern Rome,
> Where tribunes rule, where dusky Davi bow,
> And what was Goose-Creek once is Tiber now!—
> This fam'd metropolis, where fancy sees
> Squares in morasses, obelisks in trees;
> Which travelling fools and gazetteers adorn
> With shrines unbuilt and heroes yet unborn,
> Though nought but wood and [Jefferson] they see,
> Where streets should run and sages *ought* to be!

It was Moore's *Melodies*, not his political satire, that carried the day. Stephen Foster, whose family originated in Ulster, was brought up on them and, Hamm claims, it is "inconceivable" that his "Jeanie with the Light Brown Hair" could "have been written had there not been a Thomas Moore." In the late twentieth century, Jim Flannery, the *Melodies'* ablest vocal interpreter, records singing one of them to a racially mixed audience and having a West African drummer remark enthusiastically: "Man, I never thought any white man had that much soul."[10]

Moore was of middle-class Irish Catholic background and born early enough to witness and be cautioned by the reprisals against his countrymen

9. Charles Hamm, *Yesterdays: Popular Song in America* (New York, 1979), 58–59. In her 1913 memoir, *My Beloved South* (New York, 1914), Mrs. T. P. O'Connor, a native of Texas and wife of the Irish Home Rule parliamentarian of the same name, observes: "Every old library in the South, no matter how meagre, contains *Chambers' Journal* . . . Byron, Moore, Keats, Shelley, Tennyson, Thackeray, a complete set of Scott and Dickens, and several Books of Beauty" (263); James W. Flannery, *Dear Harp of My Country: The Irish Melodies of Thomas Moore* (Nashville, 1997), 117; E. Lawrence Abel, *Singing the New Nation: How Music Shaped the Confederacy, 1861–1865* (Mechanicsburg, Pa., 2000), 178.

10. Thomas Moore, from "Epistle VI. To Lord Viscount Forbes. From Washington," and from "Epistle VII. To Thomas Hume, Esq, M. D. From the City of Washington," excerpted in *Amazing Grace: An Anthology of Poems about Slavery, 1660–1810,* ed. James G. Basker (New Haven, 2002), 594; Flannery, 119; Hamm, 219.

that followed the 1798 rebellion. The songs that he later composed speak wistfully of a buried rather than a living culture. It is likely that his work was so enormously popular among the English elite precisely because it romantically evoked the past in a way that was unlikely to promote revolution in the present. Still, some of the more conservative elements in British society considered his lyrics treasonous. Above all, Moore is the poet of memory, of Faulkner's desire "to never forget" (though there's more edge in the latter) rather than of the need for present action:

> Let Erin remember the days of old,
> Ere her faithless sons betray'd her,
> When Malachi wore the collar of gold,
> Which he won from her proud invader;
> When her Kings, with standards of green unfurl'd,
> Led the Red-Branch Knights to danger,
> Ere the em'rald gem of the western world
> Was set in the crown of a stranger.

Here the "pride" of the invading English is acknowledged, while the last line both exalts Ireland (it is ensconced in a crown) and also reassures the possessors of that crown that they are threatened by no more than regretful resentment—even, indeed, that Ireland is now truly "set" within the Union. Little wonder that this popular song was to be adopted in 1901—and still remains—as the regimental march for the newly-created Irish Guards of the British Army.[11]

To what extent Moore was a political conformist rather than a covert revolutionary has long been a matter of debate. His wildly successful Orientalist writings show that he could imperialistically "other" the East as much as any writer before or after him (in 1868 the New Orleans Comus Krewe based their Mardi Gras "procession of horsemen, complete with Oriental costumes and scimitars, reenacting 'The Departure of Lally Rookh from Delhi'" on Moore's famous poem on the subject). Certainly, whatever the nuances of Moore's own views were, the more militant Young Ireland movement that developed toward the end of his life saw him as both an inspiration and as a writer that had to be surpassed for political effectiveness. Thomas Davis, the most important of the Young Irelanders who, with Gavan Duffy, was a founder and editor of the *Nation,* was intent on making Irish nationalism popular through the medium of song. Davis complained

11. Flannery, 158.

that Moore "does not speak of the stronger passions, spoils some of his finest songs by pretty images, is too refined and subtle in his dialect." While he "is immeasurably our greatest poet . . . he has not given songs to the middle and poor classes of Ireland." For Duffy, Moore's poems "dating from the unsuccessful insurrection of '98 and the Union were the wail of a lost cause" whereas "the songs of the *Nation* vibrated with the virile and passionate hopes of a new generation."[12]

Davis himself wanted to overcome this situation. He complained of the songs, both in English and Gaelic, then available: "Their structure is irregular, their grief slavish and despairing, their joy reckless and bombastic, their religion bitter and sectarian, their politics Jacobite, and concealed by extravagant and tiresome allegory." Thus, in "Penal Days," Davis declared that such earlier times should be forgotten because "All creeds are equal in our isle." Even the strong sentiments expressed in his "notorious poem" titled "Celt and Saxon," where the opening line runs, "We hate the Saxon and the Dane," quickly urges that those of Irish birth and sentiment need not worry since "We heed not blood, nor creed, nor clan." According to Mary Helen Thuente, "The song is actually a celebration of 'How every race and every creed / Might be by love combined.'" Davis criticized Augustine Thierry, a French thinker sympathetic with the Irish cause, for laying too much emphasis on race: "We must sink the distinctions of blood as well as sect. The Milesian, the Dane, the Norman, the Welshman, the Scotchman, and the Saxon, naturalised here, must combine, regardless of their blood . . . This is as much needed as the mixture of Protestant and Catholic."[13]

But Davis knew all too well that a broad public just then acquiring literacy through the medium of the English taught in the recently established national schools—where the speaking of Irish Gaelic was suppressed through a regulated system of corporal punishment—needed to hear its own history retold in accessible terms. Such retelling would act as an antidote to the British version being disseminated through the new national schools. Long afterward, W. B. Yeats was to express his ambivalence about Davis's legacy, being both envious of his popularity and critical of his submission to the needs of a cause. But it was a style of writing that had imme-

12. See Leith Davis, "Irish Bards and English Consumers: Thomas Moore's 'Irish Melodies' and the Colonized Nation," *Ariel* 24, no. 2 (1993): 7–25, for an account of how Moore's work "both paved and blocked the way to the decolonization which is still in process in Ireland." James Gill, *Lords of Misrule: Mardi Gras and the Politics of Race in New Orleans* (Jackson, Miss., 1997); Mary Helen Thuente, *The Harp Re-strung* (Syracuse, N.Y., 1994), 201.

13. Thuente, 205, 213.

diate appeal for nationalists in Ireland, as well as for Father Ryan in the American South and that obviously influenced his poetry on behalf of the Confederate cause.

The popular balladry of the *Nation* in post-famine Ireland and the Home Rule advocacy of the Fenian Charles Kickham's sentimental writing about "The Homes of Tipperary" in *Knocknagow*—one historian has called him the Maxim Gorky of the Irish revolution—have their southern (if somewhat grander) parallel in what Allen Tate has referred to rather unfairly, perhaps, as the "Confederate prose" of the now politically defensive plantation novels of the post–Civil War era. Augusta Evans Wilson's *Macaria; or Altars of Sacrifice,* published in Richmond just before the war's end—and deeply influenced by the progressive views of John Stuart Mill on women's education—concludes with the following emblematic passage:

> Irene raised her holy violet eyes and looked through the window toward the cemetery, where glittered a tall marble shaft which the citizens of W—— had erected over the last quiet resting-place of Russell Aubrey. Sands of Time were drifting stealthily around the crumbling idols of the morning of life, levelling and tenderly shrouding the Past . . . The rays of the setting sun gilded her mourning-dress, gleamed in the white roses that breathed their perfume in her rippling hair, and lingered like a benediction on the placid, pure face of the lonely woman who had survived every earthly hope; and who, calmly fronting her Altars of Sacrifice, here dedicated herself anew to the hallowed work of promoting the happiness and gladdening the paths of all who journeyed with her down the chequered aisles of Time.

In all, the second half of the century consisted of four or five decades of remarkably unaesthetic writing, but writing nevertheless that had a marked influence on its readers: Wilson's novel, however stilted its style, gave courage and comfort to those who survived. One has only to browse through those ten volumes of the aforementioned 1904 collection, *Irish Literature,* or the sixteen volumes of the *Library of Southern Literature,* which began publication in 1907, to see numerous examples of this kind of writing, a style that the cultural studies emphasis in recent decades has partly restored to at least scholarly interest.[14]

14. Allen Tate, "A Southern Mode of the Imagination," in *Essays of Four Decades* (Chicago, 1968), 579. See Susan V. Donaldson's criticisms of Tate in "Gender, Race, and Allen Tate's Profession of Letters in the South," in *Haunted Bodies: Gender and Southern Texts,* ed. Anne Goodwyn Jones and Susan V. Donaldson (Charlottesville, Va., 1997), 492–518; Augusta Evans

All was not bleakness, however, from either an aesthetic or a sociological point of view. In both places a literature emerged that, while not always highly regarded in its own time since it did not contribute directly to the national cause, is now seen as significant. In the Irish case, this literature was produced by writers such as William Carleton and Gerald Griffin; in the South, by those authors collectively known as the Southwest humorists. For example, one can see that Carleton's satiric depictions of rapacious Catholic clergy as they visit their parishioners in their homes or extort ec-clesiastical fees from indigent laborers, or the various tricksters that he meets on a pilgrimage in 1817, have a parallel in J. J. Hooper's satires on the camp revival meetings with their equally self-aggrandizing evangelists. It is clear also in the two cases that they represent a different genre from both Anthony Trollope's *Barchester* novels dealing with sophisticated par-sonage intrigue and from Hawthorne's critiques of New England Puritan-ism. There is much more sense in the Irish and southern cases of an unformed society, or at least of one that has become unsettled and is in the process of reforming itself with all the confusion and mayhem that under-taking implies.

In Carleton's autobiographical "The Lough Derg Pilgrim" from 1833—the reference is to the centuries-old custom of making a penitential journey to a lake island in Donegal associated with St. Patrick—the skeptical, but rather innocent, narrator encounters a world of characters far more wily than himself. A nineteen-year-old Catholic aspirant to the priesthood when he made the pilgrimage in 1817 but a confirmed Protestant when he wrote his account some fifteen years later, Carleton now looks upon the place as guilty of "the monstrous birth of a dreary and degraded superstition . . . destined to keep the human understanding in the same dark unproductive state as the moorland waste that lay outstretched around." Among the pil-grims themselves, there was "every description of guilt, and every degree of religious feeling": "I could see the man of years, I thought, withering away under the disconsolation of an ill-spent life, old without peace, and gray without wisdom, flattering himself that he is religious because he prays, and making a merit of offering to God that which Satan had rejected; think-ing, too, that he has withdrawn from sin, because the ability of committing

Wilson, *Macaria; or, Altars of Sacrifice* (Richmond, 1864), 183. In many ways *The Field Day Anthology of Irish Literature* is a return to this model, though more inclusive and less senti-mental.

it has left him, and taking credit for subduing his propensities, although they have only died in his nature."[15]

At night the narrator finds himself "wedged in a shake-down bed with seven others, one of whom was a Scotch-Papist—another a man with a shrunk leg, who wore a crutch—all afflicted with that disease which northern men that feed on oatmeal are liable to." Later, in the darkness of the island's chapel, some of the sleep-deprived pilgrims emit "groans and shrieks" or convulse in "sudden paroxysms." Prayers are said in English by pilgrims "totally ignorant of that language" with so many malapropisms that even the priests laugh outright at the poor perpetrators. The narrator is gulled out of his silver by a professional pilgrim who offers to pray for him, and, finally, loses even his clothes to a well-known female masquerader.[16]

Compare this scene with J. J. Hooper's 1845 story, "The Captain Attends a Camp Meeting," where we get some of the flavor of a similar occasion, though the satire is more biting and there is less of the sense of reporting than we find in Carleton:

> When [Captain Simon Suggs] arrived there, he found the hollow square of the encampment filled with people, listening to the mid-day sermon and its dozen accompanying "exhortations." A half-dozen preachers were dispensing the word . . . The excitement was intense. Men and women rolled about on the ground, or lay sobbing or shouting in promiscuous heaps. More than all, the negroes sang and screamed and prayed. Several, under the influence of what is technically called "the jerks," were plunging and pitching about with convulsive energy. The great object of all seemed to be, to see who could make the greatest noise . . . "Keep the thing warm!" roared a sensual seeming man, of stout mould and florid countenance, who was exhorting among a bevy of young women, upon whom be was lavishing caresses. "Keep the thing warm, breethring!—come to the Lord, honey!" he added, as he vigorously hugged one of the damsels he sought to save.

Hooper's work was regarded as only marginally literary in its day, yet it is he and other writers like him who now seem fresh and vigorous where the more genteel and politically defensive voices have been all but obliterated.[17]

Of course, as was argued earlier in the case of Father Ryan—who certainly belongs with the sentimental and nationalistic—that genteel writing is not without justification or appeal. Indeed, recent criticism has been

---

15. William Carleton, *The Works of William Carleton* (New York, 1970), 797, 806, 807.

16. Ibid., 810, 813.

17. J. J. Hooper, *Adventures of Captain Simon Suggs* (Tuscaloosa, Ala., 1993), 119–20.

quite sympathetic to such nineteenth-century southern novelists as John Pendleton Kennedy and William Gilmore Simms (partly a mocking imitator of the Irish Lady Morgan), much as Irish criticism is reexamining Carleton and Kickham. Simms's short stories, with their relatively nuanced awareness of the African origins of, and social distinctions among, the slaves, suggest instabilities that went unrecognized in earlier readings. Poe's stories are now seen by some as remarkable predictions of the fall of the southern big house, just as Joseph Sheridan Le Fanu's horrors mirror an anxiety about the precariousness of his Anglo-Irish class status in a predominantly Catholic and peasant culture aggressively pursuing social advancement. The fact too that *Dracula*, which on the surface doesn't seem in any way Irish, was written by an exile of Anglo-Irish origin born in "black '47" (the worst year of the potato blight) is of more than merely coincidental interest: it can be interpreted in part as a cry of postcolonial horror in the presence of the living dead of the famine era.[18]

Meanwhile, Simms's four historical novels, beginning with *Guy Rivers* in 1834, are now understood as serious examinations of their respective periods, attempts to create a history for the South that would be both complex and accurate. John Banim too, Ireland's first Catholic novelist and known as "the Irish Scott," had attempted the same for his nation, especially with his tale of the Williamite wars, *The Boyne Water*, in 1826. There is even the intriguing case of Joel Chandler Harris, son of an unknown Irish itinerant laborer who almost immediately abandoned the family: Harris's acute shyness and depression have been attributed to this traumatic experience, as has his creation of black Uncle Remus as a kind of substitute father figure. At the same time, Harris wrote about Irish characters in a number of his other stories—"The Comedy of War" and "Captain McCarthy" (described by a contemporary reviewer as "the soul of Confederate intrigue")—and his collecting of African slave folktales is not unlike John Millington Synge's empathetic, if also potentially condescending, fascination with the people of the Aran Islands, an exploration that has recently been compared too to James Agee's visit to poor whites in Alabama's Hale County as described in *Let Us Now Praise Famous Men*.[19]

Kennedy, Simms, and another Scotch-Irishman, William Alexander

18. See Kiberd's chapter, "Undead in the Nineties: Bram Stoker and *Dracula*," in *Irish Classics*, 379–98.

19. See especially Joseph M. Griska Jr., "In Stead of a 'Gift of Gab': Some New Perspectives on Joel Chandler Harris Biography,'" in *Critical Essays on Joel Chandler Harris*, ed. R. Bruce Bickley Jr. (Boston, 1981).

Caruthers, author of *The Cavaliers of Virginia*, were among the novelists responsible for giving to the South—emerging in the 1830s and 40s as an entity separate from the rest of the country—its foundational myth of having been descended from the English Cavalier tradition that had fought for Charles I in their Civil War against the Puritan forces of Oliver Cromwell. Kennedy and Simms are especially interesting because both these writers had immigrant Irish fathers to whom they stood in ambiguous relation, while they also devoted a small portion of their writing to Irish characters. One important consideration about both of them is that they felt compelled by the larger culture to identify with their English inheritance (or rather sought to identify with a heritage that was only marginally theirs since they were both *arrivistes*), much as was to be the case with F. Scott Fitzgerald a hundred years later. Kennedy's immigrant father was a wealthy merchant until his business collapsed, his mother a member of a distinguished Virginia family. His "Irish" writing, such as it was, lay in his interest in the early history of Maryland and the Catholic-Protestant tensions of those years (the 1680s), and his identification with the Cavalier Catholic tradition (though this was more of a refined English tradition than an Irish raucous one) in those stories. This material is to be found in "A Legend of Maryland" and in both his 1835 novel *Horse-Shoe Robinson* and his 1838 *Rob of the Bowl*. Ben Forkner and Patrick Samway remark of *Horse-Shoe Robinson* that "the title character epitomizes the ideal Southerner—half Scotch-Irish-backwoodsman and half-chivalric cavalier."[20]

William Gilmore Simms was undoubtedly the greatest of the pre–Civil War southern novelists, and it is his *Paddy McGann; or, The Demon of the Stump*, first published serially in 1863 in *The Southern Illustrated News*, that is of most interest in making an Irish-southern comparison, though there are also a couple at least of his short stories that Gerald Donovan recently has argued have some of their sources in the folklore of his father's County Antrim. Simms was often praised by his contemporaries for his "Irish eloquence," while his father was referred to as "Celtic to the core," which is explained rather stereotypically as his being "by family testimony and the evidence of his actions—rash, courageous, bold, and resolute." Mary Ann Wimsatt also claims that this Celtic strain predominated in Simms. While most critics have seen *Paddy McGann* as an example of Simms's ongoing concern with the theme of the blending of settled and frontier traditions,

20. Ben Forkner and Patrick Samway, eds., *Stories of the Old South* (New York, 1989), xv.

an opportunity for withering commentary on the contemporary literary establishment in the Northeast (where his books were published), and an attempt to establish a distinctive and "historical" South, James P. Cantrell, partly basing himself on the Celtic South thesis of McWhiney and McDonald, has argued strongly for the all-importance of the Irish aspects of *Paddy McGann*.[21]

The frame for the story is a dialogue between two gentlemen southerners, Wharncliffe, a planter, and Stylus, a writer not unlike Simms himself. Wharncliffe is arguing against Stylus's anxiety that "the South has produced little literature because 'our people have no past'"—as Richard Henry Wilde had argued too—and as part of his defense introduces the writer to Paddy McGann, "an uneducated Edisto raftsman who is a natural poet and storyteller." Paddy (whose full name is Patrick McGarvin) is "really a smart fellow, and a curiosity besides."[22]

Early on there is an incantatory praising of the southern land to which "Sometimes there came the stately Englishman, and the canny Scot, and the free-handed son of green Erin, and the gallant Frenchman." In such a context, according to Robert Bush, Paddy—"at his best"—"is an emblem of the essential character of the Southern masses, representing values that Simms wished to see preserved." In the South, "All the old British superstitions are retained, and you may trace them, in different sections, to an English, Scotch, or Irish source." Paddy, of course, is an exemplar of such a superstitious trait.[23]

However, Cantrell's claim that "In his rollicking analysis of Southern culture, an allegory that suggests that the seeds of a great Southern literature have already been planted in the folklore of the Paddys, Simms chooses as his quintessential Southerner an Irishman" is excessive. Thus, for example, in the middle section of the story a Scottish sea captain who saves Paddy from drowning and who also despises Yankees is seen as a fellow Celt, emphasizing that the South needs its Celtic element to survive. Can-

21. See Gerald Donovan, "Irish Folklore Influences on Simms's 'Sharp Snaffles' and 'Bald-Head Bill Bauldy,'" in *William Gilmore Simms and the American Frontier*, ed. John Caldwell Guilds and Caroline Collins (Athens, Ga., 1997), 192–206; Mary Ann Wimsatt, *The Major Fiction of William Gilmore Simms: Cultural Traditions and Literary Form* (Baton Rouge, 1989), 3, 14, 15; James P. Cantrell, "Irish Culture and the War between the States: *Paddy McGann* and *Gone with the Wind*," *Éire-Ireland* 27 (1992): 7.

22. William Gilmore Simms, *Paddy McGann; or, The Demon of the Stump*, ed. James B. Meriwether (Columbia, S.C., 1972), 222.

23. Ibid., 223, Robert Bush, introduction to *Paddy McGann*, xix; Simms, 228.

trell even adds that the South "must turn not to the Wharncliffes and Sty-luses but to the Paddys and Wilsons. At the heart of Southern culture, this allegory says, is an Irishman, not an Anglo-Norman cavalier, and the South will not develop an expansive, great literature until the Paddys become the Styluses." Southern letters need to be reinvigorated by "the reality of the Celticness of the South, with all of its violence and earthiness of language and action."[24]

Although the above elements are certainly present in the story, which is surprisingly complex with even a Joycean turn in places, and although Wimsatt refers to the novel as indicating Simms's "interest, doubtless partly autobiographical, in the idiosyncrasies of the Celtic character," it is obvious that Paddy, for all his endearing qualities and the genuine respect in which he is held (he is self-educated but anonymously writes wonderfully satiric letters to the newspapers and to offending individuals; he is to be relied upon in a crisis, is basically honest, and treats his two slaves justly), serves as a figure of amusement for his Anglo listeners. His account of his being haunted by the devil in various forms is persistently attributed to his drink-ing, though Paddy himself vehemently denies this. There is indeed an Ar-noldian condescension in the presentation despite that Paddy is identified explicitly with Ferdinand rather than Caliban. In New York, P. T. Barnum even invites Paddy to join his show as an exhibit, an invitation Paddy vigor-ously declines, though this offer is based more on his fame as a shark killer than on any other of his attributes.[25]

The reader is clearly told, however, that it is not from his Northern Irish father, once a hod carrier in Charleston, that Paddy receives his wit but rather from his ethnically unidentified mother: "His father was Irish—a regular bogtrotter—and Paddy inherits some of the brogue, which, as you see, he blends curiously with our native backwoods *patois*. But the brogue is only strongly apparent when Paddy has been rather free in his potations. At all other times it is unobtrusive." While a culture needs its Paddys, they also seem—in Simms's complicated scheme of social construction—to form an early stage of development: his audience claims to find Paddy's tales in more sophisticated form in the medieval Froissart.[26]

From the narrator's point of view, Paddy is an exceptionally good exam-ple "of our simple forest population" since he has the gifts of "fancy and

24. Cantrell, 10.
25. Wimsatt, 205.
26. Simms, 238, 235.

imagination." They only need "the *attrition* of society, the provocation of enterprises, and a growing passion for more various enjoyments and luxuries, to become a thoughtful and producing people; as much as any peasantry or rustic population in the world. *No purely rustic population, by the way, has ever yet been known to achieve what is called a high civilization*—that is, as shown in the development of letters, science and the arts. These must always come from the great marts and the densely packed communities of States." In other words, Paddy is a beginning rather than an end. At the conclusion of Paddy's tale, despite their respect for his veracity, his more sophisticated audience remains suspicious of the marvelous.[27]

It is noteworthy that in spite of the reference to his father coming from Ulster, it is almost impossible to tell whether Paddy is "Irish" Irish or Scotch-Irish: he drinks to "the blessed memory of the Holy St. Patrick," reads his Bible, impressively defends his belief in the devil, and liberally uses such words as "poteen," "masthur," "drhames," "argyment," "wather," and the very Gaelic "spalpeen" (a generic word for an itinerant laborer). Indeed, his presentation as generic Irishman without distinction seems to point to an instability at the core of the Irish/Scotch-Irish antithesis, at least in its more rigid forms. In any case, the Scottish captain tells Paddy that he sees him as southern rather than American, and "of a different nation" from the people in New York. More significantly, perhaps, one of the ethnically unidentified planters listening to Paddy is Wharncliffe's neighbor Charles Carroll, possibly of Irish Catholic Maryland ancestry, while a direct reference to another Wharncliffe friend, the real-life poet Richard Henry Wilde, who, like Paddy, was duped in a New York restaurant, makes no allusion to his having come from Ireland and in that sense being even more "Irish" than South Carolina–born Paddy. Clearly, Paddy's characterization is one of class as much as of ethnicity. When he reluctantly marries Susan Heffernan Pogson at the end of the novel, it is her slovenly Pogson father who is condemned by all, especially Paddy, for being "a poor crathur, that either didn't know his business, or didn't attend to it."[28]

What one should probably conclude from all this is that those who were identifiably Irish were relatively marginal in southern society. For the most part, persons of such background had blended in with the larger society of their own class, becoming "Anglo" at the upper end, generically white at the lower levels. However, on occasion a "Celtic" inheritance might still be

27. Ibid., 495.
28. Ibid., 385, 393, 473.

invoked to explain an idiosyncrasy of behavior, good or bad as the case might be.

What is happening in the nineteenth century, then, is that for both the Irish and southerners, who are increasingly self-conscious of themselves *as* southerners, there is a kind of laying of the foundations of a new national or sectional identity after a more cosmopolitan, but somewhat socially exclusive late 1700s and early 1800s. The plain people of Ireland, largely Catholic, are beginning en masse to speak and write in English rather than in Irish Gaelic, uncertain sometimes of the proper register or usage. In a book appropriately titled *The New Word,* Allen Upward has described such "debased" popular language among colonized people thus: "they spell our words correctly, and they have some notion of what the words mean; but English has not replaced their native speech, and hence it fits them like a borrowed garment, and they are betrayed into awkward and laughable mistakes in using it, which have given rise to the term Babu English."[29]

Nor is such a description merely another instance of English condescension: even by the end of the century, when Irish Gaelic was spoken by only a tiny fraction of the population on the western seaboard, Joyce's Stephen Dedalus was highly self-conscious of his own English speech. In *A Portrait of the Artist as a Young Man,* in the presence of an English Jesuit dean at college, Stephen reflects that "The language in which we are speaking is his before it is mine. How different are the words *home, Christ, ale, master* on his lips and on mine! I cannot speak or write these words without unrest of spirit. His language, so familiar and so foreign, will always be for me an acquired speech. I have not made or accepted its words. My voice holds them at bay. My soul frets in the shadow of his language." Well into the twentieth century, Myles na gCopaleen (Flann O'Brien) was to make fun of the same phenomenon in his Gaelic language work, *An Béal Bocht.*[30]

Declan Kiberd, in discussing Carleton, has put his finger on the essence of the problem:

> If an Irish literature in English is a myth of consolation erected upon the grave of the Gaelic tradition, this may prompt a still more radical thought: that expression may compound the deeper sense of desolation. The more

29. Quoted in Donald Davie, *Ezra Pound* (New York, 1975), 55. Frank O'Connor refers to Babu in *A Short History of Irish Literature: A Backward Look* (New York, 1967), 139.

30. James Joyce, *A Portrait of the Artist as a Young Man* (New York, 1982), 189; Myles na gCopaleen, *An Béal Bocht* (Dublin, 1975).

the people master the English language, the more meaningless and painful is that mastery without a similar access to English law, careers, capital and freedoms. If the unexpressed life is bad, the expressed life may be even more humiliating, because to poverty is added the consciousness of it as such . . . The books by Defoe and Smollett kept in peasant cabins were supposed to be promissory notes against a future culture, which would replace the ebbing Gaelic one, but that culture never really seemed to come or to fulfil its rich potential.

It could be objected here that the average English worker was also deprived of access to such benefits—and perhaps was even less likely to have Defoe and Smollett on his shelves. In any case, it was this very difference that was to reinvigorate and renew the English language in the early twentieth century. The South too was uncertain in its registers, its more genteel speech disturbed but eventually invigorated by a mountain dialect that possibly had its roots in Elizabethan English and by African American crossings, achieving one of its major culminations in Twain's work at century's end. By then, what had recently been a distinct disadvantage had become a noteworthy benefit.[31]

In 1892, Douglas Hyde, son of an Anglican clergyman and professor of Irish at Trinity College in Dublin, delivered his landmark lecture on the need to "de-anglicize" his country since, with the loss of their language, the people had ceased "to be Irish without becoming English." His agenda was to be a motivating force for Irish nationalists, though he himself explicitly claimed that it was not intended to be political and should even appeal to cultural nationalists who yet remained Unionists in that they wished to keep the British connection. Yeats and Joyce and most of the significant writers of the early twentieth century, though deeply critical of Hyde, found inspiration for their own creative endeavors in his words; when Ireland became independent in 1921, it was Hyde's agenda that was formally put in place as a national ideal, even if the realities of Irish society and politics were substantially different.[32]

Also in 1892, Virginia's Thomas Nelson Page published his defense of the "Old South," which he had been giving as a lecture throughout the region since 1887, appealing to the conservatism and Civil War pride of his exclusively white auditors without calling the restored Union into question. His South had "combined elements of the three great civilizations which since the dawn of history have enlightened the world"—the Grecian,

31. Kiberd, 269.
32. Hyde, 153.

Roman, and Saxon—brooded over by "a softness and beauty, the joint product of Chivalry and Christianity." His short story "Marse Chan," a romantic
recreation of prewar plantation society especially commended for its "faith-
ful" rendering of Negro dialect, was a staple of southern education and a
prime example of the "local color" school into which so much southern
and Irish writing of the period was cast. While Page's agenda too provoked
opposition later on, it also solidly crystallized an outlook to which vigorous
objection could be made. Kate O'Flaherty Chopin—who seems artistically
to have been almost totally a product of her Creole inheritance, though her
"energy" is sometimes ascribed to her entrepreneurial Irish father—and the
southern writers, female and male, after her would use Page's patriarchal
and plantation idyll model to fuel their opposition to it.[33]

Hyde and Page, each the culmination of particular nineteenth-century
trends in his respective region, thought of themselves as presenting laud-
able plans for the future, as defenders of true traditions against the "filthy
modern tide" of materialism and vulgarity emanating from the popular British and American media. In retrospect, it seems more accurate to see them
as laying the foundations for their own surpassing. At the very least, one
can say that there was change in the air. T. P. O'Connor, the Irish journalist
and MP for Galway, who was born in 1848, knew Oscar Wilde, Henry
James, and Joyce; wrote about Thomas Hardy; and published the early
music reviews of George Bernard Shaw. O'Connor's wife, in marked contrast, a southerner from Texas (and much admired by Wilde for her beauty),
dedicated a memoir about the region's "bounteous hospitality, its quixotic
chivalry . . . its spotless honour" to her friend Thomas Nelson Page, dutifully quoting Father Ryan along the way. At all events, by the early twentieth century, a literary heritage had been established in both places that,
however inadequate, provided traction on what had once been no more
than a slippery slope on the edge of a cultural abyss.[34]

---

33. Thomas Nelson Page, "The Old South," 393. Fred Hobson, in *Tell about the South: The
Southern Rage to Explain* (Baton Rouge, 1983), 140, has pointed to some important revisions
of the text in different editions; Emily Toth, *Kate Chopin* (New York, 1990).

34. In his *Memoirs of an Old Parliamentarian* (New York, 1929), O'Connor also explains that
he had supported the South because to a young Irish Home Ruler such as he was, "the fact
that the Southern States demanded what might be called Home Rule established an analogy
between their demand and that of Ireland" (25); Mrs. T. P. O'Connor, *My Beloved South*.
O'Connor stayed on in the Westminster parliament after Irish independence, became the first
British film censor, and banned D. W. Griffith's *America*, a movie about the Revolutionary
War, in 1924 as threatening to endanger the good relations between England and the United
States.

CHAPTER 9

THE EXPERIENCE OF REALITY

> I go to encounter for the millionth time the reality of experience and to forge
> in the smithy of my soul the uncreated conscience of my race.
>
> —JAMES JOYCE, *A Portrait of the Artist as a Young Man*

> Nowhere today, saving in parts of Ireland, is the English Language spoken with
> the same earthy strength as it is in the United States . . .
>
> —WILLIAM FAULKNER, book review, 1922

It is a commonplace that twentieth-century literature in English has been
marked by the surprising emergence, and even periodic dominance, of writers from two unlikely areas of the Anglophone world: Ireland and the
American South. In the Irish case, one thinks of W. B. Yeats, James Joyce,
John Millington Synge, Seán O'Casey; in the southern, of William Faulkner, Tennessee Williams, Flannery O'Connor, and, if in a somewhat different way, Richard Wright. Both places experienced what has generally been
referred to as a "renaissance"—more obviously in the Irish case with its
Gaelic literary heritage, though southerners and even outsiders too would
argue that the early contributions of William Byrd and Thomas Jefferson
represented an impressive "naissance" that was now being revived
there—of a vigorous and above all self-critical, conscience-forging literature
following a century of amateur, overly sentimental, and politically defensive discourse.

While the previous chapter has suggested that such dramatic opposition
between old and new may not have been quite as sharp as is conventionally
assumed, the twentieth century undoubtedly saw a marked change both in
style and in substance. "Thirty years ago," Yeats declared in his 1923 acceptance speech for the Nobel Prize, "a number of Irish writers met together
in societies and began a remorseless criticism of the literature of their
country." In short, at least in literary terms, by the early and mid twentieth

century, both Ireland and the American South had left behind the narrow confines of "local color" and stepped boldly into the international arena.[1]

In achieving their new literary status, the two areas were once again linked together, if much more in terms of broad influence than of immediate historical association. Unlike the situation in the nineteenth century, none of the new southern writers had recent Irish ancestry, though Faulkner's family variously identified itself as of "Scottish, Ulster Irish, and French Huguenot" background and even had a Gaelic-speaking sire in Mississippi, while Flannery O'Connor also had remote Irish connections. In the main, however, the emergence and trajectory of the Irish renaissance, generally thought of as beginning in the 1890s, served as a functional model or reassuring example for its southern counterpart, which for all practical purposes began sometime after World War I, even if it was prepared for a good two decades earlier. As Robert Penn Warren noted, he and his fellow Agrarians in Nashville in the 1920s and 1930s "used to talk about Yeats and Ireland vis-à-vis England as having a sort of parallel to the writer in the South, in a retarded and depressed society facing a big, booming, dominating society."[2]

Indeed, Faulkner had set out to be a poet somewhat in the manner of Yeats, an obvious influence on his arcadian verse in *The Marble Faun*, published in 1924. So engaged was he subsequently with the innovations of Joyce's *Ulysses* that he is reported to have clandestinely taken that volume with him on his ill-fated honeymoon. Certainly *Ulysses*' famous stream-of-consciousness technique influenced the Mississippian when he came to write his great modernist fictions—*The Sound and the Fury, As I Lay Dying,* and *Absalom, Absalom!*—in the late 1920s and early 1930s, while a high point of his 1925 pilgrimage to Paris had been his sighting of the master himself. Faulkner's Quentin Compson is legitimately seen as a more obsessed version of Joyce's Stephen Dedalus, the former "an empty hall echoing with sonorous defeated names" of southern military heroes, the latter trying to awaken from the "nightmare" of Ireland's history. There are remarkable echoes of Joyce's *A Portrait of the Artist as a Young Man* as well as of *Ulysses* in several parts of Thomas Wolfe's *Look Homeward, Angel* too, and he even named a Catholic priest in one of his short stories "Father Dolan," possibly in homage to the Irish writer.[3]

1. *Nobel Lectures, Literature, 1901–1967,* at www.nobel.se.

2. Joseph Blotner, *Faulkner: A Biography* (New York, 1991), 24, 9; Terence Diggory, *Yeats and American Poetry* (Princeton, 1983), 135.

3. Faulkner, *The Marble Faun* (Boston, 1924); Blotner, 159; Faulkner, *Absalom, Absalom!* (New York, 1990), 7; Joyce, *Ulysses* (New York, 1961), 34. Wolfe was quite hostile toward the

Nor was such influence confined to white writers. In Ralph Ellison's *Invisible Man,* set in the 1930s, the black narrator recalls a literature class at his alma mater in Alabama—a thinly fictionalized Tuskegee—with the professor,

> half-drunk on words and full of contempt and exaltation, pacing before the blackboard chalked with quotations from Joyce and Yeats and Seán O'Casey; thin, nervous, neat, pacing as though he walked a high wire of meaning upon which no one of us would ever dare venture. I could hear him: "Stephen's [Dedalus] problem, like ours, was not actually one of creating the uncreated conscience of his race, but of creating the *uncreated features of his face.* Our task is that of making ourselves individuals. The conscience of a race is the gift of its individuals who see, evaluate, record."

The narrator himself comes to a different conclusion later, but the Joycean template is there always for either acceptance or rejection. Indeed, the influence of the Yeats-Joyce-O'Casey threesome is still present over forty years later in Ernest Gaines's *A Lesson before Dying* (1993), and its author has also observed that the paralysis of Joyce's Dublin was replicated in the stasis of the black plantation life he experienced in a Catholic parish in mid-twentieth-century Louisiana.[4]

On the other hand, the all-too-easy yoking of Yeats, Joyce, and O'Casey together simply as "Irish" writers in spite of the marked differences and even oppositions between them—political, aesthetic, religious—is a reminder of how far removed these southern writers, white and black, were from the real situation in Ireland. There is no evidence that any of the southern writers was deeply concerned with Irish matters as such, or even very knowledgeable about them beyond a sense of Ireland as a backward, agricultural, semicolonial, and romantic society somewhat like their own, which had recently established a strong literary presence in the English language by looking critically at itself, thus offering them an enabling example for their own project. They would flee the moonlight and magnolia of the sentimental past just as Irish writers had made themselves fugitives from shamrocks and round towers. Everything else about the southerners suggests that the literary tradition with which they associated themselves, if

---

American Irish, however—see Paschal Reeves, *Thomas Wolfe's Albatross: Race and Nationality in America* (Athens, Ga., 1968).

4. Ralph Ellison, *Invisible Man* (New York, 1972), 345–46; see Matthew Spangler, "Of Snow and Dust: The Presence of James Joyce in Ernest Gaines's *A Lesson Before Dying,*" *South Atlantic Review* 67, no. 1 (2002), 104–28.

not quite the country itself, was England's rather than Ireland's. The same, of course, was substantially true of the Irish writers as well, since both groups were painfully conscious of their own meager pasts and so wanted to stake a claim in the already heavily populated territories of Anglophone literature. That the sophisticated techniques of international modernism should have provided a way in may seem paradoxical, but in part the unstable cultural pasts of these writers from what were commonly acknowledged as the margins made it possible for them to forsake a tradition they never really possessed to begin with in favor of innovation, fragmentation, and disruption, an option that may have been less readily attractive or even available to writers of a more settled inheritance.

To some extent, this remarkable burst of creativity from such unexpected sources helped erase the negative stereotypes of Ireland and the South, as both were making a contribution that needed to be taken seriously. One must also admit, however, that to some extent it served to reinforce the old stereotypes too. At its best, it familiarized a northeastern and mainland British readership with southern and Irish characters that were more complex, more individual, more *human*—the word that provokes Ellison's narrator to remember his Tuskegee class. Yeats saw his Abbey Theatre in Dublin as offering a correction to the buffoonery of the stage Irishman, while Joyce wanted to put an end to the image of the Irish as "court jester[s] to the English." The Nashville Fugitives in the 1920s set out to leave behind the South of "moonlight and magnolias"—part of the Kennedy, Simms, and Page legacy—while Donald Davidson afterward saw the rebirth of southern letters as a response to the negative representations made popular by H. L. Mencken during the Scopes Monkey Trial in Tennessee in 1925.[5]

But just how much things had really changed is open to debate. W. J. Cash's criticisms—which he thought were substantiated by Faulkner's work—and Walker Evans and James Agee's *Let Us Now Praise Famous Men* come from this era also. The latter is a sympathetic portrayal, certainly, emphasizing the dignity of a handful of interconnected families in rural Alabama, but the meticulous detailing of their poverty could only have reinforced unflattering conceptions that the American public already had about the people of the rural South. Faulkner too was originally seen as presenting the Gothic and bizarre nature of southern life, thus further confirming the stereotype. Joyce's Dubliners, meanwhile, seem to spend an inordinate

5. Ellison, 337, 345; Joyce, *The Critical Writings of James Joyce* (Ithaca, N.Y., 1989), 202.

amount of time conversing in pubs or scurrying in and out of churches to the neglect of routine business responsibilities, while Yeats's and Synge's peasants wander endlessly in poetic reverie. What one should probably say, then, is that the still-poor, backward, overly religious, and undereducated Irish and southerners were now perceived as also possessing extraordinary literary talent. They existed as poets rather than pragmatists, as persons of emotion rather than intellect, thus consciously or unconsciously reinforcing Matthew Arnold's Celtic prototype instead of undermining its assumptions. On the occasion of his receiving the Nobel Prize, Yeats stressed his engagement in the "remorseless criticism" of the past literature of his country, but he was officially being praised by the Swedish Academy for "beautiful visions" and "the tales of the fairies and elves with which you have made us acquainted" to the apparent exclusion of everything else in his oeuvre. Even as late as 1995, the Irish could be perceived as displaying literary "genius" with also being stereotypically described as "thick-brained."[6]

Furthermore, while we now think of these writers as among the best representatives of their respective cultures—and in many ways they were—it is well to recall that until the last several decades they were often considered to be outlaws, disgruntled maligners who wrote largely for an English or American audience all-too-eager to read about incest in Mississippi or patricide in the west of Ireland rather than acknowledge the hard-won dignity and respectability of the inhabitants of those regions. That so many of the writers had their praises sung so vociferously abroad made them all the more suspect at home. Synge's celebrated *Playboy of the Western World* provoked riots in Dublin's Abbey Theatre in 1907 where a largely Irish Catholic audience felt it was being ridiculed by the Anglo-Irish scion of a Protestant bishop; Joyce and O'Casey opted for bitter exile because of the controversies their works aroused, and even Yeats was read selectively, condemned or commended insofar as he aligned himself, or did not do so, with national sensibilities. So many foreign and Irish writers were officially banned in the first four decades of Ireland's independence—in the name of preserving cultural and religious purity—that an Irish author's claim to seriousness almost demanded his or her unfortunate inclusion in the list of moral degenerates. Many of the writers of the Southern Renascence likewise ended up living elsewhere. Notable among those who stayed were ones—such as Donald Davidson in the South and Daniel Corkery in Ire-

6. Lawrence H. Schwartz, *Creating Faulkner's Reputation* (Knoxville, 1988), 9–37; *Nobel Lectures; New Statesman and Society*, 26 May 1995, 26–27.

land—who were more in tune with local conditions and even critical of their more famous colleagues for not telling the "true," ennobling story of the society from which they had come. Recent literary criticism preoccupied with historical context has served only to revalidate the original local objections to these so-called champions of a humanism and artistic freedom that are now themselves—and controversially—suspect as little more than self-serving bourgeois social constructions.

It should be emphasized, in addition, that the source of the Irish influence on southern writers was Ireland itself, not the Irish America of the Northeast and Midwest. After the war, Irish America was all the more repugnant to the white re-evangelized South for its idolatrous popery, love of liquor, and, to the genteel elements in the region, for what was seen as its crass vulgarity—a feature of Irish America that sometimes irritated the Irish at home also. After all, even most of the alcoholic and irreligious southern writers had pretensions to gentility. F. Scott Fitzgerald, the son of an Irish-American mother from a fairly wealthy family and an unsuccessful and impoverished father of southern genteel background, sought to escape his Irish legacy and identify instead with his southern inheritance. Tennessee Williams well expressed the causes of Fitzgerald's anxiety in *A Streetcar Named Desire* when Stella explains to her sister Blanche that her husband is Polish: "Oh, yes. They're something like Irish, aren't they?" While Stella hesitates to confirm this observation, Blanche adds, "Only not so—highbrow?" and they both laugh. Ireland at a distance, in contrast to Irish America, offered a less threatening or embarrassing model.[7]

Yet, *pace* Fitzgerald and the general southern hostility toward Catholicism, one of the curiosities of the Irish-southern literary relationship must surely be that in terms of religion, and specifically in terms of Catholicism, the writers have gone in almost totally opposite—and counterintuitive—directions. It is in the American Protestant South that one finds a large group of Catholic writers—not only Flannery O'Connor but also Caroline Gordon, Allen Tate, Katherine Anne Porter, and Walker Percy, to name just the best-known—while in Ireland itself not a single major author in the twentieth century has been an observant member of the Church of Rome.

7. See Irish-American Rosemary Mahoney's comments on a conversation she overheard about her between Lillian Hellman and William Styron in *A Likely Story: One Summer with Lillian Hellman* (New York, 1999). In fairness, it probably needs to be kept in mind that the Irish-American portrayals in *The Glass Menagerie* and *The Night of the Iguana* are more sympathetic than that in *Streetcar*.

Rather, among the "great" Irish writers, the rejection of a claustrophobic Catholicism has been the norm. Moreover, Flannery O'Connor's religious fiction, which one might initially associate with Irish Catholic pieties—and there is the occasional "Irish" character such as Father Flynn in "The Displaced Person"—seems almost more reflective of Northern Irish Presbyterian sensibilities (though hardly less "Irish" for that) than of those of Ireland's Roman Catholics. While there has been a long line of popular clerical writers of fiction in that country ultimately asserting some of the same values as she espoused, hardly any of them would be considered significant.[8]

In all, then, the Southern Renascence that began sometime around World War I, though it had been prepared for in the work of Twain, Chopin, Ellen Glasgow, and George Washington Cable also (a writer known to Yeats and whose role was not unlike that of George Moore in Ireland), rejected the kind of literature that had gone before mainly in its determination to be *critical*. Less formally organized than the slightly earlier Irish Renaissance, it exhibited many of the same features and had many of the same goals. Although there was no exact equivalent, for example, to the summons to Coole Park and the taking of tea with Lady Gregory, there was the crucial recognition in the pages of either the *Southern* or the *Kenyon Review,* and the gatherings at Allen Tate's and Caroline Gordon's Benfolly in rural Tennessee. The English novelist Ford Madox Ford, who had aided Joyce earlier in the century and published his work in his *transatlantic review,* was to be of assistance to Gordon and Eudora Welty during his time in America in the 1930s. Finally, as was mentioned in the last chapter, from one perspective at least one might legitimately trace the Southern Renascence's origin to Thomas Nelson Page's 1892 lecture on "The Old South" (rather than to the World War I era)—even if often by way of opposition to his ideals—every bit as much as the Irish Revival originated with Douglas Hyde's proclamation of the same year on "The Necessity of De-Anglicizing Ireland" (which also both inspired and repelled subsequent writers). Both movements produced a literature that was, as Tate observed of the southern outpouring, "conscious of the past in the present." Moreover, the greatest products of the two renaissances—Yeats, Joyce, Faulkner—were troubled by the traditions that at the same time they themselves so remarkably embodied.[9]

8. See James H. Murphy's *Catholic Fiction and Social Reality in Ireland, 1873–1922* (Westport, Conn., 1997).

9. "Renascence" is the form commonly used in the Southern case, the more traditional "Renaissance" in the Irish—no significant difference is implied by the variant usages; see Caroline Gordon's letter to Ford Madox Ford from Benfolly in December 1931 about the Southern Writers' Convention at the University of Virginia with Tate, Ellen Glasgow, Paul Green, and

*   *   *

The most cohesive group of southern renascence writers, the Nashville Fugitives and Agrarians—John Crowe Ransom, Donald Davidson, Allen Tate, and Robert Penn Warren—were particularly impressed by Yeats and the Irish scene because it seemed to them that this was a situation in which poetry as such had had perceptible political consequences. It was not Ireland's traditional opposition to England that especially interested them, much less its just-completed struggle for independence, but rather Yeats's apparent nostalgia for an older, hierarchical society, a sentiment close to their own desire for a return to a lost agrarian past, an aspiration that initially rendered Joyce's work less relevant. For them, according to Terence Diggory, the "wealthy planter and yeoman farmer" stood in for "Yeats's noble and peasant. The South, in the Agrarian image, offered precisely that 'concrete relation to life undiluted by calculation and abstraction' that Tate credited . . . to Yeats's pastoral." The past they sought, of course, was not the sentimental Old South of Thomas Nelson Page's conception but rather one in which men lived in full awareness of the contingencies of life, the fulfillment of the Jeffersonian ideal that "Those who labour in the earth are the chosen people of God, if ever he had a chosen people, whose breasts he has made his peculiar deposit for substantial and genuine virtue." In practice, this re-creation of an agrarian past was never achieved, even its ideal being in time abandoned.[10]

But the work itself was what had initially attracted all of them to Yeats, and they were as anxious as he had been not to produce mere propaganda for any cause, however worthy. Ransom was less knowledgeable about Yeats's career than was Tate and so tended to see him as a stereotypical Celt preoccupied with what Ransom referred to in a late poem as the "ancestral arts" of a strange Irish "theogony." Tate, by contrast, though disappointed with the Irish poet when he read in Nashville in 1920 because all his selec-

---

Faulkner present, in *A Literary Friendship: Correspondence between Caroline Gordon and Ford Madox Ford*, ed. Brita Lindberg-Seyersted (Knoxville, 1999); Allen Tate, *Essays of Four Decades* (Chicago, 1968), 545. In its early stages at least, while the southern writers were certainly aware of the Irish revival and partly imitated it, the Irish do not seem to have paid much attention to this development in American culture. In *Faulkner: International Perspectives* (Jackson, Miss., 1984), Joseph Blotner comments on the lack of interest in Faulkner in Britain and then adds: "(As for Irish reactions, parenthetically, the single notice from an Irish journal made the least cordial British ones seem hospitable.)" (309).

10. Diggory, 144; Thomas Jefferson, *Notes on the State of Virginia* (Chapel Hill, 1955), 164–65; Kieran Quinlan, *John Crowe Ransom's Secular Faith* (Baton Rouge, 1989), 81.

tions were from the late nineteenth century (the "fairies and elves" period of the Nobel commendation), would soon come to appreciate the later Yeats, even using the opening image of "The Second Coming"—"Turning and turning in the widening gyre, / The falcon cannot hear the falconer"—in "The Eagle" that "Hears no more, past compass / In his topless flight," to criticize a culture unmoored from its origins. The two poets were seeking order in the midst of contemporary chaos, Yeats more oriented to the grim future, Tate still wanting to recycle—critically—the chivalrous past.[11]

However, it was an inheritor of the Fugitive-Agrarian legacy who was to meditate most extensively on the Irish-southern literary connection. In the 1960s and 1970s, Cleanth Brooks explored the similarity in outlook that one finds in the two revivals, deriving it from a similarity in the social conditions that produced them. He prefaced his remarks with Seán O'Faoláin's now familiar comparison between Faulkner's Mississippi and his own County Cork, a comparison first made in the Irish writer's Gauss lectures at Princeton in 1953:

> There is the same passionate provincialism; the same local patriotism; the same southern nationalism—those long explicit speeches of Gavin Stevens in *Intruder in the Dust* might, *mutatis mutandis,* be uttered by a southern Irishman—the same feeling that whatever happens in Ballydehob or in Jefferson has never happened anywhere else before, and is more important than anything that happened in any period of history in any part of the cosmos; there is the same vanity of an old race; the same gnawing sense of old defeat; the same capacity for intense hatred; a good deal of the same harsh folk-humor; the same acidity; the same oscillation between unbounded self-confidence and total despair.

Brooks was interested in the comparison because it offered a starting point for his argument that just as Yeats had turned the seeming limitations of his provincial background into a source of strength for a poetry of universal import, so too had Faulkner transformed the "postage stamp" of his northern Mississippi locale into a map of the world. A later Irish writer, Louis MacNeice, was to draw attention to another reward of focusing on a limited terrain, a reward not necessarily in opposition to the universalist impulse: "on this tiny stage with luck a man / Might see the end of one particular

---

11. John Crowe Ransom, "Birthday of an Aging Seer," in *Selected Poems* (New York, 1969), 139; Allen Tate, *Poems* (New York, 1960), 113.

action." There is indeed a satisfaction, grim at times as Dilsey in *The Sound and the Fury* knew, of seeing "de beginnin . . . en . . . de endin," which the small stage allows one to do more easily.[12]

Certainly, the quotation from O'Faoláin reads like a reprise of the whole history of both Ireland and the American South, histories characterized by defeats rather than victories, by the kind of "burden" that C. Vann Woodward has so memorably emphasized in relation to the southern experience, by an incapacity to forget "old times" either down in the land of cotton or in Tara's ancient halls, be they in County Meath or in Georgia. There is also the strong sense from the paragraph that the oscillating eruptions of an "unbounded self-confidence" on the parts of Irishmen and southerners are defense mechanisms against an American northeastern or London-English world that looks down on them as inhabitants of a primitive hinterland, John Bull's (George Bernard Shaw) or Uncle Sam's (Tate) other island, or, at best, smiles condescendingly at their predictable follies.

What Brooks saw Yeats and Faulkner as having in common was their attempt to shore up a traditional culture—of which each of them had had personal experience—threatened with extinction by the crass materialism of the modern world. That culture comprised both a peasantry and "the Big House with landed proprietors," as well as "the ethos that goes with such a governing class." In the Fugitive-Agrarian tradition—and partly ignoring the fact that such a stratification in the Irish case tended to be based on Protestant dominance, Catholic subservience—Brooks sought to recommend the same kind of stable, hierarchical society, though his emphasis was less on such an aristocracy's sense of its own privileged class than on its virtue of disinterested service. For him, it was an aristocracy of character (even if some property was also required) more than of class, and while overwhelmingly white was not exclusively so. A genuine community of peasants and patricians would be united in their opposition to "the filthy modern tide" of late capitalist commerce. Hence Brooks's claim that "the ethos of Faulkner's stories and novels reflects that of an older, more heroic

12. Seán O'Faoláin, *The Vanishing Hero: Studies in Novelists of the Twenties* (Freeport, N.Y., 1957). In 1958, Faulkner told Richard Ellmann that "he considered himself the heir of Joyce in his methods in *The Sound and the Fury*." Joyce was not aware of Faulkner, however; indeed, he only became familiar with *Huckleberry Finn* late in his life (1937 or so)—see Ellmann, *James Joyce* (New York, 1983), 297, 699n; Cleanth Brooks, *William Faulkner: The Yoknapatawpha Country* (New Haven, 1963), 2; O'Faoláin, 75; R. F. Foster, *The Irish Story: Telling Tales and Making It Up in Ireland* (London, 2001), 158; Louis MacNeice, *Collected Poems* (New York, 1967), xx; Faulkner, *The Sound and the Fury* (New York, 1990), 297.

society," a romantic South almost "dead and gone" like Yeats's nobler Ireland in "September 1913," to be replaced by a new world under the rule of Flem Snopes and Paudeen. Snopes and his kind could be included in Yeats's classic condemnation of "those mean and narrowminded" hucksters who "fumble in a greasy till."[13]

Brooks's classical view is laid bare in the comment that "The greatest work of both men is suffused with history . . . as a record of the striving of man—ultimately unchanging Man—to realize his true self by rising above his habitual self." Like Faulkner (and John Mitchel), "Yeats did not believe in progress, calling it 'the sole religious myth of modern man.'" Brooks argued that Yeats's and Faulkner's aristocratic and heroic understanding of man "also has close affinities to the orthodox Classical-Christian view," in spite of the fact that "both writers had some very severe things to say about the institutional Christianity of their times." Brooks concluded by associating Yeats's denunciation of Whiggery ("a levelling, rancorous, rational sort of mind") with Faulkner's backhanded commendation of Jason Compson in The Sound and the Fury as "the first sane Compson since Culloden." For Brooks, all of this amounted to a condemnation of Flem Snopes, whom "It is just as hard to imagine . . . jovially tipsy as it is to imagine him on his knees in prayer." Surely a Yeats who praised the "holiness of monks" in their prayers would have condemned Snopes too.[14]

Brooks was not unaware, of course, of similar ambivalences in the lives of these authors toward the restrictive cultures they respectively embodied: "A close look at [Yeats's] career reveals a continuing alteration of love and loathing for his native land, a conflict that closely parallels Faulkner's love-hate relation with his native region." So, for example, the protest about the South in at least the persona of Quentin Compson in the closing lines of Absalom, Absalom!—"I dont hate it! I dont hate it!"—and Yeats's confession of an ongoing conflict between his English ancestry and love of that nation's literature and his Irish identity, so that his hatred tortures him with love, his "love with hate."[15]

Such attitudes are the typical products of narrow, intensely felt, and introspective cultures that lack the escape hatches of mobility and urban anonymity, however contrary to the arcadian ideal these may be. Both Ire-

13. Brooks, Toward Yoknapatawpha and Beyond (New Haven, 1978), 332, 337.

14. Ibid., 341, 343, 344.

15. Faulkner, Absalom, Absalom! 303; W. B. Yeats, Essays and Introductions (New York, 1961), 519.

land and the South are places from which one wishes to escape, though the memory of their intensities persists long afterwards. However, Brooks implied a more romantic mystery in such attitudes than a careful historical analysis would show. Biographical evidence indicates just how much Yeats's attitudes changed from decade to decade and how precisely they were calibrated to specific political events and to his encounters with specific personalities. Still, there is no question about the phenomenon itself.

Even in the O'Faoláin text from which Brooks quoted, however, the Irish writer had offered an ultimately different understanding of both the South and Faulkner. Significantly, perhaps, Brooks omitted the rest of the paragraph: "There are, of course, differences [between Ireland and the American South]. There is, for example, no escape in Ireland through sex. But there are enough similarities to make one sympathize profoundly with any writer born into such a community, and admire any writer who, as Faulkner has not been, is not silenced by the disadvantages of birth, education and tradition." That last, maddeningly convoluted, multiple-negative sentence referring to Faulkner's "disadvantage . . . of birth, education, and tradition" suggests that O'Faoláin had little sense of the literary history of the American South, much less of Faulkner's immediate family and educational background. Nevertheless, O'Faoláin had taken his cue from "an old Southern aristocrat" who remarked that Faulkner "writes very well . . . for a man who writes about poor white trash." O'Faoláin proceeded to explain what he thought she meant:

> Faulkner is not really in the oldest Southern tradition at all, does not know it and does not understand it. The people he knows are, whether poor white trash or not, people without intelligence or culture, people with (like himself) comparatively shallow roots in the South, not people made and marked by the full force of Southern traditions. He is not, in other words, writing about a defeated South; he is writing about a wrecked and corrupted South. The Snopes[es] and their ilk are the only people he really knows. The true race of Sartoris is outside his gamut; what he produces as Sartorises are romanticizations. Not being informed by the finest traditions of the pre–Civil War South, all he has to handle are the shards and broken scraps of an old, lost, rich and complex life.

What Brooks had seen as Faulkner's merit of not romanticizing the southern aristocracy—that is, of taking a Yeatsian critical view of them—has here become his fault of not being acquainted with its traditions, a difference of opinion in which one is inclined to think that Brooks is nearer the mark. As a consequence, O'Faoláin observed less sense too of "any decline of traditional values" in the work of the Mississippian and commented—tellingly—that Faulkner "has written best of all when he has written like a Negro."[16]

The allusion to the South's supposed "sexiness," meanwhile, in contrast with Ireland's "sexlessness," implies a more liberated morality in the South than Brooks would probably have wished to acknowledge. It should be said in Brooks's favor, however, that numerous commentators have pointed to the lingering Victorian ethos that characterized both the South and Ireland long after it had receded from the wider culture.[17]

Even though much of what Brooks had to say about both Faulkner and Yeats has since been supplemented, contested, deconstructed—especially the claim that these writers were ultimately aiming, however indirectly, at the revival of Christian humanism has either provoked skepticism or lapsed into extreme neglect—new similarities of situation and purpose have emerged from the debris. Indeed, so many rival interpretations have been presented, and both authors have passed through the ideological fires so often and come out so differently at the end of each inquisition, that it is hard at times not to have some sympathy with Brooks as occupying at least a position that has its own contingent validity. For example, Yeats has gone from being lauded as proto-Irish nationalist to being condemned as a Fascist and Protestant anti-Irish aristocrat (with passing aspersions to his being, like Faulkner, a "Count No 'Count" in reference to his marginal status within the Anglo-Irish social hierarchy) who disdained the rising Irish Catholic middle classes, back to being recognized as a defender of artistic and civil liberties against a narrow-minded, clericalized Irish Catholic hegemony in post-independence Ireland. Faulkner's fortunes in regard to racial issues, meanwhile, bear a striking resemblance to Yeats's fate: lauded as an insightful and sympathetic humanist, he has been condemned as a southern traditionalist and covert racist, only to reemerge as a courageous risk-taker who has provided us with profound and permanent insights into the cultural construction of race.[18]

16. O'Faoláin, 75, 110–11, 107–8.

17. Blotner, 100; Daniel Joseph Singal, *The War Within: From Victorian to Modernist Thought in the South, 1919–1945* (Chapel Hill, 1983); Vivian Mercier, "Victorian Evangelicalism and the Anglo-Irish Literary Revival," in *Literature and the Changing Ireland,* ed. Peter Connolly (Totowa, N.J., 1982).

18. For more detail on Yeats in this regard, see Kieran Quinlan, "Under Northern Lights: Re-Visioning Yeats and the Revival," in *Yeats and Postmodernism,* ed. Leonard Orr (Syracuse, 1991), 64–79.

In all of this critical roller-coasting, a number of the similarities that Brooks established still remain; what has changed is their interpretation. For example, his associating Faulkner's criticisms of the Snopes family with Yeats's strictures on the Irish Paudeens failed to recognize that there is a bias in Yeats's lines against the rising Catholic middle classes rather than simply a disinterested objection to the materialism of the modern world. Faulkner's characterizations of the Snopeses likewise go well beyond simple philosophical critique and reflect some of his own class biases, biases illuminatingly reflected in his friend Phil Stone's remark that "the real revolution in the South was not the race situation but the rise of the redneck, who did not have any of the scruples of the old aristocracy, to places of power and wealth." In other words, the two authors remain alike—as do their cultural situations—but their agendas are seen as having been less innocent than Brooks supposed.[19]

Brooks also alluded to the trope of women as more dedicated to the national cause than men were, though by way of criticizing it, which has often been remarked on from the Irish side too. The very unfeminine Drusilla Hawk of *The Unvanquished* in particular was presented as a woman "utterly fascinated by death . . . in defence of some abstract conception of masculine honor." In one dramatic scene, Drusilla, like a figure from Greek mythology, greets Bayard Sartoris on his arrival home fully expecting that he will avenge his father's death in the traditional manner; like a priestess, she hands him the dueling pistols to do so and is even explicitly jealous that this is the privilege of the men of the tribe. "How beautiful you are," she tells Bayard, "do you know it? How beautiful: young, to be permitted to kill, to be permitted vengeance, to take into your bare hands the fire of heaven that cast down Lucifer." Her attitude, while certainly not characteristic of all of the women in Faulkner's fiction, does nevertheless express an ongoing theme of his writings: it is the women rather than the men who keep the memory of former injustices and old wrongs alive—like Rosa Coldfield in *Absalom, Absalom!* for example, who "was accumulating her first folio in which the lost cause's unregenerate vanquished were name by name embalmed"—and seek vengeance for them.[20]

The obvious Yeatsian parallel here is Maud Gonne, the ardent Irish revolutionary who was both the poet's inspiration and albatross, and about whom Yeats was as ambivalent as Faulkner about Drusilla. In "A Prayer for

19. Blotner, 192.

20. Faulkner, *The Unvanquished* (New York, 1991), 238; Faulkner, *Absalom, Absalom!* 6.

My Daughter," Yeats asks rhetorically: "Have I not seen the loveliest woman born / Out of the mouth of Plenty's horn, / Because of her opinionated mind / Barter that horn and every good / By quiet natures understood." In this case, though Yeats is certainly extending his criticism to the fanatical nature of those opinions themselves irrespective of the gender of the person holding them, there is little doubt that he is offended by their "unwomanliness." To his own intermittent dismay, Irish nationalists saw Yeats's 1902 play, *Cathleen ní Houlihan,* which starred Maud Gonne in Drusilla-like symbolic mode, as "a sort of sacrament," and, in Conor Cruise O'Brien's view, Gonne eventually "became the principal symbolic figure in a new and potent group in Irish politics: the Widows of 1916, the new guardian-Priestesses of the nationalist faith."[21]

There are other associations that Brooks either omitted or was unaware of. For instance, while it is clear that Faulkner's own focus was on a romanticized Scotland rather than on Ireland as such, the history of the creation of that romantic place as understood by those scholars concerned with the "invention of tradition" has shown it to be highly dependent on Irish sources in all kinds of complex ways. There is a hovering Irish, or at least Catholic Celtic, reference in Faulkner's 1945 "Appendix" to *The Sound and the Fury* in which he set out the genealogy of the Compsons: "There were Compsons: QUENTIN MACLACHAN: Son of a Glasgow printer, orphaned and raised by his mother's people in the Perth highlands. Fled to Carolina from Culloden Moor with a claymore and the tartan he wore by day and slept under by night, and little else." Indeed, not only had the marginalized Catholic highland culture—including that of the Inverness region with which some of Faulkner's ancestors were specifically associated—become the "official" Scottish culture at least in its externals, but Faulkner himself was also aware of the Catholic element in the Inverness tradition. In an earlier version of *Flags in the Dust,* Frederick Karl has found a deleted passage in which "Faulkner writes of a Bayard and John Sartoris who served under and then followed Charles Stuart in his attempt to recover England for the Catholics. Faulkner draws lines between present-day Sartorises and those in the past." After Culloden, Bonnie Prince Charlie, whose younger brother had been made a cardinal, resided in Rome under the protection of the pontiff, while his father, as legitimate heir to a British patrimony that included Ireland, was responsible for the appointment of Irish Catholic bishops until his death in 1766. It is a tangled history that probably would have defied

21. Conor Cruise O'Brien, *Ancestral Voices* (Chicago, 1995), 68, 80.

even Faulkner's ample imaginative powers of narration, but it remains hiddenly present for all that.[22]

It is doubtful, however, that Faulkner had a deep interest in the Irish Literary Renaissance as such. Still less, of course, was Yeats familiar with southern literary happenings, though he does mention George Washington Cable in an 1892 comment on the new national literature being created in America, had actually visited the South on his lecture tours, entertained a romantic sympathy for the Confederate cause, and was proud that a ship of his mother's family's business had been designed to run the Union blockade during the Civil War. Faulkner was aware at least that Yeats, Joyce, and other writers were part of a new Irish movement. In a 1921 review of a Eugene O'Neill play, he suggested in passing that in America "English was spoken with an 'earthy strength' matched nowhere save in parts of Ireland, as John Millington Synge has shown." Faulkner also refers to a decadent Oscar Wilde in *Absalom, Absalom!* as an "Irish poet," whereas less familiar knowledge—or sole concern with his dramatic works—might have led him to think of this sophisticate as English.[23]

What one would want to emphasize above all now in a more positive comparison of Yeats and Faulkner would be elements of uncertainty and contradiction, their not pushing toward an ultimate "unity of culture" however much that metaphor may have been invoked in the past. One might want to note how wonderfully like the career of Thomas Sutpen in pursuit of his "design" and his commandeering of a French architect to assist him is Yeats's description of "some powerful man" who built his Irish estate in the eighteenth century (possibly using one of the Palladian pattern books so common at the time in England, Ireland, and Virginia):

> Some violent bitter man, some powerful man
> Called architect and artist in, that they,
> Bitter and violent men, might rear in stone
> The sweetness that all longed for night and day,
> The gentleness none there had ever known.
>
> ("Ancestral Houses" in "Meditations in Time of Civil War")

22. See Eric Hobsbawm and Terence Ranger, eds., *The Invention of Tradition* (New York, 1983); Faulkner, *The Sound and the Fury,* 204; Frederick R. Karl, *William Faulkner: American Writer* (New York, 1989), 33. Carolly Erickson's *Bonnie Prince Charlie: A Biography* (New York, 1989) documents the Irish connections of the Young Pretender.

23. Yeats, *The Autobiography of William Butler Yeats* (New York, 1965), 32; *William Faulkner: Early Prose and Poetry,* ed. Carvel Collins (Boston, 1962), 106.

Surely, the final pages of *Absalom, Absalom!* with their references to the progeny of miscegenation and the burning of the big house are shadowed in this poem too—"But when the master's buried mice can play, / And maybe the great-grandson of that house, / For all its bronze and marble, 's but a mouse"—as also, and in more detail, in the Irish poet's late play, *Purgatory.* There, the father, himself the product of a misalliance between an aristocratic mother and a philandering servant, kills his own similarly begotten son in order to end the miscegenistic sequence. Although Faulkner considered eugenics important, his views here were by no means as radical as those of the Yeats, who commended "all / That comes of the best knit to the best" ("Upon a House Shaken by the Land Agitation") and who favored a program of selection that is still troubling to his admirers. Still, both authors saw the future as shadowed by social and racial reorganizations likely to shatter the strenuously achieved harmonies of a mythic past.[24]

Finally, although there has always seemed to be more reason to think of Joyce and Faulkner together as prime representatives of their respective literary renaissances, rather than associating Yeats with Faulkner for that purpose, Brooks and the Nashville Fugitive-Agrarians were right in their exemplary choice. It is true that Faulkner borrowed heavily from Joyce's technical example, and that as novelists they could explore their societies in a degree of detail not available to poets—hence their ostracization by most of those they so intimately depicted. But one's sense of Faulkner is that he never quite abandoned his early southern pieties—Quentin Compson's consciousness *echoes* "with sonorous defeated names" while Stephen Dedalus tries to *escape* his—in the way that Joyce, for better and for worse, did. Some part of Faulkner remained the little boy fascinated by what might have happened had the battles of Vicksburg and Gettysburg gone differently.[25]

Like Yeats too, the son of a painter, Faulkner started out not only to be a poet but an artist as well, his impressively sophisticated drawings for the Ole Miss student magazine very much reflecting the influence of Aubrey Beardsley and others of Yeats's circle that had appeared in the notorious *Yellow Book* in the 1890s. More importantly, Yeats and Faulkner had a keen

---

24. Desmond Guinness and Julius Trousdale Sadler Jr., *Palladio: A Western Progress* (New York, 1976); *Yeats's Poetry, Drama, and Prose,* ed. James Pethica (New York, 2000), 169–74; compare this too with Faulkner's description of Sutpen's French architect and his project as the "little grim foreigner" who "vanquished Sutpen's fierce and overweening vanity or desire for magnificence . . . and so created of Sutpen's very defeat the victory which, in conquering, Sutpen himself would have failed to gain" (*Absalom, Absalom!* 29).

25. Faulkner, *Absalom, Absalom!* 7; Joyce, *Ulysses,* 34.

awareness of the violence that is part of the historical process, a violence sometimes criticized, but more often simply ignored, by a pacifist Joyce: Yeats quoted a line from fiery John Mitchel's *Jail Journal* in his epitaph poem "Under Ben Bulben" in which he seems almost to recreate Mitchel's attitude when defending Richmond:

> You that Mitchel's prayer have heard,
> 'Send war in our time, O Lord!'
> Know that when all words are said
> And a man is fighting mad,
> Something drops from eyes long blind,
> He completes his partial mind,
> For an instant stands at ease,
> Laughs aloud, his heart at peace.

Yeats and Faulkner both chose to live in, or journey back and forth to, the semirural societies they so frequently and so dangerously criticized, constantly aware of the restrictions of the small worlds they sought to understand and redirect. However much reviled by the nationalists, Yeats was chosen to become a senator in his country's first independent government; Faulkner eventually became a cultural ambassador for his. The Nobel Prize Committee's recognition of both writers meant that one-time peripheries had at last achieved universal significance.[26]

While Yeats, Joyce, and Faulkner tower over most of the other writers from their regions, they were not the only ones concerned with the passing of the old order. There is some similarity, for example, between the attitudes of the Anglo-Irish Elizabeth Bowen and Mississippi's William Alexander Percy as recorded in their respective "plantation" memoirs, both incidentally published in the early 1940s—*Bowen's Court* and *Lanterns on the Levee*—by the Knopfs, though Bowen is more acknowledging of the injustices of the past. Irish critics have often been unsympathetic with Bowen, however, seeing her as a haughty Anglo-Irish colonist and mocker of the natives, technically a British spy in neutral Ireland during World War II, and condescending even to Seán O'Faoláin when he was her lover by calling him "Johnny" on her flaunting visits to his home ("Seán" is an Irish Gaelic version of "John"; O'Faoláin himself had early on Gaelicized his name from his given "John Whelan"). But Declan Kiberd has recently pre-

26. Blotner, 93; W. B. Yeats, *Collected Poems* (New York, 1977), 342.

sented a more sympathetic—if rather artfully contrived, not to say disingen-
uous—view: "in that very disavowal of a native background or identity,
[Bowen] becomes a voice for all those uprooted, dispossessed Irish, from
the Gaelic earls who fled in 1607" onward. Her own uneasy awareness of
her position is insightfully reflected at least in her remarks in *Bowen's Court*
that "my family got their position and drew their power from a situation
that shows an inherent wrong," that "We have everything to dread from the
dispossessed," and that her family's house was "built of anxious history."
Indeed, in a parallel with the displaced Irish that she herself noted, her
founding family's Welsh ancestor "had fretted under [English] colonization"
before coming to an Ireland where "*he* was to colonize."[27]

It was Bowen who would attract the attention of one of the South's
most important writers in the post–World War II period, Eudora Welty.
Welty had already been deeply influenced by Irish mythology, deriving the
title and even the themes for one of her "novels," *The Golden Apples*, from
Yeats's "The Song of Wandering Aengus." In her 1983 autobiography, *One
Writer's Beginnings*, Welty described how her discovery of Yeats when she
was a student at the University of Wisconsin "fed my life ever since":

> And I happened to discover Yeats, reading through some of the stacks in
> the library. I read the early and then the later poems all in the same one
> afternoon, standing up, by the window . . . I read "Sailing to Byzantium,"
> standing up in the stacks, read it by the light of falling snow. It seemed to
> me that if I could stir, if I could move to take the next step, I could go out
> into the poem the way I could go out into that snow. That it would be
> falling on my shoulders. That it would pelt me on its way down—that I
> could move in it, live in it—that I could die in it, maybe.

Almost prophetically in light of this, Diarmuid Russell, the son of one of
the major figures of the Irish renaissance, George Russell ("AE"), and himself an intimate of Yeats, offered to act as Welty's New York literary agent
and schooled her in matters Irish. Indeed, later, Russell's own experience
of his homeland—the many attacks on his father by Seán O'Casey, for example—was to have a direct impact on his handling of Welty's theatrical
possibilities.[28]

27. See Julia O'Faoláin's afterword to the revised version of her father's autobiography, *Vive
Moi!* (London, 1993); Declan Kiberd, *Inventing Ireland: The Literature of the Modern Nation*
(Cambridge, Mass., 1995), 378; Elizabeth Bowen, *Bowen's Court* (New York, 1964), 338, 453,
455, 457, 38.

28. Eudora Welty, *One Writer's Beginnings* (New York, 1984), 88; Michael Kreyling, *Author
and Agent: Eudora Welty and Diarmuid Russell* (New York, 1991), 149–51, 161.

When Welty was in Dublin in the late 1940s, acting almost on a whim—and a very unsouthern one at that, as she herself recognized—she wrote a note to Bowen, who had reviewed her work appreciatively, and was invited to stay at Bowen's Court in County Cork, the kind of "big house" that has figured in so much of Irish and southern writing. So began an important, emotionally intense, and lifelong friendship between them. It was there, during her second visit in 1951, that Welty worked on her one Irish story, "The Bride of the Innisfallen." It was there also that she, a veteran photographer from WPA days, took a series of pictures of her surroundings, including the ruined Kilcolman Castle, once a spoil given to Edmund Spenser for his Irish home (where Sir Walter Raleigh visited him), but from which he was to be driven out by "rebels" in 1598.[29]

Bowen's account of the general area would surely have appealed to a southerner of Welty's sensibility:

> This is a country of ruins. Lordly or humble, military or domestic, standing up with furious gauntness, like Kilcolman, or shelving weakly into the soil, ruins feature the landscape . . . and make a ghostly extra quarter to towns. They give clearings in woods, reaches of mountain or sudden turns of a road a meaning and pre-inhabited air. Ivy grapples them; trees grow inside their doors. . . . Some ruins show gashes of violence, others simply the dull slant of decline. In this Munster county so often fought over there has been cruelty even to the stones; military fury or welling-up human bitterness has vented itself on the unknowing walls.

How reminiscent all this must have been to Welty, who herself had written just a few years earlier of the decayed river country of Mississippi, the starkly beautiful Corinthian columns of the ruins of Windsor, and of a time even before that: now "there are no mansions, no celebrations . . . when there were mansions and celebrations, there were no more festivals of an Indian tribe there." There too were once heard "Irish songs . . . sung to popular requests," and there too were many "tombstones . . . marked 'A Native of Ireland,'" leading Welty to muse that "Whatever is significant and whatever is tragic in its story live as long as the place does, though they are unseen." Seamus Heaney's "Bogland" also comes to mind: "Every layer they strip / Seems camped on before."[30]

---

29. Eudora Welty, *Eudora Welty Photographs* (Jackson, Miss., 1989)—Welty's pictures of County Cork are numbered 174–187.

30. Bowen, 15–16; Welty, *The Eye of the Story: Selected Essays and Reviews* (New York, 1978), 286, 290, 292, 299; Seamus Heaney, *Opened Ground* (New York, 2002), 41.

Writing about Welty, Peggy Prenshaw has pointed out that Bowen's "description of the general perception of Ireland by non-natives, coincidentally, bears more than a passing similarity to popular and literary images of the southern United States in both the nineteenth and twentieth centuries: 'There is this about us: to most of the rest of the world we are semi-strangers, for whom existence has something of the trance-like quality of a spectacle. As beings, we are at once brilliant and limited.'" In a subsequent interview about her visit, Welty noted: "I saw that still further south [in County Cork] there were palm trees and fuchsia hedges and pink and blue plastered houses that made you think of Savannah or New Orleans. It's almost tropical." Welty added that "At any rate, Elizabeth is a *Southerner*. She said that wherever she went, in the whole world almost, the Southerners were always different from the Northerners. She always felt the congeniality." Welty's letters to Bowen before her first visit to Mississippi stress that, positively, she will be encountering a different America there—in fact, in one of them Welty has drawn a tiny Confederate flag to emphasize the separateness of her region.[31]

"The Bride of the Innisfallen," Welty's first ("my favorite") story to be published in the *New Yorker* and which later served as the title for one of her collections (dedicated to Bowen), is among the more elusive stories of an elusive writer. Even her friend and editor William Maxwell at the *New Yorker* sent her a list of twenty-six questions about details of the story, to one of which she replied that she had no idea how she knew that particular fact.[32] Most of Welty's critics have either avoided commenting on the story at all, or have very tentatively suggested possible meanings, ending up on occasion with wildly imaginative interpretations. Robert Daniel judged it "brilliant in observation" but "marred by the obscurity of its theme."[33]

The "bride" of the title appears only very briefly near the end of a story

31. Peggy Whitman Prenshaw, "The Antiphonies of Eudora Welty's *One Writer's Beginnings* and Elizabeth Bowen's *Pictures and Conversations*," *Mississippi Quarterly* 39, no. 4 (1986): 647; Albert J. Devlin and Peggy Whitman Prenshaw, "A Conversation with Eudora Welty, Jackson, 1986," *Mississippi Quarterly* 39, no. 4 (1986): 433; Welty to Bowen, 16 September [1951], Bowen Collection, Harry Ransom Humanities Research Library, University of Texas at Austin.

32. Ann Waldron, *Eudora Welty: A Writer's Life* (New York, 1998), 221; Kreyling, 155–57.

33. See Diana R. Pingatore, *A Reader's Guide to the Short Stories of Eudora Welty* (New York, 1996), 351–62; Robert W. Daniel, "Eudora Welty: The Sense of Place," in *South: Modern Southern Literature in Its Cultural Setting*, ed. Louis D. Rubin Jr. and Robert D. Jacobs (New York, 1961), 280. Suzanne Marrs offers a sensitive commentary and notes the influence of Bowen's

most of which is set on the "boat train," the British Railway service that connects London with Fishguard in Wales, where passengers then embark for an overnight sailing to Ireland. Nor does the huddled American girl "leaving London without her husband's knowledge," who sits in a compartment among an assortment of travelers, most of them Irish returning home, become the focus of interest until the end of the story either.[34]

The body of the tale consists in beginnings, strayings off, and snippets of conversations among the other occupants of the compartment: a Welshman who is only going a part of the way, a man traveling to Cork who has a "musical" voice, a pair of lovers who sit together entwined, a rambunctious boy in the care of his young aunt, a talkative woman with a raincoat that has all the colors of the rainbow, and a man from Connemara whose hair is "in two corner bushes" and who has "a full eye—like that of the horse in the storm in old chromos in the West of America—the kind of eye supposed to attract lightning," and who keeps ejaculating "*Oh* my God!" at intervals. A bible-reading Welsh schoolgirl sits in silence among them.[35]

Welty blends fantasy and whimsy with realism. Indeed, anyone who has ever made the journey from Fishguard to Ireland will be aware both of the accuracy of Welty's depictions, especially that strange sense of cosmic loneliness that comes in the night hours when one has just crossed into Wales, and at the same time the author's removal from those cruder and less pleasant aspects of the passage: the slobbering drunkards, sick children, and sodden toilets. Welty's mode rather is one of contemplative celebration of the variety and vagary of the human scene, not an exercise in recreating the grottiness of local discolor.

Various topics of conversation ebb and flow as the journey progresses. At one stage, the merits of speaking Irish are brought up, the Welshman remarking that it is "No real language," the woman in the raincoat defending it with the information that her brother is fluent in Irish and that "You cannot doubt yourself that when the English hear you speaking a tongue they cannot follow, in the course of time they are due to start holding respect for you." The Connemara man counters that he has an English wife who would not understand him at all if he began talking to her in that language.[36]

The House in Paris in her *One Writer's Imagination: The Fiction of Eudora Welty* (Baton Rouge, 2003), 149–55.

34. Eudora Welty, *The Bride of the Innisfallen and Other Stories* (New York, 1972), 48.

35. Ibid., 55, 51.

36. Ibid., 57–58.

When darkness falls, the passengers see shadowy reflections in the windows, some fantastical: "Out there, nuns, swept by untoward blasts of wind, shrieked soundlessly as in nightmares in the corridors." One of the lovers remarks that "in the windows black as they are, we do look almost like ghosts riding by," which leads the Connemara man to tell a story about a ghostly couple—almost like the doomed figures in Yeats's *Purgatory*—seen recurrently at a castle in Ireland. The woman has a dagger stuck in her lover, pulling him through the air like a hooked fish until they sail off together "cozy as a couple of kites to start it again." No obvious or even prophetic point is made, except to state that "Love was amazement now." The Welshman reads the American's passport aloud "as if it were a poem in the paper, only with the last verse missing," then gets off at the wrong station "as though a big thumb had snuffed him out." The anonymous narrator adds: "Not a soul had enquired of that poor vanquished man what he did, if he had wife and children living."[37]

When the boat reaches Cork harbor in the morning, the city seems unrecognizable because it has been transformed—possibly only in the consciousness of the American protagonist, however—into "shapes of light and color without knowledge or memory to inform them." In any case, while the people on the quay are preoccupied with the bride on board, the real focus of the story now shifts to the unspoken reverie of the American girl. "When it rained late in that afternoon, the American girl was still in Cork, and stood sheltering in the doorway of a pub. She was listening to the pub sounds and the alley sounds as she might to a garden's and a fountain's." She has crossed "swan-bright bridges," and seen "dozens of little girls in confirmation dresses, squared off by their veils into animated paper snowflakes, [as they] raced and danced out of control and into charmed traffic—like miniature and more conscious brides." The blossoming trees too "nearly had sound, as the bells did."[38]

The narrative description that "In all Cork today every willow stood with gold-red hair springing and falling about it, like Venus alive" leads to the rather enigmatic question: "In the future would the light, that had jumped like the man from Connemara into the world, be a memory, like that of a meeting, or must there be mere faith that it had been like that?"[39]

In the telegraph office, the American girl furtively writes to her hus-

37. Ibid., 60, 63, 74–76.
38. Ibid., 80.
39. Ibid., 81.

band that "England was a mistake," scratches the words out immediately, then reflects that "*I* was nearly destroyed." Her new-found secret, which she must never tell her husband, seems to be of "pure joy—the kind you were born and began with"—yet she has also to tell it in some way. She does so in language reminiscent of T. S. Eliot's *Four Quartets* or Virginia Woolf's *To the Lighthouse:*

> Is there no way? she thought—for here I am, this far. I see Cork's streets take off from the waterside and rise lifting their houses and towers like note above note on a page of music, with arpeggios running over it of green and galleries and belvederes, and the bright sun raining [sic] at the top. Out of the joy I hide for fear it is promiscuous, I may walk for ever at the fall of evening by the river, and find this river street by the red rock, this first, last house, that's perhaps a boarding house now, standing full-face to the tide, and look up to that window—that upper window, from which the mystery will never go . . . it was the window itself that could tell her all she had come here to know.

The girl decides to send a telegram to her husband not to expect her back yet, but when she takes shelter again in a pub doorway, she lets "her message go into the stream of the street." Instead of chasing it, she opens the pub's door and walks "into the lovely room full of strangers."[40]

Welty's story is unsatisfying in many ways, not least in the elusiveness of its possible meaning, but she herself was cautious about the reductiveness of much critical analysis. Perhaps a way of "holding" the story in mind is to accept an observation she made about the work of Ford Madox Ford: "Ford the Impressionist was breaking up human experience by his technique of time-shift in order to show the inner life of that experience, its essential mystery." So, at least, in the very respectfulness it shows toward the people it describes—and this is true also of Welty's stories and photographs of African Americans—in its collage of nonevaluative observations on a culture that all too often inspires witless commentary, "The Bride of the Innisfallen" too lingers as a creative and delicious evocation of almost intangible, Matisse-like perceptions.[41]

Welty's Irish visit—Bowen afterward stayed with her in Mississippi, and they remained in close communication for the rest of their lives—was to lead to at least one other Southern writer going to Cork. Carson McCullers,

---

40. Ibid., 82, 83.
41. Welty, *Eye of the Story,* 246.

described as "Welty's nemesis," arrived at Bowen's Court with the most romantic of expectations only to find that the mistress's regimen was much more austere and sober than she had anticipated—which was precisely what Welty had liked about the place. Still, Bowen chose to add a photo of an overjoyed McCullers seated in a veteran racing car belonging to one of the Irish writer's cousins in the revised edition of *Bowen's Court* in 1964.[42]

If by the time Eudora Welty and, to a lesser extent, Elizabeth Bowen arrived on the literary scene, the great phase of both revivals was over—a thesis currently being vigorously contested as a quintessentially male perception, though the fact that Yeats and Joyce were dead and that Faulkner had long since completed his best work gives some plausibility to the claim—there were still a surprising number of important writers in both places keeping the tradition alive. This was the case most of all in the short story, that genre that Frank O'Connor has described as the voice of "submerged population groups," and as "romantic, individualistic, and intransigent." However much of the romance still remained, all these writers had brought a disconcerting criticism—what Joyce described acidly as a "scrupulous meanness"—to the hallowed myths and certainties of their respective communities, painfully exposing them to the possibility of even greater self-examination in the future. C. Vann Woodward has written frequently and eloquently about the influence that writers such as Faulkner and Warren have had on his thinking about the southern past, freeing him imaginatively from the rigidities of defensive interpretations. In questioning—in very different ways—traditional assumptions about the Irish legacy, Yeats and Joyce too prepared the way for a reopening of the annals of Ireland's historical masters. In short, the writers helped both Irish people and southerners to engage creatively and critically with the nightmare of the past. Historians would contentiously, and often courageously, carry on the work. It is to their very similar preoccupations, fates, and conclusions that we must now turn.[43]

---

42. Based on the passion of some of Welty's letters to Bowen, Ann Waldron, Welty's unofficial and controversial biographer, speculates that the relationship between the two writers may have been more intimate (*Eudora Welty*, 225); Josyane Savigneau, *Carson McCullers: A Life* (New York, 2001), 202–3.

43. See the essays in *Haunted Bodies: Gender and Southern Texts*, ed. Anne Goodwyn Jones and Susan V. Donaldson (Charlottesville, Va., 1997); Frank O'Connor, *The Lonely Voice: A Study of the Short Story* (New York, 1963), 20–21.

CHAPTER 10

REMEMBERING THINGS PAST

The past is never dead. It's not even past.

—WILLIAM FAULKNER, *Requiem for a Nun*

Bíonn dhá insint ar gach scéal [There are two sides to every story].

—Irish proverb

Almost as much as he found them excessively religious, W. J. Cash also saw southerners as extraordinarily concerned with genealogy, and, as a product of this, with the injuries that had been done to them in their history. Hence the truth of "Dixie" (which, in that disruptive way so disconcertingly frequent throughout the human record, may have been originally composed by a black couple in Ohio rather than by the white Daniel Decatur Emmett to whom it is routinely attributed): "in de land ob cotton, / Old times dar am not forgotten." If certain southerners "were of English descent," Cash commented, "then their forebears had infallibly ridden, not only with Rupert at Naseby, but also with William at Senlac; if Scotch or Scotch-Irish, they were invariably clansmen of the chieftain's family . . . ; if plain Irish, they stemmed from Brian Boru." Memory retreated back to the civil war (England's in the 1640s) before the Civil War, and even to all the wars before that. In any case, while it is noteworthy that Cash decided to include the "plain" Irish at all in this litany—he obviously considered them players in the game—his purpose was to debunk such notions about ancestry. According to him, it was the shame and guilt of the Old South over slavery that provoked such defense mechanisms. So the southerner "told himself that he was noble, chivalrous, and kind, and that the Yankee, particularly the critic of slavery, was 'low-bred, crass, and money-grubbing.'"[1]

That, however, cannot be the full truth of the matter. How much guilt

---

1. W. J. Cash, *The Mind of the South* (New York, 1969), 66; Howard L. Sacks and Judith Rose Sacks, *Way up North in Dixie: A Black Family's Claim to the Confederate Anthem* (Washington, D.C., 1993), 63.

there ever was over slavery is subject to debate. More importantly, Zora Neale Hurston's bold, debunking statement in 1928 that she was "the only Negro in the United States whose grandfather on the mother's side was *not* an Indian chief" suggests how widespread claims to noble descent were among her African American contemporaries too. Alex Haley's celebrated, and berated, *Roots* betrays the same syndrome much more recently. All such claims must partly be explained as the cries of the defeated protesting their defeat and asserting their dignity against the indignity of their suppression; they are a plea for recognition by those for whom status has come to matter, the very human and understandable self-making acts of those who find it intolerable to have no ascertainable ancestry distinct from that of the unwashed masses—to identify with which requires considerable, Hurston-like self-confidence.[2]

Some observers have found it remarkable—or have *claimed* to find it remarkable—that such beliefs exist at all and have lamented how tenaciously they have persisted in certain communities and regions. Thomas Nelson Page's confident assertion in 1892, derived from such notions of ancestry, that the Old South combined the best of Greek, Hebrew, Roman, and Anglo-Saxon cultures may be a source of amusement to nonsoutherners, but it is clear that it was not so to many of the people in the region, even if their own families had never been associated with the plantation aristocracy, an aristocracy that itself appears to have had rather modest origins.

The Irish too, whatever their class, declared that they were the true ancient and noble race as opposed to their upstart and mercenary invaders from England. As Seamus Deane has stated in an attack on W. B. Yeats's Protestant pretensions to social superiority, "The Anglo-Irish were held in contempt by the Irish-speaking masses as people of no blood, without lineage and with nothing to recommend them other than the success of their Hanoverian cause over that of the Jacobites." Such claims too provoked cosmopolitan England's scorn. And just as from within the fold even a southern Cash called this supposed cultural superiority into question, claiming that it had been "a superficial and jejune thing, borrowed from without and worn as a political armor," so too an Irish James Joyce, or a contemporary historian such as J. J. Lee, has mocked his countrymen's historical assumptions and their massive self-deceptions (which is not to claim, however,

2. Zora Neale Hurston, *I Love Myself When I Am Laughing* (Old Westbury, Conn., 1979), 155.

that generic British assertions of aristocracy were any less tenuous or self-deceiving).[3]

For Cash, in addition, in a passage in which he himself deeply and even romantically identifies with his own southern heritage, the mind of the South is even more that of a victim than is the case with the Irish—surely an extraordinary achievement in itself!: "Not Ireland nor Poland, not Finland nor Bohemia, not one of the countries which prove the truth that there is no more sure way to make a nation than the brutal oppression of an honorably defeated and disarmed people—not one of these, for all the massacres, the pillage, and the rapes to which they have so often been subjected, was ever so pointedly taken in the very core of its being as was the South. And so not one ever developed so much of fear, of rage, of indignation and resentment, of self-consciousness and patriotic passion." Such somber preoccupations have led to what is most typical of southern culture: "Imagination there was in plenty in this land with so much of the blood of the dreamy Celts and its warm sun, but it spent itself on puerilities, on cant and twisted logic . . . and the feckless vaporings of sentimentality." Indeed, in Cash's view, during the traumatic period of Reconstruction southerners became "the most sentimental people in history."[4]

Such sentimental—in the fullest sense of the word—attachment to the painful past is passionately and movingly evoked in Faulkner's *Absalom, Absalom!* in the scene at Harvard in 1910 where the Canadian Shreve McCannon contrasts his history-impoverished background with the multilayered inheritance of Quentin Compson (whose very body was described earlier in the novel as "a barracks filled with stubborn back-looking ghosts"):

> We dont live among defeated grandfathers and freed slaves . . . and bullets in the dining room table and such, to be always reminding us to never forget. What is it? something you live in and breathe in like air? a kind of vacuum filled with wraithlike and indomitable anger and pride and glory at and in happenings that occurred and ceased fifty years ago? a kind of entailed birthright father and son and father and son of never forgiving General Sherman, so that forever more as long as your children's children produce children you wont be anything but a descendant of a long line of colonels killed in Pickett's charge at Manassas?

3. Cash, 97; Seamus Deane, *Celtic Revivals* (London, 1985), 30; J. J. Lee, *Ireland, 1912–1985* (New York, 1989).

4. Cash, 108, 130.

This passage—in which Shreve confuses Manassas with Gettysburg and is immediately (*instinctively* would be a more accurate description) corrected by Quentin, who adds that one would have to be born there to understand such matters (though he is quickly driven to concede that even that advantage might not suffice)—has the ring of a rather more prosaic remark on the Irish attitude toward their history by Lloyd Praeger: "We Irish can never let the past bury its dead. Finn McCoul and Brian Boru are still with us . . . the Battle of the Boyne was fought last Thursday week, and Cromwell . . . slaughtered in Ireland towards the latter end of the preceding month."[5]

Of course, one might legitimately question whether such tendencies make either southerners or their Irish counterparts any more knowledgeably conscious of history than others are. Perhaps all that is happening is that in situations where a community experiences either little change or little immigration, memory is not dispersed and so feeds upon itself: an impoverished South after the war and a retrenched Ireland after the famine could attract few newcomers and so local memory remained static. But, for whatever reason, remain it did. In fact, from time to time, professional historians studying Ireland or the South have commented on the satisfaction of having an engaged audience, one even a little more engaged at times than personal comfort would wish.[6]

In the same vein, Allen Tate has pointed out that while the southern mind was "not much given to introspection," it *was* meditative, "which is something quite different." Tate's analysis suggests a southern propensity to mull over the injustices of the past without ever finding release from them, to have a sense of ongoing persecution, and to cultivate a siege mentality in response. Hence too a trait that was of enormous concern to Cash: the South's extraordinary sensitivity to criticism, which he dated from the region's strident defense of slavery in the 1830s and its unwillingness to allow a difference of opinion on the issue. It was an attitude that was to be intensified rather than dispersed by defeat in 1865. Cash famously identified this syndrome as the "savage ideal" whereby "dissent and variety are completely suppressed and men become, in all their attitudes, professions, and actions, virtual replicas of one another." It was this narrow-mindedness that led Cash himself to fear the consequences when *The Mind of the South*

---

5. William Faulkner, *Absalom, Absalom!* (New York, 1990), 7, 289; E. Estyn Evans, "Introduction: The Irish—Fact and Fiction," in *The Irish World: The History and Cultural Achievements of the Irish People,* ed. Brian De Breffny (London, 1977), 8.

6. See, for example, interview with Roy Foster in *History Today* 51, no. 10 (2001): 30–32.

was finally published in 1941—Donald Davidson, one of the Nashville Fugitives, had suggested rather ominously, if jokingly, in a newspaper review that perhaps he should be "railroaded" for expressing such opinions—and so to flee the region for Mexico.[7]

In his 1940 study, *The Irish*, Seán O'Faoláin too, like Cash, set out both to clarify and debunk his fellow-countrymen's perceptions of their history. Less concerned than the nationalists (his former associates when he was a member of the anti–Free State Republicans) with the long litany of invasions and persecutions, O'Faoláin rather saw the course of Irish history as "the battleground of a racial mind forced on each new occasion to struggle afresh with itself." So, for him, while ancient Irish society had a life that was "aristocratic, regional and personal, and all three to an extreme degree," the incursions from the British mainland had ultimately enriched and broadened the Irish mind, however painful the process may have been. The growth of a narrow nationalism and pious clericalism in the nineteenth century had served to restrict freedom of thought, however, confining it within various cultural "nets" as Joyce put it, so that, as with Cash in the American South, many of those who chose to think otherwise were driven into an exile that was not wholly voluntary. Forging "the conscience of [one's] race" was best done outside the region itself—so much so that even an Irish writer who was a Jesuit seminarian in the 1940s has since confessed his relief at being sent out from neutral Ireland to wartime England for his advanced studies.[8]

O'Faoláin noted, in language that could also be applied to the southern states of America vis-à-vis the U.S. government: "If the Celtic tradition has given us anything in this field what it has given is that old atavistic individualism which tends to make all Irishmen inclined to respect no laws at all; and though this may be socially deplorable it is humanly admirable, and makes life much more tolerable and charitable and easy-going and entertaining." It could be said that O'Faoláin, as founder and editor of *The Bell*, spent the 1940s and 1950s trying to keep that ancient individualism—now

---

7. Allen Tate, *Essays of Four Decades* (Chicago, 1968), 581; Charles Reagan Wilson's comment in *Judgement and Grace in Dixie: Southern Faiths from Faulkner to Elvis* (Athens, Ga., 1995) that "the South through much of its history was a society held in the grip of orthodoxies to be questioned only at profound risk" (115) smacks of Cash; Cash, 93–94. In *Tell about the South: The Southern Rage to Explain* (Baton Rouge, 1983), Fred Hobson cautions, however, that it would be wrong to attribute Cash's subsequent suicide to the same motive (270).

8. Seán O'Faoláin, *The Irish* (New York, 1967), 9, 43; James Joyce, *A Portrait of the Artist as a Young Man* (New York, 1977), 203; John O'Meara, *The Singing-Masters* (Dublin, 1995).

in the guise of modern liberalism—alive in the teeth of dull, rather than dangerous, opposition by publishing a new generation of controversial Irish writers.[9]

In her 1942 autobiography, *Dust Tracks on a Road*, Zora Neale Hurston also demythologized an important aspect of her own race's received history:

> But the inescapable fact that stuck in my craw, was: my people had sold me and the white people had bought me. That did away with the folklore I had been brought up on—that the white people had gone to Africa, waved a red handkerchief at the Africans and lured them aboard ship and sailed away. I know that civilized money stirred up African greed. That wars between tribes were often stirred up by white traders to provide more slaves in the barracoons and all that. But, if the African princes had been as pure and as innocent as I would like to think, it could not have happened.

The claim that things may not have been quite as they once seemed—either ancestries or injuries—was bound to upset those who had drawn sustenance from such myths to tide them over in difficult times. Hurston was to remain a controversial figure in the black community.[10]

The production of historical interpretation, then, has always been a highly contested enterprise in both places. While Cash and O'Faoláin, neither of whom was a professional historian, represent a creative effort at changing the public mind-set in the 1940s in a more open direction, they belong in a line of popular interpretations that generally had a less inclusive intent. Biographies of Jefferson Davis, Stonewall Jackson, Nathan Bedford Forrest, and John Brown, written by Allen Tate, Donald Davidson, and Robert Penn Warren, respectively, in the previous decade, for example, were aimed at the same audience but with a more conservative purpose. In Ireland, nationalist histories produced by Alice Stopford Green, A. M. Sullivan, and Dorothy McArdle enjoyed great success. It was not necessarily that nonprofessional histories had greater appeal in these regions than in Britain or in the larger United States but that their effects were more immediately palpable in them.

Even if the extent to which a broad American southern nationalism, as opposed to simple identification with one's own state, existed before the war

9. O'Faoláin, 45–46.

10. Zora Neale Hurston, *Dust Tracks on a Road* (Urbana, Ill., 1984), 200. In *Slaves in the Family* (New York, 1998), Edward Ball also reports encountering a hesitancy among the descendants of African slave traders as late as the 1990s to discuss the injustices of the past.

is a matter of some debate, it seems clear that the war reinforced the sense of being "southern" rather than Virginian, or Georgian, or Carolinian. Paradoxically, the "South" truly came into being after its wartime defeat. It did so first among the enthusiasts for the Lost Cause. The memory of having had wrong done to them as defeated, impoverished, and disenfranchised whites, rather than the accusation that they had done wrong to others through the institution of slavery, was dominant in their minds. In general, white southerners felt that the original secession had been morally and legally justified and that God was on their side. They refused to see slavery as the central issue, since several noted biblical figures had practiced the same. Thus, as Gaines M. Foster points out in *Ghosts of the Confederacy*, with their strong sense of the importance of honor, southerners of the post-1865 era were upset with the need to seek pardons for their wartime activity. What they wanted was vindication, not forgiveness.[11]

This defensiveness about the issues of the war resulted in the endless commemorating and statue-building of the 1880s and afterward, when almost every courthouse square boasted its often generic Confederate soldier and when Monument Avenue was laid out in Richmond as a shrine to the honorably defeated. Father Ryan was emblematic of the mind-set, as exemplified in his reading of "The Sword of Robert E. Lee" ("a nation's dirge") at the unveiling of a statue over the general's tomb on June 28, 1883, at Washington and Lee College. Ryan, according to Foster, represented the old attitudes of the pre-reconciliation era, but his influence, and that of the Veterans and Daughters of the Confederacy, lasted into the beginning of the twentieth century, when, though professional historians began to take over, even these "maintained a tenuous peace with the leaders of the Confederate celebration and indeed participated in it." It could be argued that this mind-set is still not totally uncommon in the American South, having been preserved by generations of oral history and lore, as well as by a good deal of college instruction.[12]

So strong were the feelings of righteousness at the end of the nineteenth century that the veterans controlled the texts used in schools and colleges and thereby ensured that they expressed a white southern bias. Patrick Cleburne's worst fears about the victorious enemy writing the history seemed not to have been fulfilled. The restrictive cohesiveness of southern

11. Gaines M. Foster, *Ghosts of the Confederacy: Defeat, the Lost Cause, and the Emergence of the New South, 1865–1913* (New York, 1987), 6.

12. Ibid., 180.

culture at the time is also shown by the kind of trouble that arose when William P. Trent, in an 1892 critical biography of William Gilmore Simms, denounced the South's war for slavery and saw the conflict as being "between southern 'primitives' and the forces of progress": his mother was shunned; he himself worried about visiting his hometown of Charleston; and there was an attempt made to remove him from the faculty at the University of the South. After all, his presentation went against the very conscious determination to deemphasize the importance of slavery in accounts of the war.[13]

Even later when nonsouthern professional historians took over—William A. Dunning at Columbia University most prominent among them—they also saw their task as a kind of missionary labor, although of a somewhat different stripe. They thought "the 'redemption' of the South would come through a combination of strong nationalism, industrial development, education, and progressive social engineering." While they argued for freedom of thought and a more scientific approach to southern history, and attacked an excessively sentimental view of the South's past, as missionaries, Foster claims, "they themselves displayed little objectivity." As defenders of the white southern cause, they too downplayed the matter of slavery.[14]

The same was even more true of southern professional historians' attitudes. In a 1985 essay, Robert F. Durden could claim that "sullen, defensive sectionalism has markedly receded among us," while also showing how painfully slow that process had been.[15] Thus, while the first president of the Southern Historical Association, E. Merton Coulter, in 1935 argued that the history of the South was largely unwritten "because southerners and especially the Scotch-Irish, who played such an influential role in the region, 'were individualistic and greatly lacking in self-consciousness,'" five years later Frank L. Owsley famously attacked Lincoln's Gettysburg speech as "the most eloquent statement of what the war was not fought" about, since, according to him, it was the South and not the North that exemplified authentic American nationalism. A year later, Benjamin B. Kendrick argued that the postwar South had been made into a colony, that the North had been antislavery only because in a society where there weren't many blacks

13. Ibid., 182.

14. Ibid., 181.

15. Robert F. Durden, "A Half Century of Change in Southern History," *Journal of Southern History* 51, no. 1 (1985): 3–14.

anyway, it was an "inexpensive method for . . . a conscientious nonslave-holding middle class to pay their debts to God." In this way of looking at things, the subsequent policy of Reconstruction was interpreted as an exercise in brutal imperialism, a foregone decision to subjugate the agricultural South, as Avery Craven argued in 1951, not a crusade to end Negro slavery.[16]

A marked change of attitude, however, came about in 1952 with C. Vann Woodward's famous essay "The Irony of Southern History." In it he showed how the South had once been the home of antislavery societies and had only later become defensive of the institution. He pleaded for "a critical yet sympathetic—an ironic—approach to the South's past," something that has especial interest when looking at the Irish case. But Francis B. Simkins's presentation in 1954, "Tolerating the South's Past," was a kind of throwback to an earlier view, and it was only in 1963 with James W. Silver's "Mississippi: The Closed Society" that the changed attitude could be said to be permanent, since he actually condemned white supremacy cloaked in states' rights and fundamentalism. Subsequent developments in the civil rights movement saw southern historians by and large refusing to support continued segregation, while the growing prosperity of the region made the "colonial" argument less persuasive than before.[17]

Nevertheless, in spite of this development in a generally more open direction, it is instructive to look in greater detail at Simkins' 1954 talk, as it represents an important and ongoing aspect of the white southern mindset. Simkins argued that the past must be evaluated by the standards of the past. For example, the founders of the South simply did not accept the notion of equality on any level. The separation of the races was "the most important fact in Southern history," without which "the region . . . would be just a geographical expression." The plantation system helped to civilize blacks: "The slave was so well inoculated with Anglo-American culture that almost all elements of his African background disappeared." Simkins repeated a famous, and probably sincerely held, bromide: "A majority of Southerners believes that the nearest approach to heaven this side of the grave is that aristocratic perfection known as the Old South," a belief that "has brought about a unity of spirit which results in a friendly tie between the masses and the classes."[18]

16. Ibid., 4, 7, 10.

17. Ibid., 12.

18. Francis B. Simkins, in *The Pursuit of Southern History*, ed. George B. Tindall (Baton Rouge, 1964), 311, 314, 315.

Simkins concluded by arguing for a position that was to be especially resonant with Irish historians some years later: he attacked those southern scholars who demythologized the history of the region, suggesting that it was not as aristocratic as previously thought but rather more middle class, with both poor whites and blacks suffering from its intrinsic inequities. In particular, he attacked the then-emerging C. Vann Woodward, commenting:

> This revision of Southern legends is factually correct, based as it is upon much research in manuscripts and other original documents. But it carries with it the danger of equating facts with truth . . . Sometimes Southern historians forget that what is often important to Southerners is not what actually happened but what is believed to have happened. Southerners want their historians to do them concrete good by revealing or creating ancestors for them . . . Disillusioning researches in the records of the South's past have not generally impressed the Southern people. This sort of revelation must go unheeded if the South is to survive as a cultural entity.

This is a remarkable statement in its unequivocal acceptance of findings that contradict the author's ideology and in its determination nevertheless to assert the need for such views to persist—in this case, of course, a white understanding of such history. It is at once a last-ditch defense of a disappearing mind-set and an unintended justification for other groups to do likewise, African Americans not least among them. History, it would seem, can be selectively presented as a means of shoring up a valued culture.[19]

The emergence of C. Vann Woodward in the 1950s, in contrast, marked the advent of what seemed then to be a "scientific" history of the South, or at least one that placed more emphasis on fact. In *The Burden of Southern History,* he went through the various representations and myths, dismissing each of them in turn, including the myths of the Cavalier and necessarily segregated South. Very much as Conor Cruise O'Brien was to argue later regarding the Irish situation, Woodward came to the conclusion that their history itself, "the collective experience of the Southern people," was what united them. That experience made them different from the general run of other Americans because it included defeat in war (not replicated for the rest of America, in Woodward's view, until the Vietnam debacle), a "preoccupation . . . with guilt [over slavery], not with innocence, with the reality

19. Ibid., 317.

of evil, not with the [American] dream of perfection," and "Generations of scarcity and want . . . an experience too deeply embedded in their memory to be wiped out by a business boom." Different from the American norm in their defeat, guilt, and poverty, southerners also were seen as having a sense of place, unlike the larger American society, which stressed change and mobility. In all, their experience had been so different from the American norm, Woodward concluded, that—positively—it should make southerners cautious about uncritically embracing "all the myths of [American] nationalism." In other words, the acknowledged evils of the past could engender a chastened present, making southerners in the process—though this wasn't the overt intent—more morally perceptive than their all-too-complacent fellow countrymen.[20]

Although Woodward stressed poverty and place as important in the southern experience, his correction of previous interpretations is remembered most of all for its emphasis on the South as having undergone defeat in a way quite unlike any other part of America. Such an interpretation, while provocative and liberating in its way, requires caution however, not least because it has been so readily accepted among white southerners. Alice Walker has given the classic retort: "I was invited to speak at a gathering of Mississippi librarians and before I could get started, one of the authorities on Mississippi history got up and said she really *did* think Southerners wrote so well because 'we' lost the war. She was white, of course, but half the librarians in the room were black . . . So I got up and said no, 'we' didn't lose the war. '*You* all' lost the war. And you all's loss was our gain."[21]

Perhaps one might want to compromise and say that for a hundred years after the Civil War, both white and black southerners were locked into a spiral of self-defeating tension and conflict that retarded the ordinary development of the region (though "ordinary" and "normal" are words that need their own scrutiny in this case), mainly for bad but with some elements of good, in comparison with the rest of the nation. No one had really "won" the war in any great triumphant sense, though blacks were undoubtedly better off because of it. Whites were too, but their defeat had been so massive and the devastation, material and psychological, so vast that that

20. C. Vann Woodward, *The Burden of Southern History* (Baton Rouge, 1993), 16, 21, 17–18, 25.

21. Alice Walker, *In Search of Our Mothers' Gardens* (New York, 1983), 48–49.

was not apparent except to the consciences of the more societally rebellious among them.[22]

The real irony of most southern history was that it tried to ignore the past of a very large minority of its people—those whose ancestors had been slaves before the war—for a very long time. White and black histories were segregated almost as much as the races themselves, but black history too, as we saw in chapter 6, had its own sentimental and religious phase and only got under way as a "scientific" enterprise early in the twentieth century with Carter G. Woodson, who founded the *Journal of Negro History* in 1915. Unfortunately, this development coincided with the rise of the white professional approach noted above, one deeply influenced by "racist thinking among American intellectuals." For example, Charles Beard, a leading influence on both American and Irish historians, was not concerned with race as a moral issue. Woodson noted too of Ulrich B. Phillips, an expert on slavery, that "In just the same way as a writer of the history of New England in describing the fisheries of that section would have little to say about the species figuring conspicuously in that industry, so has the author treated the negro in his work."[23]

W. E. B. Du Bois's *Black Reconstruction in America* (1935) was to provide a major contribution to this new "scientific" approach in regard to the place of African Americans in U.S. history that had been advocated by Woodson. There, in a concluding chapter entitled "The Propaganda of History," he attacked the textbooks and encyclopedias of the day for their falsification of history, their failure to distinguish between "fact and desire": "In the first place, somebody in each era must make clear the facts with utter disregard to his own wish and desire and belief . . . Then with that much clear and open to every reader, the philosopher and prophet has a chance to interpret these facts." Seeing evil where earlier white historians had observed only biblical and classical precedent, Du Bois criticized a situation in which "We must forget that George Washington was a slave owner, or that Thomas Jefferson had mulatto children . . . and simply remember the things we regard as creditable and inspiring."[24]

22. Some former slave owners thought that they would be freed from reliance on black labor and even attempted to recruit new workers in Germany and Italy. See Don H. Doyle, *Faulkner's County: The Historical Roots of Yoknapatawpha* (Chapel Hill, 2000).

23. August Meier and Elliott Rudwick, *Black History and the Historical Profession, 1915–1980* (Urbana, Ill., 1986), 3, 4.

24. W. E. B. Du Bois, *Black Reconstruction in America* (New York, 1956), 722.

For Du Bois, it was absolutely clear that the issue of slavery had been the main cause of the war, though white historians would have one believe that "a great nation murdered thousands and destroyed millions on account of abstract doctrines concerning the nature of the Federal Union." The history of the freedmen had been either "misstated" or "obliterated," government documents on Reconstruction being totally ignored in favor of "selected diaries, letters, and gossip." Du Bois acknowledged his own interest:

> I write then in a field devastated by passion and belief. Naturally, as a Negro, I cannot do this writing without believing in the essential humanity of Negroes, in their ability to be educated, to do the work of the modern world, to take their place as equal citizens with others. I cannot for a moment subscribe to that bizarre doctrine of race that makes most men inferior to the few. But, too, as a student of science, I want to be fair, objective and judicial; to let no searing of the memory by intolerable insult and cruelty make me fail to sympathize with human frailties and contradiction, in the eternal paradox of good and evil. But armed and warned by all this, and fortified by long study of the facts, I stand at the end of this writing, literally aghast at what American historians have done to this field.

Again and again Du Bois insisted that what he was seeking was simply the truth of the matter. He even recognized that the actions of those white people "who hated and despised Negroes and regarded it as loyalty to blood, patriotism to country, and filial tribute to the[ir] fathers to lie, steal or kill in order to discredit these black folk . . . may be a natural result when a people have been humbled and impoverished and degraded in their own life," though of course he did not accept that the process should continue.[25]

Du Bois explained the then-current understanding of Reconstruction, which saw the period as anarchic and disastrous, with freedmen either driven by their own lusts and ignorance or subject to the manipulation of Yankees, thus: "they cannot conceive Negroes as men; in their minds the word 'Negro' connotes 'inferiority' and 'stupidity' lightened only by unreasoning gayety and humor. Suppose the slaves of 1860 had been white folk . . . [Then] Ignorance and poverty would easily have been explained by history, and the demand for land and the franchise would have been justified as the birthright of natural freemen." He blamed Dunning and others for this state of affairs because they influenced a whole generation of young

25. Ibid., 722, 723, 725.

white history students from the South at a time when relations between the races were at their lowest point. American scholarship "when it regarded black men, became deaf, dumb and blind. The clearest evidence of Negro ability, work, honesty, patience, learning and efficiency became distorted into cunning, brute toil, shrewd evasion, cowardice and imitation, a stupid effort to transcend nature's law." For a few years after the war, "a majority of thinking Americans in the North believed in the equal manhood of black folk" but then, during the economic crisis of the 1870s, began to pay more attention to "the simple moving annals of the plight of a conquered people."[26]

Du Bois concluded his assessment with great passion in a passage very similar to one found in a famous Irish history:

> The most magnificent drama in the last thousand years of human history is the transportation of ten million human beings out of the dark beauty of their mother continent into the new-found Eldorado of the West. They descended into Hell; and in the third century they arose from the dead, in the finest effort to achieve democracy for the working millions which this world had ever seen. It was a tragedy that beggared the Greek; it was an upheaval of humanity like the Reformation and the French Revolution. Yet we are blind and led by the blind. We discern in it no part of our labor movement; no part of our industrial triumph; no part of our religious experience. Before the dumb eyes of ten generations of ten million children, it is made mockery of and spit upon.

Du Bois's approach had its limitations too—as a number of black scholars pointed out at the time—but it served notice that a different history could be told than that which then prevailed.[27]

Still, the major turning point did not come until the mid-1950s, when a series of events—the *Brown vs. Board of Education* decision in Arkansas, Martin Luther King Jr.'s Montgomery bus boycott, the publication of Woodward's *Strange Career of Jim Crow*, and Kenneth Stampp's account of slavery, *The Peculiar Institution*—all conspired to reshape the nation's thinking on the subject. Woodward wrote pointedly that Stampp's book ripped off "a lot of blindfolds we have used to shut out realities," demolishing "the myth 'of racial harmony under slavery.'"[28]

26. Ibid., 726–27.
27. Ibid., 727.
28. Woodward, 139.

The situation had changed so much by the late 1960s that it was now the liberal white historians who had to justify to a new cadre of militant black academics their own engagement with black history. In a turbulent 1969, Woodward himself felt compelled to respond to the idea that only black scholars could interpret black history since white scholars had already betrayed them. Acknowledging that it is always good to be sympathetic with the victims and skeptical of the "dominant mythology" of the victors, Woodward defended yet again the ironic approach to historical events, which, he noted caustically, is "an abomination to revolutionaries." He argued instead for the acceptance of "mixed motives, ambivalence, paradox, and complexity," cautioning that "the passion for justice is not a substitute for reason . . . race and color are neither a qualification nor a disqualification for historians," and that "myths, however therapeutic, are not to be confused with history." Woodward acknowledged the "moral obtuseness" in past historical writing by Beard and others which had failed to see any significance in the existence of slavery.[29]

Woodward also criticized history written from the point of view of white guilt, quoting British historian Herbert Butterfield on the matter: "since moral indignation corrupts the agent who possesses it and is not calculated to reform the man who is the object of it, the demand for it—in the politician and the historian for example—is really a demand for an illegitimate form of power"; it is "a tactical weapon . . . to rouse irrational fervour and extraordinary malevolence against some enemy."[30]

Woodward recognized the problem with a white approach that all too often inclined "to present to the Negro as *his* history the record of what the white man believed, thought, legislated, did and did not do *about* the Negro," but he pointed out that it was both white and black scholars who once thought that the African past did not matter since they were Americans. He effectively quoted a comment that Du Bois himself had written in 1919: "Once for all, let us realize that we are Americans, that we were brought here with the earliest settlers, and that the very sort of civilization from which we came made the complete adoption of Western modes and customs imperative if we were to survive at all. In brief, there is nothing so indigenous, so completely 'made in America' as we."[31]

29. C. Vann Woodward, *The Future of the Past* (New York, 1989), 49, 31.

30. Herbert Butterfield, *History and Human Relations* (London, 1951), 110; Woodward, *Burden of Southern History*, 34.

31. Woodward, *Burden of Southern History*, 35, 10; W. E. B. Du Bois, *Dusk of Dawn: An Essay Toward an Autobiography of a Race Concept* (New York, 1940), 275.

Woodward anticipated that since blacks had recently begun to take more pride in Africa following the gaining of independence by many of its countries, new and different historical accounts would be created, some of which "may seem rather bizarre." He cautioned his auditors, however, not to forget that "the 'scientific' school at the end of the last [nineteenth] century placed great emphasis on 'Teutonic' and 'Anglo-Saxon' tribal customs and institutions and that in doing so it was dipping several centuries deeper into the past for primitive origins than the Afro-Americans are now. The Irish nationalists of the twentieth century in decreeing the use of Gaelic were attempting the revival of a language a good deal less alive than Swahili." Woodward elaborated on the point:

> The priests who taught the children of the Irish slums that St. Brendan, Bishop of Clonfert, discovered America in the sixth century, or the rabbis who taught their charges in the Jewish slums that the Indians were the lost tribes of Israel, or the Bohemians and Poles and Swedes and Italians who assured the children that it was *their* countrymen who saved the day at Bunker Hill or Bull Run or the Bloody Angle were not advancing the cause of history. But they *were* providing defenses against WASP myths of the schoolbooks and some sense of group identity and pride and self-esteem to slum dwellers who were, in their turn, regarded by the Best People as the scum of the earth.

In the end, however, as one would expect, Woodward argued that black history could not be segregated and left to black historians alone.[32]

Although they were taking place at a national level, the roots of these intense confrontations lay in specifically southern history. Even in the case of historians of the same ethnic group, just how seriously southerners still take their history can be seen in a remark of British academic Michael O'Brien's in 1988 in reply to criticisms of his work that had appeared in the *Southern Partisan* journal: "the final court of appeals for ideas in the South is a bar" rather than a faculty gathering, he complained, but he added wisely that "Each has marked disadvantages." As recently as 1991, Ken Burns's appearances in the South to promote and receive commendation

---

32. See, for example, a letter to the editor of the *Birmingham News* from D. Miller, an African American who has returned to Alabama after twenty-five years and finds little racial change: "We are direct descendants of kings, queens, princes, princesses and slaves. We have a history rich in cultural gifts lost through slavery, a mighty people who have endured more than our share of inequality, poverty and family division," *Birmingham News*, 6 July 1997, 2C; Woodward, *Burden of Southern History*, 39, 40.

for his PBS *Civil War* documentary series—considered by some historians to be far too sympathetic to the Southern side—provoked enough of a politely hostile response on at least one campus that the university afterward offered a program of scholarly introductions to current thinking on the subject. In this context too, the present emphasis on the existence of a Celtic South, however legitimate some of its aspects may be, is also part of a vigorous white backlash against a revisionism that wants to deconstruct its historical myths.[33]

Many of the same problems of contesting historical understandings and mythologies, though in a rather different setting and with different nuances, appear in the Irish case. Its historical records go back much farther, of course, beginning with the eleventh-century compilation known as the *Book of Invasions* (*Lebor Gabála*) which traces Ireland's history from the creation of the world through Noah to its own time. Geoffrey Keating, the Roman Catholic priest of Anglo-Norman ancestry that we met in the opening chapter, wrote his seventeenth-century *Foras Feasa ar Éirinn* in Gaelic as a defense of Ireland against the accounts of foreign historians, though its author also believed that the English conquest of the country had been a divine punishment for sin. So-called modern Irish history writing originates with the Romantic movement and Anglo-Irish antiquarianism in the late 1700s, and, as Roy Foster has noted, stresses "the capacity of the land to assimilate its invaders, [which had been] a matter for censure in earlier commentaries."[34]

In the period that parallels the creation of the American South, Irish history writing too has experienced much of the same tension between "sentimental" and "scientific" accounts of events, a tension driven by the perception that interpretations can have very palpable consequences for the immediate political situation.

33. Michael O'Brien, *Rethinking the South: Essays in Intellectual History* (Baltimore, 1988), 214. O'Brien also notes a telling reference from Woodward himself in which the latter remarks of Eugene Genovese and others like him: "they fought out their battles in the South though not for the South" (211). O'Brien cautions in passing, however, that "As usually practiced the search for Southern distinctiveness is a logical nightmare" (216). The campus in question was Auburn University in Alabama. For criticism of Burns as excessively sympathetic to the South, see Eric Foner, *Who Owns History? Rethinking the Past in a Changing World* (New York, 2002), 189–204.

34. Foster, in *Interpreting Irish History: The Debate on Historical Revisionism*, ed. Ciarán Brady (Dublin, 1994), 124.

Much of the popular imagery associated with Irish history—shamrocks, wolfhounds, round towers, the cult of Brian Boru—come from the Romantic period and the collecting efforts sponsored by the Royal Irish Academy, which was founded in 1796. This is not to question the matter of their historical existence but rather to point out that the constellation of their present arrangement is not necessarily one with which a meticulous historian would be completely satisfied. The Romantic Ireland that such images inspire was made even more popular in the balladry of Thomas Moore. While Moore called to mind "the warrior bard" who "to the war has gone" on behalf of his country's defense, his evocations were generally received, as we saw in chapter 8, as nostalgic—like the Scottish lays of the same period—rather than politically threatening, though they undoubtedly nourished nationalist patriotism.

Soon, however, Foster laments, "even as the materials for studying Irish history were slowly being collected and arranged in a way that might facilitate dispassionate analysis, a biased and political priority was taking over." Whether a "dispassionate analysis" was either possible or even desirable has frequently been called into question. In any case, the disparate events of Irish history were constructed into a continuous whole—the story of a free people becoming subjugated by a foreign power but never giving up the struggle for their liberation—to form "the Irish nationalist myth." This myth, Foster claims, was accepted even by an unsympathetic British historian such as Lord Macaulay, was unintentionally reinforced by Matthew Arnold with his lectures on Celticism, and persuaded Prime Minister Gladstone in developing his policies on Irish land tenure and Home Rule in much the same way that the Washington government after the 1870s came to accept the white southern "myth" of the evils of Reconstruction.[35]

The nineteenth and early twentieth centuries eventually saw Irish historians, professional and popular, dividing between Unionist and nationalist sympathies in their accounts, which may not be very different from today, though now at least everyone is aware of these biases. Nationalists sacralized the separatist tradition of Tone, Emmet, Davis, Mitchel, and Pearse, basing their interpretations on the highly successful volumes of such writers as Stopford Green and Sullivan; Unionists looked to Edmund Burke and Edward Carson and popularized their pantheon in similar, if less widely known, fashion.

In the 1930s, just a decade or so following Irish independence, an

---

35. Foster, 127, 133.

achievement that seemed to vindicate a nationalist reading of past events and one that also resulted in lots of generic, rifle-bearing military statutes in the centers of Irish towns and villages, a more "scientific" approach based on German, French, British, and American models was initiated by T. W. Moody and R. Dudley Edwards. Moody would subsequently describe the Irish school textbooks of the period when he began his work as "narrow in sympathy, amateur in treatment, uninformed by new research and often unreadable." The new government was attempting to teach Irish history without its English context, stressing the impact of the 1916 Easter rising, for example, while completely ignoring the numerically far more significant Irish involvement in World War I.[36]

Moody and Edwards, by contrast, set out to get rid of "two equally destructive myths": the sectarian myth of Ulster loyalism and the nationalist myth of southern republicanism. Forty years later, in 1977, Moody attacked a whole series of myths that he felt still bedeviled the field: the idea that one must be Catholic to be Irish, that Orangeism should be seen as part of the great European struggle for freedom, the Thomas Davis myth of 700 years of struggle for an independent Irish nation, presenting the famine as genocide, the myth of predatory rather than apathetic landlords. Moody especially rejected P. S. O'Hegarty's Du Bois–like "story of a people coming out of captivity, out of the underground, finding every artery of their life occupied by her enemy, recovering them one by one, and coming out at last in the full blaze of the sun." History, he concluded bitterly, should not be required to edify students.[37]

This general approach—which began with a series of studies of specific events from Irish history—soon became known as "revisionism," though its full implications were not felt until the 1960s, when the crisis in Northern Ireland renewed old animosities and made the general public more aware of changed interpretations of a handful of crucial historical episodes.

In a 1978 essay with a very Woodwardian title, "The Burden of Our History," and recommending a procedure that Du Bois would have recognized, F. S. L. Lyons argued that historical revisionism "is proper revision-

36. The Irish went against the historicism of European theorists in favor of the tradition of Americans Charles Beard and Carl Becker and the British A. F. Pollard. Nevertheless, though in their preface to the first issue of *Irish Historical Studies* in 1938, T. W. Moody and R. D. Edwards set out to undertake the "scientific study of Irish history," they also dedicated their work "as did the historians of old: *dochum glóire Dé agus onóra na hÉireann* [for the glory of God and the honor of Ireland]" (Brady, 37, 38).

37. Brady, 7, 75, 83, 84.

ism if it is a response to new evidence which, after being duly tested, brings us nearer to a truth independent of the wishes and aspirations of those for whom truth consists solely of what happens to coincide with those wishes and aspirations." Seeing Irish history as a set of tensions between those of Gaelic nationalist, English, Anglo-Irish, and Scots-Presbyterian backgrounds, he concluded that there was a need to recognize that "cultural unity and cultural diversity constitute the burden of our history." In particular, he mentioned how difficult it was for the Anglo-Irish, mainly Protestants, to identify with a history based on the triumph of Catholic nationalism.[38]

Inevitably, however, revisionism provoked strong reactions even among professional historians, who themselves might well be revisionists in regard to certain aspects of that same history. The signature statement in this argument is by Brendan Bradshaw, an Irish historian at Cambridge University who also happens to be a Roman Catholic priest. Bradshaw questions the "value-free" tradition of the previous fifty years because it downplays the sense of catastrophe in the Irish historical experience. He notes that especially in regard to the three episodes that have most deeply influenced Irish history over the last four centuries—"the conquest of the early modern period [i.e., circa 1607]; the accompanying process of dispossession and colonisation, and the calamitous nineteenth-century famine"—the revisionist approach that stresses nuance, subtlety, and irony in interpretation has "the effect of filtering out the trauma." Although Bradshaw himself doesn't say so, it is as if the revisionists had set out, in Yeats's words, "to sweeten Ireland's wrong" by sugaring over its original sourness. In these revisionist approaches, for example, Cromwell's brutality is seen as not being exceptional to the pattern of the period. Colonization, in turn, is presented as "a mere matter of internal British migration." Finally, the famine is either neglected or is treated with "an austerely clinical tone."[39]

According to Bradshaw, one simply cannot present this kind of history in this kind of way; the Irish experience, like the Jewish holocaust or American slavery, requires a certain sensitivity and empathy that the purely scientific approach denies. Bradshaw points out, moreover, that even Herbert Butterfield, the British historian who first attacked the Whig view of history (that England was somehow providentially destined for imperial greatness)

38. Brady, 91, 102.

39. Brendan Bradshaw, "Nationalism and Historical Scholarship in Modern Ireland," in Brady, 210, 204.

and has long been an icon of the revisionists, himself fell back on such an interpretation when his own country was threatened during World War II. In other words, a country needs an enabling myth in order to survive in times of crisis. It might be added that recent Jewish revisionist historians of Israel's creation have encountered many of the same dilemmas.[40]

Most controversial about Bradshaw's position is the extent to which he is willing to sacrifice truth to such a myth, though his approach here is one with which C. Vann Woodward would not be wholly unsympathetic: "The historian's role of mediation must begin . . . by acknowledging the burden of the past. Having done so, ways must then be sought, as Butterfield suggests, to communicate an understanding of the tragic past that is both historically true and humanly responsive." The revisionist agenda, according to Bradshaw, is to debunk the nationalist historical narrative that sought "to provide an origin-legend for the twentieth-century nation-state." For him, however, this is a necessary "form of public history in which the historical consciousness of the community was expressed and transmitted."[41]

For Bradshaw, Butterfield's wartime reversal offers a significant model for the Irish situation: "In a nutshell, the issue raised by Butterfield's exposition of the positive values of English public history is whether the received version of Irish history may not, after all, constitute a beneficent legacy—its wrongness notwithstanding—which the revisionists with the zeal of academic puritans are seeking to drive out." Not unlike Simkins in the white southern case, Bradshaw therefore recommends a "purposeful unhistoricity," a kind of history that would enable the nation to cope with present needs. Rather than being racist, however, as the revisionists claim—and here Bradshaw differs radically from Simkins—nationalist history has been precisely the opposite: "by the skilful deployment of anachronism and idealisation the Gaelic origin-legend has been reworked and developed in order to graft on successive waves of new settlers to the native stock and to enable a progressively more heterogeneous national community to appropriate the rich heritage of the aboriginal Celtic civilisation." He even sees Hyde, Griffith, and Pearse, who sought "to mould a notion of Irishness which would establish continuity between themselves—*arrivistes* to a man, as their [English] names indicate—and the Gaelic past," as stand-

40. See Benny Morris, *Righteous Victims: A History of the Zionist-Arab Conflict, 1881–2001* (New York, 2001).

41. Bradshaw, 205, 210, 211; the reference is to Butterfield, *The Englishman and His History* (London, 1944), 4–11.

ing "in a tradition stretching back to Geoffrey Keating and, indeed, beyond him to the Gaelic recensionists of the tenth century with whom the myth originated."[42]

Seamus Deane has taken an even more extreme view than that of Bradshaw. He sees the problem as one of bias against southern Irish interpretations of history in favor of Unionist ones. He remarks caustically, with a passing reference to the American South where arch-Unionist Ian Paisley took his doctorate: "Maybe they have classes on the hermeneutics of suspicion in Glengall Street or at the Bob Jones University."[43]

Deane elsewhere declares that he does "not regard the word 'mythology' as an insult" since all societies need myths for purposes of legitimization and change or replace them as the occasion demands. Taking his cue from Hayden White, Deane declares that "There is no such thing as an objective factual history which has somehow been distorted by a series of mythologies invented by various bigoted groups. There is no such thing as objective history, and there is no innocent history. All history and literature . . . are forms of mythology." Thus, he denies that "there is such a thing as an Irish national character or an Irish fate or an Irish destiny." For him, in the end, Ireland is a colonial society with a sectarian issue that cannot be avoided. But then it is rather confusing when he rejects the kind of "pluralism" that would seek to respect diverse and even antagonistic traditions as being "scandalously unintelligent," though "it has a wonderful ethical appeal to those who want to avoid political repercussions." Such a statement seems to point to a desire for a cultural and political cohesiveness that is no longer possible in either Irish or British terms since the simple polarities of nationalist and unionist are themselves what is now in question.[44]

Whether, and to what extent, Ireland has been a colony of England is an extremely vexed one, as is the case also of the American South vis-à-vis the United States. It may even be the wrong question to ask since it forecloses nuanced interpretations of complex facts. Conquest, dispossession, and religious oppression (which, of course, also occurred on the British mainland) suggest one answer, while assimilation and participation in the "march of

42. Bradshaw, 212, 213, 214. Bradshaw even suggests that the writing of Northern Irish history has been equally ill served by the revisionists.

43. Seamus Deane, "Wherever Green Is Read," in Brady, 236.

44. Seamus Deane, "Cannon Fodder: Literary Mythologies in Ireland," in *Styles of Belonging: The Cultural Identities of Ulster,* ed. Jean Lundy and Aodán Mac Póilin (Belfast, 1992), 25, 26, 21, 32.

empire" suggests another. Current historical focus is on how the Irish, Catholic and Protestant, served at every level of the British administration in India and other colonized areas in a way that would not have been open to a subjected people, and how even after Irish independence in 1922, the empire, especially in Africa, still provided major routes of passage and support for Irish Catholic missionary endeavors. The answer, then, would seem to be that a simple polarity of colony or not-colony does not apply in this situation, which calls for a more historically sensitive approach.[45]

On the other hand, even if one does not accept the 700-year occupation model of Irish history (beginning with the Norman arrival in 1169 and ending with Irish independence in 1922), and even if one acknowledges Irish collusion in British hegemony at home and abroad, it can still be argued that Ireland, Protestant and Catholic, has often felt itself to be a colony rather than a constituent part of the United Kingdom. From this point of view, the Irish mind during the last several centuries has been a colonial one, embittered by its subjection to the imperialism of another culture, slowly finding its tentative expression in the language of the conqueror, but never absolutely confident in itself and always awaiting the personal slight (when the Irish parliament, all Protestant, was abolished in 1800, some expressed the fear that because of their Irish accents even its ablest orators wouldn't get much of a hearing when they transferred to Westminster). However inaccurately, the Irish felt that they had been forced to change from being first-class Gaels to becoming second- or third-class Englishmen—without even making, or wishing to make, the transition.

Hence too their deep, generally unspoken resentment that their development has not been that of a "normal" European country, and the startling immediacy with which they refer to their seventh-century glory days, when Irish missionaries helped preserve the remnants of European civilization so that the country was known as "the island of saints and scholars." Hence even James Joyce's great rebellion against his enslavement to imperial Britain, his searing consciousness that the words *Christ, Ale, Master,* were different on his lips than on an Englishman's. It is from such a sense, the handed-down lore of one's ancestors having been pushed onto "scraggy acres" while the "promised furrows" were taken over by others (Seamus Heaney, "The

45. See, for example, Keith Jeffrey, ed., *An Irish Empire? Aspects of Ireland and the British Empire* (Manchester, 1995). Also Thomas Bartlett, "'An [sic] Union for Empire': The Anglo-Irish Union as an Imperial Project," in *Hearts and Minds: Irish Culture and Society under the Act of Union,* ed. Bruce Stewart (Gerrards Cross, UK, 2002), 249–59.

Other Side") that resentment of foreign rule has persisted over the centuries. The economic dominance of a Protestant minority until recently in the Republic of Ireland itself has tended to make Irish Catholics feel that that they were second-class citizens even in their own independent country.[46]

Ulster, still a festering sore in the Irish consciousness, is where the ancient oppositions manifest themselves most acutely and where they are least avoidable. In many of the essays in *Styles of Belonging: The Cultural Identities of Ulster* (1992), one sees some of the consequences of the Bradshaw-Deane school of thought, as well as an analysis of many of the same problems and tensions that are present in the American South. Gerald Dawe refers to "the terrible urge towards destiny that has been handed down, often *via* the women of the house, generation to generation, like an incurably blighted idealism which cyclically fails in identifying, inspiring or strengthening change." He argues insightfully that "the chief enemy of positive change has always been piety: the need we have to sanctify and ritualise ourselves by way of compensation for what may well be the impoverished reality of our politics and culture."[47]

Edna Longley, by contrast, writing from her divided Catholic-Presbyterian family background, is critical of the Deane school, which she sees as traditional, bankrupt nationalism with a gloss of contemporary continental theory. Her profound irritation at an Irish Roman Catholic cardinal's symptomatic remark that "Many Protestants love Ireland as devoutly as any Catholic does" makes her, like Donald Akenson, want to banish the idea that "some Irish writers are more Irish than others." Terence Brown's reference to the importance of "theories of Calvinist destiny" in Ulster Presbyterianism and its production of "mind different from that of the nationalists" suggests less a choice between Irish and British nationalisms as Deane would have it but rather an independence from both—though the British connection remains important because it guarantees freedom from potential Catholic dominance and, less commendably, a sense of cultural superiority over the minority Catholic population.[48]

Deane is right to point out that the Ulster situation gives an edge to the nationalist versus revisionist debate that is sometimes absent in the Irish

---

46. The justice of the latter title, however, is affirmed in Cahill's book—unlike the illusory nature of some of the southern glorious past.

47. Lundy and Póilin, 7.

48. Ibid., 15, 44.

Republic; in that sense, one might even want to say that British Ulster in some ways is more "Ireland"—or more "old" Ireland—than its increasingly bland, independent neighbor to the south. There is a keen awareness in Ireland too that, as John Wilson Foster has noted, "whereas revisionist historians *tend* to be Protestants questioning Irish nationalist history, revisionist critics *tend* to be Catholics questioning Protestant nationalism which they see as disguised unionism." In other words, the interpretations are politically loaded.[49]

In light of this, it is interesting to see how Seamus Heaney, a contemporary of Deane's who suffered many of the same intimidations from Protestant militia in Northern Ireland in the 1950s, has commented on the enterprise in a review of a book by arch-revisionist Roy Foster in 1997:

> What the revisionists want to revise is a narrative put in place by successive generations of "Nationalist" historians which reads Irish history as the gradually successful emergence of the Gaelic nation from foreign domination, culminating in the reinstatement of native government and the official recognition of the native language and majority [Catholic] religion after Irish independence was gained, in 1921. The imposition of this narrative, it is argued, suppresses other "varieties of Irishness" (especially those alloyed with Britishness), and is therefore detrimental to any move toward a more politically workable, culturally pluralist future for the country, north and south. The revisionists would espouse a new narrative, conducive to a reconciliation of all the traditions on the island; and, indeed, the currency of those very words—"reconciliation" and "traditions" (in the plural)—is a testimony to the way they have changed the intellectual climate during the past thirty years, a period in which the activities of the Provisional Irish Republican Army have been a vehement reminder of where the freedom narrative can lead.

Heaney's hopeful idea—he has referred to himself as "less furious about British impositions than Deane"—seems to be less that the diverse cultures of the present can be integrated into a unitary narrative about the past but rather that new narratives must be created that will lead to a future in which these traditions coexist and interact with one another in creative but unpredictable ways. It is in this sense that Heaney can both assert his family's long and painful tenure in Ulster, and at the same time recognize and even admire Protestant poet John Hewitt's lines in "The Colony": "We have rights drawn from the soil and sky; / the rain against the lips, the changing

49. Ibid., 13.

light, / this is our country also, no-where else." It is probably misdirected to think in terms of an ultimate and satisfactory resolution to such disunities. Rather, on a more mundane level, what one can hope for is a tenuous equilibrium of interests protected by a legal and administrative system that aspires to justice and which itself is its own not-insignificant cultural achievement.[50]

In examining this sense of acute historical consciousness in Ireland and the American South, it needs to be said also that while these areas, unlike their larger neighbors, are endlessly perceived as excessively preoccupied with such matters, even to the extent of surviving as tribal enclaves of frozen development, they would argue that they, like lots of smaller nations and ethnic groupings, have a greater need to defend their self-interpretations against alien and more powerful characterizations, ones indeed that are no less self-absorbed, though their wide acceptance and continuous reinforcement make them appear "normal." As former Canadian journalist and current cultural critic Michael Ignatieff has commented recently, England itself is an extremely nationalistic country, though it took him years of residence there to notice this fact. Americans too often seem almost exclusively concerned with their own political arena, puzzled at most that the rest of the world chooses to live differently.[51]

Still, even while acknowledging such cautions, one can claim, I think, that whereas a British prime minister might be ridiculed by professional historians for the many inaccuracies of asserting that "This British nation has a monarchy founded by the Kings of Wessex over eleven hundred years ago, a Parliament and universities formed over seven hundred years ago, a language with its roots in the mists of time," all of which "is no recent historical invention," his words do not carry the same measure of risk that an Irish prime minister or the governor of a southern state might encounter in a passing reference to historical events. It is precisely because the interpretation of such events can have immediate consequences in these areas that one cannot expect the degree of detachment that one finds in the larger cases of Britain and the United States.[52]

50. Seamus Heaney, review of Roy Foster's Yeats: The Apprentice Mage (New York, 1997), in Atlantic Monthly, November 1997, 155–60; Heaney, Finders Keepers (New York, 2002), 400; Heaney, Preoccupations (New York, 1980), 147.

51. Michael Ignatieff, Blood and Belonging: Journeys into the New Nationalism (New York, 1994).

52. The prime minister was John Major in a 1994 speech, quoted by David Cannadine in "British History as a 'New Subject': Politics, Perspectives and Prospects," in Uniting the King-

The interesting parallel between the southern and Irish cases, then, lies in the intimacy with which each has had to deal with problems that also affected the larger United States and Britain in other ways: coping with defeat and survival required more lock-step adherence and piety than was needed in the larger, more secure nations. A very similar pattern can be observed in the still-struggling black community, where dissent from the received account of uninterrupted victimhood is routinely and vigorously ostracized. In all of these cases, historical interpretations needed to be guarded zealously for current political purposes.

As an extension of the above explanation, it is important to realize too that, in spite of regular observations to the contrary, there is nothing especially "mysterious" about the history of either Ireland or the American South and that some of the same questions that agitate these regions have their resonances also in the larger entities. Thus, British historian David Cannadine has noted that the problem with the traditional histories of the British Isles is that they have been written from an Anglocentric perspective that, especially with the decline of the empire and the new immigrants (there are now more Muslims than Methodists in the United Kingdom), is no longer relevant. He concludes that "the presumptions and presuppositions which characterized English history-writing in the heyday of the nation-state, and of Britain as top nation" are no longer valid. "Globally, it is no longer convincing to depict the history of England as the successful and still unfinished epic of the rise of a great power and the winning and consolidation of a great empire. Continentally, it is no longer convincing to depict the history of England as the process whereby it inexorably assimilated the rest of the British Isles. And academically, it is no longer convincing to write the history of England without some awareness of the separate but interlocking histories of Ireland, Scotland, and Wales."[53]

Much the same can be said of U.S. history as it reexamines its presumptions about first discovery, frontiers, assimilation, manifest destiny, and so forth. Again, the sense of these issues is much more immediate for Irishmen and southerners because of the possible consequences of a shift in interpretation. Hence the long tradition of controlling interpretations, penalizing those who did not conform their public views to them, and the slow acceptance of a more "scientific" approach to past events. That "de-

---

dom? The Making of British History, ed. Alexander Grant and Keith J. Stringer (New York, 1995), 12.

53. Cannadine, 21.

tachment" is itself still very much in debate in both places, opposed in al- most equal parts by reactionary nationalism and healthy, antihegemonic skepticism, and also subject to ongoing economic and social developments. In other words, there is no getting outside of or beyond the contingencies of history in order to create a wholly disinterested master narrative.

The problem peculiar, if by no means unique, to both Ireland and the South is this: how do we affirm major but contradictory traditions? How can the Irish accept the validity of both nationalist and Unionist aspirations without lapsing into blandness? How can the Old Confederacy and black civil rights be celebrated without ridiculous contradiction? The South's semi-covert celebrating of Robert E. Lee in the same month as its much more overt homage to Martin Luther King Jr. only appears like a failure of nerve or an exercise in political hypocrisy when Nelson Mandela's decision to allow two national anthems commemorating often opposed traditions to be played in sequence in South Africa is forgotten. Yet there is both an emotional and practical need for such uncomfortable compromises.

Is there any way, then, of reconciling these diverse traditions—black and white in the American South, Unionist and nationalist in Ireland? John Shelton Reed, former sociology professor at the University of North Caro- lina, and generally perceived as a kind of down-home southern philosopher, basically conservative, but with a keen eye for the ridiculous in all parties, has interesting things to say about the display of Confederate symbols on public occasions. Although attached to them himself, and quoting a poll that showed that "a majority of black Georgians said the current flag was all right with them," he admits that "the symbols of the Confederacy these days signify and inspire mostly discord." The conclusion he reluctantly comes to is that "the South needs and deserves *some* sort of symbols," but that "the Confederate flag won't do anymore." He notes the changing com- position of the southern population as represented in a 1992 Southern Focus Poll in which "something under 20 percent of today's white South- erners have an exclusively Confederate heritage." A Confederate flag that insults or excludes many southerners won't do, and "other symbols of re- gional identity, more inclusive ones that can be saluted by anyone of good- will" are needed. His final solution eschews contemporary chamber of commerce blandness, referring back instead to some of the same issues that have been going on in southern history for over a hundred years:

> Let those who honor the Confederate heritage do so privately. But let's not go overboard. The symbols of the Confederacy shouldn't be denied to those

who are entitled to them and moved by them . . . Indeed, those whose grandfathers fought with Lee must often feel these days that they *are* being asked to apologize for their heritage, if not to renounce it altogether. As the Marxist historian Eugene Genovese observed during an exchange on this subject at a recent meeting of the American Studies Association, no one should be required to spit on his ancestors' graves. We should all wish the latter-day Confederates luck in rescuing their symbols from the racist trash who have lately sought to appropriate them.

More recently, it has been suggested that the Confederate flag be kept in greatly reduced size on certain insignia of southern states as a recognition of their complex histories, much as Nelson Mandela's proposal keeping the Afrikaner and ANC anthems in South Africa, and—a matter of ongoing debate—as the new Northern Ireland executive has tried to incorporate a diminished crown into the uniforms of a reconstituted, nonsectarian Ulster police force.[54]

Meanwhile, the Irish dilemma, Ciarán Brady agrees, is only their local version of the American problem with interpreting slavery, Germany's with accounting for the Third Reich, or France's with the Vichy regime. Still, Brady claims (echoing Michael O'Brien's comments on southern historians) that an approach to history such as that recommended by Bradshaw can "degenerate into a high-sounding version of unarguable bar-room abuse." Joyce's Cyclopean Citizen in *Ulysses* comes to mind. Brady's own remedy, therefore, reflects a more tentative, post-"scientific" approach:

> The fact that professional historians share a common problem with those whose conscious sense of history is rudimentary or those who have extracted from the past all the select history they need may seem disturbing. But it nevertheless reveals a further requirement concerning the way in which the historians should express themselves in presenting their vicarious experience of the past. Again what is needed "to connect" is not the voice of the prophet or the scientist, nor even the ironist; but of the experienced intelligence whose engagement with history has been tempered by the realization that what we must demand of the past is necessarily too much, and what we can ultimately know too little.

There is a humility here about the power of historians to understand the past that corresponds to Hayden White's emphasis on its selective and con-

54. John Shelton Reed, *Kicking Back: Further Dispatches from the South* (Columbia, Mo., 1995), 42–43.

structed nature, or to Raphael Samuel's idea that "popular understandings of history tend to be non-teleological," unfinished, which is to say that they often differ from those of ideologically driven historians, whether of the left or the right. It seems responsive also to an emphasis on the nonteleological understanding of history in the work of those Irish and southern female historians who argue that their gender has been written out of the narrative—or never included to begin with. For them, both nationalist and revisionist versions indulge in confrontations that are peculiarly male.[55]

All of this will seem to some to veer too much in the direction of an injudicious comment made recently by the vice-chancellor of Oxford University: "History is mostly a matter of opinion anyway, isn't it?" Already, for example, there has been criticism of the Irish commemoration of the 150th anniversary of the famine, and of the African American reparations movement, as based not only on distortions of the historical record—which is to say that mere unsubstantiated opinion about the past is not enough—but as self-serving indulgences in the politics of victimhood. Nevertheless, new histories are needed—and are being created—that call into question many of the assumptions of current representations, even if it is difficult to see how they can rule out all of the traditional issues. They will be more than supplementary, however, for they will reveal previously unnoticed fissures and light up some of the unexamined areas and understandings of the past. Meanwhile, historians of Ireland and of the American South, separately, report both elation at the responsiveness their work receives in these communities—"we have an engaged audience," Foster comments joyfully— and dismay at the belligerence they still sometimes encounter. Truly, the past is "not even past" and there are always at least "two ways of telling every story."[56] How illusory it was for anyone ever to have thought otherwise.

55. Brady, 27, 30; see J. C. D. Clark, "British America: What If There Had Been No American Revolution?" in Virtual History, ed. Niall Ferguson (New York, 1997), 173; also Raphael Samuel, Theatres of Memory (London, 1994).

56. Quoted in David Cohen, "Is 'Modern Oxford' a Sign of the Times or an Oxymoron?" Chronicle of Higher Education, 25 January 2002, A38.

COΠCLVSiOΠ

Strange Kin has looked at matters Irish and southern and found several direct connections and even more striking similarities between them. But it
looked at them also, some would contend, as they *were* rather than as they
are. More recent commentators would note that the two places have
changed considerably, and generally for the better, in the last decade—
which, of course, from one point of view, would only lend them yet another
similarity. At all events, Seán O'Faoláin's comment that Ireland would be a
wonderful place in which to live in two hundred years' time has received a
kind of early fulfillment in the many exiles returning to it in the last few
years, while on the other side of the Atlantic numerous relocating African
Americans have confessed that they now find the South—though there is a
preferential hierarchy among its states—the most congenial part of the
United States in which to live. Certainly the economies of both places have
improved dramatically, even if large areas of acute poverty still exist. By
one reckoning—not at all easy to believe—it is estimated that the southern
states now have the fourth largest economy in the world. Indeed, as long
ago as 1966, Walker Percy's Will Barrett in *The Last Gentleman* returned
from New York to a South that was "happy" and "victorious," "rich" and
"patriotic." Meanwhile Ireland is regularly, if rather provincially, touted as
the "Celtic Tiger" that came from far behind to catch up with, and occasionally outpace, many of its European allies in economic activity. County
Cork too has been transformed from a rural backwater, now vaunting itself,
among other achievements, as the gourmet capital of Ireland, and without
the irony that such an appellation might suggest to those unacquainted with
recent developments in British Isles cuisine (nor, happily, would Terry
Eagleton's quip about "Alabaman [*sic*] *haute cuisine*" being a "contradiction
in terms" any longer pass muster in informed gourmet circles). In a 1993
lecture at Oxford as the university's newly elected Professor of Poetry, Seamus Heaney confessed that "unlike Oscar [Wilde], I have been unable to
mislay my Irish accent," a remark at once ingratiatingly deferential and assertively patriotic, and very much reflective of a new confidence under-

girded, not inconsequentially, by his country's commercial as well as creative success.[1]

Contemporary Irish novelist Dermot Bolger has strongly objected to the "postcolonial" label beloved of academics as it is applied to Ireland, nor does he see present-day Irish writers as being preoccupied with matters of religion and nationalism in the Joycean mode. Rather, there has been an attempt in more recent Irish and southern writing—and the continuance of strong literary traditions in both places has often been noted as being remarkably similar—to get away from such issues to deal with the very mundane realities of people's actual lives. Thus Bolger in Dublin is more concerned with cocaine than with Cromwell, while the characters in many of Bobbie Anne Mason's Kentucky stories are unaware of most of the details—what one of her characters calls the "inner workings"—of their region's past as they negotiate their way between health club, community college, and shopping mall.[2]

The question naturally arises, then, that if the Old Ireland was like the Old South (somewhat), will the new versions have equally striking similarities? The prospect does not seem wholly bizarre or irrelevant. Indeed, from a negative perspective, in both places there is a lingering fear that the economic bubble may burst and that the old despondency and sense of defeat may return. Should the American South continue to prosper, it is likely that it will attract a new generation of Irish immigrants as it already has done in regard to Latinos and set off a new cycle of comparisons. Ireland is faced with new challenges to its received conceptions of race and nationality as a diversity of immigrants reach its shores. It will likely take some time before R. V. Comerford's claim that "a baby born yesterday in the Rotunda Hospital to a Nigerian asylum-seeker is no less Irish than the oldest native speaker in Connemara" becomes an indisputable reality.[3]

As accepted categories are called into question, almost forgotten hierarchies attempt to renew themselves. Descendants of the Gaelic aristocracy abolished under the Tudors receive heightened recognition—albeit merely honorary in a democratic Republic of Ireland—though not without the oc-

1. Walker Percy, The Last Gentleman (New York, 1966), 149; Peter Applebome, Dixie Rising: How the South is Shaping American Values, Politics, and Cultures (New York, 1997), 9; Terry Eagleton, After Theory (New York, 2003), 74; Seamus Heaney, The Redress of Poetry (New York, 1995), 86.

2. Dermot Bolger, in The Oxford Book of Ireland, ed. Patricia Craig (New York, 1998), 15; Bobbie Ann Mason, Shiloh and Other Stories (New York, 1982).

3. R. V. Comerford, Inventing the Nation: Ireland (New York, 2003), 267.

casional bogus claim, proving that the Irish themselves aren't always certain where they came from or that they can fool their fellow countrymen about the matter just as easily as they have others. Armed with a master's degree in history, Terence McCarthy, son of a Belfast dance teacher, was for a time recognized by the Irish government (and made it into *Debrett's*) as "The MacCarthy Mór, Prince of Desmond and Lord of Kerslawny"; exposed, he "abdicated" in 1999, though not before he had been "made colonel of the South Carolina State Guard and given an honorary colonelcy in Alabama." J. J. Hooper's Captain Simon Suggs would have enjoyed the deception.[4]

Meanwhile, both places are being vigorously marketed as tourist destinations in ways that might disconcert an earlier generation: Selma, Alabama, as—and on the same highway hoarding—a place where one can see streets of gracious antebellum homes and also visit the Edmund Pettis Bridge from which Martin Luther King Jr., set out on his famous march in 1965 to challenge the inheritors of such hegemony; an Irish past repackaged to create (in the words of a Tourist Board memorandum) "a strong brand image of Ireland as quality heritage destination, with unique heritage attractions." In 2001, a Spanish descendant of the O'Neills, Britain's Prince Andrew, and Ulster-born Irish President Mary McAleese, all sit together on a windy platform in Kinsale to commemorate the watershed battle there in 1601, the real beginning of Ireland's political trauma, while in a press interview afterward the town's mayor glosses over the battle's historical significance in the hope that the occasion will attract more revenue-enhancing visitors to the area.[5]

But blandness has not yet fully prevailed. Day-to-day life is much more untidy. I visit the gift shop in Selma with its improbable array of Confederate and civil rights memorabilia and, from a random overheard remark perhaps inaccurately understood, feel uncertain about the politics of the elderly white man behind the counter as I sheepishly purchase my Edmund Pettis Bridge cap. I sit in the pew of a local Birmingham Episcopal church for a Lenten lecture to be given by an Irish Anglican bishop and cringe when he asks, referring to the Irish nationalists in Ulster, "What more do they want? We've given them all we can." I know that he is arguing for peace—and afterward he proves personally congenial and unassuming—but his words prick; I had expected more repentance and self-criticism. I read

4. Peter Berresford Ellis, *Erin's Royal Blood: The Gaelic Noble Dynasties of Ireland* (New York, 2002), ix.

5. Roy Foster, *The Irish Story* (London, 2001), 24.

Father Andrew Greeley on the "Achievement of the Irish in America" and find that Irish Catholics "are the most successful gentile ethnic group in America," while Irish Protestants, in the main, "ended up in a backwater of the changing nation."[6] As a current resident of that "backwater," I am not encouraged. I listen to an African American colleague (whose mother is French) lecture enthusiastically on black female *agit-prop* theatre in an elegant library room dominated by a portrait of the donor's Confederate ancestor, who had himself contributed "585 books from their original home in Ireland," and ponder both wistfully and uncomfortably Roy Foster's remark on the "variety and ambivalence of historical experience."[7] As I enter our university's student center for lunch, I am met by an amplified electronic voice broadcasting that "the glory that was Greece and the grandeur that was Rome" were in fact white thefts from an originary African culture, leading me to reflect on what I have been teaching in my last class and on the relevance of all demythologizing efforts.

And, unfortunately, from time to time—often when quiet seems finally to have settled over the controversial issues of the past—churches are burned, schoolchildren harassed, innocent people killed in the name of racial, tribal, and sectarian absolutes. The unexpected also happens: Southern Baptist President Bill Clinton has probably done more than any other American before him to try to bring reconciliation to Northern Ireland. While Ireland likes to think of itself as more liberal than the Bible-thumping American South, there are probably greater social freedoms in the latter: in 2001, an estimated 7,000 pregnant Irish women, representing one in ten Irish births, had to go to England to have abortions.[8] Meanwhile, the *New York Times* reports that the seemingly positive changes in Northern Ireland are not ones that hold much attraction for Protestants, any more than the successes of the civil rights movement in the South were welcomed by a white working class that saw its traditional entitlements to jobs in the police, as firemen, or in factories severely restricted. Religious and religious, religious and secular ideologies still clash, and the economic consequences of legal decisions are painfully and bitterly felt. Ireland has not yet become unlike the South, nor the South unlike Ireland. The past does not fade gently into the present, and the future remains largely unknown.

6. Andrew Greeley, "Achievement of the Irish in America," *Encyclopedia of the Irish in America*, ed. Michael Glazier (Notre Dame, 1999), 1, 3.

7. Roy Foster, *Paddy and Mr. Punch* (New York, 1993), 305.

8. *USA Today*, 7 March 2002, 1A.

CHRONOLOGIES

(The events listed here are confined to those mentioned in the text.)

10,000–5,000 BC   Original settlement of American Southeast by peoples from Asia; original settlement of Ireland by peoples from Central Europe.

500 BC   Presumed arrival of the tribes afterward known as "Celts" in Ireland.

432 AD   Christianization of Ireland by St. Patrick and other missionaries from Europe.

600s–700s AD   Irish monks re-Christianize British Isles and Europe after barbarian invasions.

1014   Brian Boru defeats invading Danes/Vikings at the Battle of Clontarf.

1169   Norman invasion of Ireland (thought of by Irish nationalists as the beginning of the 700-year occupation; seen by "revisionist" historians in a less monolithic way).

1539   Arrival of Hernando de Soto in Florida and exploration of the Southeast.

1580   Edmund Spenser and Sir Walter Raleigh in Ireland as part of plantation of Munster after Irish rebellions; Spenser's home, Kilcolman Castle, burned down in 1598.

1601   Irish under Ulster chiefs/earls O'Neill and O'Donnell defeated at the Battle of Kinsale.

1607   Flight of the earls (O'Neill and O'Donnell); Jamestown settlement in Virginia.

1610   Plantation of Ulster mainly with Scots settlers; Irish survive on marginal lands or convert to new Protestant faith to retain their properties.

1619   First African slaves imported into American colonies.

1640s   English Civil War; Irish Catholic leaders ally with King Charles I against Puritans; Cromwell subdues Irish.

1690   Irish fighting with Catholic Stuart king James II defeated at the Battle of the Boyne by William of Orange; remaining Catholic aristocracy flee to Europe; period of Protestant ascendancy aided by Penal Laws against Catholics begins.

1700s   French penetration of American Southeast; Scots-Irish emigration from Ulster to British North America.

1746   Defeat of Bonnie Prince Charlie at Culloden dashes Irish Catholic hopes of restoration.

1767   Birth of Andrew Jackson to Irish immigrant parents from Ulster.

1776   American Revolution.

1798   Wolfe Tone's unsuccessful Irish rebellion partly modeled on those of the Americans and the French, and aided by France; effort to unite Irish Catholics, Anglicans, and Protestants in a common cause—an exceptional alliance, though one that has served as an ideal for Irish Republicans since then.

1801   Ireland becomes part of United Kingdom of England, Scotland, and Wales.

1808   Cessation of African slave trade.

1829   Catholic Emancipation won under Daniel O'Connell.

1831   Forced removal of southeastern Indians to Oklahoma.

1845–   Irish famine and mainly Catholic emigration to the United States; Mexican war; 1848 rebellion in Ireland.

1861–   American Civil War; emancipation of slaves.

1865–   Reconstruction begins in 1867—votes for freed slaves—ending in 1877; development of "Lost Cause" culture to ensure proper commemoration of Civil War dead, control school instruction on the reasons for the war, etc.

1880s   Charles Stewart Parnell prominent in Irish politics to win restoration of land (successful) and Home Rule (unsuccessful); beginnings of literary revival.

1912   Ulster (Protestant) Covenant signed in opposition to possible British imposition of Home Rule administered from (Catholic) Dublin.

1914–   World War I; Irish parliamentary leaders urge enlistment in British army—to which thousands respond—in the expectation of Home Rule being granted after war is over.

1916   Easter Rebellion led by Patrick Pearse, one of the minority dissenting from call to enlist; unsuccessful but pivotal event in Irish nationalist history and precursor of future independence.

1921–22   Southern Ireland becomes independent; Ulster/Northern Ireland remains part of UK but with separate internal administration.

1950s/1960s   Civil rights movements in American South and Northern Ireland.

SELECTED BIBLIOGRAPHY

Abbott, Shirley. *Womenfolks: Growing Up Down South*. New York: Ticknor & Fields, 1983.

Abel, E. Lawrence. *Singing the New Nation: How Music Shaped the Confederacy, 1861–1865*. Mechanicsburg, Pa.: Stackpole Books, 2000.

Agee, James, and Walker Evans. *Let Us Now Praise Famous Men*. Boston: Houghton Mifflin, 1969.

Akenson, Donald Harman. "The Historiography of the Irish in the United States of America." In *The Irish in the New Communities*, edited by Patrick O'Sullivan, 99–127. London: Leicester University Press, 1992.

————. *If the Irish Ran the World, 1630–1730*. Montreal: McGill-Queen's University Press, 1997.

Anderson, Benedict. *Imagined Communities: Reflections on the Origins and Spread of Nationalism*. 2nd ed. New York: Verso, 1991.

Applebome, Peter. *Dixie Rising*. New York: Harcourt Brace, 1996.

Archdeacon, Thomas J. *Becoming American: An Ethnic History*. New York: Free Press, 1983.

Ardagh, John. *Ireland and the Irish*. London: Penguin, 1994.

Ball, Edward. *Slaves in the Family*. New York: Farrar, Straus & Giroux, 1998.

Barclay, Anthony. *Wilde's Summer Rose; or, The Lament of the Captive*. Savannah: Georgia Historical Society, 1871.

Bartlett, Thomas, and Keith Jeffrey. *A Military History of Ireland*. New York: Cambridge University Press, 1996.

Basker, James G. *Amazing Grace: An Anthology of Poems about Slavery, 1660–1810*. New Haven: Yale University Press, 2002.

Bernstein, Iver. *The New York City Draft Riots*. New York: Oxford University Press, 1990.

Berthoff, Rowland. "Celtic Mist over the South." *Journal of Southern History* 52, no. 4 (November 1986): 523–46.

Bickley, R. Bruce, Jr., ed. *Critical Essays on Joel Chandler Harris*. Boston: G. K. Hall & Co., 1981.

Blassingame, John W., ed. *New Perspectives on Black Studies*. Urbana: University of Illinois Press, 1971.

Blethen, H. Tyler, and Curtis W. Wood Jr., eds. *Ulster and North America: Transatlan-*

tic Perspectives on the Scotch-Irish. Tuscaloosa: University of Alabama Press, 1997.

Blotner, Joseph. *Faulkner: A Biography.* New York: Random House, 1984.

Boles, John B., and Evelyn Thomas Nolen, eds. *Interpreting Southern History: Historiographical Essays in Honor of Sanford W. Higginbotham.* Baton Rouge: Louisiana State University Press, 1987.

Boskin, Joseph. *Sambo:The Rise and Demise of an American Jester.* New York: Oxford University Press, 1986.

Bowen, Elizabeth. *Bowen's Court.* New York: Knopf, 1964.

Brady, Ciaran, ed. *Interpreting Irish History: The Debate on Historical Revisionism.* Dublin: Irish Academic Press, 1994.

Brooks, Cleanth. *William Faulkner: The Yoknapatawpha Country.* New Haven: Yale University Press, 1963.

———. *William Faulkner: Toward Yoknapatawpha and Beyond.* New Haven: Yale University Press, 1978.

Brown, Malcolm. *The Politics of Irish Literature: From Thomas Davis to W. B. Yeats.* Seattle: University of Washington Press, 1972.

Cahill, Thomas. *How the Irish Saved Civilization.* New York: Doubleday, 1995.

Cairns, David. *Writing Ireland: Colonialism, Nationalism, and Culture.* Manchester, UK: Manchester University Press, 1988.

Cantrell, James P. "Irish Culture and the War between the States: *Paddy McGann* and *Gone with the Wind.*" *Éire-Ireland* 27 (summer 1992): 7–15.

Carleton, William. *The Works of William Carleton.* Volume 2. Freeport, N.Y.: Books for Libraries Press, 1970.

Cash, W. J. *The Mind of the South.* 1941. Reprint, New York: Vintage, 1969.

Clark, Dennis. *Hibernia America: The Irish and Regional Cultures.* New York: Greenwood Press, 1986.

Clinton, Catherine. *Tara Revisited: Women, War, and the Plantation Legend.* New York: Abbeville Press, 1996.

Connelly, Thomas L. *The Marble Man: Robert E. Lee and His Image in American Society.* New York: Knopf, 1977.

Connolly, Sean. *Religion and Society in Nineteenth-Century Ireland.* Dublin: Dundalgan Press, 1985.

Cullingford, Elizabeth. *Ireland's Others: Gender and Ethnicity in Irish Literature and Popular Culture.* Notre Dame: University of Notre Dame Press, 2001.

Cunliffe, Barry. *The Ancient Celts.* New York: Oxford University Press, 1997.

Curtis, L. Perry, Jr. *Apes and Angels: The Irishman in Victorian Caricature.* Rev. ed. Washington, D.C.: Smithsonian Institution Press, 1997.

Deane, Seamus. *Celtic Revivals: Essays in Modern Irish Literature.* London: Faber, 1985.

Diggory, Terence. *Yeats and American Poetry.* Princeton: Princeton University Press, 1983.

Dillon, William. *Life of John Mitchel*. London: Kegan Paul, Trench & Co., 1888.

Dolan, Jay P. *Catholic Revivalism:The American Experience, 1830–1900*. Notre Dame: University of Notre Dame Press, 1978.

Donovan, Gerald. "Irish Folklore Influences on Simm's 'Sharp Snaffles' and 'Bald-Head Bill Bauldy.'" In *William Gilmore Simms and the American Frontier*, edited by John Caldwell Guilds and Caroline Collins, 192–206. Athens: University of Georgia Press, 1997.

Dooley, John. *John Dooley, Confederate Soldier: His War Journal*. Edited by Joseph T. Durkin, S.J. Washington, D.C.: Georgetown University Press, 1945.

Douglass, Frederick. *Narrative of the Life of Frederick Douglass, an American Slave, Written by Himself*. Edited by William L. Andrews and William S. McFeely. New York: Norton, 1997.

An Duanaire, 1600–1900: Poems of the Dispossessed. Edited by Seán Ó Tuama, translated by Thomas Kinsella. Dublin: Dolmen Press, 1981.

Du Bois, W. E. B. *Black Reconstruction in America*. 1935. Reprint, New York: Russell & Russell, 1956.

———. *The Souls of Black Folk*. 1903. Reprint, New York: Norton, 1999.

Durden, Robert F. "A Half Century of Change in Southern History." *Journal of Southern History* 51, no. 1 (February 1985): 3–14.

Eagleton, Terry. *Crazy John and the Bishop and Other Essays on Irish Culture*. Notre Dame: University of Notre Dame Press, 1998.

———. *The Truth about the Irish*. New York: St. Martin's, 2000.

Eagleton, Terry, Frederic Jameson, and Edward Said. *Nationalism, Colonialism, and Literature*. Minneapolis: University of Minnesota Press, 1990.

Eid, Leroy V. "The Colonial Scotch-Irish: A View Accepted Too Readily." *Éire-Ireland* 21 no. 4 (winter 1986): 81–105.

Elliott, Marianne. *The Catholics of Ulster: A History*. London: Penguin, 2001.

Ellis, Mary Louise. "Improbable Visitor: Oscar Wilde in Alabama, 1882." *Alabama Review* 39 (October 1986): 243–60.

Ellison, Ralph. *Invisible Man*. New York: Random House, 1952.

Ellmann, Richard. *Oscar Wilde*. New York: Vintage, 1988.

Encyclopedia of the Irish in America. Edited by Michael Glazier. Notre Dame: University of Notre Dame Press, 1999.

Evans, Eli N. *The Provincials: A Personal History of Jews in the South*. 1973. Reprint, New York: Free Press, 1997.

Faherty, W. B. *The Fourth Career of John B. Bannon*. Portland, Ore.: C & D Publishing, 1994.

Fair, John D., and Cordelia C. Humphrey. "The Alabama Dimension of the Political Thought of Charles Stewart Parnell." *Alabama Review* 52 (January 1999): 21–50.

Faulkner, William. *Absalom, Absalom!* 1946. Reprint, New York: Vintage, 1990.

———. *Early Prose and Poetry*. Edited by Carvel Collins. Boston: Little, Brown, 1962.

Faust, Drew Gilpin. *The Creation of Confederate Nationalism: Ideology and Identity in the Civil War South.* Baton Rouge: Louisiana State University Press, 1988.

The Field Day Anthology of Irish Literature. Edited by Seamus Deane. New York: W. W. Norton, 1991.

Fitzgerald, Sally. "Root and Branch: O'Connor of Georgia." *Georgia Historical Quarterly* 64 (winter 1980): 377–87.

Flannery, James W. *Dear Harp of My Country: The Irish Melodies of Thomas Moore.* Nashville: J. S. Saunders & Co., 1997.

Foley, Albert S. *Beloved Outcaste: The Story of a Great Man Whose Life Has Become a Legend.* New York: Farrar, Straus, & Young, 1954.

———. *Dream of an Outcaste: Patrick F. Healy.* Tuscaloosa, Ala.: Portals Press, 1989.

Foner, Eric. *Who Owns History? Rethinking the Past in a Changing World.* New York: Hill & Wang, 2002.

Foster, Gaines M. *Ghosts of the Confederacy: Defeat, the Lost Cause, and the Emergence of the New South, 1865 to 1913.* New York: Oxford University Press, 1987.

Foster, Roy. *The Irish Story: Telling Tales and Making It Up in Ireland.* London: Penguin, 2001.

———. *Paddy and Mr. Punch: Connections in Irish and English History.* New York: Penguin, 1993.

Gallagher, Gary W. *The Confederate War.* Cambridge, Mass.: Harvard University Press, 1997.

Gallier, James. *Autobiography of James Gallier, Architect.* New York: Da Capo, 1973.

Gleeson, David T. *The Irish in the South, 1815–1877.* Chapel Hill: University of North Carolina Press, 2001.

———. "Parallel Struggles: Irish Republicanism in the American South, 1798–1876." *Éire-Ireland* (summer 1999): 97–116.

Green, E. R. R., ed. *Essays in Scotch-Irish History.* Belfast: Ulster Historical Society, 1992.

Guilds, John Caldwell. *Simms: A Literary Life.* Fayetteville: University of Arkansas Press, 1992.

Guilds, John Caldwell, and Caroline Collins. *William Gilmore Simms and the American Frontier.* Athens: University of Georgia Press, 1997.

Hamm, Charles. *Yesterdays: Popular Song in America.* New York: W. W. Norton, 1979.

Harper, Jared Vincent. "The Irish Travelers of Georgia." Ph.D. diss., University of Georgia, 1977.

Harwell, Richard, ed. *Gone with the Wind as Book and Film.* New York: Paragon House, 1987.

Heaney, Seamus. *Finders Keepers.* New York: Farrar, Straus & Giroux, 2002.

———. *Poems, 1965–1975.* New York: Farrar, Straus & Giroux, 1980.

———. *The Redress of Poetry.* New York: Farrar, Straus & Giroux, 1995.

Hernon, Joseph M., Jr. *Celts, Catholics, and Copperheads: Ireland Views the American Civil War.* Columbus: Ohio State University Press, 1968.

Heyrman, Christine Leigh. *Southern Cross: The Beginnings of the Bible Belt.* New York: Knopf, 1997.

Hickman, Mary. "'Binary Opposites' or 'Unique Neighbors'? The Irish in Multi-Ethnic Britain." *Political Quarterly* 71, no. 1 (January–March 2002): 50–59.

Hobsbawm, Eric, and Terence Ranger, eds. *The Invention of Tradition.* New York: Cambridge University Press, 1983.

Hobson, Fred. *Tell about the South: The Southern Rage to Explain.* Baton Rouge: Louisiana State University Press, 1983.

Hoffman, Ronald. *Princes of Ireland, Planters of Maryland: A Carroll Saga, 1500–1782.* Chapel Hill: University of North Carolina Press, 2000.

Hooper, J. J. *Adventures of Captain Simon Suggs.* Tuscaloosa: University of Alabama Press, 1993.

Howe, Stephen. *Ireland and Empire: Colonial Legacies in Irish History and Culture.* New York: Oxford University Press, 2000.

Hoy, Suellen, and Margaret MacCurtain, eds. *From Dublin to New Orleans: The Journey of Nora and Alice.* Dublin: Attic Press, 1994.

Hughes, Nathaniel Cheairs, Jr., and Thomas Clayton Ware. *Theodore O'Hara: Poet-Soldier of the Old South.* Knoxville: University of Tennessee Press, 1998.

Hurston, Zora Neale. *Dust Tracks on a Road: An Autobiography.* New York: Harper, 1991.

———. *I Love Myself When I Am Laughing.* Edited by Alice Walker. Old Westbury, N.Y.: Feminist Press, 1979.

Hyde, Douglas. *Language, Lore, and Lyrics.* Dublin: Irish Academic Press, 1986.

Hyde, Samuel C., Jr., ed. *Plain Folk of the South Revisited.* Baton Rouge: Louisiana State University Press, 1997.

Ignatiev, Noel. *How the Irish Became White.* New York: Routledge, 1995.

Jacoby, Russell, and Naomi Glauberman, eds. *The Bell Curve Debate: History, Documents, Opinions.* New York: Times Books, 1995.

James, Simon. *The Atlantic Celts: Ancient People or Modern Invention?* Madison: University of Wisconsin Press, 1999.

Jeffrey, Keith, ed. *An Irish Empire? Aspects of Ireland and the British Empire.* Manchester, UK: Manchester University Press, 1995.

Jones, Katharine W. *Accent on Privilege: English Identities and Anglophilia in the U.S.* Philadelphia: Temple University Press, 2001.

Jordan, Winthrop D. *Black over White: American Attitudes toward the Negro, 1550–1812.* Chapel Hill: University of North Carolina Press, 1968.

Joyce, James. *A Portrait of the Artist as a Young Man.* 1916. Reprint, New York: Penguin, 1982.

Keegan, John. *Fields of Battle: The Wars for North America.* New York: Knopf, 1996.

Keller, Morton. *The Art and Politics of Thomas Nast.* New York: Oxford University Press, 1968.

Keneally, Thomas. *The Great Shame and the Triumph of the Irish in the English-Speaking World.* New York: Doubleday, 1999.

Kiberd, Declan. *Irish Classics*. Cambridge, Mass.: Harvard University Press, 2001.

Kinealy, Christine. "Potatoes, Providence and Philanthropy: The Role of Private Charity during the Irish Famine." In *The Meaning of the Famine,* edited by Patrick O'Sullivan, 140–71. London: Leicester University Press, 1997.

King, Richard H., and Helen Taylor, eds. *Dixie Debates: Perspectives on Southern Cultures.* New York: New York University Press, 1996.

Kirby, Jack Temple. *Media-Made Dixie: The South in the American Imagination.* Rev. ed. Athens: University of Georgia Press, 1986.

Kreyling, Michael. *Author and Agent: Eudora Welty and Diarmuid Russell.* New York: Farrar, Straus & Giroux, 1991.

Lankford, Nelson D., ed. *An Irishman in Dixie: Thomas Conolly's Diary of the Fall of the Confederacy.* Columbia: University of South Carolina Press, 1988.

Lester, DeeGee. "John Mitchel's Wilderness Years in Tennessee." *Éire-Ireland* 25, no. 2 (summer 1990): 7–13.

Levine, Lawrence W. *The Unpredictable Past: Explorations in American Cultural History.* New York: Oxford University Press, 1993.

Lewis, David Levering. *W. E. B. Du Bois: The Fight for Equality and the American Century, 1919–1963.* New York: Henry Holt, 2000.

Leyburn, James G. *The Scotch-Irish: A Social History.* Chapel Hill: University of North Carolina Press, 1962.

Lott, Eric. *Love and Theft: Blackface Minstrelsy and the American Working Class.* New York: Oxford University Press, 1993.

Lundy, Jean, and Aodán Mac Póilin, eds. *Styles of Belonging: The Cultural Identities of Ulster.* Belfast: Lagan Press, 1992.

McCrum, Robert, William Cran, and Robert MacNeil. *The Story of English.* New York: Viking, 1986. Revised ed., New York: Viking, 2002.

McFeely, William S. *Frederick Douglass.* New York: W. W. Norton, 1991.

McGraw, Eliza Russi Lowen. "A 'Southern Belle with Her Irish Up': Scarlett O'Hara and Ethnic Identity." *South Atlantic Review* 65, no. 1 (winter 2000): 123–31.

McWhiney, Grady. *Cracker Culture: Celtic Ways in the Old South.* Tuscaloosa: University of Alabama Press, 1988.

McWhiney, Grady, and Perry D. Jamieson. *Attack and Die: Civil War Military Tactics and the Southern Heritage.* Tuscaloosa: University of Alabama Press, 1982.

Marrs, Suzanne. *One Writer's Imagination: The Fiction of Eudora Welty.* Baton Rouge: Lousiana State University Press, 2002.

Meier, August, and Elliott Rudwick. *Black History and the Historical Profession, 1915–1980.* Urbana: University of Illinois Press, 1986.

Mencken, H. L. *Prejudices: A Selection.* New York: Vintage, 1958.

Miller, Kerby A. *Emigrants and Exiles: Ireland and the Irish Exodus to North America.* New York: Oxford University Press, 1985.

Miller, Kerby A., et al. *Irish Immigrants in the Land of Canaan* (New York: Oxford University Press, 2003).

Miller, Randall M., and Jon L. Wakelyn. *Catholics in the Old South: Essays on Church and Culture*. Macon, Ga.: Mercer University Press, 1983.

Miller, Randall M., et al., eds. *Religion and the American Civil War*. New York: Oxford University Press, 1998.

Mitchel, John. *Jail Journal*. 1854. Reprint, Dublin: University Press of Ireland, 1982.

Mitchell, Margaret. *Gone with the Wind*. 1938. Reprint, New York: Avon, 1973.

Naipaul, V. S. *A Turn in the South*. New York: Knopf, 1992.

Neely, Mark E., Jr., et al. *The Confederate Image: Prints of the Lost Cause*. Chapel Hill: University of North Carolina Press, 1987.

Niehaus, Earl F. *The Irish in New Orleans, 1800–1860*. Baton Rouge: Louisiana State University Press, 1965.

O'Brien, Conor Cruise. *Ancestral Voices: Religion and Nationalism in Ireland*. Chicago: University of Chicago Press, 1995.

———. *The Long Affair: Thomas Jefferson and the French Revolution, 1785–1800*. Chicago: University of Chicago Press, 1996.

O'Brien, Michael. *The Idea of the American South, 1920–1941*. Baltimore: Johns Hopkins University Press, 1979.

———. *Rethinking the South: Essays in Intellectual History*. Baltimore: Johns Hopkins University Press, 1989.

O'Connor, Áine, ed. *Hollywood Irish*. Dublin: Wolfhound Press, 1997.

O'Connor, Flannery. *The Habit of Being*. New York: Farrar, Straus, & Giroux, 1979.

———. *Mystery and Manners*. New York: Farrar, Straus, & Giroux, 1969.

O'Driscoll, Robert. *The Celtic Consciousness*. New York: George Braziller, 1982.

O'Faoláin, Seán. *The Irish*. New York: Penguin, 1967.

———. *The Vanishing Hero: Studies in Novelists of the Twenties*. Freeport, N.Y.: Books for Libraries Press, 1957.

O'Neill, Charles Edwards. "Toward American Recognition of the Republic of Ireland: De Valera's Visit to New Orleans in 1920." *Louisiana History* 34, no. 3 (summer 1993): 299–307.

Opie, Iona. *The People in the Playground*. New York: Oxford University Press, 1994.

O'Toole, James M. *Passing for White: Race, Religion, and the Healy Family, 1820–1920*. Amherst: University of Massachusetts Press, 2002.

Prenshaw, Peggy Whitman. "The Antiphonies of Eudora Welty's *One Writer's Beginnings* and Elizabeth Bowen's *Pictures and Conversations*." *Mississippi Quarterly* 39, no. 4 (fall 1986): 639–50.

Purdue, Howell, and Elizabeth Purdue. *Pat Cleburne: Confederate General*. Hillsboro, Texas: Hill Junior College Press, 1973.

Pyron, Darden Asbury. *Southern Daughter: The Life of Margaret Mitchell*. New York: Oxford University Press, 1991.

Quinlan, Kieran. "The Memory of Defeat: Ireland and the American South." In *Perspectives on the American South*, 17–28. New York: Gordon & Breach, 1985.

———. "Under Northern Lights: Re-Visioning Yeats and the Revival." In *Yeats and*

Postmodernism, edited by Leonard Orr, 64–79. Syracuse, N.Y.: Syracuse University Press, 1991.

Quinn, David B. *The Elizabethans and the Irish*. Ithaca: Cornell University Press, 1966.

Ray, Celeste. *Highland Heritage: Scottish Americans in the American South*. Chapel Hill: University of North Carolina Press, 2001.

Remini, Robert V. *Andrew Jackson and the Course of American Empire, 1767–1821*. New York: Harper & Row, 1977.

Rubin, Louis D., Jr., ed. *The Literary South*. Baton Rouge: Louisiana State University Press, 1979.

Ryan, Abram J. *Poems: Patriotic, Religious, Miscellaneous*. New York: P. J. Kenedy, 1895.

Said, Edward. *Orientalism*. New York: Pantheon, 1978.

Sawyers, June Skinner. *Celtic Music: A Complete Guide*. New York: Da Capo, 2000.

Simkins, Francis Butler. "Tolerating the South's Past." *Journal of Southern History* 21 (February 1955): 3–16.

Simms, William Gilmore. *Paddy McGann*. Columbia: University of South Carolina Press, 1972.

Solnit, Rebecca. *A Book of Migrations: Some Passages in Ireland*. New York: Verso, 1997.

Stradling, R. A. *The Spanish Monarchy and Irish Mercenaries: The Wild Geese in Spain, 1618–68*. Dublin: Irish Academic Press, 1994.

Strode, Hudson. *Jefferson Davis, Tragic Hero: The Last Twenty-Five Years, 1864–1889*. New York: Harcourt, Brace, 1964.

Symonds, Craig L. *Stonewall of the West*. Kansas City: University Press of Kansas, 1997.

Takaki, Ronald. "The Tempest in the Wilderness: The Racialization of Savagery." *Journal of American History* 79, no. 3 (December 1992): 892–912.

Tate, Allen. *Essays of Four Decades*. Chicago: Swallow Press, 1968.

Taylor, Helen. *Circling Dixie: Contemporary Southern Culture through a Transatlantic Lens*. New Brunswick: Rutgers University Press, 2001.

Thuente, Mary Helen. *The Harp Re-strung: The United Irishmen and the Rise of Irish Literary Nationalism*. Syracuse, N.Y.: Syracuse University Press, 1994.

Tompkins, Jane. *Sensational Designs: The Cultural Work of American Fiction, 1790–1860*. New York: Oxford University Press, 1985.

Tucker, Phillip Thomas. *Father John B. Bannon: The Confederacy's Fighting Chaplain*. Tuscaloosa: University of Alabama Press, 1992.

Vance, Norman. *Irish Literature: A Social History*. Oxford: Blackwell, 1990.

Waldron, Ann. *Eudora Welty: A Writer's Life*. New York: Doubleday, 1998.

Walker, Alice. *In Search of Our Mother's Gardens*. New York: Harcourt, Brace, 1983.

Walker, Clarence E. *Deromanticizing Black History: Critical Essays and Reappraisals*. Knoxville: University of Tennessee Press, 1991.

Washington, Booker T. *Up from Slavery*. New York: Penguin, 1986.

Welty, Eudora. *The Bride of the Innisfallen and Other Stories*. New York: Harcourt, Brace, 1972.

———. *Eudora Welty Photographs*. Jackson: University of Mississippi Press, 1989.

———. *One Writer's Beginnings*. New York: Warner Books, 1984.

Wilde, Oscar. *The Complete Letters of Oscar Wilde*. Edited by Merlin Holland and Rupert Hart-Davis. New York: Henry Holt, 2000.

Wilson, Andrew J. *Irish America and the Ulster Conflict, 1968–1995*. Washington, D.C.: Catholic University of America Press, 1995.

Wilson, Charles Reagan. *Baptized in Blood: The Religion of the Lost Cause, 1865–1920*. Athens: University of Georgia Press, 1980.

———. *Judgement and Grace in Dixie: Southern Faiths from Faulkner to Elvis*. Athens: University of Georgia Press, 1995.

Wimsatt, Mary Ann. *The Major Fiction of William Gilmore Simms: Cultural Traditions and Literary Form*. Baton Rouge: Louisiana State University Press, 1989.

Woodward, C. Vann. *The Burden of Southern History*. Baton Rouge: Louisiana State University Press, 1993.

———. *Thinking Back: The Perils of Writing History*. Baton Rouge: Louisiana State University Press, 1986.

Wright, Frank. *Northern Ireland: A Comparative Analysis*. Dublin: Gill & Macmillan, 1992.

Wright, Richard. *Black Boy*. 1936. Reprint, New York: HarperCollins, 1993.

———. *Native Son*. 1941. Reprint, New York: HarperCollins, 1993.

Wyatt-Brown, Bertram. *Hearts of Darkness: Wellsprings of a Southern Literary Tradition*. Baton Rouge: Louisiana State University Press, 2003.

———. *The House of Percy: Honor, Melancholy, and Imagination in a Southern Family*. New York: Oxford University Press, 1994.

———. *Southern Honor: Ethics and Behavior in the Old South*. New York: Oxford University Press, 1982.

Yaeger, Patricia. "Race and the Cloud of Unknowing in *Gone with the Wind*." *Southern Cultures* 5, no. 1 (spring 1999): 21–28.

Yeats, W. B. *Autobiography of William Butler Yeats*. New York: Macmillan, 1965.

———. *Collected Poems*. New York: Macmillan, 1977.

———. *Essays and Introductions*. New York: Macmillan, 1961.

Young, Robert J. C. *Colonial Desire: Hybridity in Theory, Culture, and Race*. New York: Routledge, 1995.

INDEX

Abbott, Shirley, 183

Abel, E. Lawrence, 76

Abolitionists, 9, 47, 48, 63, 65, 68, 69, 141, 153, 170; anti-Catholicism of, 50, 51, 53–54, 55, 84

Agee, James, 202, 213

Akenson, Donald Harman, 33–34, 38, 43, 258

Allen, Richard, 53

Allen, Theodore W., 52n

Anderson, Alister C., 106n

Anderson, Benedict, 44n

Andrew, Prince, 267

Andrews, John H., 194n

Anglicans, 46, 49, 65, 136, 143, 147, 148, 267

Appalachia, 42, 166

Applebome, Peter, 266n

Archdeacon, Thomas J., 30n

Ardagh, John, 188

Arnold, Matthew, 184, 214

Arthur, Richard, 24

Austen, Jane, 191, 194

Bach, Rebecca Ann, 67n

Ball, Edward, 38n, 240n

Banim, John, 202

Bannon, John, 83–87, 99, 103, 113, 147, 155, 183

Baptists, 21, 116, 143, 146, 152, 268

Barnum, P. T., 205

Bartlett, Thomas, 257n

Beard, Charles, 246, 249

Beardsley, Aubrey, 226

Becker, Carl, 253

Beecher, Henry Ward, 68–69

Benjamin, Judah P., 86

Benson, Ciarán, 177

Bermuda, 67

Bernstein, Iver, 81n

Bertelson, David, 183n

Berthoff, Rowland, 43

Black, Hugo, 17

Blackett, R. J. M., 79n

Blanchard, Mary Warner, 114n

Blotner, Joseph, 217n, 223n

Boas, Franz, 74

Boles, John B., 150n, 152–53, 155

Bolger, Dermot, 266

Böll, Heinrich, 168

Bonnie Prince Charlie, 8, 25, 224–25

Booraem, Hendrik, 43n

Boru, Brian, 235, 238, 252

Boskin, Joseph, 172, 181

Bouccicault, Dion, 195

Bourke, Angela, 131n

Bowen, Elizabeth, 5, 149, 188, 227–30, 233–34

Bracken, Brendan, 178

Bradshaw, Brendan, 254–56

Brady, Ciarán, 263–64

Bragg, Braxton, 89

Brenan, Joseph, 65

Brontë, Charlotte, 194

Brooks, Cleanth, 218–23

Brosnan, Pierce, 178

Brown, John, 240

Brown, Malcolm, 67

Brown, Terence, 154, 258

Bryson, Bill, 166n

Bull Run (Manassas), Battle of, 80–81

Burke, Edmund, 252

Burns, Ken, 250–51

Bush, Robert, 204

Butler, Ben, 105
Butler, Pierce, 38, 82, 134n
Butterfield, Herbert, 249n, 255–56
Byrd, William, 210
Byron, George Gordon, Lord, 191, 195

Cable, George Washington, 216, 225
Cahill, Thomas, 167, 258
Cairns, David, 169n
Caldwell, Erskine, 167
Calhoun, John C., 68
Cambrensis, Giraldus, 168
Canada, 59, 98, 140
Cannadine, David, 261
Canny, Nicholas, 25n
Cantrell, James P., 123–24, 126, 204–205
Carleton, William, 193, 195, 200–201, 207
Carlyle, Thomas, 66, 68, 69, 71, 173
Carroll, Charles (the Settler), 25, 31, 51, 58, 118
Carroll, Dr. Charles, 25–26
Carson, Edward, 160, 252
Caruthers, William Alexander, 202–203
Casement, Sir Roger, 145
Cash, Johnny, 103
Cash, W. J., 4, 25, 32, 42, 59, 124, 141, 142–43, 165, 185, 187, 235, 236–37, 238–39, 240
Catholic Church, 6–7, 84, 86, 102, 134, 141–49, 153–54, 157, 160; and devotional revolution, 28, 60, 146–47; and slavery, 50–52, 56, 83
Catholic Emancipation, 47, 49, 56, 88, 147, 170
Celtic South thesis, 4, 12, 39–44, 80, 251
Celts, 43–44
Charles I (king of England), 22, 203
Charleston, S.C., 55, 56, 76, 134, 146, 242
Cherokees, 70
Chesnutt, Mary, 127
Choctaws, 10, 59
Chopin, Kate (O'Flaherty), 209, 216
Civil War, 76–95
Clark, Dennis, 37, 37n, 43, 120
Clark, J. C. D., 264n

Cleburne, Patrick Ronayne, 87–92, 100–101, 241
Clinton, Catherine, 121–22
Clinton, William Jefferson (Bill), 3, 268
Commerford, R. V., 266
Conley, Carolyn, 187n
Connelly, Thomas, 110
Connolly, James, 72
Connolly, Seán, 146
Connor, "Bull," 162
Conolly, Thomas, 82
Corby, William, 102
Corkery, Daniel, 214
Coulter, E. Merton, 3, 242
Craig, James, 160
Cran, William, 167n, 190n
Craven, Avery, 243
Cromwell, Oliver, 22, 25, 42, 58, 65, 66, 82, 130, 203, 238, 254
Cullen, Paul, 146
Cullingford, Elizabeth, 195n
Cunliffe, Barry, 44
Curtis, L. Perry, Jr., 169, 171–73, 174, 175–76, 182
Curzon, Lord, 173

Daniel, John Moncure, 78
Davidson, Donald, 213, 217, 239, 240
Davie, Donald, 207n
Davis, Graham, 153
Davis, Jefferson, 78, 79, 82, 86, 91, 93, 99, 100, 196, 240; Oscar Wilde visits, 114
Davis, Leith, 198n
Davis, Richard, 59n
Davis, Thomas, 108, 145, 171, 197–99, 252
Davis, Varina Anne, 115–16
Davison, Neil R., 172
Dawe, Gerald, 258
Deane, Seamus, 108, 236, 256, 258–59
Defoe, Daniel, 208
De Valera, Eamon, 39, 157, 161
Devine, T. M., 29n
Devlin, Bernadette, 162
Dickens, Charles, 194
Dickinson, Emily, 194
Diggory, Terence, 217

Dixon, Thomas, 116–17, 121
Donaldson, Susan V., 199n
Donnelly, James S., Jr., 11n
Donovan, Gerald, 203
Dooley, John, 94
Douglass, Frederick, 4, 53, 54, 55–56, 60, 67, 69, 87, 149, 152; Irish visit, 48–49
Doyle, David N., 27
Doyle, Don H., 246
Doyle, Sir Arthur Conan, 178
Du Bois, W. E. B., 106, 143–44, 152, 156, 246–48, 249, 253; on Irish, 74–75
Duffy, Sir Charles Gavan, 58, 66, 197
Dunne, Tom, 50n
Dunning, William A., 242, 247
Durden, Robert F., 90n, 242–43
Durkin, Joseph T., 94n
Dwyer, Richard, 127

Eagleton, Terry, 148, 154, 179–80, 186, 265
Eaton, Clement, 40n
Edgeworth, Maria, 194
Edwards, R. Dudley, 58n, 253
Eid, Leroy V., 42
Eliot, George, 194
Eliot, T. S., 233
Elliott, Marianne, 27–28, 41, 156–57
Ellis, Mary Louise, 73n
Ellis, Peter Berresford, 267n
Ellison, Ralph, 212
Ellmann, Richard, 112n, 219n
Emerson, Ralph Waldo, 194
Emmet, Robert, 17, 115–16, 133, 145, 159, 252
Emmet, Thomas Addis, 17
Emmett, Daniel Decatur, 235
England, John, 50–51, 55
English, Richard, 175n
Enya, 44
Erickson, Carolly, 225n
Evans, E. Estyn, 238n
Evans, Eli N., 52, 156
Evans, Walker, 168, 213
Eysenck, H. J., 177

Faber, Frederick W., 148
Faherty, William B., 84n, 99

Fair, John D., 17n
Fallis, Richard, 184
Famine, Irish. See Great Famine
Fanon, Franz, 171
Farwell, Byron, 173n
Faulkner, William, 5, 8, 61, 164, 167, 186, 210, 218–27; Absalom, Absalom!, 13, 59, 128, 197, 211, 225–26, 237–38; The Sound and the Fury, 211, 219, 220, 224
Faust, Drew Gilpin, 105, 128–29
Fenians, 45, 88, 98, 139, 140, 157, 172
Fiedler, Leslie, 127
Finke, Roger, 147
Finney, Albert, 178
Fischer, David Hackett, 42
Fitzgerald, F. Scott, 32–33, 215
Fitzgerald, Phillip, 119
Fitzgerald, Sally, 38
Fitzhugh, George, 68
Flannery, James W., 196
Foley, Albert S., 59–62, 64
Foley, John Henry, 100
Foley, T. P., 104n
Foner, Eric, 251n
Ford, Ford Madox, 216, 233
Forkner, Ben, 203
Forrest, Nathan Bedford, 240
Fort Sumter, S.C., 78, 83
Foster, Gaines M., 103n, 241–42
Foster, John Wilson, 259
Foster, Roy, 18, 173–74, 177, 179, 238n, 251, 267n, 268
Foster, Stephen, 196
Franklin, Battle of, 92
Fredericksburg, Battle of, 83
Freeman, Douglas Southall, 94
Friel, Brian, 194n
Froissart, Jean, 205
Fugitive slave law, 60, 69

Gaines, Ernest, 212
Galbally (Ireland), 35
Gallagher, Gary W., 96
Gallier, James, 35
Garrison, William Lloyd, 9, 48n, 53, 63, 87
Gates, Henry Louis, Jr., 171

Genovese, Eugene, 150, 151, 251, 263

Georgetown University, 61, 64

Gerster, Patrick, 166

Gettysburg, Battle of, 83, 102, 226, 242

Gibran, Khalil, 108

Gilbert, Sir Humphrey, 23

Giles, Paul, 48n, 57n

Gill, James, 97n, 198n

Gilley, Sheridan, 148

Glasgow, Ellen, 216

Gleeson, David T., 8–9, 52, 54, 77n, 104, 125

Gone with the Wind, 4, 118–36

Gonne, Maud (MacBride), 223–24

Gordon, Caroline, 146, 215, 216

Gorki, Maxim, 199

Great Famine, 10, 36, 48–49, 53, 66, 67, 84, 88, 95, 109, 170, 195, 199, 202, 238, 253, 254, 264; religious explanations for, 141, 153

Great Revival, 146

Greeley, Andrew, 268

Greeley, Horace, 67

Green, Alice Stopford, 240, 252

Green, Paul, 216n

Gregory, Lady Augusta, 82, 216

Gregory, Sir William Henry, 82

Grenville, Sir Richard, 22

Griffin, Gerald, 194, 200

Griffith, Arthur, 72–73, 255

Griska, Joseph M., Jr., 202n

Guinness, Desmond, 226n

Haley, Alex, 236

Hall, Jacquelyn Dowd, 120

Hamm, Charles, 196

Hardy, Thomas, 164, 209

Harper, Jared Vincent, 37

Harris, Joel Chandler, 30, 33, 202

Harris, Richard, 178

Haughton, James, 68

Hawaii, 58

Hawthorne, Nathaniel, 193, 200

Hayden, Tom, 113

Heagney, H. J., 114

Healy, James, 59–65, 72

Healy, Patrick, 61–65

Healey, Denis, 177–78

Heaney, Seamus, 5–6, 12, 12n, 14, 113, 115, 145, 172, 229, 257, 259, 265

Hecht, Ben, 124

Heisser, David C. R., 56n

Helper, Hinton Rowan, 55

Hemings, Sally, 48, 196

Henry, Patrick, 47

Hernon, Joseph M., 53, 55, 65, 77, 81n, 83

Herrenstein, Richard J., 182

Hewitt, John, 259–60

Heyrman, Christine Leigh, 146

Hibernian Hall (New Orleans), 34

Hickman, Mary, 176, 177

Hobsbawm, Eric, 225n

Hobson, Fred, 56n, 209, 239n

Hoffman, Ronald, 34

Holmes, Janice, 147n

Home Rule, Irish, 170

Hooper, J. J., 200, 201, 267

Hotze, Henry, 87, 182–83

Howe, Julia Ward, 114

Howe, Stephen, 175, 176

Hoy, Suellen, 72–73

Hughes, Nathaniel Cheairs, Jr., 101n

Hughes, John, 51

Hume, John, 161–62

Humphrey, Cordelia C., 17n

Huntley, Chet, 162

Hurston, Zora Neale, 13–14, 236, 240

Hyde, Douglas, 9, 171, 208, 209, 255

Ignatieff, Michael, 260

Ignatiev, Noel, 52, 52n, 63

Jackson, Alvin, 160

Jackson, Andrew, 10, 25, 27, 35, 39, 216

Jackson, Henry E. R., 82

Jackson, Thomas J. "Stonewall," 82, 89, 100n, 156, 163, 240

Jacobs, Harriet, 60, 69, 149, 152

James, Henry, 209

James, Simon, 43

James I (king of England), 40

James II (king of England), 22–23

Jefferson, Thomas, 47, 48, 146, 159, 170, 185, 196, 210, 246
Jeffrey, Keith, 59n, 257n
Johnson, James Weldon, 9
Jones, Katherine W., 165n
Jonson, Ben, 168–69
Jordan, Michael, 165
Jordan, Winthrop D., 169
Joyce, James, 5, 99, 164, 184, 208, 209, 210, 213, 214, 216, 236, 257; *A Portrait of the Artist as a Young Man*, 141–42, 144, 211, 212, 257; *Ulysses*, 211, 219n
Joyner, Charles, 43n

Kane, Hartnett T., 166–67
Karl, Frederick, 224
Kay, Jackie, 16
Keating, Geoffrey, 21–22, 251, 256
Keegan, John, 11, 11n
Keillor, Garrison, 164
Keller, Cozette, 110n
Keller, Morton, 184n
Kelly, James, 187n
Kemble, Fanny, 38, 70, 82, 134n
Kendrick, Benjamin B., 242
Keneally, Thomas, 50n, 83n
Kennedy, John Pendleton, 202–203, 213
Kiberd, Declan, 57n, 193, 195, 207–208, 227
Kickham, Charles, 199
Kinealy, Christine, 11n, 59n
King, Martin Luther, Jr., 161, 163, 248, 262, 267
Kingsley, Charles, 168
Kirby, Jack Temple, 167–68
Know Nothing Party, 36, 50, 79, 84, 89. *See also* Nativism
Koger, Larry, 63n
Kreyling, Michael, 228n
Ku Klux Klan, 17, 116–17, 127, 136, 149, 156, 162

Lane, Ralph, 22
Lange, Dorothea, 168
Lankford, Nelson D., 78, 82
Larkin, Emmet, 29n
Laughton, Charles, 178

Lee, J. J., 236
Lee, Robert E., 82, 93, 97, 99, 110, 155, 156, 159, 241, 262
Le Fanu, Joseph Sheridan, 195, 202
Leigh, Vivien, 122, 178
Lester, DeeGee, 70, 97n, 99n
Levine, Lawrence W., 150–51, 152
Leyburn, James G., 43n
Lincoln, Abraham, 38, 96, 242
Lindberg-Seyersted, Brita, 217n
Lipscomb, Oscar H., 103
Lloyd, David, 149n
Longfellow, Henry Wadsworth, 104, 108
Longley, Edna, 258
Longstreet, Augustus Baldwin, 195
Lost Cause, 79, 103, 105, 109, 111, 116, 156, 158, 184, 241
Lott, Eric, 12, 181n
Luddy, Ailbe J., 154n
Luther, Martin, 155
Lynch, John Roy, 38
Lynch, Patrick, 56, 87
Lyons, F. S. L., 253

Mac an tSaoi, Máire, 39n
Macarthy, Harry, 76–77
Macaulay, Lord, 57, 252
MacCaig, Norman, 12n
MacDaniel, Hattie, 122
MacDonagh, Thomas, 191
MacNeice, Louis, 218–19
MacNeil, Robert, 167n, 190n
Macpherson, James, 195
Madison, James, 47
Maffitt, John Newland, 82
Magee, Thomas Darcy, 59
Mahoney, Rosemary, 215n
Major, John, 260n
Malone, Bill C., 6n, 38
Mandela, Nelson, 262, 263
Mangan, James Clarence, 194, 195
Marrs, Suzanne, 230n
Martin, Harold, 128n
Martin, John, 87
Mason, Bobbie Anne, 266
Mathew, Theobald, 147

Maturin, Charles, 195
Maxwell, William, 230
McAleese, Mary, 267
McAnally, Ray, 178
McArdle, Dorothy, 240
McCarthy, Terence, 267
McClean, Sorley, 12n
McCrum, Robert, 167n, 190n
McCullers, Carson, 233–34
McDiarmid, Hugh, 12n
McDonald, Forrest, 39, 40, 204
McFeely, William S., 49n
McGarahan, James, 54
McGovern, Bryan, 69n
McGraw, Eliza Russi Lowen, 126
McPherson, James M., 86n, 111
McWhiney, Grady, 39–44, 74, 80, 123, 186, 204
Meadows, Dennis, 175n
Meagher, Thomas Francis, 59, 67, 79–80, 81
Meier, August, 246n
Melville, Herman, 194
Memphis, Tenn., 97
Mencken, H. L., 4, 142, 185–86, 213
Mercier, Vivian, 222n
Methodists, 4, 143, 147, 152, 261
Michaels, Walter Benn, 12
Miller, Kerby A., 24, 29, 30n
Miller, Randall M., 51, 52, 84n, 102
Mitchel, James, 98
Mitchel, John, 4, 59, 83, 97–99, 104, 115, 145, 153, 159, 171, 173, 183, 194, 227, 252; defense of slavery, 65–73, 93; defense of South, 77–79, 92–94
Mitchel, John C., 4, 78, 83, 101–102
Mitchel, Willy, 83
Mitchell, Margaret, 8, 32, 102, 118–36
Montague, John, 7
Montserrat, 58, 164
Moody, Dwight Lyman, 107n, 147n
Moody, T. W., 253
Moore, George, 216
Moore, Thomas, 47, 174, 194, 195–98, 252
Moran, D. P., 148
Moran, John, 109

Morgan, Hiram, 22
Morgan, Lady, 202
Morris, Benny, 255
Morrison, Blake, 176–77
Morrison, Toni, 165
Mulholland, St. Clair Augustin, 102
Murray, Albert, 2
Murray, Charles, 182

Naipaul, V. S., 168
Nashville Agrarians, 161, 211, 217
Nashville Fugitives, 185, 213, 217, 226, 239
Nast, Thomas, 183–84
Nation, the, 58, 66, 92, 108, 112, 145, 197
Nativism, 56, 63–64, 80, 84. See also Know Nothing Party
New Orleans, Battle of, 35
New Orleans, La., 7, 34–37, 52, 73–74, 76, 108, 181, 195, 197
Newport, Christopher, 23, 24
Niehaus, Earl F., 34, 36
Nietzsche, Friedrich, 72

O'Brien, Conor Cruise, 158n, 159, 224, 244
O'Brien, Flann, 207
O'Brien, Michael, 250, 251
O'Brien, William Smith, 59, 67, 79, 145
O'Callaghan, Seán, 23n
O'Casey, Seán, 141, 210, 212, 214, 228
Ó Ciosáin, Niall, 149
O'Connell, Daniel, 68, 76, 100, 157; on slavery, 36–37, 47, 48, 53–56, 72
O'Connor, Feargus, 174
O'Connor, Flannery, 14, 119, 120–21, 144–45, 146, 148–49, 210, 215, 216; on Irish, 38, 39n
O'Connor, Frank, 188–89, 207n, 234
O'Connor, Mrs. T. P., 196, 209
O'Connor, T. P., 209
O'Conor, Charles, 97
O'Donnell, Rory, 21, 25, 157
O'Faoláin, Julia, 228n
O'Faoláin, Seán, 141, 142, 186, 187, 227, 239–40, 265; compares Ireland with South, 5, 186, 218–19; on Faulkner, 221–22
O'Gorman, Richard, 104

O'Hara, Frank, 32
O'Hara, Theodore, 101
O'Hegarty, P. S., 253
O'Kelly, Patrick, 192–93
Ó Longáin, Micheál Óg, 50n
O'Meara, John, 239
O'Mores, the, 25
O'Neill, Charles Edwards, 39n
O'Neill, Eugene, 225
O'Neill, Hugh, 21, 22, 25, 157
O'Neill, Jeremiah, Sr., 54
O'Neill, Kevin, 81n
O'Neill, Owen Roe, 21
Onkey, Lauren, 9n
Opie, Iona, 175–76, 177
Orangism, 66, 160, 162, 174, 253
Ó Riordáin, Seán, 157
Ó Súilleabháin, Eoghan Rua, 57, 132–33
O'Toole, James M., 62–65
O'Toole, Peter, 178
Owsley, Frank L., 242

Page, Thomas Nelson, 42, 159, 208–209, 213,
    216, 217, 236
Paisley, Ian, 7, 154, 256
Parker, Geoffrey, 23n
Parks, Rosa, 14
Parnell, Charles Stewart, 16–17, 73, 109, 145,
    158
Patterson, Orlando, 12
Pearse, Patrick, 158, 160, 163, 252, 255
Penal Laws, 46, 146
Percy, Walker, 146, 215, 265
Percy, William Alexander, 182, 227
Percy family, 31–32
Phillips, Ulrich B., 246
Pittock, Murray G. H., 13n
Pius IX (pope), 86, 113
Poe, Edgar Allan, 79, 108, 191, 193, 195, 202
Pollard, A. F., 253
Pollard, Edward, 79
Porter, Katherine Anne, 146, 215
Powhatan, 23
Praeger, Lloyd, 238
Prenshaw, Peggy Whitman, 230

Presbyterians, 7, 8, 46, 65, 143, 146, 147, 154,
    216, 254, 258
Presley, Elvis, 1
Punch, 171–74, 178
Purdue, Elizabeth, 88n, 101
Purdue, Howell, 88n, 101
Pyron, Darden Asbury, 119, 124–26, 130

Quinn, David, 24

Raleigh, Sir Walter, 22, 228
Randall, Alice, 127
Ransom, John Crowe, 5, 161, 185, 217
Ray, Celeste, 8n, 12
Read, Benedict, 100n
Reconstruction, 38, 96–97, 114, 130, 243,
    246–48
Reed, John Shelton, 262–63
Reeves, Paschal, 212n
Religion, 6–7, 139–63. See also Anglicans;
    Baptists; Catholic Church; Methodists;
    Presbyterians
Rhett, Claudine, 78, 101–102
Rhett, Robert Barnwell, 78
Richmond, Va., 78, 80, 83, 156
Ripley, Alexandra, 180
Robbins, Keith, 30
Robinson, Mary, 10
Roe, Micheál D., 166n
Roediger, David R., 52n
Ruffin, Edmund, 71, 78
Russell, Diarmuid, 228
Russell, Lord John, 174
Ryan, Abram J., 102–17, 118, 159, 201, 209,
    241
Ryan, Ray, 12n

Sacks, Howard L., 235n
Sacks, Judith Rose, 235n
Said, Edward, 171, 174–75, 182
Samuel, Raphael, 264
Samway, Patrick, 203
Sankey, Ira David, 147
Savanorola, 155
Scallon, Rosemary ("Dana"), 18n
Schivelbusch, Wolfgang, 139n

Schwartz, Lawrence H., 214n
Scotch-Irish, 3, 7, 10, 26, 34, 65, 70, 76, 116, 132, 135–36, 142, 156, 202–203, 206, 235, 242
Scott, Sir Walter, 116, 194–95, 202
Secession, 76–77
Shakespeare, William, 171
Shankman, Arnold, 9n, 55n
Shaw, George Bernard, 209
Sheridan, Phil, 98
Sherman, William T., 130, 237
Shiloh, Battle of, 89
Shuttlesworth, Fred, 161
Simkins, Francis Butler, 243–44, 255
Simms, William Gilmore, 202, 203–206, 213, 242
Singal, Daniel Joseph, 222n
Silver, James W., 243
Slavery, 46–75; Catholic Church on, 50–52, 56; Irish on, 47–48, 49–50, 53, 55–58, 65, 72–75; John Mitchel on, 67–70; Daniel O'Connell on, 47, 48, 53–56
Smith, R. T., 10
Smollett, Tobias, 208
Solnit, Rebecca, 6
Spangler, Matthew, 212n
Spenser, Edmund, 168, 228
Stampp, Kenneth, 248
Stephens, John, 119
Stereotypes, 164–90; of blacks, 165, 166, 169–70, 180–83; of Celt vs. Saxon, 184–86; of Irish, 126, 133–34, 165, 167, 168–69, 170–80; of white southerners, 165, 166, 167–68, 183–84
Stoker, Bram, 202
Stone, Phil, 223
Stonequist, Everett, 61
Stowe, Harriet Beecher, 68, 106–107
Strode, Hudson, 97n, 115n
Sullivan, A. M., 240, 252
Sumner, Charles, 65
Sword, Wiley, 89n, 92
Symonds, Craig L., 88n, 89
Synge, John Millington, 9, 202, 210, 214

Takaki, Ronald, 22
Tandy, Napper, 177

Tate, Allen, 146, 185, 187, 215, 216, 217–18, 238, 240
Taylor, Hannis, 106
Taylor, Helen, 11n
Temple, Shirley, 167
Tennyson, Alfred Lord, 106n, 108, 194
Thierry, Augustine, 198
Thomas Aquinas, St., 119
Thoreau, Henry David, 194
Thuente, Mary Helen, 57n, 198
Tóibín, Colm, 148
Tompkins, Jane, 106–107
Tone, Wolfe, 58, 145, 159, 177, 252
Travelers, Irish, 37
Trent, William P., 242
Trollope, Anthony, 174, 194, 200
Tucker, Phillip Thomas, 84, 87
Turner, Nat, 152
Twain, Mark, 107–108, 193, 216
Tyndall, George B., 40n

Upward, Allen, 207

Vance, Norman, 101n
Vaughn, Bernard, 99
Vaughn, J. Barry, 156n
Vicksburg, siege of, 85, 226
Virginia, 23–24

Wakelyn, Jon L., 51n
Waldron, Ann, 230n, 234n
Walker, Alice, 14, 121, 135, 245
Walker, Clarence E., 151
Walmesley, Charles, 147
Ware, Thomas Clayton, 101n
Warren, Craig A., 81n
Warren, Robert Penn, 4, 211, 217, 240
Washington, Booker T., 151
Washington, George, 47, 54, 246
Waters, Maureen, 174
Watson, Tom, 117, 119
Welty, Eudora, 5, 216, 228–34
Wesley, John, 155
White, Hayden, 255, 263
Whitman, Walt, 194
Wilde, Lady, 112, 115

Wilde, Oscar, 4, 108, 114–15, 209, 225, 265
Wilde, Richard Henry, 191–93, 206
Wilde, Sir William Wills, 82
William of Orange (king of England), 23, 130
Williams, Richard Dalton, 112, 115
Williams, Tennessee, 210, 215
Williamson, Joel, 126n
Wilson, Andrew J., 162n
Wilson, Augusta Evans, 107, 199–200
Wilson, Charles Reagan, 103, 155, 156, 239n
Wimsatt, Mary Ann, 203
Wogan, Terry, 178
Wolfe, Thomas, 141, 211
Woodson, Carter G., 246
Woodward, C. Vann, 5, 234, 243, 244–45,
    249–50, 255

Woolf, Virginia, 233
Wordsworth, William, 194
Wright, Frank, 11n
Wright, Richard, 8, 141, 185, 210
Wyatt-Brown, Bertram, 31–32, 110

Yaeger, Patricia, 126, 127
Yeats, William Butler, 38, 184, 188n, 189,
    194–95, 198, 208, 210, 212, 214, 217–18,
    228, 232, 236, 254; compared with
    Faulkner, 218–27
Young, Elizabeth, 121
Young, Robert J. C., 183
Young Ireland, 56, 57, 66, 81, 88, 110. See
    also Mitchel, John

bitter disputes as to the interpretation of their respective "lost causes." Quinlan also examines the unexpected twentieth-century literary flowering in Ireland and the South—as exemplified by Irish writers James Joyce, W. B. Yeats, and Elizabeth Bowen, and southern authors William Faulkner, Eudora Welty, and Flannery O'Connor.

Sophisticated as well as entertaining, *Strange Kin* represents a benchmark in Irish-American cultural studies. Its close consideration of the familial and circumstantial resemblances between Ireland and the South will foster an enhanced understanding of each place separately, as well as of the larger British and American polities.

KIERAN QUINLAN is the author of *Walker Percy, the Last Catholic Novelist* and *John Crowe Ransom's Secular Faith*. Born in Dublin, he spent several years as a Trappist monk and is currently writing an account of that experience. He is an associate professor of English at the University of Alabama at Birmingham.